The Rationalist Reader

Architecture and Rationalism
in Western Europe
1920–1940/1960–1990

Edited by Andrew Peckham
and Torsten Schmiedeknecht

Routledge
Taylor & Francis Group

LONDON AND NEW YORK

First published 2014
by Routledge
2 Park Square, Milton Park, Abingdon, Oxon OX14 4RN

Simultaneously published in the USA and Canada
by Routledge
711 Third Avenue, New York, NY 10017

Routledge is an imprint of the Taylor & Francis Group, an informa business

British Library Cataloguing in Publication Data
A catalogue record for this book is available from the British Library

Library of Congress Cataloging in Publication Data
The rationalist reader : architecture and rationalism in Western Europe 1920–1940
and 1960–1990 / [edited by] Andrew Peckham and Torsten Schmiedeknecht.
    pages cm
  Includes index.
    1. Architecture–Europe, Western–History–20th century. 2. Rationalism
    (Architecture)–Europe, Western. I. Peckham, Andrew, editor of compilation.
    II. Schmiedeknecht, Torsten, editor of compilation.
  NA958.R38 2013
  720.94′0904–dc23   2013008517

ISBN: 978-0-415-60435-2 (hbk)
ISBN: 978-0-415-60436-9 (pbk)

Typeset in MetaPlus and Perpetua
by Keystroke, Station Road, Codsall, Wolverhampton

Printed and bound in Great Britain by
TJ International Ltd, Padstow, Cornwall

For Penny, Rachel, Danny, and Julia, Henri and Kate

Contents

Preface

The concept for an anthology, or 'reader', focused on rationalist architecture was originally conceived independently and subsequently evolved in mutual collaboration.

It was Torsten Schmiedeknecht's invitation to write on the subject of Aldo Rossi's reputation in *An Architect's Guide to Fame* (edited with Paul Davis and published in 2005) that revived Andrew Peckham's interest in the Neo-rationalist movement, dormant during the 1990s in the face of a contrary architectural culture.

Torsten subsequently broached his long-standing 'project' for a *Rationalist Reader*, serving a didactic purpose in providing a model to reconnect design theory and practice, and acting as a sourcebook for architectural students. Prescient, since he was unaware of his prospective co-editor's 1979 review published in *International Architect* comparing Leon Krier's *Rational Architecture Rationelle 1978* and *The Rationalists: Theory and Design in the Modern Movement* (edited by Dennis Sharp), which suggested a comparative anthology of rationalist texts from the two periods. It would have remained no more than a speculative comment, without our fortuitous meeting of minds twenty-five years later.

Academic commitments intervened but an edition of Architectural Design, *Rationalist Traces* (edited with Charles Rattray in 2007) kept our rationalist trajectory on track. Meanwhile others were publishing significant research that had implications for our project, and we hope we have done their work justice in the 'retrospective' sections of the Reader – as also to Alan Colquhoun's essay on *Rationalism: a Philosophical Concept in Architecture*. Meeting with Alan in April 2011 to confirm approval to publish extracts from his text, our conversation and his instructive critical advice actively influenced what followed – so we dedicate this book to his memory: Alan Colquhoun 1921–2012.

The Editors

Acknowledgements

The Editors express particular thanks to the various people, in addition to our contributing authors, who made significant contributions to the conception, research for and the production of this Reader.

Peter Jenkins in London and Hans van der Heijden in Rotterdam have been consistently supportive of our efforts throughout what has been a lengthy process.

Luka Skansi provided key advice with his knowledge and close reading of a wide range of Italian sources, and without Luciano Lazzari's professional contacts there would have been a significant gap in our coverage of Italian Neo-rationalism.

Our translators Kevin Cook, Stefania Boccaletti and Julien Denis all worked patiently beyond any reasonable call of duty or recompense, in negotiating the, often opaque, linguistic habits of architectural writing in different national cultures.

We were fortunate to eventually find a path through the tangled world of copyright permissions, but without the efficient professionalism of Melanie Lazar at the Getty Research Institute and Pamela Quick at MIT Press in particular, we might well have lost our way at key points. The help and advice of publishers, archivists, architects, authors and their representatives in dealing with our persistent enquiries was greatly appreciated, as also the generosity of those who waived, or moderated, fees for many of the texts involved. We would like to thank the following individuals: Madleen Lamm, Sofia Ungers, Anja Sieber-Albers, Chiara Spangaro, Thomas Flierl, Martin Steinmann, Helen Castle, Stephanie Coleman, Roman Vesely, Frau Eggebrecht, B. Ravelli, Daniel Weiss, Veronika Darius, Ursula Bein, Alex Winiger, Nikolaus Kuhnert, Ute Barba, Ute Zoerbach, Karina Danulat, Levente Koltai, Heinz Wirz, Elodie Cadiou, Pia Solcà, Cornelia Ruhland, Dan Simon, Kate Nesbitt, Sheik Safdar, Karen Lee, Ellen Grimes, Kevin Mitchell, Susanne Schindler, Jon Goodbun, Giovanni Bonfanti, Daniela Meggiorin, Silvia Sala, Maurice Culot, Wilfried Wang, Richard Burdett, Alfred Marks, Thomas Weaver and Estate Mies van der Rohe.

Danny Peckham made a major contribution to the onerous task of text processing, formatting and editing.

Finally Fran Ford our architectural editor at Taylor and Francis always responded to our questions and momentary crises with unhesitatingly sound advice, which served to reinforce our confidence in the enterprise when this was needed. Laura Williamson looked after us on the final straight, and our production editor Alanna Donaldson coordinated the proof stages while patiently incorporating any changes and requests until the very last minute – many thanks.

We would also like to thank the University of Liverpool and the University of Westminster for their generous financial support, particularly in relation to the translation work, specialist research and teaching relief.

Introduction

Andrew Peckham and Torsten Schmiedeknecht

The rationalist legacy: complement and contradiction

An architectural Reader is concerned with what architects (and their critics or apologists) write, which may, or may not, correspond with their design practice and the buildings with which they are identified. A meta-language is an unstable condition, paralleling its subject, more or less close to its specific referent. Writing about Rationalism in architecture, or indeed Rational Architecture, has an ambiguous status, seeking to explain but at the same time justify its subject.

This gap between narration and practice is instructive in that the concept of rationalism infused the rhetoric of what came to be understood as generic Modern Architecture, largely synonymous with the label Rationalist Architecture. In contrast the theoretical practice identified with the Neo-rationalist movement during the later post-war period sought initially to construct a 'critical architecture', which metamorphosed into a design methodology. A distinction is apparent between an accumulative narrative, which by persistent repetition becomes attached to its subject, and a didactic discourse which, insisting on its theoretical acumen, construes a form of architecture which acquires, in the shadow of ideas, a more mundane life of its own.

While chronological anthologies have a scholastic relevance in preparing the explanatory way for students of architecture, incorporating contextual introductions to each text or theme, our intent was not to over-interpret our sources. No anthology is complete; no 'reader' offers an unquestionably definitive view of its subject. What we did aim for, though, was to expand the implication of our previous publication *Rationalist Traces* to more fully engage the thinking behind twentieth-century rationalist architecture, its contemporary reception and retrospective critical interpretation.[1]

The Reader's primary content is a selection of twentieth-century texts by European architects and theorists of the 'interwar' and 'later post-war' periods. Organized in two sets of 'Documents' these are introduced by architects or academics with a particular knowledge of the legacy of Rationalism. The anthology is limited to Western Europe, and generally to those countries where rationalist thinking during both periods was most prevalent, that is Germany, Italy and France. Nonetheless, European architects looked to developments in America during the earlier period when commercial and industrial architecture was of particular interest, and principal rationalist architects emigrated to the US in the late 1930s. The publication of Aldo Rossi's texts in the early 1980s by the IAUS in New York was similarly a sign of an active American connection, but this Reader is confined to the formulation of a rationalist architecture in Western Europe.

The trajectory of Rationalism in twentieth-century architecture veers between a 'scientific' methodology identified with generic models, and a formal paradigm of typological consistency related in the later post-war period to an 'architecture of the city'. With philosophical origins in Enlightenment culture, the development of Rationalist thinking in nineteenth-century architecture points to a certain volatility in its later re-interpretation in different periods of the twentieth century, where our intention was to promote an understanding of attitudes both towards an everyday architecture and more self-conscious architectural design.

› Agenda

The Reader is structured as a comparative documentation of texts on rationalist architecture in Western Europe from two periods, broadly 1920–1940 and 1960–1990. This was informed by a didactic concern to examine the relationship between the two periods, where attitudes towards rationalism in the Modern Movement and to what was latterly termed Neo-rationalism have tended from an Anglo-American perspective to be seen in opposition to one another (while in Italy links between the two periods were more apparent).

Wary of repeating chronological collections of architectural theory where a linear historical narrative tends to subsume discontinuities, one 'movement', 'school' or set of ideas, following on from those before, our comparison between rationalism in architecture during the two periods accepts a break between interwar concerns and those of the considerably later post-war era. One may question how directly post-war reconstruction in fact followed a trajectory set in the interwar period, given the fracture of wartime experience and the uneven cultural formation attached to different conceptions of rationalism in architecture.[2]

Our intention, recognizing the vicissitudes of architectural culture during the two periods, was for readers to form their own opinion about what, particularly in terms of attitudes to the city, was apparently a fundamental dichotomy. The comparison involved value judgments, not only in our choice of thematic categories, but also in the assumption that the relationship between the two periods retained a contemporary purchase (against a grain unsympathetic to reinvention of Enlightenment values or categories).[3]

Concerned not to pigeonhole the rationalist strands of the Modern Movement, or circumscribe the inclusive identity of Neo-rationalism as an exclusive product of the earlier Italian *Tendenza*, we sought to avoid prescribing too neat compartments into which rationalism, together with other styles, movements and groups, should be placed. This was to recognize the cogency of particular episodes within each period, and also the distinct thinking and writing of individual architects, critics and theorists.

If modernism was itself relegated to the status of 'history' with the onset of post-modernism in architecture around 1970, then Neo-rationalism has acquired its own patina of dust. With the 'movement' consigned to the archive, research consequently focused on the presumptions of its protagonists and critics, and the significance of the social and political context in which it was formed. We aimed to respond to a revival of academic interest in the legacy of rationalism in both periods, which suggested re-examining their relationship. While the arrival of post-modernism stimulated a critique of the idealism and instrumentality inherent in the Modern Movement, it also encouraged the assumption of a critical distance from that ideology, which in fact persisted in many aspects of everyday practice.[4]

To return to the concept of Rationalism is to adopt a revisionist perspective, but one that re-examines an aspect of modern architecture too readily conflated with Functionalism (to which it was fundamentally opposed). Both terms became synonymous within the identity of the Modern Movement – while a rationalist architecture was explicitly 'made their own' by the exponents of 'Italian Rationalism'. The converse is true of Neo-rationalism, where the thinking behind the critical project of the Italian *Tendenza* was expanded to correlate with projects beyond its ambit.

Neo-rationalism as a loose term came to represent a broad range of work in Europe and the US, an influence reflected in Aldo Rossi's growing international reputation. Various strands emerged from under its general umbrella: Leon Krier's polemical urbanism and classicist urbanity;[5] O. M. Ungers's conception of an (increasingly) abstract architecture, but one attached to a historical legacy,[6] or a French conception of urbanism represented by different protagonists and reflected in Bernard Huet's nuanced assessment of the Athens Charter.[7] Recent studies have better understood the political and economic context of the *Tendenza*'s urban critique and its evident parallels with its antithesis – the contemporary Italian neo-avant-garde of the 1960s – as well as the association Rossi cultivated with Hans Schmidt's rationalist move towards a Socialist Realism.[8] Pier Vittorio Aureli has also revisited the concept of 'autonomy' in architecture, through political critique in his *The Project of Autonomy*, the conception of an 'absolute architecture', and most recently in his instructive rehabilitation of Ludwig Hilberseimer.[9]

› Structure: documents and contributors

The Reader is organized in two main sections, Documents One and Two, which incorporate texts primarily written within their respective periods. Four themes identify predominant issues: Rationalism and Type; The City; Construction; and Production. These constitute the parallel sub-sections of each set of documents.

In the first section, these are elaborated as: 'Rationalist Architecture: Type-Form and History; 'The New City'; 'The Logic of Construction – Rationalization', and 'Industrial Production and the Collective'. Correspondingly in the second section: 'Neo-Rationalism: Type and Typology'; 'Architecture and the City'; 'Logical Construction and Autonomy' and 'Reproduction and Tradition', complete the paired sequence.

The selected documentation was written variously by architects, critics, theorists and historians, and we have avoided identifying texts as exclusively theoretical or concerned purely with applicability in practice. A number are well known but essential to discussion of rationalism in architecture. Others are translated here for the first time or stem from less well-known sources. The two main documentary sections are each complemented by a following 'retrospective' sub-section concerned with more recent critical studies of each period.

At the outset we approached the late Alan Colquhoun for permission to reprint substantial extracts from his essay 'Rationalism: a philosophical concept in architecture' which provides direct access to the historical legacy of the Enlightenment.[10] Written in 1987 at the point when the dynamic of Neo-rationalism had begun to fade, it provides a relativistic view of the adventures of rationalism in architecture, re-interpreted in different circumstances, but also according to a changing relationship with a philosophical tradition imbued with the logic of its conflict with empiricism. The circular, not to say tautological, argument inherent in Viollet-le-Duc's ambivalent identification with reason – posing sincerity against falsehood, 'appealing to subjective feeling to justify the rational, and to the rational to justify subjective feeling' – influences the architectural avant-garde at the turn of the nineteenth century.[11] A paradigm shift consequently becomes evident in an association between the logical atomism of Bertrand Russell and the new architecture's literal embrace of Functionalism (mediated by the schematic formalism of *neue Sachlichkeit* architects or Le Corbusier and Mies van der Rohe's interpretations of a classically orientated rationalism). The former, Colquhoun contends, gave 'artistic expression to the conflict between . . . the *a priori* and the empirical, which in the hands of

ANDREW PECKHAM AND TORSTEN SCHMIEDEKNECHT

the Italian Rationalists both expressed this divide but also, particularly, in Terragni's work sublimated it'. He closes his own circle in viewing the Neo-rationalism of later post-war Italian architects, epitomized by Aldo Rossi, as a return to an eighteenth-century conception of reason, one undercut in his view by the schism between 'modern scientific conceptual thought' and 'sensuous images of order'.

Thilo Hilpert[12] and Henk Engel[13] were invited to introduce the interwar and, later post-war, periods. In addition Charles Rattray[14] takes an overview of rationalism in nineteenth-century architecture and Nicholas Bullock[15] provides a bridging piece on the immediate post-war experience in France. Each author developed their own perspective towards what constituted a rationalist architecture in the period concerned, bearing in mind our selection of texts, but with an open agenda.

Rattray examines the differing roles and approaches of Étienne-Louis Boullée and 'his favourite pupil' Jean-Nicolas-Louis Durand,[16] as points of departure. Durand's concern with classification and categorization is set against Boullée's 'dramatic forms, extravagant scale and spooky renderings' emphasizing the 'simplest and most primitive form'. Citing Durand's conviction that 'if one concerns oneself solely with the fulfilment of practical requirements, it is impossible that it should not be pleasing', Rattray contends that the 'linking of beauty to the disciplines of utility and structural honesty is a recurring theme in French Rationalism . . . crucially encapsulated by Marc-Antoine Laugier, in his *Essai sur l'architecture* of 1753'. He argues that Durand's '*Précis* received its most elegant and powerful application – in the *Altes Museum* by Karl Friedrich Schinkel'. Classification (by type), and tectonics (of construction) are set out as sometime coincident and sometime contradictory strands within rationalism. Following Schinkel and then Semper,[17] whose theory of cladding was perhaps best exemplified by Wagner in his Post Office Savings Bank in Vienna, Rattray arrives at the inception of modernism, and its diverse articulation in the work of pivotal figures such as Berlage or August Perret[18] at the beginning of the twentieth century.

Professor Hilpert's subsequent introduction to the initial Documents reflects on the genealogy or 'family tree' of the architects of 'classic' modernism, and the progressive texts with which it was associated (primarily in Germany and France).[19] His contention is that August Perret's garage in Paris of 1906, was 'the first [modernist] building' as it 'revealed the new form of construction, combining it with a novel function, which only through modernism would become a programme "worthy" of architecture'. Classifying modernist architects and writers on architecture into 'precursors'; those instituting 'classic' modernism; 'modernism's children' and 'grandchildren', his discussion of key texts moves to consider the 'sociology of the new forms', examining the differences between 'individualism', implicitly rationalist 'collective' endeavour, and 'internationalism'. Developed with reference to the Weissenhof Siedlung in Stuttgart this argument investigates parallels between Hannes Meyer's design for the school for the *ADGB* (German Trade Union Federation) near Berlin and Max Bill's design of the *Hochschule für Gestaltung* (School of Design) in Ulm. Hilpert highlights the contrariness of the texts that 'define' modernism, and hence the problems of a conventional historiography that tends to categorize architectural movements as 'homogeneous' entities.

In his introduction to Neo-rationalism, Dutch architect Henk Engel examines developments in Italy, arising from the earlier post-war period.[20] His discussion investigates the attitudes towards the city which inform Neo-rationalist thinking: 'Postulating "a science of the city" as Rossi did – that is a science of its construction over time confirmed in processes of transformation and conditions of permanence – challenges the ideological legacy of Modern Architecture'.[21] Engel examines the chronology of Neo-Rationalism in Europe, and its inception in the project of the Italian *Tendenza*,[22] whose aim 'was nothing less than a re-founding of architecture as an attempt to instigate "a new design method, rational and transmittable"'. Tracing initial differences between the positions of Ungers and Rossi[23] on the one hand and Leon and Rob Krier[24] on the other, he observes that: 'public space became the main focus of Neo-Rationalism. Urban morphological analysis had created a critical distance from the new discipline of territorial planning, underpinning the claim of autonomy for the architectural project.' Comparing Scolari's contemporary explanation[25] of the work of Rossi and Grassi,[26] with its deeper philosophical sources in the theories of Croce, Carnap and Geymonat, Engel places the architects' critique of Lynch and Alexander's respective conceptions of environmental planning, and design methodology, in direct opposition to the empirical sciences that had during the 1960s invaded the 'domain' of architecture. Taking issue with the received view of Rossi's debt to Structuralism – privileging the evolution of myth and language – he contends that the conception of a rule-based practice, where architectural 'events' (or projects) parallel individual speech acts, is the key to this relationship. Identifying with Grassi's view of the limits of logical analysis, he argues that 'the rule as norm' reveals itself 'in the act of design'; proposing a 'new rationalism' in architecture that accepts this distinction between analysis and design.

Nicholas Bullock examines rationalism in the historical context of post-war reconstruction in France. His interest is in how the need for mass housing, at a time of scarce materials and skilled labour, impacted on contemporary architecture. Tracing developments from *'Reconstruction and the Industrialisation of Building'* to a *'rational architecture'* Bullock investigates attitudes towards the industrialization of the building industry post-war, contrasting Lods and Prouvé – infused with the legacy of modernism in seeking 'a radical programme of reform'– with the mainstream who favoured 'the cautious pragmatism of the Vichy years'. His discussion centres on the choice of different types of prefabrication, informed by conceptions of tradition and progress, and the consequent debate concerning 'heavy' (concrete) or 'light' (steel) construction. Concluding with Perret's reconstruction of Le Havre, Bullock notes that 'the "structural classicism" of Le Havre's reconstruction was rooted in Perret's rationalist beliefs',[27] and that 'Perret's architecture answered perfectly the ambiguities of a reconstruction called upon to privilege both the ties of the past and the promise of the future'.

A subsequent 'Postscript' presents four different responses to the significance of rationalism for contemporary architecture today. These range from discussion of the need for rational negotiation between the collective interests of the public, and the demands of the private, sector in urban renewal; the case for a rationalist tectonic, correcting misconceptions about Semper's ideas which provide a model for mediating constructive facts and visual appearance in the 'contemporary' façade, and the legacy of Neo-rationalism in redefining the concepts of 'rationalism' and the 'science' of building. To conclude, Leon Krier re-examines the Neo-rationalist catalogues of 1973 and 1978[28] which generalized an inclusive Neo-rationalist architecture, highlighting Cervellati's 'formidable and forgotten' book of 1974 on 'The Typology and Morphology of the Historic City'. Focused on restoration and repair, this might have acted, he argues, as a model for his own historical revivalism.

> ## Four themes: rationalism and type/the city/construction/production

Rationalist architecture: type-form and history /Neo-rationalism:
type and typology
Discussion of a rationalist conception of the issues surrounding type and typology separates out the culture of the two periods as distinct, but also points to an underlying relationship. In

ANDREW PECKHAM AND TORSTEN SCHMIEDEKNECHT

each case a concern with historical tradition underpins the respective argument. Modernist architects, in particular Le Corbusier who exerted a canonical influence, seemingly aimed to make it 'new' as the first English translation of *Towards a New Architecture* emphasized. But an accurate translation, *Toward an Architecture*,[29] is more reticent than is the contemporary 'Five Points towards a New Architecture'[30] where a putative objectivity, as Frampton notes, is tempered by an 'underlying classical affinity'. For all his radical exhortations, just as Wagner's conception of Modern Architecture accepted the transformations of modern life yet conceived *Modern Architecture*[31] as a 'style' aligned with those of the past, it is Le Corbusier's polemical juggling with *object types,* contrasting paradigms of a machinist present with those of Greek and Roman antiquity, that stands out.

From the more technocratic perspective of Gropius,[32] or later Schmidt (particularly post-war),[33] it became routine to complement summary of the exigencies of industrial production with concluding pleas for a respect for tradition (whether in a modest vernacular or the serial form of the grand urban ensembles of the eighteenth or nineteenth century). Adolf Loos, misconstrued as a mainstream modernist by early historians of the Modern Movement, pointed to the sobriety of tradition as the antithesis of the artistic licence evident in the 'applied arts'. Characteristically he avowed that 'only a very small part of architecture belongs to art: the tomb and the monument'.[34] A double-edged observation this comment, since although set in the context of everyday building ('the house is conservative') and accepting the representative 'artistic' value of symbolic architecture – these received archetypes were unlikely to be fundamentally altered. Loos's satirical writings were often raided indiscriminately by critics and architects from both Modernist and Neo-rationalist periods, who implicitly identified with their discursive conviction. It was, however, Quatremere's conception of type in classical architecture that served Rossi more directly as a model for tradition in architecture.[35] There was a charac-teristic oscillation within Neo-rationalism between type as ideal, and a generic typological realism (sought by Giorgio Grassi), where an operative conception of architectural 'history' was held to condition formal composition.[36] This 'belief' was also reflected in the 'unarguable' density and the rhetorical tropes of much of the writing associated with the *Tendenza* – as a consequence these ideas have been too readily consigned to history. A substantial body of theoretical discourse on typological issues and urbanism grounded the emergence of the *Tendenza*. Variously pursued, reiterated and re-interpreted by Italian, French, German and Spanish theorists and critics alike, these texts are perhaps the most substantive legacy of Neo-rationalism.[37]

Anthony Vidler's short articulate essay 'The Third Typology,[38] published in *Rational Architecture Rationnelle 1978*, was in contrast readily anthologized. Like its host it provides a window into the 'moment' when a Neo-rationalist movement had been consolidated beyond its origins in the Italian *Tendenza*. Leon Krier's contemporary survey of European projects, with its symmetrical title and given date, represented a homage to, and a deferral from, its name-sake *Architettura Razionale* of 1973. Manfredo Tafuri criticized that book and the accompanying exhibition, for their associative inclusion of work beyond the ambit of the *Tendenza*,[39] and in 1978 a similar generosity (or expediency) accompanied Krier's polemical conviction about the Reconstruction of the European City.

The critical fortunes of Italian Rationalism have been revived by the research of David Rifkind and Michelangelo Sabbatino[40] (following the monographs on Modern Architecture in Italy by Richard Etlin and Dennis Doordan).[41] Where earlier studies emphasized Gruppo 7's debt to Le Corbusier, it is clear that the Rationalists reformed his polemic while accepting the contemporary Fascist claims being made on national identity (a position well publicized in the journal *Quadrante*).[42] Gruppo 7 were more explicit than Corbusier about the relevance (if not the detail) of the transformation of historical types for a prospective 'new archaic era' (which aptly summarized their predicament). Giuseppe Pagano's thoughtful attitude towards construction and traditional typologies (balancing his acerbic anti-formalist stance towards Terragni),[43] are mirrored in the later Neo-rationalist attention Grassi gives to vernacular building as a typological model, but one about which he is objectively 'descriptive'.[44]

The new city / architecture and the city

The two respective sections representing a rationalist conception of the city present a polarity between the New City (of the future), typically identified with Le Corbusier, and *The Architecture of the City* (as mental artifact) – Aldo Rossi's Neo-rationalist text addressing the transformation of the city over time. This contrast is distinct but not unmediated. Rossi's position, though antithetical to the 'Functionalist City' (enshrined in the conclusions to CIAM's *Athens Charter*), is positive about Le Corbusier's attention to housing and adamant that: 'the construction of a more complex rationalism than the schematic one offered by the historiography of modern architecture . . . entails a confrontation with modern architecture's own tradition . . .' He cites Ludwig Hilberseimer whose analyses 'are rigorously interdependent aspects of a general theory of rationalism in architecture.'[45]

Le Corbusier's apopleptic 'Lesson of Rome'[46] in *Toward an Architecture* vacillates between extremes, fixated by monumentality, drama, measure and order, but denigrating Rome's 'exhibitionist' status. Rossi's contrasting view of 'The Roman Forum' represents his view that architecture is 'both contingent on and determinative of the constitution of urban artifacts'.[47] Le Corbusier's urban logic gels in his *The City of Tomorrow* (Urbanism)[48] where the individual cell and its social hierarchy exhibit 'freedom through order' and 'winding' streets are replaced by 'straight roads'. His conception of urban architecture presents a dichotomy between permanence or monumentality ('it is only architecture which can give all the things that go beyond calculation'), and the 'repetition' intrinsic to mass production and standardization; 'to build on a clear site' enables the construction of 'standardized houses with standardized furniture'. In the conclusions to the Athens Charter[49] this age of production is represented by four key functions: housing, work, recreation and traffic (whose 'autonomy' is mobilized through the application of technology and an efficient transport infrastructure). These nonetheless are balanced in the Charter's main text by comments on the virtues (and limitations) of the traditional city.[50]

Wagner's *Großstadt*[51] placed a polemical gloss on the burgeoning economy of the expanding city foregrounded in his regulation plan for Vienna, while Hilberseimer's direct engagement with the scale, alienation and economic realities of the contemporary metropolis staked out territory beyond Le Corbusier's immediate influence. Hilberseimer's architecture is as generic as the grey metropolitan atmosphere where, his writing argued, glass and steel construction revealed the parameters of a new social order.[52] For Rossi, attracted both to the temporality of the city and its 'permanences', time may appear suspended in his projects but not 'backdated' as in Leon Krier's conception of the 'Reconstruction of the European city'. Inverting the 'conclusive' logic of the Athens Charter, arguing 'housing is not a monument', Krier proposed the rehabilitation of the city *quartier* as the antithesis of Functionalist zoning.[53] His identification with a classical tradition, also emphasized within Neo-rationalism, is less apparent in Rossi's earlier work where Italian critics noted a rationalist dimension of modern architecture. O. M. Ungers's parallel urban strategies were indebted to typological studies that transformed the study of functional types in housing, into the autonomous realm of an independent analysis of form.[54]

Rossi sought a celebral and 'scientific' theoretical stance in order to construct a theory of the city. Conceptualizing typological questions; the pathological tendencies of the functional

ANDREW PECKHAM AND TORSTEN SCHMIEDEKNECHT

city; the nature of urban artifacts; the efficacy of monuments; urban geographers' theories of permanence, and finally the concept of *locus*, he marshalled the theoretical credentials of the Italian *Tendenza* (just as his own work was also departing from them). Taken individually these concepts were deployed beyond Italy (in Rob Krier's essentially descriptive 'Urban Space' for example)[55] lacking the grounding of Ernesto Rogers's long-standing conception of 'continuità' (which provided direction for the various groups researching urban history and theory in post-war Italy). A Neo-rationalist footfall may be found among the polemical strictures of the earlier Italian Rationalists Gruppo 7 manifestoes[56] (about which Vittorio Gregotti's speculative 'The Thin Red Thread of Italian Rationalism' is informative).[57] David Rifkind has traced how Rationalist urbanism following the Athens Charter realigned CIAM's four categories to accord with the corporatavist priorities of Italian Fascism while incorporating an archaeological sensibility (shared later by Rossi).[58] In parallel Mary Louise Lobsinger[59] has taken a measured look at the debate on the practice of urbanism that was the immediate context of *The Architecture of the City*. Each of these retrospective views provides insights into the specific history of rationalist urbanism that retains consequence for the city of the twenty-first century.

The logic of construction / logical construction and autonomy

The rationality of the reinforced concrete frame preoccupied modern architects from the outset. This may retain, or part company with, classical order. For August Perret the concrete 'framework' assigned to his modern museum should not only demonstrate a visible constructive integrity, but also assert a lasting presence when the building falls into ruin – imbued with a classical connotation but not with a directly figurative order.[60] Le Corbusier's 'Five Points'[61] reinvents a classical syntax for reinforced concrete construction, while Mies's famous dictum concerning 'Office Building' of 1923, is in contrast bluntly matter of fact: 'maximum effect with minimum expenditure of means' achieved in 'skin and bone buildings'.[62] 'We know no formal problems, only building problems' he notes laconically.[63] The following year, discussing the industrialization in the building industry (and its limits) he conceived the manufacture of an all-purpose building material reducing building to 'assemblage' – Hilberseimer's thoughts on 'Construction and Form' followed a similar trajectory, but sought verification in antiquity.[64] The latter's tone is circumstantial, metropolitan (economic) necessity ensures: 'Construction and form have become one: clear, logical, simple, unambiguous, and regular.' Thoughtful, if metaphysically inclined, Giuseppe Pagano's 'Structure and Architecture'[65] written eleven years later, followed the mantra 'construction is born out of necessity' but asserted that aesthetic and moral choice precede 'technique'. Tongue in cheek he writes: 'Reason! The demon of rationality invoked by men of refined artistic sensibility!' His model is 'in nature', yet tradition is seen 'as a springboard towards the future' and his nuanced analysis of frame construction projects a disregard for (fascist) 'academic' historicism. Much overlaps with the earlier Group 7 manifestoes, but an empirical directness permeates his writing on vernacular tradition.

Neo-rationalists privileged the logical construction of architecture at the philosophical heart of the discipline, inverting Mies's choice of 'building' over 'form'. Habitually referred back to Schinkel or Von Klenze, the legacy of Mies remains – referenced by Ungers, and informing the 'classical' resolve with which Hans Kollhoff negotiates the imperatives of contemporary 'building'.[66] Grassi's *The Logical Construction of Architecture*[67] was focused both on 'the syntactic aspect of architecture' and contrastingly the 'theoretical paradigms of deductive thinking'. The language, and classification, of form, is removed from its empirical referent. Rossi in his 'Architecture for Museums' elaborates: 'Architecture was born out of need, now it is autonomous', presenting an ambiguous analogy where architecture in its 'highest form' 'creates museum places . . . drawn upon by technicians to be transformed and adapted to the multiple functions and needs to which they have to be applied'.[68] 'One has to educate oneself about the analysis of the basic constructive character of a project' he claims. What sounds empirical is in fact a theoretical proposition. The introduction to *Architettura razionale* is more direct: 'A sort of heraldry, perhaps, could list the different possibilities in the same fashion Klein used to list all the possible movements'.[69] Grassi's description of the design of a portico by Tessenow in his essay 'Architecture as Craft', moves in a similar vein to argue that 'structure becomes modified in the project', its load-bearing function annihilated to produce 'a completely autonomous figuration'. All that remains 'is a *heraldic emblem*'.[70] Inverting empirical logic in the spirit of philosophical rationalism serves to emphasize the mythology that constitutes architecture, not its empirical reality. Mario Vigano in *La Tendenza*, the catalogue accompanying the 2012 exhibition at the Centre Pompidou,[71] looks at the specificity of 'autonomy': in the self-contained intellectual work that appealed to Communist architects; in Rossi's anti-utopian conception of a zero-point architecture 'without ideological trappings', and in the way that architecture, urban planning and design became separate disciplines during the 1970s. Henk Engel in this Reader proposes a new rationalism in architecture, distinguishing between what is separately applicable in analysis and to design. The concept of 'autonomy' occupies an ambiguous location, essential to a critical understanding of architectural form but inclined to formalism in practice.[72]

Industrial production and the collective / reproduction and tradition

If one theme serves to highlight the distance between Rationalism and Neo-rationalism in architecture, it could well be modern architecture's identification with industrialization (endorsed by Le Corbusier and Mies)[73] given Neo-rationalism's general antipathy to the urban consequences of prefabrication in post-war Europe. An important exception was Rossi's identification with Hans Schmidt's socialist 'catalogue architecture',[74] where prefabrication and serial repetition are justified as antithetical to free-market choice and somewhat disingenuously compared to the 'uniformity' of classic historical precedents ('why don't we speak of monotony here?'). Schmidt claims that this is a social, not an aesthetic issue. He adopts a different tone from the rhetorical verve of Hannes Meyer's view, in 1926,[75] of the collective virtues of industrialized architecture, but is closer to the intentions of the production line assembly attempted by Gropius at the Siedlung Törten of 1926–1928. Aligned to the standard prototypes emphasized in his Dessau 'Principles of Bauhaus Production',[76] the model estate proved to have serious limitations.

If Neo-rationalism shied away from issues of 'production', typological 'reproduction' and the legacy of tradition were another matter; a literal retrieval of tradition in the form of the model 'European City' was sought by Leon Krier whose influence during the 1970s should not be underestimated. Setting out his initial argument in the 1978 'Rational Architecture' catalogue, by 1980 he had consolidated a more explicitly classicist agenda. This moved away from the catalogue's earlier association with Unger's work: for example the influential 1964 project at Köln Grünzug Süd (worked on by Rob Krier and applauded for its typological diversity), which presented a 'relational' rather than literal 'contextualism'. The historical model of the 'museum' as a building type and paradigm, recurs in later rationalist thinking, whether as Perret's model of a building 'without use', a frame for Unger's compositional strategies, or in analogical terms in Rossi's writing.[77] In the museum of architects, Adolf Loos is an architect whose paradoxical thinking and contradictory buildings reside uneasily in the territory between Modernism and Neo-rationalism, but it was his view of tradition that increasingly preoccupied Rossi. The title of the résumé 'Regarding Economy'[78] appears matter of fact, but his aphoristic

ANDREW PECKHAM AND TORSTEN SCHMIEDEKNECHT

wit extols the virtues of tradition in clothing, furniture and architecture, where an ironic contention presents the modernist virtues of 'functional' durability and economy as traditional qualities shared by his interiors, in fact characterized by a comfortable sensuality.

What attracted Rossi to Loos is this characteristic swerve that takes the rhetoric of modernity and inverts its logic, promoting tradition as a typological continuity. This everyday vernacular, or sublimated classicism, resisted the call of an avant-garde 'art' of architecture. Loos's 'honesty' is disingenuously ironic, however, in over-emphasizing the inevitability of tradition. Rossi's empathy with Loos[79] was strengthened by his move away from the 'authentic rationalism' (constructing a logic of architecture) proposed in his 1967 'Introduction' to Boullée's *Architecture essai sur l'art* – at odds, he notes, with the 'extremes' of a 'conventional' or alternately a 'fanatic', 'emotional' or 'metaphoric' rationalism.[80] But Loos's conception of tradition consistently held to a pattern of unexceptional reproduction, whereas Rossi's relationship to the concept of rationalism in architecture, and hence tradition, became more volatile.

› Symptomatic rationalism

If the term 'rationalist architecture' came to stand in for modern architecture or later the Modern Movement, then in Otto Wagner's text *Modern Architecture* of 1896, for all its episodic structure and tendency to digression, we first find a relationship proposed between rational construction and social democracy: 'All modern creations must correspond to the new materials and demands of the present if they are to suit modern man; they must illustrate our better, democratic, self-confident, ideal nature . . .' just as 'this new style' should express 'an almost all-encompassing appearance of reason in all our works.'[81] That 'almost' is advisory and the mark of ambivalence.

By 1908 H. P. Berlage's parallel discourse had moved further in establishing the *sachlich* credentials of the 'Modern Movement'.[82] These nonetheless in his case remained set in the context of a structural rationalism aligned to craftsmanship and local tradition. Oscillating between artistic and rational polarities, a slippage occurs in both architects' thinking between an incipient idealism (whether aesthetic, political or spiritual) and a contemporary realism. They recognize rationalization as a condition of modernity, but one tempered by traditional values.

Within the later canons of Modern Architecture the *sachlich* connotation becomes more marked in emphasizing standardization and economy. It is to become axiomatic, then, when Adolf Behne clarifies the distinction between rationalist and functionalist attitudes in a book titled *The Modern Functional Building*.[83] Considering mechanization's typical pattern of serial repetition, he distinguishes between a 'functionalist' concept of the individual building as a natural organism, a 'utilitarian' concern with the 'economic principle', and a rationalist's representative view of the virtues of standardization and typification. Purposefully, Behne lists rationalist prerogatives: a predilection for the 'general case' against a functionalist concern for the 'unique'; an acceptance of purposefulness but a disregard for the 'tyranny' of instrumentality; a search for the 'most appropriate' general solution as opposed to the most specifically adept, and an assertion of the collective 'norm' in contrast to individual particularity.

Behne's conclusion paradoxically blurs the boundaries between these structural oppositions, arguing that 'formlessness' is the outcome of a functionalist 'selflessness', and that the personal conviction ascribed to a rationalist position is equally identified with 'play' *and* 'form' (seemingly a formalist conviction). It is not the exactness of Behne's categories that stands out, but rather the grey area between them. This comes to mean that within the tradition of Modern Architecture one stands in for the other within a general perception of modernity, an ambiguity that productively marked the thinking of Adolf Loos and Le Corbusier. Mies's abstractly rational classicism and Hilberseimer's generic metropolitan rationalism offered more forthright positions. Behne's dialectical view of rationalism as a strand of modernism parallels something of Neo-rationalism's own agenda post-war, distanced from the urban consequences of a rationalized modern architecture but not immune to aspects of its formulation.

Aldo Rossi was explicit in questioning the urban consequences of Functionalism in *The Architecture of the City*. The Neo-rationalist position was to reflect on the past, appealing to 'history' in order to acquire its formal repertoire – and evolving a variety of typological methodologies. In this sense it read modernism itself as an antithetical 'history', but one with which it could identify – if only in the work of selective rationalist architects.

› Notes

Note: numbers in brackets refer to texts in this Reader where full details and pagination are given.

1 A. Peckham, C. Rattray and T. Schmiedeknecht (ed.), *Architectural Design: Rationalist Traces*, London: Wiley, 2007.
2 See this Reader: Nicholas Bullock, 'Architecture, Rationalism and Reconstruction: the example of France 1945–55'.
3 See Tzvetan Todorov, *In Defence of the Enlightenment*, London: Atlantic Books, 2009; John Bender, *Ends of Enlightenment*, Stanford CA: Stanford University Press, 2012, pp. 4–18 and C. Siskin and W. Warner, *This is Enlightenment*, Chicago: The University of Chicago Press, 2010 pp. 1–33.
4 Environmental functionality (the pivot of a sustainable architecture) and the new technologies once again promoting prefabrication in housing, being cases in point.
5 (56) Leon Krier, 'The Reconstruction of the City', and (69) Leon Krier, 'The Age of Reconstruction'.
6 (67) O. M. Ungers, 'Was ist Architektur?', and O. M. Ungers 'The Criteria of Architecture', in *Architecture as Craft*, Amsterdam: SUN, 2010, pp. 95—108.
7 Bernard Huet, 'The City as Dwelling Space', *Lotus*, 41, 1984, pp. 6–17.
8 (74) Angelika Schnell, 'The Socialist Perspective of the XV Triennale di Milano. Hans Schmidt's Influence on Aldo Rossi'.
9 (73) Pier Vittorio Aureli, 'Rossi: The Concept of the Locus as a Political Category of the City', and his (42) 'Architecture for Barbarians—Ludwig Hilberseimer and the Rise of the Generic City'.
10 See this Reader: Alan Colquhoun, 'Rationalism: a Philosophical Concept in Architecture'; complete text in his *Collected Essays in Architectural Criticism*, London: Black Dog, 2009, pp. 163–177.
11 See also this Reader: Charles Rattray, 'Rationalist Tendencies in Nineteenth-century Architecture'.
12 See this Reader: Thilo Hilpert, 'The Architects of Modernism and Their Texts: an introduction to the history of modern architecture'.
13 See this Reader: Henk Engel, 'The Neo-rationalist Perspective'.
14 See note 11.
15 See note 2.
16 See also (52) Werner Oechslin, 'Premises for the Resumption of the Discussion of Typology'.
17 See also in this Reader: Hans Kollhoff, 'Tectonics'.
18 (1) Julia Bloomfield, Thomas F. Reese and Salvatore Settis (ed.) *Hendrick Petrus Berlage: Thoughts on Style 1886–1909*; (8) August Perret, 'Le musée moderne'; and (11) Auguste Perret, 'Les besoins collectifs et l'architecture'.
19 See note 12.
20 See also Henk Engel, 'Autonomous Architecture and the Project of the City', *OASE*, 62, 2003, pp. 20–69.
21 (55) Aldo Rossi, *The Architecture of the City*.
22 (47) Massimo Scolari, 'The New Architecture and the Avantgarde'; also see Frédéric Migayrou (ed.), *La Tendenza: Architectures Italiennes*, 1965–1985, Paris: Editions du Centre Pompidou, 2012 (French/English text).
23 (64) O. M. Ungers, 'Architecture's Right to an Autonomous Language'; (67) O. M. Ungers, 'Was ist Architektur?', and (55) see note 21, and (68) Aldo Rossi, 'Architecture for Museums'.

24 (56) See note 5; (69) Leon Krier, 'The Age of Reconstruction'; and (57) Rob Krier, *Urban Space*.

25 (47) See note 22.

26 (55) See note 21; (61) Aldo Rossi, 'Introduzione'; (68) see note 23; (46) Giorgio Grassi, 'Architettura e razionalismo'; (59) Giorgio Grassi, *La costruzione logica dell'architettura*; and (63) Giorgio Grassi, 'Architecture as Craft'.

27 (8) (11) See note 18.

28 (56) See note 5; (48) Anthony Vidler, 'The Third Typology' and (49) Bernard Huet, 'Small Manifesto'.

29 (3) Le Corbusier, *Toward an Architecture*.

30 (24) Le Corbusier and Pierre Jeanneret, 'Five points towards a new architecture'.

31 (19) Otto Wagner, *Modern Architecture*.

32 (29) Walter Gropius, *The New Architecture and the Bauhaus*; and (33) Walter Gropius, 'Principles of Bauhaus production [Dessau]'.

33 (13) Hans Schmidt, 'Die Beziehung der Typisierung zur Architektur'; and (37) Hans Schmidt, 'Modularkoordination in der Architektur'.

34 (2) Adolf Loos, 'Architecture (1910)'.

35 (55) See note 21; (52) Werner Oechslin, 'Premises for the Resumption of the Discussion of Typology'.

36 (59) See note 26.

37 (47) Massimo Scolari, 'The New Architecture and the Avantgarde'; (52) see note 35; (53) Micha Bandini, 'Typological Theories in Architectural Design'; (54) Guido Francescato, 'Type and the Possibility of an Architectural Scholarship'; (60) Ezio Bonfanti, 'Elementi e Costruzione: note sull'architettura di Aldo Rossi'; (70) Manfredo Tafuri, *Storia dell'architettura italiana*; (72) Mary Louise Lobsinger, 'The New Urban Scale in Italy'; and (73) Pier Vittorio Aureli, 'Rossi: The Concept of the Locus as a Political Category of the City'.

38 (48) Anthony Vidler, 'The Third Typology'.

39 (70) Manfredo Tafuri, *History of Italian Architecture*.

40 (43) David Rifkind, 'Everything in the state, nothing against the state': corporative urbanism and Rationalist architecture in fascist Italy'; and (41) Michelangelo Sabatino, 'The Politics of *Mediterraneità* in Italian Modernist Architecture'.

41 (40) Richard Etlin, *Modernism in Italian Architecture*; (39) Dennis P. Doordan, *Building Modern Italy 1914–1936*.

42 See David Rifkind, *The Battle for Modernism: Quadrante and the Politicization of Architectural Discourse in Fascist Italy*, Venice: Marsilio, 2012.

43 (12) Guiseppe Pagano and Guarniero Daniel, *Architettura Rurale Italiana*; (28) Giuseppe Pagano, 'Struttura ed architettura'; and (41) see note 40.

44 (63) Giorgio Grassi, 'L'architettura come mestiere'; see also Giorgio Grassi, 'The Licence of Obviousness', *Lotus*, 15, 1977, pp. 26–27.

45 Aldo Rossi, *The Architecture of the City*, 'Preface to the Second Italian Edition 1969', Cambridge MA: MIT Press, 1982, p. 166.

46 Le Corbusier, *Toward an Architecture*, London: Francis Lincoln, 2008, pp. 193–212.

47 Rossi, *The Architecture of the City*, (see note 45) p. 116 and pp. 119–126.

48 (15) Le Corbusier, *The City of Tomorrow and its Planning*; see also Le Corbusier, *The Radiant City*, London: Faber, 1967.

49 (18) CIAM / Le Corbusier, 'The Athens Charter: Conclusions'.

50 (17) CIAM / Le Corbusier, *The Athens Charter*.

51 (14) Otto Wagner, *Die Großstadt*.

52 (16) Ludwig Hilberseimer, *Großstadtarchitektur*; (42) Pier Vittorio Aureli, 'Architecture for Barbarians'.

53 (69) Leon Krier, 'The Age of Reconstruction' and 'The Reconstruction of the European City'.

54 (64) O. M. Ungers, 'Architecture's Right to an Autonomous Language'.

55 (57) Rob Krier, 'Typological and Morphological Elements of the Concept of Urban Space'.

56 (7) Gruppo 7, 'Architettura I'.

57 (38) Vittorio Gregotti, 'Il filo rosso del razionalismo italiano'.

58 (43) See note 40.

59 (72) See note 37.

60 (8) See note 18.

61 (24) Le Corbusier and Pierre Jeanneret, 'Five points towards a new architecture'.

62 (21) Mies van der Rohe, 'Office Building'.

63 (22) Mies van der Rohe, 'Building'.

64 (31) Mies van der Rohe, 'Industrial Building'; and (23) Ludwig Hilberseimer, 'Construction and Form'.
65 (28) Giuseppe Pagano, 'Struttura ed architettura'.
66 See note 17.
67 (59) Giorgio Grassi, *La costruzione logica dell'architettura*.
68 (68) Aldo Rossi, 'Architecture for Museums'.
69 Aldo Rossi, 'Rational Architecture', *Aldo Rossi: selected writings and projects*, London: Architectural Design / Dublin: Gandon Editions, 1983, p. 57.
70 (63) See note 44, and also (46) Giorgio Grassi, 'Architettura e razionalismo'.
71 (47) See note 22.
72 (59) See note 67; (47) ibid; and (64) see note 54.
73 (3) See note 29, and (31) see note 64.
74 (13) See note 33.
75 (34) Hannes Meyer, 'The New World' and (35) 'Building'.
76 (33) See note 32.
77 (8) See note 18; O. M. Ungers, 'Architecture of Collective Memory', *Lotus*, 24, 1979 and (68) see note 23.
78 (4) Adolf Loos, 'Regarding Economy'.
79 See Aldo Rossi, 'Introduction', in Adolf Loos, *Spoken into the Void: collected essays 1897–1900*, Cambridge MA / London: MIT Press, 1982, pp. viii–xiii, and Aldo Rossi, 'Preface', in Benedetto Gravagnuolo, *Adolf Loos*, Milan: Idea Books, 1982, pp. 11–15.
80 Aldo Rossi, 'Introduction to *"Architecture, essai sur l'art"'*, *UCLA Architecture Journal*, 2, 1989, pp. 42–3.
81 (19) See note 31.
82 (1) See note 18.
83 (20) Adolf Behne, *The Modern Functional Building*.

Alan Colquhoun

Rationalism: a philosophical concept in architecture (1987)

First published in *Das Abenteuer der Ideen: Architehtur und Philosophie seit der Indusriellen Revolution*, Claus Baldus (ed.), Berlin: International Bauausstellung, 1987. Text extracts.

› From classical rationalism to the Enlightenment: the search for beauty

There is a common-sense view that divides mental activities into the scientific, depending on reason, and the artistic, depending on feeling or intuition. Such a simple dichotomy fails to take account of both the role that intuition plays in scientific thought and the role that the judgment-forming intellect plays in artistic creation. Nevertheless, the distinction contains an element of truth—less as a way of distinguishing between science and art than as a way of distinguishing between different aspects of the artistic process.

Of all the arts, architecture is the one in which it is least possible to exclude the idea of rationality. A building has to satisfy pragmatic and constructional criteria, which circumscribe, even if they do not determine, the field within which the imagination of the architect works. Therefore the degree to which architecture can be said to be rational depends less on the presence or absence of 'rational' criteria than on the importance attributed to these criteria within the total process of architectural design and within particular ideologies. The rational in architecture never exists in isolation. It is not an art historical category like neo-classicism. It is one side of a complex system that can be expressed only dialectically in terms of a series of more or less homologous oppositions: reason/feeling, order/disorder, necessity/freedom, universal/particular, and so on.

But having made this initial distinction, we are immediately faced with another. The definition of the 'rational' in architecture has not remained constant throughout history. We are dealing not with a simple, static concept, but with one that has varied according to the constellation of ideas dominating particular historical phases. These changes of meaning are dependent on changes in ideology and cannot be considered independently of either economic or social factors or philosophical ideas.

As a preliminary step in the definition of architectural rationalism, it is necessary to note the sense in which the term is used in the history of philosophy. In philosophy the primary distinction is that between rationalism and empiricism, or reason and experience. While the opposition of reason/feeling cannot be reduced to these philosophical categories, there is nonetheless a relation between them. In both cases *reason* implies the intervention of rule or law between the direct experience of the world and any praxis or *techné* such as architecture. It is this notion—that architecture is the result of the application of general rules, established by the operation of reason—that may be taken as the most general definition of rationalism in architecture.

The conflict between rationalism and empiricism is one between two concepts of knowledge (or science), that define it as *a priori* or *a posteriori*. To the extent that knowledge is held to be *a priori,* empirical knowledge appears to be random, unfounded, and subject to contingency. To the extent that knowledge is held to be *a posteriori,* the terms are reversed and it is *a priori* knowledge that becomes unsure and dependent on authority, received ideas, or habit. The history of architectural theory during the last two hundred years has been the history of the conflict between these two concepts of architectural knowledge. But more than this; the dominance of one or the other has determined the role ascribed to those other mental processes that cannot be subsumed under the operation of reason or science. When discussing rationalism in architecture, therefore, we are discussing two sets of varying relationships: those that come from different concepts of knowledge itself, and those that come from the distinction between knowledge and intuition or feeling.

The rationalist philosophy of the seventeenth century, which we take here as represented by Descartes, Spinoza, and Leibnitz, absorbed within its system the traditional view that there are innate ideas and that 'science' is a fundamentally *a priori* enterprise based on these ideas. Innate ideas must be thought of as implanted by God, and, as such, they may be enshrined in a wisdom that has been revealed to mankind in the past and that constitutes valid authority. Knowledge gained by experience and induction has, ultimately, to be measured against this authority.

Cartesian rationalism did not abandon this tradition, but it inaugurated a search for clarity of concept, rigor of deduction, and intuitional certainty of basic principles. This is reflected in seventeenth century academic artistic theory, of which Nicolas Boileau-Despréaux's *L'art poetique,* Jean-Philippe Rameau's *Traité de l'harmonie réduite à ses principes naturels,* and François Blondel's *Cours d'architecture* may be taken as examples.

The principles enunciated in these works were themselves based on an older body of ideas. When, in the late fifteenth century, architecture was first constituted as a separate branch of science, an important part of the knowledge forming this science depended on the authority of the ancients and the precepts found in the only surviving ancient architectural treatise, that of Vitruvius. At the same time, architectural theory began to be inscribed within a general artistic doctrine derived from Aristotle, Horace, and Cicero, on the one hand, and neo-Platonism on the other. The most important component of this doctrine was the idea that art was an imitation of nature, and that the art of the ancients, being derived from this law, was also worthy of imitation. Thus, nature was chiefly approachable through the authority of the ancients. This notion of authority is closely linked to the seventeenth century doctrine of *a priori* knowledge and innate ideas.

One of the sources of the concept of imitation can be found in Aristotle's *Physics*. He says:

> If a house were one of the things provided by nature, it would be the same as it is now when produced by art. And if natural phenomena were produced not only by nature but also by art, they would in this case come into being through art in the same way as they do in nature. . . . In short, art either completes the process that nature is unable to work out fully, or it imitates nature.

Here we see two ideas which, to the modern mind, seem quite different, if not contra-dictory: the idea that architecture and other artefacts are extensions of nature's laws, and the idea that this entails a process of imitation or representation. In fact, throughout the eighteenth

ALAN COLQUHOUN

and nineteenth centuries there is a progressive separation between these two ideas and the concept of architecture becomes split between its constructive and 'scientific' and its representational and 'artistic' functions, *reason* being reserved for the former and *feeling,* or *sentiment,* for the latter.

Such a split, however, would have been inconceivable to the classical mind. Access to the truth and beauty was by way of laws that were already inscribed—however obscurely—in nature. Truth was the revelation of what already existed, and if it depended on revelation it must equally be based on truths already revealed to previous men. All truth was therefore a re-presentation. This view is still found in certain writers until the end of the eighteenth century. The English architect John Wood the Elder held that the science of architecture was its speculative or metaphysical part, while the *art* of architecture was the knowledge of its specific causes and its application to human uses. It is the final cause that gives meaning to architecture, not the efficient cause or the solutions to specific problems. The distinction we find here between science and art is the opposite of the one generally made today; science for Wood belonged to the realm of metaphysics and the unchanging, and art to the realm of the practical and the contingent. Quatremère de Quincy is equally adamant that architecture should imitate the *idea* of nature. This imitation results in a building having a certain 'character', which may be of three kinds—essential, relative, and accidental—according to whether one is imitating nature in her more generic and timeless aspects or in her more specific and momentary aspects. (The idea of character comes from the theory of genres in Aristotle's *Poetics*, but de Quincy turns it into something rather neo-Platonic.)

But a new attitude was developing within the ethos of seventeenth century Rationalism, which emphasised the role that both empirical science and individual intelligence played in the discovery of truth and which tended to throw doubt on the status of *a priori* knowledge and innate ideas, as much as on the authority of the ancients or of the Bible. The quarrel between the 'ancients' and the 'moderns' gave rise to an increasingly critical dispute as to which architectural rules belonged to the realm of innate ideas and which belonged to the realm of empirical experience. The 'lawful' now become split between what was eternal and absolute and what was customary—the latter coming increasingly under the guidance of 'taste'.

*   *   *

In Laugier's *Essai sur l'architecture* of 1753, the rules of good architecture are presented as self-evident to the uncorrupted mind and eye; *a priori* reason is confirmed by empirical experience and by sensation. In this way, untutored reason confirms the truth of the earliest architecture and no longer depends on the guidance of particular antique models. But reason and truth were still tied to the purification of the tradition, of which more or less imperfect models already existed. Just as it was the task of the painter or sculptor, in classical and neo-classical doctrine, to imitate the idea lying behind the imperfect appearances of nature, so it was the task of the architect to uncover the types lying concealed in the manifold, but imperfect, examples presented by the history of architecture. Architecture is treated exactly as if it were a natural phenomenon. Even Carlo Lodoli, whose functionalism, *avant la lettre,* has often been mistaken for a pure empiricism, adhered to a concept of architectural ornament in which there is a clear distinction between what is normative and typical and what is due to 'accidental' cultural differences. The Enlightenment may have wanted to replace *l'esprit du système* by *l'esprit systèmatique,* in order to free practice from the domination of authority and received ideas, but its aim was still to discover the universal and unchanging laws underlying empirical experience. A building such as Soufflot's Sainte-Geneviève, uniting 'the noble decoration of the Greeks and the lightness of the Gothic Architects', and the rationalism of a Lodoli or a Laugier both pointed to the need to free architecture from the arbitrary and tasteless rules to which it had succumbed under the Baroque and bring it back to nature, whose laws were simple and eternal.

This project was similar in many ways to the Grammarian's search for the universal and rational laws of language. Architecture was also a rational 'language', subject to the variations of character demanded by climate, custom, and decorum, but capable, nevertheless, of being reduced by the exercise of reason to a universal system, whose laws even genius could not escape. The eighteenth century is marked by the opposition reason/caprice, reason alone being capable of discerning universal truths. But this *reason* is now in alliance with subjective experience; empirical experience is no longer set in opposition to a reason that has been implanted in us by God and that constitutes an unquestioned authority. It is used as a supplementary proof of the existence of Natural Law.

› Utilitarian and eclectic rationalism: the search for utility

With the growth of utilitarianism the structure of thought on which the alliance between rationalism and classicism depended became increasingly tenuous. 'Scientific' reason became increasingly directed to instrumental efficacy rather than metaphysics. Efficient causes replaced final causes. There was now no theory that could withstand the growth of caprice and eclecticism, or the proliferation of what Quatremère called 'accidental character'. JNL Durand, though still working within the formal language of classicism, justified a rational architecture purely on the grounds of economics and utility. The efforts of architects and theorists like Durand, Legrand, Thomas Hope, and Schinkel were now directed to an irenic eclecticism which would select, in a system of combinations and permutations, appropriate stylistic elements from the panorama of history or from buildings of a utilitarian nature. There were now as many 'architectures' (the word is Legrand's) as there were times and peoples; classicism was reduced to a specific tradition (admittedly 'our own') whose use was purely justified by convention.

*   *   *

› Structural and organic rationalism: the search for authenticity

From the second half of the eighteenth century onward the conceptual split between architecture as construction and architecture as representation had begun to undermine seriously the unitary doctrine of classicism. But a weak form of classical doctrine nonetheless persisted, in which it was possible to think of the use of different styles as permissible within the classical notions of character and decorum.

The development of a rationalism based on the logic of structure took place chiefly in France, where, as far back as the seventeenth century, architects had recognised in Gothic architecture a rational constructive principle. The structural rationalists of the late eighteenth century did not reject classicism; they sought to subject it to more stringent functional analysis in terms of the new science of the strength of materials and in terms of use. This tradition continued well into the nineteenth century, even after the impact of Comtian positivism. The belief, characteristic of the positivists, that science provides us with the only valid knowledge and that facts are its only objects, was quite compatible with a form of idealism that promoted all that was not reducible to experimental science to a vaguely neo-classicism realm of 'Beauty'.

*   *   *

This debate, however, took a different form among the Gothic revivalists. According to them, Gothic architecture was not a style that could he used eclectically, as a way of eliciting literary associations *within* the classical definition of 'character'; it should be seen as an *alternative* tradition to that of classicism. The difference between the Gothic Revivalists and the classical eclectics was that for the former structure itself became the basis of architectural meaning. Ornament and 'representation' were now thought of as emerging from the structure of a building, rather than as arbitrary clothing that could be added to it. It followed that, of the three kinds of character described by Quatremère, only the first—essential character—was kept.

The chief spokesman for this school of thought and possibly the most influential architectural writer of the nineteenth century was Viollet-le-Duc. For him technique becomes the basis for an architecture that is rational in its very essence. He sees in Gothic architecture a constructional principle that should become the methodological paradigm of a future architecture. In spite of a predominance of restorations in Viollet's oeuvre and his nostalgia for Medieval culture, his writings exhibit the same adherence to positivism as those of the opposing school of classical eclectics, and an even stronger belief in the open-ended progress of mankind, which, it was supposed, would follow in the wake of the Industrial revolution. But for Viollet the history of architecture is a continuous technological development, which excludes the possibility of repeating the 'perfect' forms derived from antiquity. The morphology of architecture is no longer determined by a taxonomy of external and historical *forms,* but by a system of underlying *functions.* 'That which is generally regarded as a matter of true art, namely symmetry, the apparent form, is quite a secondary consideration.'

This 'evolutionary' rationalism, which tied architecture to an implacable and objective historical destiny, was combined with a subjective moralism. The principles of Gothic architecture were both rational *and* moral.

*   *   *

› Rationalism and the twentieth century avant-garde: the search for transparency

It has often been argued that it was not until the twentieth century that positivism and the structural rationalism of the nineteenth century bore fruit. If the law of historical evolution and progress was to be demonstrated, architecture would have finally to sever its ties with past styles and draw its meaning and its language exclusively from the objective conditions of technique and programme.

It was not until the end of the nineteenth century that certain architects began to put these principles into operation. Among these, HP Berlage and Otto Wagner were outstanding in the way in which they were able to transform their stylistic inheritance (Gothic Revival and neo-classical, respectively) by the application of rational constructional principles. The two paradigmatic 'halls' of the early twentieth century, the Amsterdam Exchange and the Post Office Savings building in Vienna, both assimilate the nineteenth century exhibition or railway shed to socio-cultural programmes and embed them in an architecture, which, though recognisably traditional in overall form, tries to develop a new kind or ornament derived from construction.

However, although the craftsman-like principles embodied in these buildings were incorporated into the doctrine of the twentieth century avant-garde, the rationalism of the Modern Movement cannot be understood in these terms alone. Twentieth century rationalism differs radically from that of the nineteenth century, and to understand this difference it is necessary to analyse it in terms of three concepts: *logical atomism, functionalism,* and *formalism* which, while not absolutely new, now take an entirely new form.

› Logical atomism

Logic was stressed in positivistic thought, but we have seen that for Viollet-le-Duc: there was always a passage from logic, via technique, to subjective feeling and organic nature. Viollet had talked about the machine as a paradigm for architecture, but for him mechanisation did not imply any change in the relation between the components of architecture and the building as a whole. Iron could be substituted for wood or stone, but this substitution, though it entailed substantial formal transformations, depended on the fact that these materials had analogous properties and could still be 'worked' in a craftsman-like way. It was precisely such linking of 'logic' and 'technique' that enabled Viollet to see architecture as a continuous process of evolution, whose principles remained constant, even if their material embodiment changed.

A series of developments in aesthetic theory, in philosophy, in construction, and in production in the late nineteenth and twentieth centuries intervened to alter quite radically this fundamentally traditional conception of architecture.

*   *   *

› Functionalism

The idea, fundamental to the Modern Movement, that there is an overriding causal relation between functions and forms in architecture is part of a tradition going back to Vitruvius. Until the end of the eighteenth century, as we have seen, this idea was closely united with the idea of imitation in the sense given by Aristotle. But in the first half of the nineteenth century, under the influence of romanticism and historicism, it became associated with the notion of genetic development. An *inner necessity* took the place of *analogy* as the generator of forms expressive of the programme or the structure of a building. This 'inner necessity' was capable of either an idealist interpretation (an invisible spirit giving direction to material causality) or a 'scientific' or materialist interpretation (based on efficient causes and empirical evidence).

*   *   *

The leftists among the *Neue Sachlichkeit* architects present, in their theory, an extreme example of this kind of 'functionalism'. When Hannes Meyer defined architecture as *function x economics* he was trying to reduce architecture to an absolutely primitive system excluding all *a priori* 'values'. But of course the nature of this system was already given by his own arbitrary restriction of the relevant facts: those, like structure, economy, and fundamental 'need', which could he empirically tested by the 'scientific' method. In a fully axiomaticised field of knowledge such as mathematics, such arbitrary limitations are justified, and indeed essential. But in an affective and ideological field like architecture, their rigid application can he explained only by hidden ideological motives.

The term *functional;* as used in modern architecture, was coloured by this arbitrary limitation as to what could be logically deduced or empirically verified. The results, instead of being understood as aspects of a purely formal operation, as they are in mathematics, were taken as objectively true descriptions of the real world.

A similar situation pertained to 'functionalism' in anthropology, where the recording of empirically observable behaviour was considered to be the only way of arriving at truth statements about a particular society.

In the 1940s, in anthropology and somewhat later in architecture, a structuralist critique was developed, whose purpose was to demonstrate that there was no necessary correlation between forms and structures on the one hand and 'functions' and 'behaviour patterns' on the other. Forms, it was claimed, were independent of the empirical situations which lent them 'meaning' at any one time or place.

› Formalism

We can define formalism as that type of thought which stresses rule-governed relationships rather than relationships of cause and effect.

*   *   *

While one of the aims of formalist art history was to break the hold of normative classical aesthetics, these aims could only be achieved by establishing more general norms which would apply to all art, of whatever period. It thus tended toward the establishment of ahistorical laws, and in doing so resembled classical theory itself. Formalist art theory concentrated on the 'how' of art because it rejected the kind of 'why' explanations always given to justify a particular system of values (or a particular style). But classical doctrine also concentrated on the 'how' (the rules of good poetry and of rhetoric, etc.) precisely because it *accepted,* without question, a particular system of values.

The formalist tendencies of the twentieth century avant-garde therefore contradicted the historicist interpretations of modern architecture given by Viollet-le-Duc and his followers. Instead of seeing architecture as continuously developing according to a historical law of technical and social evolution, they carry the implication that modern architecture is a radical break with history—that it has reached a threshold which enables it to give form to the eternal laws of aesthetics. In this way it can be seen as a type of classicism, but one which rejects the specific, historically determined forms of the classical style. This view was, nonetheless, closely connected to developments in constructional techniques, which were seen as freeing the architect from those technical constraints that had previously tied architectural aesthetics to particular times and particular craft traditions.

*   *   *

In the 1920s most of the avant-garde architects began to accept the replacement of craft by the machine as the price architecture had to pay if it was to tackle the urgent social tasks presented to it. But, although this involved a certain simplification of masses and the stressing of the typical over the individual, its incipient classicism was overshadowed by the elementarist and montage-like compositional principles that denied the formal hierarchies of the classical *system*. This was particularly true of the left-wing architects like Hannes Meyer, Ernst May, Mart Stam, and Hans Schmidt, among others.

There is, in the work of these architects, and especially in the city layouts by Ludwig Hilbersheimer, an extreme schematicism, which transposes diagrams resulting from purely analytical operations into objects of the real, perceptual world. This is a primitive kind of formalism which halts the process of abstraction midway, as it were, without allowing it to work toward an adequate image.

In the work of Le Corbusier and Mies van der Rohe, however, this schematic formalism was combined with more overt classical tendencies. Le Corbusier's classicism, in particular, was quite explicit and was based on a rather generalised acceptance of the French classical tradition. In the greater part of his work he was concerned with reconciling the classical idea of an *a priori* artistic order with the idea of continuous progress inherited from historicism and positivism. His drawing of the Domino frame was a demonstration of the dialectical principle that was to inform all his later work. Here the concrete frame has all the certainty of the Cartesian *a priori*. Within this frame, the volumes and the equipment of the house can be independently arranged, according to practical needs. The organisation of these needs is supposed to follow an empirical necessity whose laws are as rigorous as those of the Platonic frame and its implied cubic envelope (though, in fact, it is precisely here that the invention of the architect/artist comes into play, with all its freedom of metaphorical allusion). The dialogue between the frame and its infill is made apparent by means of Cubist techniques of spatial simultaneity, themselves made possible by new constructional techniques.

Le Corbusier's architecture gives artistic expression to the conflict between the two traditions of rationalism we have traced: the *a priori* and the empirical. On the one hand we find those 'clear and distinct ideas' which, translated from a Cartesian metaphysics into the sensuous objects of art, have been promoted by French classical theorists from Boileau to Durand. On the other, we find the empirical and scientistic ideas of positivism, which are expressed as the functional, the accidental, and the contingent.

*   *   *

> ### › Postmodernism: the search for meaning

*   *   *

In the mid-1960s, a new architectural discourse emerged, which, instead of trying to reform architecture from within a specifically modernist tradition, sought rather to define rationalism in terms of an autonomous tradition of architecture. This movement originated in the circle of young architects grouped around Ernesto Rogers, the editor of the magazine *Casabella*. The specific transformations to which rationalism had been subject in historical development were seen as secondary to, and dependent upon, a deeper tradition according to which what is 'rational' in architecture is that which conserves architecture as a cultural discourse throughout history. These ideas were based on an analogy with structural linguistics, which had stressed the paradigmatic value of the typical and invariant structures underlying individual speech acts.

Although there is an evident historical connection between this view and the formalistic aspects of modernism, they differ in one crucial aspect. Modernist formalism had assumed that architecture could be reduced to forms which corresponded to the structure of the human mind, whereas the new formalism we are describing sees the invariant elements of architecture as derived from architecture itself, as a social and cultural reality.

The implication of this view is that we should look upon the history of architecture—or at any rate a large segment of it—as if it were a continuous instant in which thought and memory are coextensive. The model for such a view is Enlightenment thought, which looked on progress not as the unpredictable and open-ended development it was to become for positivism, but as the rational rearrangement and exploitation of existing material. According to such a view, the typological characteristics of a rational architecture are not those that are created by technology or by specifically modern forms of social behaviour, but those that persist through technological and social change and anchor us to a permanent image of man. There is return to an eighteenth century view of reason, as the faculty which is, itself, outside history.

The architects who exemplify these attitudes most clearly are Giorgio Grassi and Aldo Rossi. The former emphasises the more ontological and tectonic aspects of the rationalist tradition, while the latter stresses those subjective and poetic images to which it can give rise. As part of a more general 'postmodern' technology, this type of rationalism must be seen as a defensive reaction to the current social conditions of production and consumption. It is not an accident that in both cases this output is small and deliberately modest in scale. Its protagonists seem to be saying that we have reached a stage of social evolution in which the products of man's reason are increasingly divorced from the experience of making, constructing or imagining.

Charles Rattray

Rationalist tendencies in nineteenth-century architecture

'Centuries as cultural entities often begin and end decades before or after the hundred-year mark' said Henry-Russell Hitchcock, but he approved of the title of his *Architecture: Nineteenth and Twentieth Centuries* because the years around 1800 were different: they had 'inherited the tradition of a completed architectural revolution'.[1] What was this revolution? It was the abandonment of those objective standards of beauty epitomised by Vitruvian Classicism in favour of relative values, of subjectivity, of associationism, of a trust in the Sublime. In short, the last decades of the eighteenth century marked a decisive cultural shift away from the ideas of the Enlightenment – the 'Age of Reason' – towards Romanticism.[2]

In such circumstances one might be forgiven for confusing the timescale of Étienne-Louis Boullée and his favourite pupil, Jean-Nicolas-Louis Durand. Boullée, after all, was the visionary one, entranced by dramatic forms, extravagant scale and spooky renderings; even his belief that architecture was at its purest and best when in its simplest and most primitive form evokes a mythical, rather than factual, history. By comparison, the work of Durand reflects his background as an engineer in Napoleon's army: dispassionate, practical to the point of mechanistic, and rather dry. His key contributions to architecture are two theoretical works. The first, published in 1800, is the *Recueil et parallèle des édifices de tout genre, anciens et modernes* (Collection and Parallel of Every Building Type, Ancient and Modern), an eclectic selection of Egyptian, Classical, Gothic and Renaissance buildings plus some 'almost entirely of my own invention' as he put it. In this miscellany all are drawn to the same scale and treated as of equal importance – a significant, not to say anti-authoritarian, move, since it implied that architecture was no longer synonymous with Classicism. The second work is his lecture summaries, published in 1802 and 1805 – the *Précis des leçons données à l'École polytechnique* – which forms an architectural methodology, a guide to composing architecture from its constituent parts. The crucial characteristics of both are that the selected buildings are almost invariably drawn in two dimensions (a simplification that made use of the descriptive geometry developed by Durand's mathematics colleague at the *Polytechnique*, Gaspard Monge) and that they are categorised by *type* rather than style.

The presentation is symptomatic of intellectual detachment, and the contrast with that of Boullée or Ledoux is sharp. Pérez-Gómez[3] has commented that:

> Durand and his students [...] proud of their new scientific and specialized architecture, took pains to emphasise the *differences* between their own eminently rational profession and the other fine arts, which were ruled by intuition. For them, architectural drawing was no more and no less than an instrument for precisely representing a building.

The interest in classification and categorisation that accompanied this marks Durand as a taxonomer – and one living in an age of taxonomy. One may point to the eighteenth-century development of the modern encyclopaedia with its exposition of human knowledge (notably Diderot's *Encyclopédie* from the 1750s) and suggest, as Vidler has,[4] that these architectural publications – these *musées imaginaires* – are its visual counterparts. More precisely, one may suggest that, just as Durand's compatriot and contemporary, the zoologist Georges Cuvier, was extending the systematisation of natural history begun by Linnaeus in the previous century, Durand was producing a 'natural' story of architecture – a straightforward evolution founded on economy, utility and structural rationale that fitted well in the post-Revolution and anti-aristocratic French state.

In so doing, Durand seemed unmotivated by personal interest and rather appeared to be pursuing a higher, educational, duty. And the effect was considerable. In the case of the *Précis* in particular, the conceptual presentation promised wide applicability and the reliance on apparently universal rules had wide appeal; it became the most influential architectural treatise of the first half of the nineteenth century even as its join-the-dots method was mocked by others such as Gottfried Semper who, in 1834 (the year of Durand's death), described it as blank sheets of paper 'divided into many squares in the manner of a knitting pattern or chessboard, on which the plans of buildings arrange themselves quite mechanically [. . .] with them, the first-year polytechnical student in Paris becomes a complete architect within six months'.[5] By his own account, Durand would not have understood the problem: 'one should not strive to make a building pleasing', he had written in the first volume of the *Précis,* 'since if one concerns oneself solely with the fulfilment of practical requirements, it is impossible that it should not be pleasing'.[6]

This linking of beauty to the disciplines of utility and structural honesty is a recurring theme in French Rationalism,[7] a theme aired by Cordemoy (in 1706) and Blondel (from 1750), for example, before being crucially encapsulated by Marc-Antoine Laugier, in his *Essai sur l'architecture* of 1753. Nevertheless it was six hundred miles east of Paris, in the Prussian capital, Berlin, that the *Précis* received its most elegant and powerful application – in the *Altes Museum* by Karl Friedrich Schinkel, designed in 1823 and completed in 1828. Schinkel took Durand's prototypical museum plan, split it in half, retaining the peristyle, rotunda and courtyards, and then departed from it in a spatial orchestration involving, *inter alia*, the ends holding the giant-order stoa, and the entry sequence of steps, secondary columns and diagonals of the paired stairs. The resultant finesse is hard-won, and is therefore particularly appreciated by practitioners.[8] It may seem ironic, then, that this is the very building most often cited as being derived from Durand's method[9] since, in fact, the museum demonstrates both its possibilities *and* insufficiency. But then Schinkel's imagination was guided by two contrasting influences. On the one hand was indeed the pragmatism of Durand, supported by Laugier's ideas of Greek architecture as truthful structure evolved from the economies of the primitive hut. On the other, however, was his young teacher Friedrich Gilly, whose project for a monument to Frederick the Great of 1797 recalled the drama of Boullée[10] and whose own education owed much to those Parisian architect-scholars who had come under the influence of that romantic lover and imaginative portrayer of Roman architecture, Piranesi, at the French Academy in Rome. With Schinkel, then, the apparent objectivity associated with Rationalism is paired with intuitive speculation and with art. As he wrote after the completion of the *Altes Museum*:

> Every work of art, of whatever kind, must always bring a new and living element into the world of art. [. . .] This is the moral value of a work of art from which the individual

soul of the artist speaks [. . .] In architecture everything must be true, and any masking or concealing of the construction is an error. [. . .] Every perfect construction in a specific material has its own very distinct character, and cannot be rationally carried out in the same way in another material.[11]

This reminds us that Laugier's 'primitive' Classicism was not so simple after all; it also recalls Durand's observation in the second volume of the *Précis* of the delightful paradox that creative freedom may thrive in conditions that are themselves not free:

Many architects say that rules and method are shackles of genius. Far from sharing that opinion, we think on the contrary that they facilitate its development and assure its progress; besides, reason can do without genius, whereas genius cannot avoid error unless it is led and enlightened by reason.[12]

Or, as Goya's then recently published (1796) etching had it, 'The sleep of reason begets monsters'.

In Schinkel's work, the structural rationalism advocated by Laugier was most evident in the utilitarian brick-clad Bauakademie, Berlin of 1836 – a building influenced by a trip to the UK in 1826 during which he drew factories and gas-works in his notebooks. However, in mid-century, the most elegant demonstration of the *néo-grec* was by Henri Labrouste at the Bibliothèque Nationale in Paris, where insertions into an existing enclosure include frankly expressed wrought-iron stacks and an apparently gravity-defying reading-room roof, resting on sixteen slender columns. Here, of course, 'it is of the utmost importance that *each* of these columns is a freestanding element, including those lining the perimeter, for this further exemplifies the Greco-Gothic tradition'.[13]

If, in the mastery of work by Labrouste and Schinkel, the inadequacy of pure utilitarian functionalism is implicit, then what makes us smile at the projects of Eugène-Emmanuel Viollet-le-Duc is the fact that the shortfall is so very clearly evident; David Watkin, for example, describes his illustrations for the *Entretiens sur l'architecture* (Lectures on Architecture) of 1863 and 1872 as 'painfully ham-fisted',[14] John Summerson as 'at once unattractive and fascinating'.[15] One imagines a retort phrased along the lines of Viollet-le-Duc's praise of the steam locomotive:

Some will call it an ugly machine. But why ugly? Does it not exhibit the true expression of the brute energy which it embodies? Is it not appreciable by all as a thing complete, organised, possessing a special character [. . .]? There is no style but that which is appropriate to the object.[16]

and no style, he wrote later, without 'an intervention of reason'.[17] Summerson understood these illustrations as 'demonstrations of how the rational theory can inflect contemporary design, not necessarily how it should'; for Viollet-Le Duc himself, they demonstrated first principles: the architect, he argued, should analyse precedents, abstract their arguments and then apply them to the problem in hand using technology appropriate to the time. The fact that the language of this rationality was Gothic is almost beside the point. He loved Gothic architecture as a practitioner involved with historic buildings and was fascinated by its openness to 'scientific' analysis (both interests demonstrated extensively in his ten-volume *Dictionnaire raisonné de l'architecture française du XIe au XVIe siècle* of 1854–68) but inherent – and essential – in his architectural theory is the principle of what one may describe as *tectonic independence*: he presented a method liberated from historicism and open to originality. It also meant that he was free to approve developments of his own times, a startling example of which was his advocacy of prefabrication as early as 1878, the year before his death.[18]

These messages of structural logic and of analogy rather than imitation were particularly appreciated in the Low Countries and particularly evident in the work of Victor Horta in Belgium and Hendrik Petrus Berlage in the Netherlands. While Horta's lyrical structural ironwork at the Hôtel Tassel, Brussels, of 1892 is a rather wilful by-product of the *Entretiens,* the façade and interior of the *Maison du peuple* in Brussels (1897–1900) shows their debt clearly – perhaps too clearly – in an articulated construction of iron and masonry that is both impressive and slightly awkward. Berlage's older associate, Cuypers, had corresponded with Viollet-le-Duc and, as one would expect, Berlage's work initially showed a Gothic stylistic inheritance; its significance derives from the way successive schemes chart a progressive development towards something else: an idea of decoration arising quasi-naturally through sober consideration of construction methods. One can trace this shift through the designs for the Amsterdam Exchange, from the (fourth-placed) competition scheme of 1883, to the final, built, design of 1897 in which, as he later wrote, he was especially concerned with the primacy of 'spatial enclosure [. . .] achieved through walls'. This demanded that the walls be flat, with decoration on the wall-plane:

> Projecting elements remain limited to those that are suggested by the construction, such as window lintels, water spouts, gutters, single cornices, and so on. It follows from this [. . .] that the possible supports, such as pillars and columns, are not given projecting capitals, but rather that the transition is accomplished within the plane of the wall.[19]

The resultant load-bearing structure with its unfinished brickwork, constructive stone highlights and exposed roof trusses is a virtuoso demonstration of Viollet-le-Duc's principles, and the way they seem to permeate the building is what Mies van der Rohe described in conversation with Peter Carter:

> The idea of clear construction came to me there [at the Exchange], as one of the fundamentals we should accept. We can talk about it easily but to do it is not easy. It is very difficult to stick to this fundamental construction, and then to elevate a structure. [. . .] By structure, we have a philosophical idea. The structure is the whole, from top to bottom, to the last detail – with the same idea.[20]

In such a monolith what we see is what we get. An entirely different theoretical thread leads from Viollet-le-Duc's contemporary, Gottfried Semper who, in his *Die vier Elemente der Baukunst* (The Four Elements of Architecture, 1851) and two-volume *Der Stil* (Style, 1860 and 63) describes the notion of a woven wind-break, or textile, hung on the wooden frame of a primordial structure to provide enclosure, shelter and division of space. His writing, at once atavistic and radical, is described by Edward R. Ford as:

> the second major theory of building of the late nineteenth century, one that was in practice the opposite of the Gothic Rationalist school of monolithic exposed construction. Semper was able to make explicit what was only implied in the teaching of the Beaux-Arts: that rational building could be achieved by means of analogous structural systems, by finish materials that describe the true structural systems they conceal (or, as Semper would put it, 'cladding').[21]

The development of Semper's ideas passed to a younger generation. Even in the Amsterdam Exchange, Kenneth Frampton points to the 'hanging, castellated relief' at high level on the walls of the main space as early evidence of Berlage's interest in those ideas[22] (and an interest that would endure, for example in the woven appearance – Semper might have called it 'wickerwork' – of non-structural brickwork at the Municipal Museum in The Hague, 1935). But it was Otto Wagner who came to grips with Semper's theory of *Bekleidung* – or cladding – in practice. If what we see can do no more than allude to what we really get, then begins an 'oscillation between the tectonic of the structure and the skin', as Frampton puts it.[23] In this gap between the appearance and the making of a building – what Hans Kollhoff has called the 'myth of the structure and the architectonic'[24] – Wagner pursued the idea that the skin would assume more than a practical role. In his inaugural professorial address at the Vienna Academy of Fine Arts in 1894 he said that 'methods of construction must be fully and completely expressed if architecture is not to be reduced to caricature';[25] then, two years later he explained how this 'modern way of building' might be progressed (and, typically, emphasised his main point by using capitals):

> for the exterior cladding [. . .] a panel system will be used [. . .] Since these panels can be assumed to have significantly less cubic volume, they can be designed for a nobler material [. . .] fastened by bronze bolts (rosettes) [. . .] the money spent will decrease enormously, and the production time will be reduced [. . . but] the greatest advantage is that IN THIS WAY A NUMBER OF NEW ARTISTIC MOTIFS WILL EMERGE.[26]

The clearest built demonstration of this is in his Post Office Savings Bank of 1903, where Kollhoff's 'myth' may indeed be understood as a story with a veiled meaning, the exterior skin being the top layer in a synthetic constructional system and one that just might communicate something of what lay between it and the wallpaper of the interior.

As nineteenth-century Rationalism in architecture began with the work of a systematic Frenchman with an engineering background who illustrated his work in a very particular way (Durand) so it ended with one too. Auguste Choisy's *Histoire d'architecture* of 1899 treats architectural history entirely in terms of construction with a winning combination of clear and concise writing and 1700 drawings by the author – uniformly monochrome, isometric up-views that show the plan, section and elevation in a single, diagrammatic image. Along with this, Banham notes 'his favourite method of correct appraisal from which the answer logically derives [:] *La question posée, la solution était indiquée*'.[27] There is something of his fictional contemporary, Sherlock Holmes, about this. Less rational is Choisy's relaxation about material transcription in the examples he chooses (primarily Greek and Gothic). This is to some extent concealed by his drawing style, as Frampton observes: 'in one upward-looking isometric after another, in which the corporeal volume was depicted as being homogenous with its columnar supports, Choisy seems to have anticipated reinforced concrete as the sole technique that would prove capable of overcoming the age-old schism and fusing into a single entity the two great lines of Western building culture'.[28]

Teleology is a dubious practice in the writing of history, but in both the theory of Choisy and the practice of Wagner we do see ideas that were maintained and developed in the twentieth century: Choisy was the key early influence on Auguste Perret and Le Corbusier; Wagner is the seminal figure in a century of wrapped structure and layered construction, the virtual revolution in architecture's plasticity and tectonic.

But before all that was a hiatus: there was a real revolution in Russia and, in the West, the 'war to end all wars'. It didn't, but for architecture entering the machine age, just as for almost everything else in society, things were never the same again.

› Notes

1   H.-R. Hitchcock, *Architecture: Nineteenth and Twentieth Centuries*, Harmondsworth: Penguin Books, 1975, p. 13.
2   See, for example, E. Kaufmann, *Architecture in the Age of Reason*, Cambridge MA: Harvard University Press, 1955.
3   A. Pérez-Gómez, *Architecture and the Crisis of Modern Science*, Cambridge, MA: The MIT Press, 1983, p. 311.
4   A. Vidler, *The Writing of the Walls*, Princeton, NJ: Princeton Architectural Press, 1987, p. 166.
5   G. Semper, *Vorläufige Bemerkungen über bemalte Architektur und Plastik bei den Alten* (Preliminary remarks on polychrome architecture and sculpture in antiquity), Altona, 1834, trans. H. F. Mallgrave and W. Herrmann (ed.), in *Gottfried Semper: the Four Elements of Architecture and other writings*, Cambridge: Cambridge University Press, 1989.
6   J.-N.-L. Durand, *Précis des leçons données à l'École polytechnique*, vol. 1, Paris, 1802.
7   And was a leitmotiv of both nineteenth-century and modern architecture, too: Pugin, Viollet-le-Duc, Wagner, Lubetkin and Buckminster Fuller – to name but a few – all replayed Keats' maxim (from the end of *Ode on a Grecian Urn*, 1820) that 'Beauty is truth, truth beauty'. For Modernists, the theme was subjected to unrestrained variation since their functionalism no longer operated within the established architectural languages of Classical or Gothic.
8   See, for example, M. Goalen, 'Schinkel and Durand: The Case of the Altes Museum', in M. Snodin (ed.) *Karl Friedrich Schinkel: A Universal Man*, New Haven, CT and London: Yale University Press, 1991, and C. St.J. Wilson, *Architectural Reflections*, Oxford: Butterworth, 1992.
9   To give just one example, Hitchcock, op. cit., describes the museum within a chapter entitled 'The Doctrine of J.-N.-L. Durand'.
10 Seeing this design at an exhibition that year is said to have inspired Schinkel to study architecture. See H. F. Mallgrave, *Architectural Theory, volume 1*, Oxford: Blackwell, 2006, p. 401.
11 K. F. Schinkel, *Das architektonische Lehrbuch* (Notes for a Textbook on Architecture), c.1830, G. Peschken (ed.), Berlin: Deutscher Kunstverlag, 1979, pp. 114–115, trans. H. F. Mallgrave, ibid., p. 412.
12 Durand, op. cit, vol 2, 1805.
13 K. Frampton, *Studies in Tectonic Culture*, Cambridge, MA: The MIT Press, 1996, p. 47–48.
14 D. Watkin, *Morality and Architecture*, Oxford: Oxford University Press, 1977, p. 2.
15 J. Summerson, 'Viollet-le-Duc and the Rational Point of View', in *Heavenly Mansions and other Essays on Architecture*, New York: W. W. Norton, 1963, p. 154.
16 E.-E. Viollet-le-Duc, *Entretiens sur l'architecture* (Lectures on Architecture), lecture 6, trans. B. Bucknall, New York: Dover, 1987.
17 E.-E. Viollet-le-Duc, *Dictionnaire raisonné de l'architecture française du XIe au XVIe siècle*, 1866, trans. K. D. Whitehead (in *The Foundations of Architecture: Selections from the* Dictionnaire raisonné, New York: George Braziller, 1990). In H. F. Mallgrave, *Architectural Theory, volume 1*, Oxford: Blackwell, 2006, p. 526.
18 E.-E. Viollet-le-Duc, *Les bâtiments de l'Exposition Universelle de 1878* (The Buildings of the Universal Exposition of 1878), trans. C. Contandriopoulos and H. F. Mallgrave, in Contandriopoulos and Mallgrave (ed.), *Architectural Theory volume 2*, Oxford: Blackwell, 2008, p. 33.
19 H. P. Berlage, *Gedanken über Stil in der Baukunst* (Thoughts on Style in Architecture) 1905, trans. Iain Boyd Whyte, in *Hendrik Pertrus Berlage: Thoughts on Style 1886–1909*, Santa Monica, CA: Getty Publication Programs, 1996, p. 152.
20 P. Carter, 'Mies van der Rohe: An Appreciation on the Occasion, This Month, of His 75th Birthday'. In *Architectural Design* 31, 3 (March 1961): 97.
21 E. R. Ford, *The Details of Modern Architecture*, Cambridge, MA: The MIT Press, 1990, p. 205.
22 Frampton, op. cit., p. 337.
23 Ibid., p. 340.
24 H. Kollhoff, 'Der Mythos der Konstruktion und das Architektonische', in H. Kollhoff (ed.), *Über Tektonik in der Baukunst*, Wiesbaden: Braunschweig, 1993. Quoted in translation in H. Van der Heijden, 'The Diagram of the House', in *Architectural Research Quarterly*, 5, 2: 111. See also No. 66 in this Reader.
25 O. Wagner, 'Inaugural Address to the Academy of Fine Arts' 1894, trans. H. F. Mallgrave, in *Otto Wagner: Modern Architecture*, Santa Monica, CA: Getty Publication Programs, 1988. Quoted in Contandriopoulos and Mallgrave (ed.), *Architectural Theory volume 2*, Oxford: Blackwell, 2008, p. 89.
26 O. Wagner, *Moderne Architektur*, 1896, ibid., p. 94–95.
27 R. Banham, *Theory and Design in the First Machine Age*, London: The Architectural Press, 1972, p. 26
28 Frampton, op. cit., p. 58.

DOCUMENTS ONE
1920–1940

Thilo Hilpert

The architects of modernism and their texts: an introduction to the history of modern architecture 1922–1934

The renewal of architecture leading up to the Heroic Period of Modernism after the First World War arrived so inconspicuously that its revolutionary importance was easily overlooked.

› The first building

August Perret's garage of 1906 constructed in Paris on Rue de Ponthieu was, like his apartment building on Rue Franklin three years earlier, a concrete frame building. But its appearance was more elemental, and, except for the large glass window above the entrance drive, the building was without ornamentation. Consequently it revealed the new form of construction, combining it with a novel function, which only through modernism would become a programme 'worthy' of architecture. Le Corbusier later reminisced that only since 1900 had the first cars paraded through the streets of Paris and not until 1907 were the first planes seen in the skies above the city. Within fifteen years he had proposed – in his first theoretical urban project – to locate an airport in the city centre, accessed by elevated, traversing highways for cars. In his book *Vers une architecture* (Toward An Architecture) of 1923, he would demonstrate to architects the precision required by these modes of transport, the car and the plane, and accusingly refer to 'Eyes That Do Not See',[1] his brash style reminiscent of Brecht's phrase 'don't stare so romantically'. The car had conquered the city and Le Corbusier adapted his concept for the future city accordingly, naming his 1925 plan for a new centre of Paris *Plan Voisin* after the famous luxury automobile brand.

The first metro line had opened in Paris in 1900 and the 'fée electrique' illuminated the site of the world expo, where visitors on travelators became accustomed to experiencing the new dynamics of travel. In summary, and seen retrospectively 100 years later, it is notable that the transformations of modernism in architecture were all inherent in the garage in the Rue de Ponthieu. Le Corbusier had worked for Perret during 1908 (but only later acknowledged him as a teacher). The legendary 'Five Points Towards a New Architecture' of 1927, identified with his houses for the *Weissenhofsiedlung*, demanded a three-dimensional freedom for the modernist structural frame – developed from Perret's 'school' of building with concrete, and modified with reference to Le Corbusier's experiments with abstract Cubist painting (after 1914). The 'checkerboard or grid', which he declared in 1922 was to be the 'generator' for the facades of modernist buildings,[2] was not derived from observation of 'American factories', implied by the photographs associated with the concept of 'a machine for living in' published in *L'Esprit Nouveau*, but rather from Auguste Perret.

The building in the Rue de Ponthieu must have been demolished without great fuss sometime after 1965 (when I photographed it); in any case, conducting research one always comes across the lapidary remark 'demolished'. However, for later 'classic' Modern Architecture after 1922 there was another expression of the idea of 'permanence' beyond the life of the individual, and one within the European culture of architecture as of equal importance to that of the individual building – the text – whether manifesto, essay or book. Written discourse was crucial to the idea of Rationalism in architecture, particularly after 1968 and for the generation following Aldo Rossi.

› The architects of modernism: 1920 – departure and precursors

The influential architects of the period between the two wars, understood today as the architects of 'classic' modernism, were all born around 1885: Le Corbusier (1887–1965),[3] Mies van der Rohe (1886–1969)[4] and Walter Gropius (1883–1969),[5] together with lesser known figures like Ludwig Hilberseimer (1885–1967), Ernst May (1886–1970), Hannes Meyer (1889–1954), Hans Schmidt (1893–1972), El Lissitzky (1890–1941) and also Arthur Korn (1891–1978).

In subsequent depictions of Modern Architecture Auguste Perret has typically been seen as a 'precursor', albeit without the conviction that his architecture would warrant (after the Second World War). The problem of assigning Perret is not untypical for the generation of 'the precursors of modernism' born around 1870, for example Tony Garnier (1869–1948), Peter Behrens (1868–1940), Adolf Loos (1870–1933), Hans Poelzig (1873–1935), Heinrich Tessenow (1876–1950) or Henry van de Velde (1863–1957). Some, like Perret or van de Velde, continued to work well into the post-Second World War era. While their thinking was related to the philosophy of the architects of 'classic' modernism like Le Corbusier, Mies, Gropius or J.J.P. Oud, they can only be counted with the earlier generation. Nonetheless, Perret not only organised the rebuilding of Le Havre after the Second World War but also influenced the rebuilding of the devastated German inner cities with his 'model' concrete grids – more significantly in fact than the less 'exotic' Le Corbusier.

In my youth during the 1970s it was still common to classify famous architects like Le Corbusier or Mies according to their preferred construction systems: Le Corbusier was held to be synonymous with building in concrete and Mies with steel building. Later their cultural significance would be recognised: South America, primarily Brazil, represented an important area of Le Corbusier's influence, whereas North America, in particular Chicago, enacted Mies' conception of building in steel.

There does not seem to have been any significant formal written dialogue between the two architects; at least not in comparison to the regular and open exchanges Le Corbusier had with Walter Gropius or with the painter Willi Baumeister. Le Corbusier knew Mies' work very well, having already met him in 1911 in Peter Behrens' office in Berlin; Mies literally 'paid court' to Le Corbusier, who was living in Paris, by granting him two projects for the *Weissenhofsiedlung* in Stuttgart. However, this did not prevent him in his obituary for Le Corbusier from accusing his former, now famous, 'comrade in arms' of certain 'baroque' tendencies. Gropius, on the other hand, who kept a bluntly arrogant distance from Mies, was friendly with Le Corbusier whom he had most likely met in 1923, and they continued to work closely following the founding of CIAM (Congrès Internationaux d'Architecture Moderne) in 1928.

There was unlikely to have been a rationalist architect uninfluenced by Le Corbusier's theories, and many would also have known him personally. Ludwig Hilberseimer for example, the most influential urban theorist of the Weimar Republic period, was invited to the Bauhaus by Hannes Meyer, and having emigrated to Chicago, assisted Mies in teaching at the Illinois Institute of Technology (IIT), becoming in effect Mies' spokesperson. With a recommendation from the art historian and publicist Paul Westheim, Hilberseimer visited Le Corbusier in Paris during the early 1920s and assured him of his admiration. The eerily bold drawings for a vertical *Großstadtarchitektur* which Hilberseimer published in Germany, were nothing more than stacked elements from Le Corbusier's vision of the city: streets for automobiles, pedestrian bridges and high-rise buildings for dwelling and working, arranged in a vertical mega-structure.

While Mies' and Hilberseimer's projects were not too far removed from CIAM's concepts, they never took part in CIAM congresses. The same is true of Bruno Taut, who could claim to have designed and built almost 1500 flats in Berlin[6] – no less successful an outcome than Ernst May's equivalent housing in Frankfurt. In contrast to the self-satisfied May, who in 1929 organised the Second CIAM Congress on 'Die Wohnung für das Existenzminimum' (The Minimum Subsistence Dwelling), Taut was capable of self-critical reflection on the subject of modernism. His article 'Gegen den Strom'[7] (Against the Grain), typified this desire to think through, and argue his case. In contrast to the later reception accorded to the celebrated May – to whom few gravitated at the CIAM congresses after 1945 – a well-received monograph on the work of the strident Prussian Taut was published in East Berlin by Kurt Junghanns (a member of the resistance).

› Theory and text: from manifesto to the theory of history – Giedion and Behne

The most emphatic period of Modernist culture was framed by the two World Wars, initially encompassing the larger European nation states in a vibrant axis between Berlin and Paris. However, its influence continued into the mid 1960s, by then including the USA and Japan, after the Second World War parts of North Africa, and later also India and Brazil.

Reyner Banham dates the end of the efficacy of 'classic' theories of Modern Architecture to around 1960, when he published his book *Theory and Design in the First Machine Age* and when, with the influence of Japanese Metabolism, a fundamental change in the structure of architectural thinking became evident. It does make sense, given the 1932 exhibition 'The International Style' in New York, to locate the main period of conceptual productivity between 1922 and 1932, the short period of ten years preceding the exhibition; that is before the US cultural elites appropriated these concepts for themselves. It still makes sense, if we consider that the Fourth CIAM Congress engaging 'The Functional City' took place in 1933; that Le Corbusier's important book *La Ville Radieuse* (The Radiant City) was not published until 1935, and that the concluding text by Laszlo Moholy-Nagy (1895–1946), *Vision in Motion*, only appeared in Chicago after the war in 1947 (and remains relatively unknown today in Germany).

Vers une architecture

Le Corbusier's 'instructive' text of *Vers une architecture* (Toward an Architecture) was published in 1922,[8] shaking up traditional architectural thinking like no other modernist publication. It set out the definition of a 'new architecture' which from the 1920s onwards provided the basis for [most] of the polemic and buildings of Modern Architecture: 'Architecture is the masterful, correct, and magnificent play of volumes brought together in light ... cubes, cones, light reveals well; the image is clear and tangible for us, without ambiguity. That is why these are *beautiful forms, the most beautiful forms.*'[9]

Le Corbusier's contributions to *L'Esprit Nouveau* were typical of modernist texts at the onset of the decade; they were 'manifestos' in the form of essays, consciously incorporating opinionated statements like those of the Futurists rather than objective reports on the international state of architectural developments. The 'Programme of the Staatliches Bauhaus in Weimar' from 1919 has significantly been referred to as 'Founding Manifesto' ('The ultimate aim of all visual arts is the complete building!').[10] Only the later 'programmes' of CIAM, like the 1928 'La Sarraz Declaration', have a genuinely collective character, as the product of mutual opinion formed by a homogeneous group of architects. Even in the 1943 Athens Charter, where Le Corbusier imprinted his individual stamp on the reworked version, the influence of the different national representatives remained evident at the heart of the declaration.[11]

Typically, the texts of 'classic' modernism in architecture move between manifesto, programme and declaration. However, from the mid 1920s onwards they also included more comprehensive studies such as those by Adolf Behne (1885–1948) and Siegfried Giedion (1888–1968) who claimed for their contemporaries – the architects of modernism – a place in history, and for their buildings the formal characteristics of a new epoch or a new style.

Paying attention to their impact as publicity, Le Corbusier republished various texts – written between 1920 and 1926 as a significant part of the contents of the journal *L'Esprit Nouveau* – in three consecutive books. Each referred to a different field that would become integral to the conception of 'modern design': *Vers une architecture* addressed architecture; *Urbanisme* town planning, and *L'art decorative d'aujourd'hui* furniture and everyday objects (which at the Bauhaus were seen as the products of 'industrial design').[12] The chronology of the translation of architectural texts always registers the nuances of their reception and the interests prevalent in particular countries. In Germany the first two were translated and published in 1926 soon after their appearance in French (but only *Vers une architecture* was later republished in the series 'Bauwelt Fundamente' in the 1960s). In Russia the translation of *Urbanisme* in the late 1920s prompted a broader and more emphatic but superficial 'Corbusianisme'. The third book *L'art decorative d'aujourd'hui*, linguistically and intellectually the most intriguing text of the three, was initially only published in France and then, years after Le Corbusier's death, in the USA.

Giedion and Behne

In his treatise of 1928, *Building in France, Building in Iron, Building in Ferroconcrete*, Giedion delivered a model explanation for the genesis of Modernism. The architectural innovations of Le Corbusier, Mies or Gropius consequently acquired the justification of historical necessity, declared to be inseparable elements of technological progress. According to this model the new architecture had, so to speak, matured within the aspect of traditional architectural forms, just as a revolution matures in the context of outdated societies, until the new technical foundations compelled their adequate expression in newfound contemporary form. As a consequence during the post-war era whole generations of students were subjected to dull lectures in which the development of the great train stations was held to exemplify a fundamentally natural and necessary process in the genesis of modernism.

Giedion and Behne emerged from the same generation as the architects of 'classic' modernism and were each similarly influential, but with different emphases and embedded in distinct architectural milieus. They both initially wrote and published in German. Later, when Giedion, at the beginning of the 1940s published his work in the USA, Behne had become virtually silent in Berlin. In 1928 Giedion was appointed secretary general of CIAM. He organised their congresses, edited their public announcements (into the 1950s), and provided CIAM with a uniform effectiveness which, given the changing constellation of its members, was effectively a chimera. His book of 1940, *Space, Time and Architecture*, was for many years regarded as the 'standard history of modern architecture'. It has the character of a concluding and valedictory account of Modernism, which by then had acquired the character of an operative doctrine – one opaque to contradiction or deviation. Twelve years after CIAM's foundation, one could already speak of the 'growth of the new tradition', the sub-title of Giedion's book.

In opposition to Giedion, however, it was Adolf Behne in Berlin who had a more lasting impact on the development of Modern Architecture, but only his book *The Modern Functional Building* is well known internationally. Despite being educated as an art historian and as an architect, he had directly engaged with aspects of Modernism in architecture well before Giedion – in particular with the work of Bruno Taut. Aiming for populist 'enlightenment' he had, in 1928, written a short introduction to contemporary architecture *Eine Stunde Architektur* (One-hour Architecture)[13] for the expanding population of the modern housing estates in Berlin.

For Behne, Modern Architecture's fundamental 'break' with the forms of a representational eclecticism was less a consequence of technological progress than the social consequence of a changing way of life – architectural theory, for the first time, was grounded in behaviourism. Modernism, according to Behne, was the spatial negation of the 'knights' who had thus far existed in representative shells, removed from reality. Modern architecture, he argued, emerged from a new societal desire for sociability and communication. At the same time as Giedion, in his intelligent book *Mechanisation Takes Command*, documented the origins of modern furniture in banal appliances – presenting an 'anonymous history' of American civilisation – Behne in 1947, one year before his death, was motivated to portray a genuine 'image of the working class' in an exhibition for the 'new' trade unions.[14] This displayed paintings by Meunier, Kollwitz and Waldschmidt, to an audience poisoned by the misconceived pathos of '*Arbeit macht frei*'.

› The grandchildren of modernism: 1960 – rediscovery – Frank Lloyd Wright and the Futurists

To write history involves the assessment and selection of what to retrieve from obscurity or leave as the received view; this is how critical consciousness and objectivity are linked.

The most influential studies on the history of Modernism in architecture emerged from the 'generation of the grandchildren' – from Reyner Banham (1922–1988), Peter Blake (1920–2006) and Bruno Zevi (1918–2000); there were also the contributions of Ulrich Conrads (b. 1923) in Germany and the Frenchman Michel Ragon (b. 1924): all were written after 1960 when the work of the Metabolists in Japan, and the founding of the Bauhaus archive in Darmstadt, marked a clear break with the past.

Michel Ragon's treatise in three volumes, promisingly titled *Histoire mondiale de l'architecture et de l'urbanisme modernes*, an opulent book, differed from the others in its later publication in 1971. The author had little contact with the architects or artists of the 1920s. Having written extensively on Parisian post-war painting (the 'Ecole de Paris'), he only later concentrated on architecture, in 1965 forming the group GIAP around architects such as Yona Friedman. Viewed retrospectively his work appears to be a source and chronicle of the period's technological fantasies (architectural futurology and 'Utopias from the Blue Planet') rather than a depiction of twentieth-century modernism.

Ulrich Conrads' (who had been the editor of the popular *Bauwelt* magazine) collection of projects on 'Fantastic Architecture' which reach back to the roots of Expressionism, was the internationally most successful contribution from Germany. Conrads had even accessed documents from Behne's widow in the process. His most important achievement, however, was the republication, from 1964 onwards, of neglected books by Le Corbusier, Behne and El Lissitzky, in the series 'Bauwelt Fundamente' (later also followed with publications by Jane Jacobs, Aldo Rossi and Robert Venturi). Whether it was Conrads, or Professor Jürgen Joedicke (b. 1925), who first fell for the myth disseminated by Häring that he as a critic of Le Corbusier should be recognised as the alternative hero of CIAM, is unclear.

First corrective

It was the 'generation of grandchildren' born around 1920 that first attempted to reconstruct the relationship between the modernist architects, their polemic and their contradictions.

Peter Blake who emigrated, early post-war, to the USA, prompted a shift in the assessment of the 'fathers' of Modernism, instituting appreciation of Frank Lloyd Wright as a 'modern' architect. His 1960 book *The Master Builders* places Wright next to Le Corbusier and Mies, aligned with the architects of classical modernism.

One has to remember that Wright was already twenty-one years old and working in the office of Sullivan (his 'lieben Meister') – as a draughtsman on the auditorium building for 25 dollars a week[15] – when Mies was born in 1886. Wright was obviously from a different generation than the modernists in Europe, and shaped by different experiences. Not only the earliest 'forerunner', his Guggenheim Museum in New York was completed one year after his death (at the grand age of ninety-two). He witnessed what had so fascinated the Europeans about the America of the 1920s – extremely rapid urbanisation (by almost five times from 38m to 180m, between 1867 and 1959) increasing the ratio of city dwellers to 75 per cent of the population. The America from which Mendelsohn reported in his 1926 *Amerika: Bilderbuch eines Architekten*, seemed as strange to Frank Lloyd Wright as were Le Corbusier's vision of urbanism and his interest in Henry Ford's conveyor belt production.

Wright's own vision of Broadacre City, his concept for the suburban development of America (published in his 1932 book *The Disappearing City*), was not only a radical answer to the country's urban transformation but also a reaction to its fascination for European architects. It is not surprising that Hans Schmidt and the other delegates at the founding of CIAM in La Sarraz refused the proposal to invite the American Wright onto an advisory committee of the precursors of the Modern Movement. Walter Gropius, who had moved to England in 1934, still called Wright a 'romantic'. From this perspective Wright's Sibylline note explaining his reluctance to meet Le Corbusier becomes understandable: 'I hope Le Corbusier will find America as he hopes to find it. Yours humbly, Frank Lloyd Wright'.[16]

Without this knowledge of Wright, his hospitable welcome for the immigrant Mies van der Rohe, on his arrival in Chicago in 1938, is even more surprising. But Wright appreciated in Mies a mutual quality. Both were architects rooted in craft, with a love for detail and a wary suspicion of Le Corbusier's intellectual inclinations (which Gropius followed).

Second corrective: retrieving Futurism

Aside from Blake's book, during the 1960s it was Reyner Banham's comprehensive *Theory and Design in the First Machine Age* that particularly shaped the understanding of Modernism. Many critics even saw it as the 'definitive' text. Through detailed textual analysis and citations, it compared the conceptualisation of *L'Esprit Nouveau,* via the Bauhaus to that of *De Stijl.* The emphasis of the book, however, was its focus on the texts of early Modernism.

The book's main achievement in 1960 was the rediscovery of Futurist theories for the history of modernism; it included Sant'Elia's sketches from before 1914 and Marinetti's manifestos; but this also became problematic. Previously undervalued, Futurism was now being overvalued and the Futurists' excitement for technology acquired prophetic significance for an emerging Second Machine Age. But, as a consequence of Futurism's only brief influence on the Modernism of the First Machine Age, it became stylised into a tragic 'movement' in Banham's book.

Banham consequently underpinned his historic examination with an intellectual finality that inevitably led on to the technical inventions of Buckminster Fuller (1895–1983) – his Dymaxion car and metal roundhouses. He concludes that Fuller, despite having been the real inventor of the house as 'a machine for living in', was duplicitously ignored by the European modernists. His proposition spans 'classic' Modernism with an arch of technologically determined thinking, instigated by the Futurists and concluded with Fuller's inventions. According to Banham these inventions, around 1960, prepare the way for novel technological thinking about electronic environmental systems.

It is surely no coincidence that Reyner Banham, with his enthusiasm for Buckminster Fuller's design practice, was at the end of the 1950s welcomed at the *Hochschule für Gestaltung* in Ulm by Tomas Maldonado and Claude Schnaidt – and soon the 'master' himself, Buckminster Fuller, would travel from the United States to his first seminar in Ulm.

Remarkably Banham, whose exclusions prevented the book from becoming a 'definitive' history of architecture, had not only excluded Bruno Taut but also refrained from any mention of Russian Constructivism (whether that of Tatlin or that of Rodchenko). After all it had been the Constructivists who had followed most faithfully the directives of the Italian Futurists. Bruno Zevi's *Storia dell architettura moderna* of 1950 had remained the only hint of this formerly influential field of practice in Russia. This remained the case when Claude Schnaidt published his monograph about Hannes Meyer, Gropius' unrecognised successor, looking for further information in El Lissitzky's book of 1930 *Russia: An Architecture for World Revolution*, which had been published in Germany. It was Anatole Kopp (1915–1990) who not only broke the silence with his book *Ville et Revolution (Town and Revolution)* in 1967, to bring to light forgotten projects and debate, but who also, probably unintentionally, had an impact on the generation of young architects participating in the events of May 1968.

> ## › Caesura: sociology of the new forms – individualism, the 'collective' and internationalism

To displace history is also part of a strategy of remembering. Given a particular focus on developments during the years after 1928, however, critical research is mainly confronted with 'displacement'. But 1928 was as important for architecture as 1925 had been, the year Taut's *Hufeisensiedlung* in Berlin was handed over to its tenants; the Bauhaus in Dessau opened, and the Pavilion de L'Esprit Nouveau was exhibited in Paris. Each – whether to do with urban design, building, form or text – concerns 'Individualism', the 'Collective', and an 'International' dimension: the housing exhibition at the *Weissenhofsiedlung* in Stuttgart; the competition for the *ADGB* (Federation of German Trade Unions) school in Bernau, and the founding of CIAM in La Sarraz.

Weissenhofsiedlung: *individualism and urban space*

Mies van der Rohe was commissioned by the Deutsche Werkbund to plan the *Weissenhofsiedlung*; it would demonstrate a range of different programmatic solutions to the problem of planning small flats, designed by 'prominent European architects'. On 1 May 1927 the local issue of a worker's newspaper willingly appropriated this statement to their own ends: 'prominent architects of Europe unite!' What was 'new' about the *Weissenhofsiedlung* was not only its Internationalism but also the evident individualism of its architectural fabric.

In contrast to contemporary German Siedlungen – Ernst May's *Römerstadt* or Gropius' *Siedlung Törten*, and later larger estates like *Weisse Stadt* and the *Ringsiedlung* in Berlin – Mies had granted the individual architects like Oud, Gropius, Le Corbusier, Stam, Taut, Scharoun, and others, the licence to allow their buildings to stand out exceptionally from the framework of the master plan. The overall arrangement was largely contradicted by the spatial logic of individual buildings.[17] Mies' central 'block', already completed in 1927, stood out as an apartment building from the other, mostly two storey, individual houses.

The question arises why, despite its prominence as a collection of model buildings, Erich Mendelsohn, one of the first German modernists, did not contribute to the *Weissenhofsiedlung*. Quite apart from his much-vaunted aloofness, the architect with the most experience of urban building would have been a rather unsuitable choice for a *Siedlung*. There may have been other reasons for this. Towards the end of 1928 Mendelsohn had designed and built the *Kaufhaus* (Department Store) Schocken in Stuttgart, responding to the local urban context with a differentiated volumetric arrangement. In this regard, Mendelsohn was the architect who most skilfully heightened pedestrians' and motorists' perception of the dynamics of contemporary urban space, as the most able architect of the urban context. Mendelsohn's particular urban achievement is no longer evident since the *Kaufhaus* Schocken was demolished in 1958 with the agreement of Egon Eiermann; the building obstructed the priority given to the demands of traffic in the planning of the post-war city. Consequently the only alternative, in Stuttgart, to the urban strategy of the Weissenhofsiedlung was the thorough but stolid urban conception of Paul Schmitthenner's neighbouring Kochenhofsiedlung from 1933.

From Bernau to Ulm: collective and group-form

The year 1928 was perhaps the most productive year of Hannes Meyer's career. On 1 April he had been announced to succeed Gropius as director of the Bauhaus, and later the same month he won the competition for the residential school of the *ADGB* (German Trade Union Federation), a building larger than the Bauhaus complex in Dessau.

The design of the school for the *ADGB* at Bernau near Berlin was in no way the circumscribed architecture one might have expected from a 'functionalist' like Meyer. Comparison of his proposal with the other competition entries, those of Taut or Mendelssohn for example, highlights the qualities of Meyer's solution. The proposal was in spatial terms undoubtedly the most intelligent, and fully justified the jury's decision to award him the project. Rather than deploying lengthy schematic corridors and 'representative facades'; referring to urban typologies or resorting to plans reminiscent of barracks; Meyer had chosen a different route. He integrated the orthogonal geometry of the whole complex into its topographical situation and emphatically incorporated a sequence of different activities into the landscape.

The composition of the jury for this competition was almost as interesting as its outcome. The jury protocol from April 1928 cites three 'renowned' architects as expert jurors – the Berlin building councillor Martin Wagner (who emigrated in 1935), the publicist Adolf Behne (silent after 1933) and, astonishingly, the architect Heinrich Tessenow (Professor at the TU Berlin) to whom Le Corbusier attributed the role of a precursor to Modernism in the early 1920s, and who, much later, was to inspire Aldo Rossi's elementary house forms.

The role of the Bernau complex in serving as a model for the Swiss architect Max Bill's design of the *Hochschule für Gestaltung* (School of Design) in Ulm is clearly evident; it would succeed the Bauhaus after the Second World War. Bill studied under Meyer in Dessau towards the end of the 1930s, but always concealed his professor's influence. Meyer's project had qualities not to be found in other subsequent or immediately post-war projects. Offering only a short-term residency the school needed (according to Behne) to convey a sense of community to its students. The competition brief stipulated that the design should 'strengthen the feeling of identity and community' and contribute to the unique aspiration that 'via its spatial structure' it could 'influence everyday life and achieve a pedagogic impact'.[18] Effectively, Meyer's resolution of the project predated by 30 years CIAM's demand for 'group-form', which evolved in the late 1950s.

The founding of CIAM: Neues Bauen and internationalism

The *Congrès Internationaux d'Architecture Moderne* was founded in Switzerland at the end of June 1928 as a response to the rejection of schemes by modernists like Le Corbusier but also Meyer in the competition for the Palace of Nations. Constituting the first international organisation of modern architects CIAM paralleled the trans-national organisation of the League of Nations, placing itself in direct opposition to the stolid and inappropriate character of the League's international representation.

During this period, before the Second World War, German was still the second language of CIAM congresses. It was therefore not only a matter of translation, but a conscious shift of emphasis, when CIAM was not called *Kongresse für Moderne Architektur* in German, but rather, *Kongress für Neues Bauen*. *Neues Bauen* (New Building) referred to a different kind of architecture, an architecture that, beyond stylistic orientation and aesthetic criteria, should be capable of finding specific and (rationalist) formal solutions to any 'problem'.

Without Hannes Meyer's and Mart Stam's contributions there would have been no definition of a contemporary urbanism at La Sarraz, and without Hans Schmidt, no discussion, either, about industrial building beyond Le Corbusier's conception of the mass production of concrete 'cells'. The fundamental definition of 'Town Planning' was not from Le Corbusier, but from Meyer – 'Town planning is the organization of all functions of collective life . . .'.[19]

Because the CIAM protocols remained unpublished, Hugo Häring, chairman of the Berlin Ring, could persistently claim in his post-war memoirs that his conception of 'the organic' had unsuccessfully confronted the geometric 'rule' of Le Corbusier at the 1928 CIAM congress in La Sarraz. Given the wording of the meeting's protocol this seems to be a complete invention by Häring, one which reflected the polarities of the post-war architectural debate, but not that concerning the *Neues Bauen* at the end of the 1920s.

Building and conceiving Neues Bauen

Meyer's manifesto *Bauen*, published in the Bauhaus journal in the last quarter of 1928, would prove to be as radical as Le Corbusier's texts, which had thrust the term 'a machine for living in' at his audience six years earlier. Meyer now demanded that the 'machine for living' be a 'biological apparatus'. Without being able to foresee the consequences of his claim for a multi-disciplinary approach to architectural form, he demanded: 'all art is composition and, hence, is unsuited to achieve its goals – all life is function and therefore un-artistic – . . . building is not an aesthetic process.'[20]

The term 'building' – '*construire*' in French – as Meyer employs it, acquires a functional emphasis. His formulation became, in 1929, the core of one of the most wide-ranging polemics written by the publicist and painter Karel Teige (1900–1951). Teige had not taken part in the congress at La Sarraz but was the spokesman of a particularly active group of modern architects in Czechoslovakia. He directed the logic of Meyer's polemic against Le Corbusier's project in 1928 for a Mundaneum, which was intended to form a cultural centre for the League of Nations. One of Le Corbusier's most intransigent projects, it was composed strictly according to the rules of the golden section and proposed that most monumental of all elemental geometries, the pyramid, for the complex's spiralling museum.

Not for four years would Le Corbusier answer Teige; he did so in a special issue of *L'Architecture d'Aujourd'hui* published at the turn of 1933–1934. The text, however, had been spontaneously written back in 1929 on a train journey to Moscow (Le Corbusier travelled there for the first time in 1928, to supervise the Centrosoyuz project). He had encountered an architectural context where a whole nation sought to define itself artistically, 'claiming' the intellectual freedom and vision that he had sought himself – to 'conceive, invent, plan', and not simply to 'build, execute, function'. By 1934 that was all behind him, his journeys to Russia and the Fourth CIAM Congress in Athens in 1933 on the 'Functional City' (which had originally been planned to take place in Moscow).

The eventual publication of Le Corbusier's response to Teige at the beginning of 1934 may be seen as the summation of a conflict which had been brewing since 1928, and was in fact primarily aimed at Ernst May's town planning in Russia while at the same time defending his own thinking (which had been reviled as 'utopian'). The manner of his riposte, referring to Leonidov, a leading architect from the generation of the 'sons', invoked the undertone of a melancholic and almost tender sense of personal identification, something seldom found in Le Corbusier's polemic: 'If Leonidov, the poet who incarnates all the hopes of the Russian architectural "constructivists," claims he is a functionalist and rails against constructivism, I am ready to explain to him why he does so. It is because the Russian architectural movement represents a moral earthquake, a manifestation of the soul, a surge of lyricism, an aesthetic creation, an act of faith in modern life . . .'[21]

Le Corbusier stubbornly defended architecture as an artistic practice, where intellectual thought precedes craft: 'Concevoir d'abord, construire après' (conceive first, construct later),[22] setting out the continually evident polarity of architectural practice – text and craft.

› Modernism's children 1930–1933: lost years?

We only have fragmented knowledge of architectural events providing leverage for the internationalisation of modernism, which suggest a close relationship between culture and politics (aesthetic perspectives and societal processes) during the years from 1928 to 1933.

The second generation
During this period the generation of the 'pupils and sons of classic modernism' emerges, who in Germany, at least, could only begin to articulate their position after the end of the Second World War. They step out, militantly independent, but also more diffuse in their views and with fewer prospects of being able to build. They shaped the dissemination of modern architecture – both in buildings and texts – rather than its basic principles.

The historian Nikolaus Pevsner (1902–1983) can be counted among them, as can the co-founder of *L'Architecture d'Aujourd'hui* Pierre Vago (1910–2002) and the Berlin architect Julius Posener (1904–1996), who already published with Vago in Paris and who in the 1970s became friendly with Kurt Junghanns (1908–2006).

There is then also the glitzy American Philip Johnson (1906–2005), who cunningly exploited curating exhibitions like 'The International Style' in 1932, for his own ends and publicity as an architect; much as his South American opposite number Oscar Niemeyer (1907–2012) reinforced the contrary image of an architect of the left. Pierre Vago was a more typical case of the activities of an architect from the generation of 'sons' since he felt compelled to seek out Le Corbusier's goodwill in order 'to be allowed to work for the master'. He was brusquely refused, because his father, Joseph Vago, had been successful in the League of Nations competition. Vago junior had then, together with André Bloc, founded *L'Architecture d'Aujourhui*, and became, quite apart from his writing, an internationally active architect and organiser. Looking for equivalents in East Germany, Hermann Henselemann (1905–1995) planned the Stalinallee and was a pugnacious publicist; while in the West, Egon Eiermann (1904–1970), an impressive expert on concrete building, and Ernst Neufert (1900–1986), author of much-read specialist literature, should to be mentioned. Also to be counted are Hitler's later henchmen Rudolf Wolters (1903–1983) and Albert Speer (1905–1981), who was active in the university Nazi group at the TU Berlin – whose overwhelming majority had little resistance from the small group of communist students attending the seminars of Poelzig and Taut, like Gerhard Kosel (1909–2003), who later became secretary of state for building in the GDR, and Karola Bloch (1905–1994), financially supportive wife of the philosopher Ernst Bloch.

Bandstadt *and Ville Radieuse*

1929 was the year in which the two stylistically most important buildings of the Modern Movement, Le Corbusier's Villa Savoye and Mies' Barcelona Pavilion, were completed, overlapping with the Second CIAM Congress on the 'The Minimum Subsistence Dwelling', which promised a peaceful solution to the housing question. Following on in 1930 came the Third CIAM Congress 'Rational Lot Development' on high-rise housing; the Deutsche Werkbund Exhibition in Paris[23] which included debates on Russia's urbanisation; the move of Ernst May's group to Russia; and Hannes Meyer's dismissal in Dessau. During the next year, 1931, both Le Corbusier and Mies complained of being insulted by younger architects in Berlin, who claimed both individuals were only building for a rich clientele.

At this point nothing could be seen in isolation; everything was shadowed by the world economic crisis, or shaped (in architecture) by the competition for the Palace of the Soviets, which had many hopes attached to it, not the least those of Le Corbusier. Moving the Fourth CIAM Congress from Moscow to Athens in August 1933 seemed to signal the demise of 'classic' modernity in European architecture – and the 1933 Reichstag fire an invitation to the 'finale'.

After the 1931 Berlin building exhibition, contemporary architecture and politics could no longer be separated. Ernst May, the key practitioner of social housing, had lectured on his experiences in planning new cities in Russia. Meanwhile young architects and students of the Technical University – like Gerhard Kosel and Karola Bloch, influenced by Arthur Korn (1891–1978, emergent architect of the new glass architecture) – propagandised Milyutin's high-flown concept for Russia's 'linear cities' in a 'proletarian building exhibition' where a new urban classification elided the factory and hostel in a single urban continuum.[24] Korn, on whom there is still no monograph written, is, however, conserved in the memory of prominent students of the AA in London like Kenneth Frampton and Rem Koolhaas, who both have quoted Korn verbatim: 'First there was me, then there was Mies'.

Mies exhibited 'The Dwelling of our Time' and a model of a prototype house (preparing perhaps for the American post-war bungalow style) in his department. Back in Paris Le Corbusier proudly reported that one phone call to Mies had sufficed, at short notice, to obtain exhibition space to present his plans for the *Ville Radieuse*. What he did not say – or show – was that the project exhibited in 1931 (after the war to become the basis for the planning of Chandigarh), was in fact his proposal for a new plan for Moscow, which he had drawn up just before the exhibition.

The international style: New York 1932

At first unnoticed by the Europeans 'The International Style: Architecture since 1922', an exhibition in New York curated by Henry-Russell Hitchcock and the tenacious Philip Johnson, optimistically summed up the work of the new architecture. The exhibition renamed Modern Architecture, or the *Neues Bauen*, with a claim for their 'international' status. The exhibition revealed in its images and range of projects, the work of what was almost a ten-year period; this outcome, however, was linked to a shift of the axis of modernism from Central Europe to the East Coast of the United States.

Hitchcock and Johnson's exhibition catalogue was modelled on Le Corbusier's 1922 *Vers une architecture*. Le Corbusier's 'Three Reminders to Architects' from the early 1920s, was now illustrated with numerous examples from 'practice' of his exemplary characteristics: building 'volume', building 'surface' and building in 'plan'. Similarly the original chapter on 'Mass-Production Housing' had been replaced with a section on *Siedlungen* (using the German term). A third of the projects from fifteen European countries, Japan and the USA, in a summation of modernism, came from Germany, which would now, as a country, enter a long (dark) night.

The International Style became the rulebook for modern architecture. Alfred Barr, the director of the Museum of Modern Art in New York, had in his preface suggested the term 'Post-Functionalism' as a synonym for International Style. Clearly this was a reference to Hannes Meyer who had meanwhile become the incarnation of the anti-art of functionalism given a social and 'critical' orientation. Absurdly, this ideological antipathy would remain more energetic than that generated by other positions in the coming decades; it would even, at the beginning of the 1950s, remain a hostile image, this time (in reverse), for the Ulbricht government in East Berlin. A relieved Alfred Barr could still remark in his 1932 preface to the exhibition catalogue that the Bauhaus had been led by Mies since 1930.[25] But even for Mies 1930 meant a caesura, as he, and this is seldom mentioned, when taking office in Dessau had already pleaded for the creation of a Bauhaus branch in Chicago.

Summary failure – Athens 1933

At the turn of 1933–1934 Le Corbusier attempted to sum up the era in a special issue of *L'Architecture d'Aujourd'hui* – egocentric in its perception, but his projects the product of genius. Notably their representation failed to include any photographs of his buildings at the *Weissenhofsiedlung* of 1927; neither were they mentioned in explanation of his 'Five Points'. There is no report on the Fourth CIAM Congress in Athens, on town planning and 'The Functional City'. Nor even a single line on the urban analysis of four months earlier. Only the merest hint surfaced in Le Corbusier's lecture on his ideas for hermetically sealed glass facades and his universal concept of environmental control (from Moscow to Buenos Aires). He concluded with the words: 'My dear comrades of the congress, towards the adventure, the beautiful adventure. Architecture and Town Planning.'[26]

A disillusioned Le Corbusier remarked in 1933 that the enemies of modernism had gained the upper hand in Russia and in Germany. The social basis for the projects of modern architecture had been almost completely eroded in Germany and Russia. He noted that in Germany modernism was being persecuted as 'communist': 'there are martyrs, victims worthy of pity'.[27] His journeys to Italy, to the USA and to Brazil in 1934, 1935 and 1936 were an attempt to reclaim a new social basis for his work.

According to available research this much is clear: unbelievable for his many admirers, and not known to many, Le Corbusier in 1933 drew his own radical conclusions from the political context in which he had previously placed himself – between the aging Italian Futurists' cult of technology, and the *Neues Bauen* supporters' euphoric socialist planning. His stance closely resembles what the younger Italian architects like P.M. Bardi and Terragni were thinking at the time. Le Corbusier, a fascist? The malicious suspicion grows as it is ignored, only to demonstrate the manner in which a particular history of architecture is exploited. This served to trivialise Le Corbusier's status as that of an apolitical star-architect – just as did his executors in Paris.

Between January 1930 and March 1932 Le Corbusier was co-editor of *Plans*, a magazine edited by 'revolutionary Sorelians' – a group of anti-capitalist technocrats and radical Saint Simonists whose self-made philosophy only took hold in France and Italy. His series of articles on the *Ville Radieuse* were published in this magazine. Then, having moved into the attic flat of his newly completed apartment building in bourgeois Auteuil, he began contributing to the scurrilous publication *Prelude*, co-edited by his long-term friend and cohabitant Dr Pierre Winter. Winter ineptly published, in the August–September 1933 issue, together with reports on the CIAM Athens Congress, the group's self-evaluation: 'If we, with *Prelude*, stand between Fascism and Collectivism, then we demand our place on this demarcation line.'[28]

› Postscript: Rome, rationalism and rehabilitation

When Pierre Winter speaks of Collectivism in 1933 he refers to Russia and when he speaks of Fascism he refers to Italy. But because the Fascism in Italy was ten years earlier in its inception than that in Germany, it did not represent such a radical liquidation of modernism (anti-communist, anti-Semitic, anti-intellectual). Quite the opposite, it meant in 1933, with the founding of the journal *Quadrante*[29] a channelling of tendencies towards an 'Architettura Razionale' (Rational Architecture) by its supporters like P. M. Bardi (1900–1999, who emigrated with Lina Bo Bardi to Brazil in 1947), Ernesto Nathan Rogers (1909–1969, elder cousin of Richard Rogers and later a patron of Aldo Rossi), and Guiseppe Terragni the outstanding architectural talent of Italian Rationalism (1904–1943, who died on his return from the Russian front).

One has to consider these dates in order to understand the ideological differences involved; to emphasise that Gropius' generation had no equivalent in Italy, and similarly that the invitation for Le Corbusier to Italy in 1934 was part of the debate between the 'children of modernism'. This also partly applies to Alberto Sartoris (1901–1998) and his book *Gli Elementi dell' Architettura Razionale,* which in 1932 added a further term to the designation of modern architecture – *Neues Bauen*, International Style, and *Architettura Razionale*.

Le Corbusier's journey to Rome was important to him for two reasons: both concern urban planning and urban design. Superficially he was interested in a *dirigiste* economy, as this was presented in the *Prelude* articles – that is in offering a new basis for urban planning, similar to that he had experienced in a dynamic 'Moscow atmosphere', previously. On the other hand he is concerned with the Rome of antiquity, just as he had described it twelve years earlier in *Vers une architecture*. His conception of 'The Lessons of Rome' in a book also about the house as 'a machine for living in' was often misinterpreted or seen as a historical justification for modernism, lacking true sense.

But the Rome Le Corbusier had described in 1922 was an imaginary Rome which never existed. It was a Rome of a 'kit of parts', without Baroque layers or ruins, and without any mention of the monument to Vittorio Emanuele II. In fact it was a Rome that corresponded with the projections of modernism. The buildings in that model were exactly what Le Corbusier put forward as a contemporary urbanism, namely freestanding elementary building volumes: the 'Pantheon, Coliseum, Aqueducts, Cestius-Pyramid . . . No phrases, but instead order . . . The use of elementary forms. A healthy ethic.'

In Le Corbusier's drawings the antique monuments of Rome are cleared of all the additions attached to them as parasitic uses, but which are the reality of their history. This spatial ideal of freestanding volumes was realised in the well proportioned and yet empty government centre in Chandigarh. It could also lead to renewal projects like the *Plan Voisin* or the projects for the rebuilding of Berlin; one only needs to read the section on Michelangelo in *Vers une architecture* to see how Le Corbusier's renewal programme was derived from a misconceived reading of the historic city.

THILO HILPERT

Apart from the photographs showing Le Corbusier on the rooftop test track of the Fiat factory in Lingotto, which in 1923 had inspired him as a model for large urban forms, there were hardly any remaining impressions from this journey that would justify his initial euphoria. A disappointed Le Corbusier writes about P. M. Bardi and the organisation of a journey where he felt he had been dropped 'like a hot potato'.

In Le Corbusier's reports about his Rome trip of 1934 there is, astonishingly considering that it had just been completed (and invited comment), no mention of the character of the *Via dei Fori Imperiali*[30] which cut a corridor into the fabric and topography of the old city in order to provide a view to the Coliseum. Aldo Rossi, who 30 years later would become the most important architect of Neo-Rationalism identified it with the 'terrorism of modernism' and pleaded, in his book *The Architecture of the City* for a reading of the dialectic between building and urban space, for which Rome is the classic exemplar of this reciprocal relationship between internal and external urban space.

> ## › Notes

Translated by the editors.

1   'A great era has just begun. There exists a new spirit. There exists a host of works in this new spirit, they are encountered above all in industrial production . . .' Le Corbusier, *Toward an Architecture*, London: Francis Lincoln, 2008, p. 102.
2   Ibid., p. 112.
3   Thilo Hilpert, *Le Corbusier 1887–1987: Laboratory of ideas. Labor der Ideen. Laboratoire des idées*, Hamburg: Christians & Reim, Messe Frankfurt, 1987.
4   Thilo Hilpert, *Mies in Postwar Germany, The Mannheim Theater. Mies im Nachkriegsdeutschland, Das Theaterprojekt 1953*, Leipzig: E.A. Seemann, 2001.
5   Thilo Hilpert, *Walter Gropius – das Bauhaus in Dessau. Von der Idee zur Gestalt*, Frankfurt am Main: Fischer-Verlag, 1999.
6   Thilo Hilpert, 'Die andere Moderne – Bruno Tauts Stadtvision', Landeshauptstadt Magdeburg (ed.): *Bruno Taut 1880–1938*, 1995, pp. 80–89.
7   Bruno Taut, 'Gegen den Strom', Thilo Hilpert, *Hufeisensiedlung Britz 1926–1980. Ein alternativer Siedlungsbau der 20er Jahre als Studienobjekt*. Berlin: TU Berlin, 1980.
8   The contents of the book were published earlier as twelve essays in the journal *l'Esprit nouveau* from 1920–1922.
9   Le Corbusier, *Toward an Architecture* (see note 1), p. 102.
10 Ulrich Conrads (ed.), *Programmes and Manifestoes on 20th-century Architecture*, London: Lund Humphries, 1970, pp. 49–53.
11 Thilo Hilpert (ed.), *Le Corbusiers 'Charta von Athen'. Texte und Dokumente. Kritische Neuausgabe.* Braunschweig/Wiesbaden: Vieweg 1984. (Bauwelt Fundamente 56).
12 All three are collected in Le Corbusier, *Essential Le Corbusier: L'Esprit nouveau articles*, Oxford: Architectural Press, 1998.
13 This accompanied the 1927 Werkbund exhibition 'Die Wohnung' at the *Weissenhofsiedlung in Stuttgart*. Adolf Behne, *Eine Stunde Architektur*, Stuttgart: Akademischer Verlag Dr. Fritz Wedekind, 1928.
14 Adolf Behne, '150 Jahre soziale Strömungen in der Bildenden Kunst', *Kulturwoche des FDGB, Sonntag*, 9 November 1947.
15 Marco Dezzi Bardeschi, *Frank Lloyd Wright*, London, New York: Hamlyn Publishing Group, 1972.
16 Letter written in November 1935 from Talliesen Wisconsin to Leo J. Wiessenborn in Chicago. Quoted in: Thilo Hilpert, 'USA 1935: Kontroverse Wright – Le Corbusier', *Der Architekt*, 1/1993, pp. 38–42.
17 Richard Pommer and Christian F. Otto, *Weissenhof 1927 and the Modern Movement in Architecture*, Chicago: University of Chicago Press, 1991.
18 'Bundesschule des Allgemeinen Deutschen Gewerkschaftsbundes in Bernau-Berlin', E. Deines (ed.), *Bau-Wettbewerbe*, 33. Karlsruhe, December 1928.

19 'CIAM: La Sarraz Declaration (1928)', collected in Ulrich Conrads (ed.), *Programmes and Manifestoes on 20th-century Architecture*, see note 10, p. 110.

20 'building is a biological process. building is not an aesthetic process. in its design the new dwelling becomes not only a "machine for living", but also a biological apparatus serving the needs of the body and mind', Hannes Meyer, 'Building (1928)', Conrads, *Programmes*, p. 117.

21 Thilo Hilpert, *Die Funktionelle Stadt. Le Corbusiers Stadtvision – Bedingungen, Motive, Hintergründe*. Braunschweig: Vieweg, 1978 (Bauwelt Fundamente 48), p. 86: 'Der Funktionalismus-Streit', translation from Le Corbusier: 'Défense de l'architecture', *L'Architecture d'Aujourd'hui*, 10, 1933–1934, p. 38. 'Si Leonidov, le poète et l'espoir du "constructivisme" architectural russe, dans son enthousiasme de 25 ans, clame le fonctionalisme et vitupère le constructivisme . . .'.

22 Le Corbusier, 'Concevoir d'abord, construire ensuite', *L'Architecture d'Aujourd'hui*, 10, 1933–1934, p. 29.

23 In fact the 'Section Allemande' of the twentieth annual Salon of the *Societe des Artistes decorateurs*, 'Essentially a Bauhaus rather than a Werkbund exhibition . . .' See Paul Overy, 'Visions of the Future and the Immediate Past: the Werkbund Exhibition, Paris 1930', *Journal of Design History*, 4, 2004, pp. 337–357.

24 Thilo Hilpert, 'Linear Metropolis: the forgotten urban utopia of the 20th century', *Visionary Architecture and Urban Design of the Sixties Reflected by Contemporary Artists*, Berlin, Ostfildern: Hatje Cantz, 2008.

25 Henry-Russell Hitchcock and Philipp Johnson, *The International Style – Architecture since 1922*. New York: The Norton Library, 1932, pp. 11–14.

26 Le Corbusier, 'Discours d' Athènes', *L'Architecture d'Aujourd'hui*, 10, 1933–1934, pp. 81–89, 89.

27 Le Corbusier, 'Défense de l'architecture', *L'Architecture d'Aujourd'hui*, 10, 1933–1934, note 39. 'Voici 1933. Voici Hitler. En Allemagne desormais toute architecture moderne est . . . considérée comme manifestation communiste: il y a des martyres des victimes pitoyables . . .'.

28 Pierre Winter, 'Formations Nouvelles', *Prelude 7*, aout–septembre 1933, p. 3. Quoted after: Thilo Hilpert, 'Le lieu de la Ville Radieuse', *AMC*, 49, Numero Special Le Corbusier, September 1979, pp. 91–96 (describes the political background of the Ville Radieuse 1930 to 1934).

29 Francesco Tentori, *P. M. Bardi, con le cronache artistiche de l'Ambrosiano, 1930–1933*, Milan: Mazzotta, 1990.

30 Ursula Salwa and Attilo Wunderlingh, *Roma in Guerra. Rome at war – From Fascism to the World War*. Roma: Intrea Moenia, 2011.

Rationalist Architecture: Type-Form and History

1 H. P. Berlage

The foundations and development of architecture (1908)

H. P. Berlage, *Grundlagen und Entwicklung der Architektur: Vier Vorträge gehalten im Kunstgewerbemuseum zu Zürich*, Rotterdam: W. L. & J. Brusse; Berlin: Julius Bard, 1908. Extract here from: Julia Bloomfield, Thomas F. Reese, Salvatore Settis (ed.) *Hendrick Petrus Berlage: Thoughts on Style 1886–1909*, Santa Monica, CA: The Getty Centre for the History of Art and the Humanities, 1996, pp. 248–250, translation by Iain Boyd Whyte and Wim de Wit.

* * *

For if we recapitulate yet again, we come to the following observation. If you desire to create something in the visual arts that has style, the whole project must be based on a mathematical system, with no form derived from pure arbitrariness. The forms of earlier styles should not be used and should, for this reason, be done away with. If you work according to this principle, then you are ultimately working toward a formal style, yet a style that will still lack the spiritual impulse until such time as a universal idea is once more born. For this reason today's Modern Movement is to be seen only as a recasting of form, which had to come after the enervation of the nineteenth century.

But if this Modern Movement works in a rational, constructional form—clearly and *sachlich,* as was done in both great styles—then it is also working in a religious way, with a religious longing, until finally the longing becomes reality and a new universal idea is born.

How will this universal idea announce itself; which spiritual idea will serve as its foundation? Who can answer these questions? Christianity is dead, and the first quiet stirrings of a new type of universal concept derived from scientific research have barely begun to be felt. Yet man demands a certain ethical satisfaction, and from all the recent turmoil surfaces a powerful tendency to regard this as an altruistic battle. It is a question of either one or all. With the denial of morality should the individual alone be protected, or all men, according to the principle of equality?

Once again, this is not the place to analyze the worth or worthlessness of such a principle, but the powerful ethical intention behind the struggle for universal economic equality cannot be denied. A consequence will be that all men will become spiritually and intellectually independent and thus able to take advantage of all spiritual and intellectual material. For only then will, on the one hand, the actual conditions be set for the spiritual universal struggle [*Welt-Kampf*], conditions that will stimulate the deployment of the greatest ability, for intellectual results will be regarded more highly than material results are today. On the other hand, these results will reach the highest levels thanks to the mutual intellectual and spiritual accord, whereas today they have sunk to the lowest level due to the enfeebling influence of capitalism and the resulting class struggle.

In my already-cited lecture "Thoughts on Style" I tried to develop the theme of how the struggle against eclectic architecture can be compared with the workers' movement, in that they run as parallel developments: the former spiritual, the latter material. As I say in the lecture, the political initiative must first be implemented before the artistic initiative can achieve a breakthrough, and only from this moment on can work begin on the evolution of a style.

Therefore, if the modern artists work in a *sachlich,* clear way under the preconditions that I have tried to develop, they will be striving toward the modern spiritual ideal, the principle of the economic equality of all men. In doing so, they will breathe life into the formal beauty that has already been developed but which, in the last resort, needs a style in order to rise to new heights. By *sachlich,* clear work I mean a renewed awareness that architecture is the art of spatial enclosure, and, for this reason, prime value, both constructionally and decoratively, should be laid on space. It follows from this that a building should not be essentially an external manifestation.

The art of architecture resides in the creation of spaces, not in the design of facades. A spatial enclosure is produced by walls, and thus the space or the various spaces find external expression in a more or less complex arrangement of walls. It is also important in this sense that the walls should remain flat, for an overarticulated wall loses its intrinsic, wall-like character. By *sachlich,* clear work I mean that the architecture of the wall remains two-dimensional decoration, that the projecting elements are limited to those offered by the construction, such as window supports, water spouts, gutters, single cornices, and so on. It follows from this so-called wall architecture, in which vertical articulation disappears of its own accord, that the vertical supports such as piers and columns are not given projecting capitals, but rather that the development of the transitions are developed within the wall. The windows form the true decoration of the wall plane; they are installed only where necessary, and then in appropriate sizes.

By *sachlich,* clear work I mean work in which the pictorial decorations do not dominate and are employed only in those places that have shown themselves, after the most careful study, to be the correct ones.

Following the principle above, the pictorial decoration should remain surface decoration, in other words, sunk into the wall, and the figures should ultimately form decorated areas of the wall.

Above all, one should once again display the naked wall in all its smooth and simple [*schlicht*] beauty.

By *sachlich,* clear work I mean a work in which all excess is most scrupulously avoided, in which there are no useless cornices and moldings, pedestals and pilasters, shoulder pieces and fixtures—in short, no architecture of a parasitic nature.

By *sachlich,* clear work I mean, finally, an intelligible work that will stimulate interest as only natural simplicity and clarity can, whereas unnatural complexity and ambiguity remain misunderstood. Such complexity startles but does not evoke any interest, which explains why architecture was excluded from the realm of cultural progress in the nineteenth century. The *sachlich,* rational, and therefore clear construction can become the basis of the new art, but only when this principle has penetrated deeply enough and been applied widely enough, will we stand at the door of a new art. And at the same moment the new, universal spirit [*Weltgefühl*]—the social equality of all men—will be revealed, a spirit whose ideals are located not in the beyond but here on earth, confronting all of us.

2 Adolf Loos

Architecture (1910)

Adolf Loos, *Der Sturm*, 15 December 1910. Collected in Adolf Loos, *Trotzdem 1900–1930*, Adolf Opel (ed.), Innsbruck: Brenner Verlag, 1931, pp. 90–104. Extracts here from: Yehuda Safran and Wilfried Wang (ed.), *The Architecture of Adolf Loos*, Arts Council Catalogue, London: Arts Council of Great Britain, 1985, pp. 107–109, translation by Wilfried Wang with Rosamund Diamond and Robert Godsill.

*   *   *

When I was finally given the task of building a house, I said to myself: in its external appearance, a house can only have changed as much as a dinner jacket. Not a lot, therefore. And I saw how the old buildings had freed themselves from ornament, from century to century, from one year to another. I, therefore, had to begin again at that point where the chain of development bad been broken. I knew one thing: in order to continue that line of development, I had to become significantly simpler. I had to substitute the golden buttons with black ones. The house had to look inconspicuous. Had I not once formulated the sentence: he who is dressed in a modern manner is one who is least conspicuous. That sounded paradoxical. But there were brave people who were careful to remember this, and many of my other paradoxical ideas; and who put them into print. That happened so often that people in time took them to be true.

However, as far as inconspicuousness is concerned, there was one thing I had not considered. That is: what was true in the case of clothes was not the case for architecture. If architecture had only been left alone by those warped people, and if the clothes were reformed in terms of old theatrical junk or in the Secessionist manner — there certainly were attempts in this direction — then the situation would have been the other way round.

Consider this situation: everyone wears clothes that relate to a past period or to one of an imaginary, distant future. One would see men from grey antiquity, women with towering hair styles and crinoline dresses, dainty men wearing Burgundy trousers and in between, a few cheeky moderns with purple escarpins and apple-green doublets (decorated by Professor Walter Scherbel). And now a man was to enter wearing a simple suit, would he not be conspicuous? More than that, would he not cause offence? And would the police not be called, since after all, they have the duty to remove everything that causes an offence?

However, the matter is quite the contrary. The clothes are the right ones; the act of buffoonery is in the domain of architecture. My house (the Michaelerhouse in Vienna, built in the same year that this article was written), gave real offence, and the police were immediately at hand. I might be allowed to do such things in the confines of my own four walls, but it does not belong in the street!

Many will have had doubts over my last remarks, doubts which are directed against the comparison which I have drawn between tailoring and architecture. After all, architecture is an art. Granted, it is for the time being. But have you never noticed the strange correspondence between the exterior dress of people and the exterior of buildings? Is the tasselled robe not appropriate to the Gothic style and the wig to the Baroque? But do our contemporary houses correspond with our clothes? Are we afraid of uniformity? But were the old buildings within one period and one country also not uniform? So uniform that it is possible for us to place them in order according to the styles of countries, peoples and towns. Nervous vanity was alien to the old masters. Tradition determined the forms. The masters did not change the forms. The masters however, were unable faithfully to use the established, hallowed, traditional forms. New tastes changed the forms and thus the rules were broken and new forms were developed. But the people of that period were at one with the architecture of their times. The newly erected building pleased everyone. Today most houses only please two people: the client and the architect.

The house has to please everyone, contrary to the work of art, which does not. The work of art is a private matter for the artist. The house is not. The work of art is brought into the world without there being a need for it. The house satisfies a requirement. The work of art is responsible to none: the house is responsible to everyone. The work of art wants to draw people out of their state of comfort. The house has to serve comfort. The work of art is revolutionary; the house is conservative. The work of art shows people new directions and thinks of the future. The house thinks of the present. Man loves everything that satisfies his comfort. He hates everything that wants to draw him out of his acquired and secured position and that disturbs him. Thus he loves the house and hates art.

Does it follow that the house has nothing in common with art and is architecture not to be included amongst the arts? That is so. Only a very small part of architecture belongs to art: the tomb and the monument. Everything else that fulfils a function is to be excluded from the domain of art.

Only when the great misunderstanding, that art is something which can be adapted to serve a function has been overcome, only when the deceitful catch-phrase of 'applied-art' has disappeared from the vocabulary of the people, only then will we have the architecture of our period. The artist needs only to serve himself; the architect must serve the population at large.

*   *   *

Architecture arouses sentiments in man. The architect's task therefore, is to make those sentiments more precise. The room has to be comfortable; the house has to look habitable. The law courts must appear as a threatening gesture towards secret vice. The bank must declare: here your money is secure and well looked after by honest people.

The architect can only achieve this if he establishes a relationship with those buildings which have hitherto created this sentiment in man. For the Chinese, the colour of mourning is white:

for us it is black. Consequently it would be impossible for our architects to produce a happy atmosphere with the colour black.

When we come across a mound in the wood, six feet long and three feet wide, raised to a pyramidal form by means of a spade, we become serious and something in us its says: somebody lies buried here. *This is architecture.*

Our culture is based on the knowledge of the all-surpassing grandeur of classical antiquity. We have adopted the technique of thinking and feeling from the Romans. We have inherited our social conscience and the discipline of our souls from the Romans.

It is no coincidence that the Romans were incapable of inventing a new column order, or a new ornament. For they had already progressed so far. They had taken all that knowledge from the Greeks and had adapted it to their needs. The Greeks were individualists. Every building had to have its own profile, its own ornamentation. But the Romans considered things socially. The Greeks could hardly administer their cities: the Romans administered the globe. The Greeks squandered their inventiveness on the orders; the Romans wasted theirs on the plan. And he who can solve the great plan does not think of new mouldings.

Ever since humanity sensed the greatness of classical antiquity, one common thought has unified all great architects. They think: the way I build is the same as the way the Romans would have built. We know that they are mistaken. Time, place, function and climate, milieu have upset their calculations.

But every time the minor architects who use ornament move architecture away from its grand model, a great architect is at hand to guide them back to antiquity. Fischer von Erlach in the south, Schlüter in the north, were justifiably the great masters of the eighteenth century. And at the threshold to the nineteenth century stood Schinkel. We have forgotten him. May the light of this towering figure shine upon our forthcoming generation of architects!

3 Le Corbusier

Toward an architecture (1923)

Le Corbusier, *Vers une architecture*, Paris: Crès and Cie., 1924. English translation by John Goodman, from: Le Corbusier, *Toward an Architecture,* Jean-Louis Cohen (introduction), London: Francis Lincoln, 2008, extracts pp. 87, 88–89, 182–183, 185 and 266–267.

› Argument

*   *   *

AIRPLANES
The airplane is a product of high selection.
The lesson of the airplane is in the logic that governed the statement of the problem and its realization.
The problem of the house has not been posed.
Current architectural things do not answer to our needs.
Yet there are standards for the dwelling.
The mechanical carries within it the economic factor that selects.
The house is a machine for living in.

*   *   *

MASS-PRODUCTION HOUSING
A great era has just begun.
There exists a new spirit.
Industry, invading like a river that rolls to its destiny, brings us new tools adapted to this new era animated
    by a new spirit.
The law of Economy necessarily governs our actions and our conceptions.
The problem of the house is a problem of the era. Social equilibrium depends on it today. The first obligation
    of architecture, in an era of renewal, is to bring about a revision of values, a revision of the constitutive
    elements of the house.
Mass production is based on analysis and experimentation.

Heavy industry should turn its attention to building and standardize the elements of the house.
We must create a mass-production state of mind,
A state of mind for building mass-production housing.
A state of mind living in mass-production housing.
A state of mind for conceiving mass-production housing.
If we wrest from our hearts and minds static conceptions of the house and envision the question from a critical
     and objective point of view, we will come to the house-tool, the mass-production house that is healthy
     (morally, too) and beautiful from the aesthetic of the work tools that go with our existence.
Beautiful too from all the life that the artistic sense can bring to strict and pure organs.

*   *   *

› Eyes that do not see

III Automobiles

*   *   *

To establish a standard is to exhaust all practical and reasonable possibilities, to deduce a recognized type consistent with function, maximal return, and minimum expenditure of means, manpower and materials, words, forms, colors, sounds.

The automobile is an object with a simple function (to run) and complex ends (comfort, resistance, looks) that has placed major industry under an imperious necessity to standardize. All automobiles are essentially organized the same way. Through the relentless competition of the countless firms that build them, each has found itself under obligation to dominate the competition, and, on top of the standard for realized practical things, there has intervened a search for perfection and harmony outside of brute practical fact, a manifestation not only of perfection and harmony, but of beauty.

Thence is born style, which is to say the unanimously acknowledged acquisition of a unanimously felt state of perfection.

The establishment of a standard proceeds from the organisation of rational elements according to a line of conduct that is likewise rational. The enveloping mass is not preconceived, *it results:* it can look strange at first. Ader making a "Bat" that didn't fly; Wright and Farman making airfoils that were odd and disconcerting, but that flew. The standard was fixed. Then came the fine-tuning.

*   *   *

So let us put the Parthenon and the automobile on show to make it clear that it's a question here, in different domains, of two products of selection, the one having reached its outcome, the other still progressing. This ennobles the automobile. And then? Well, it remains to compare our houses and our palaces with automobiles. Here's where we get stuck, where everything *gets* stuck. Here's where we don't have our Parthenons.

* * *

› Mass production housing

(caption)
L.C., 1921. "Citroban" (not to say Citroën) mass-production house. In other words, a house like an automobile, conceived and built like a bus or a ship's cabin. Present housing necessities can be identified and require solutions. We must work against the old-world house that misused space. We must (present necessity: low net cost) look upon the house as a machine for living in or as a tool. When you create an industry, you buy the equipment; when you set up house, at present you rent a stupid apartment. Until now we made houses into barely coherent groupings of many large rooms; in the rooms there was always too much space and not enough space. Today, fortunately, we no longer have enough money to perpetuate this routine and since we don't want to consider the problem in its true light (machines for living in) we cannot build in the cities and a disastrous crisis is the result; with budgets, we could build apartment buildings that are admirably laid out, on the condition, of course, that tenants change their mindset; besides, they will conform anyway under pressure of necessity. Windows and doors should have their dimensions rectified; railway cars and limousines have proven to us that man can pass through small openings and that we can calculate space to the square centimetre; it is criminal to build four-square-meter bathrooms. Building costs have quadrupled, we must reduce old architectural pretensions by half and the square footage of houses by at least half; this is henceforth a problem for the technician; we call upon the discoveries of industry; we completely change our state of mind. Beauty! It is always present when the intention and the means *that are proportion* exist; proportion doesn't cost the owner anything, just the architect. The heart will be touched only if reason is satisfied and it can be when things are calculated. We must not be ashamed to live in houses without pitched roofs, to own walls as thin as sheet metal and windows similar to factory chassis. But what we can be proud of is having a house as practical as our typewriter.

4 Adolf Loos

Regarding economy (1924)

'Von der Sparsamkeit', compiled by Bohuslav Markalous[1] *Wohnungskultur*, 2/3, 1924. English translation by Francis R. Jones, from: Max Risselada (ed.), *Raumplan versus Plan Libre: Adolf Loos and Le Corbusier, 1919–1930*, New York: Rizzoli International Publications, 1988, extracts pp. 137–138, 138, 140 and 141.

An item becomes out-of-date the instant our feelings turn against it, as soon as we would feel ridiculous for staying faithful to it.

A top hat can take a variety of forms. Imagine a row of a hundred of them. I want to go to a funeral. I try various shapes and see that most of them are impossible, ridiculous, and that only one hat fits. The 1924 hat, let's say.

This hat is the only possible one for me and the time in which I live.

People find only possible things modern.

The 1924 top hat is definitely possible, and if I could have worn it twenty years ago and still wear it today, everything would be fine. And because I can actually wear it, this top hat is fully justified in production terms, or more generally speaking, in commercial terms.

But these are just fashions, which soon change.

But if it so happens that a desk loses its aesthetic value for me after ten years, that I find it impossible, get rid of it and buy myself a new one, then that is a gigantic waste in commercial terms.

I reject any form of innovation-mania. Only a conservative person is economical, and every innovator is wasteful.

On the other hand, someone who has a lot of clothes takes good care that they do not go out of fashion.

Someone who only has one suit has no need to be cautious. On the contrary. Through constant use, he wears out his suit in a very short time, and in so doing forces the tailor to keep inventing new styles.

The counter-argument, that these constant changes in fashion are a very useful thing in that they provide the producers with plenty of work, is actually back-to-front.

One needs to have a lot of clothes so that one can change them according to one's needs of the moment. When it is raining I wear a mackintosh, in spring I wear an overcoat, in winter a worsted suit, and in this way I treat my wardrobe with respect. Fashion is something ephemeral only because we do not make things last. As soon as we have objects which last a long time and stay beautiful, fashion ceases. We should measure beauty in terms of time. I cannot judge rails by how many trains can pass along them, but only by how long they last. They will remain good as long as they do a good, reliable job.

* * *

Every effort to reduce the durability of an item is wrong. We must make all the articles we produce last longer. This is correct.

I buy some poor-quality material and have a suit made from it: the suit lasts a third as long as a good-quality one. One to three! A good suit is economical, a bad one wasteful. This is a matter of great economic significance.

But when objects crafted from top-quality materials with consummate technical skill go out of fashion in a few years through wilfulness of form – this is waste.

Labouring for months to produce lace only to have the lace torn in a single night is also a bad thing. Such lace can be produced effortlessly and at much less cost by machine.

Let us strive for refinement and economy. I do not know who is the more economical: the man who drinks good wine or the one who quaffs great quantities of bad wine.

But I would also like to say something about the psychology of economy. If I buy a cigarette-case, that does not mean I wish to be bludgeoned, to be deprived of the joy of material and workmanship and be given the dubious pleasure of ornamentation in its stead. I want the material itself, suitably finished. A ring is a hoop-shaped piece of good gold. A cigarette-case means two flat trays of good silver, perfectly smooth. The beautiful smoothness of polished silver, so fine to the touch, is the best ornamentation.

* * *

I have no need whatsoever to draw my designs. Good architecture, how something is to be built, can be written. One can write the Parthenon.

I am against the photographing of interiors. Something quite different comes out of it. There are designers who make interiors not so that people can live well in them, but so that they look good on photographs. These are the so-called graphic interiors, whose mechanical assemblies of lines of shadow and light best suit another mechanical contrivance: the *camera obscura*. My home interiors are impossible to judge from photographs or reproductions. I am certain that, if photographed, they would look wretched and ineffective.

For photography renders insubstantial, whereas what I want in my rooms is for people to feel substance all round them, for it to act upon them, for them to know the enclosed space, to feel the fabric, the wood, above all to perceive it sensually, with sight and touch, for them to dare to sit comfortably and feel the chair over a large area of their external bodily senses, and to say: this is what I call sitting! How can I prove this to someone by means of a photograph, how can I let the person looking at this photograph feel how good my chair is to sit on, no matter how well-photographed it is?

So photography says nothing, you see. Photography draws pictures, pretty or not so pretty. Their effect is to distract people from the thing itself. To give them the wrong upbringing. Photography has on its conscience the fact that people want to furnish their homes, not so that they are good to live in, but so that they look pretty. Photography deceives. I have never wanted to deceive anybody with my activities. I reject such methods. But our architects have had their upbringing exclusively in the deceptive method, and are rooted in it; they base their reputation on pretty drawings and fine photographs. They do so consciously, for they know that people are so helpless that they find a graphic, photographic illusion enough to live in and even be proud of. And in this way the clients, living a life of self-deception in all these drawings and photographs, show so little honesty towards themselves that they refuse to admit the fact.

*   *   *

I always feel glad when I have been living for a length of time in America and England.

An English bride would be happiest if she could acquire all her parents' furniture. Our brides will hear nothing of easing their parents' financial burden by taking over some of their furniture. They want something new, "fashionable", "modern". They even want an "artistic design". And in four years they will want another "artistic design", because their furniture is already thoroughly out-of-date and completely new designs are now on the market. This is dreadful! It is a waste of energy, labour and money, and is economically ruinous.

In contrast, English furniture is the acme of comfort, and *ours* – "artistically designed by modern designers" – is a heap of nonsense and crimes against substance, purpose and workmanship.

An English lounge chair is perfection itself. Similarly shining examples of many other types of furniture are also to be found in America and England. I believe that each year, in the whole world, we produce just one good model which is able to serve for any length of time. All the rest disappear within a few years and become as unbearable for people as an old bonnet. Our so-called *Kunstgewerbe*, or art-and-craft trade, creates nothing but the ramshackle, and such "artistic interiors" only exist because they have been ordered and paid for beforehand, because they are ready-made anyway, because they are there in the home as one single package which people must suffer patiently, like it or not, once they have already fallen for something of the sort.

This is why I do not like people calling me *Architekt*. My name is simply Adolf Loos.

To the Viennese, economy is absolutely unheard-of. They have a veritable mania for constantly changing their homes, buying new things, rearranging, running from *Architekt* to *Architekt*. This chaos is a sign of the times. And anyone who can contribute a little calm to the state of our architectural design is worthy indeed.

*   *   *

It was sometime in 1895, when I was in America, that I first realized that a Thonet chair is the most modern chair there is.

Any joiner can make the objects I furnish with. I have not made a patented architect of myself. Any stonemason, any weaver or artisan can make my objects without begging me respectfully for permission. The main thing is that he do an honest job of work. And I have not been as wary of anything in life as of the production of new forms.

The role of the designer is to grasp the deepness of life, to think a need through to its most far-reaching consequences, to help the socially weaker, to equip as large a number of households as is feasible with articles of perfect utility, but never to invent new forms.

But these are all views which as many people will understand in Europe today as can be counted on the fingers of one hand.

› Note

1   This article was compiled by Bohuslav Markalous, the editor of *Wohnungskultur,* from various conversations with Adolf Loos: hence its fragmentary nature. In accordance with the author's wishes, the article has been entitled 'Regarding Economy'.

5   J. J. P. Oud

Yes and no: confessions of an architect (1925)

J. J. P. Oud, 'Ja und Nein: Bekenntnisse eines Architekten', *Europa Almanac,* Potsdam: 1925. English translation from: Jane Beckett (ed.), *The Original Drawings of JJP Oud 1890–1963*, Exhibition Catalogue, London: Architectural Association, 1978, extract pp. 25–26.

› Contribution to Maschinenromantik in architecture

On technology

I kneel before the marvels of technology, but I do not believe in comparing an ocean liner with the Parthenon.

I can be elated about the almost perfect beauty of lines of a motor car, but the aeroplane appears to me still very clumsy.

I'm longing for a dwelling which satisfies all the demands of my love for comfort, but a house is more to me than a machine-for-living-in.

I have railway bridges whose forms are similar to those of Gothic cathedrals, but the pure 'Zweckarchitektur' of many famed engineering structures I couldn't care less about. I would not like to advocate the imitation of the campanile by Giotto for the architecture of the present, but I am dreaming of a tower of the future more beautiful than the Eiffel Tower.

I do understand why American grain silos are shown as examples of contemporary architecture but I'm asking myself where, in architecture, art has been hidden.

I proclaim that artists must put themselves into the machine, but I've become conscious of the fact that the machine must be a servant of art.

I harbour the best hopes for refinement which machine production can bring to architecture, but I fear that uncritical admiration of every-thing mechanical might lead to a regrettable regression.

On analogy

I'm glad that in a time without love for work, technology created forms which were both perfect in appearance and conscientious in fulfilling their purpose, but I'm annoyed that the works of many artists who praise these characteristics are so mannered and superficial.

On the typical

I expect a crystallization of form in a distinct style, to result from the reduction to the typical of the subordinate parts of a building; but the standard house prefabricated en masse appears to me to be difficult to fit into the complex of a large city.

On materials

I thought that current architectural opinions do not do justice to materials used at the present time, but it became apparent to me that today's materials do not reach the level of the progressing development of architecture of today.

On style

I love the square in the way it rejects the decorative nonsense of disappearing eclecticism, but I do not see any reason why the new architecture should do without circular forms.

On form

I understand the craving for asymmetrical disposition in a period characterised by dissolution and destruction, but I'm not clear why a constructive period of art should not also use symmetrical forms.

On propaganda

I recognise that it is necessary to be one-sided when propagating new ideas, but I cannot see the development of a new style without comprising life in all its facets.

On modern art

I can tremble with excitement when looking at a work of modern art, but I'm not always sure whether it is because of the modern or because of the art.

On the new style

Without reservation I'm on the side of modern art out of whose vital will in time the new style will come; but I admit that sometimes I equally admire its force with which it breaks with the Old, and its talent with which it builds up the New.

On rationalism

I learned at school that a rationalist architect is somebody who honours construction, but for me an architect is only a rationalist when he honours the purpose of a building.

I'm convinced that a new architecture can only grow from rational principles, but rationalism is to me the opposite pole to art.

On truth

I was of the opinion that truth is the corner-stone of the art of our time, but I came to the conclusion that the essential new lies in its clarity.

On colour

I was under the illusion that in the evolution of painting the picture became space and space became the picture, but I was disappointed to learn that this was a development from the easel painting to the easel space.

I thought it was reasonable that the painter had to have the same status as the architect in the creation of a building, but I got a shock when I realised that the creation of an architectural work of art would be under the domination of an aesthetic workers' council if sculptors and locksmiths and carpenters etc. should claim equal rights.

I raved about the revival of colour in architecture, but I agree with those who contend that too much colour makes not for colourfulness but for garishness.

On totality

I love the driving energy of the precursors who tear everything down (the blazing trail of the precursor), but I know that beauty can only be approached through the individual's concentration.

6 Le Corbusier

Type-needs type-furniture (1925)

Le Corbusier, *L'art décoratif d'aujourd'hui*, Paris: Crès and Cie., 1925. English translation by James I. Dunnett, from: Le Corbusier, *The Decorative Arts of Today*, London: Architectural Press, 1987. Extract here from: *Essential Le Corbusier: L'Esprit Nouveau Articles,* Oxford: Architectural Press, 1998, p. 76.

*   *   *

We have now identified decorative art as commensurate with the art of the engineer. The art of the engineer extends across a wide spectrum of human activity. If at one extreme it encompasses pure calculation and mechanical invention, at the other it leads towards *Architecture*.

Can one then speak of the architecture of decorative art, and consider it capable of permanent value?

The permanent value of decorative art? Let us say more exactly, of the *objects* that surround us. This is where we exercise our judgement: first of all the Sistine Chapel, afterwards chairs and filing cabinets; without doubt this is a question of the secondary level, just as the cut of a man's jacket is of secondary importance in his life. Hierarchy. First of all the Sistine Chapel, that is to say works truly etched with passion. Afterwards machines for sitting in, for filing, for lighting, type-machines, the problem of purification, of simplification, of precision, before the problem of poetry.[1]

› Note

1   When the typewriter came into use, letter paper was standardized; this standardization had considerable repercussions upon furniture as a result of the establishment of a module, that of the *commercial format*. Typewriters, file-copies, filing trays, files, filing drawers, filing cabinets, in a word the whole furnishing industry, was affected by the establishment of this standard; and even the most intransigent individuals were not able to resist it. . . .

7 Gruppo 7

Architecture (1926)

Gruppo 7, 'Architettura I', *La Rassegna Italiana*, 18, December 1926. English translation by Ellen R. Shapiro, *Oppositions*, 6, 1976, extract pp. 89–92.

*   *   *

Current opinion holds that our time is one of confusion and disorder in the field of art. This was so, and perhaps it was so even recently, but today it is certainly not the case.

We have gone through a period of formation which has now matured, and it was the work of this formative period that caused a general sense of disorientation (perhaps even the men of the first years of the Quattrocento felt disoriented: a comparison cannot be too bold, since we are truly on the threshold of a great period).

A "new spirit" has been born[1] It exists, we would like to, say, in the air, like a thing by itself, independent of single individuals, in all countries, with different appearances and forms, but with the same foundation—a prodigious gift which not all art epochs or historical periods have possessed. We live, therefore, in privileged times since we can witness the birth of a whole new order of ideas. Proof that we are at the beginning of an epoch that will finally have its own well-defined character can be seen in the frequent repetition of the perfect correspondence of the various forms of art, and the influence that the one exercises upon the other—precisely those characteristics of periods in which a style was created.

All over Europe, such a characteristic is now well-known. The exchange of influences among Cocteau, Picasso, and Stravinsky is very evident in the way in which their works complement each other. In addition, the influence Cocteau had on the "Six" is well-known, as is his influence in general on the evolution of French music. What is striking, however, is the correspondence between Le Corbusier, who is without doubt one of the most noteworthy initiators of a rational architecture, and Cocteau. Le Corbusier writes his very clear-cut polemical books, talking about architecture in the style of Cocteau, and constructs his houses according to an identical ideal of rigid, clear, crystalline logic. Cocteau, in his turn, constructs his writings according to a completely architectonic scheme of conciseness and "Corbusian" simplicity. And also, note how a painting, say, by Juan Gris, is perfectly at home in a room by Le Corbusier—only in that kind of ambience can the new spirit appear in all its value.[2]

In their turn, Germany and Austria offer a magnificent example of another type: the example of the refinement of art which a country can attain when the sense of a new architecture is understood by an entire nation, and dominates all decorative forms, so that all objects down to the most modest carry its imprint. From the monumental building to the cover of a book, Germany and Austria possess a style. This style, more solid in Germany, more refined and precious in Austria, has an absolute personality: it may please or displease, but *it asserts itself.* What is more, it has a distinct nationalistic character, and this should suffice, where there might not have existed other reasons, to show how wrong were those who believed they were renewing architecture by transplanting German styles, which are very noble ones to be sure, but which are out of place in this country.

In an analogous fashion, in Holland there is a blossoming of architectural forms composed of the most rigorous and constructive rationality, perfectly attuned to the country's climate and landscape. And so, each with its own characteristics, the Nordic countries Sweden and Finland also contribute to the "new spirit."

A group of famous European architects—Behrens, Mies van der Rohe, Mendelsohn, Gropius, Le Corbusier—create architecture tightly connected to the necessities of our time, and from these necessities extract a new aesthetic. Therefore there *exists,* particularly in architecture, a new spirit.

And in Italy? Without doubt even here correspondences can be seen, like those cited above, among the various forms of art. There exists, for example, an affinity between certain of Bontempelli's abstractions and certain strange paintings of De Chirico, Carrà, and Sironi. Their attitude, having assumed the name "Novecento," would appear to foreshadow a coordination of forces. In any case, Italy, because of its nature, tradition, and most of all because of the victorious period it is passing through, is most worthy of the mission of renewal. It remains for Italy to give maximum development to the new spirit, to carry it to its logical conclusion, until it dictates a *style* to other nations, as it has in the great periods of the past.

There is a certain obstinacy, however, particularly in architecture, in not wanting to recognize this new spirit, at least for the moment. Perhaps only the young understand it and feel a pressing necessity for it; and this constitutes their force, and ours. In general we, youth, meet with general diffidence, which is understandable and even excusable in part; the word "avant-garde" has by now assumed an equivocal sense in art, and until now the young have not given it much definition. It is necessary to understand, to persuade oneself, that our very tightly-knit postwar generation is far from its predecessors. The Futurist and early Cubist experiences, even with their advantages, have stung the public and disillusioned those who expected a better result from them. And how far away they already seem to us, particularly the former, with its attitude of the systematic destruction of the past—still a very romantic concept.

The youth of today follows a completely different road. We all feel a great necessity for clarity, revision and order. The new generation *thinks*; and its seriousness is so unexpected that it appears as presumption and as cynicism.

The legacy of the avant-garde that preceded us was an artificial impulse—an empty, destructive fury that confused good and bad. The natural right of the youth of today is a desire for *lucidity*, for *wisdom*. We must convince ourselves of it.

It is well-known that the cultural level of the new generation is notably superior to those preceding it. Above all, the sphere of interest for art in general has been infinitely widened among students; youth whose studies lead them into totally other fields are interested in music and painting, are well informed about foreign literature; they diligently attend art exhibitions, concerts, and book sales. And only very few are an exception to this. Therefore the desire for a new spirit among the young is based on a solid knowledge of the past, and is not founded on nothing.

Particularly in architecture we have perhaps arrived at this sensation of an absolute necessity for the new, through a saturation of knowledge. In studying the past, the young have not been content simply to question built architecture, but have investigated art forms in their most hidden spirit: the Quattrocento in the wood engravings of the "Hypnerotomachia Poliphili" and in the drawings of Maso Finiguerra; Byzantium in its enamel, glass, ivories, and in a pilgrimage of admiration through the treasures of the cathedrals; the medieval East in the Armenian Codices, the Syrian Gospels, Persian miniatures, Coptic fabrics—and exactly this much culture of the museum and the old bookstore overwhelms our thought and causes us to invoke *simplicity*. This has nothing to do with our admiration for the past; nothing hinders us from admiring the Giottesque backgrounds and the illustrated Tarot cards of the Quattrocento, and to understand and defend the extraordinarily decorative part that shining advertising plays in the modern city. Nothing prohibits us from admiring the architectural marquetry of Francesco di Giorgio and the wood engravings of Serlio, and to understand the rhythm, the almost Greek purity of certain factories with walls of glass. There is no incompatibility between our past and our present. We do not want to break with tradition; it is tradition which transforms itself, and assumes new aspects, few people may recognize it.

We have had a sincere admiration for the architects who immediately preceded us. We recognize them for having been the first to break with a tradition of superficiality and bad taste, which ruled for too long. Also, we have in part followed our predecessors; but we will no longer. Their architecture has given everything new it could. In effect we can distinguish two great tendencies in Italy: the Roman and the Milanese. The former have patterned themselves after our classic great Cinquecento, achieving at times a serene nobility. But by now their style has degenerated into a too simple code, and they limit themselves to the opposition of ashlar planes and blank surfaces. The latter have turned to neo-classic elegance, and have derived from it undoubtedly refined and pleasing results. They, however, have fallen into pure decoration, into the insincerity of an architecture which varies its effects by means of expediencies, alternating broken facades, candelabra, cupolas, and crowning obelisks. Both tendencies are by now a *dead end* that repeat themselves in a sterile manner, with no way out. How frequently do buildings, even by very well-known architects and even if pleasing when finished, show while under construction, in the nudity of their skeleton, all the wretchedness of an architecture without rhythm, which saves itself only with decorative application.

We can no longer be satisfied with this. The new architecture, the true architecture, must result from a rigid adherence to logic, to rationality. A rigid constructivism must dictate the rules. The new *forms* of architecture must receive aesthetic value exclusively from the character of *necessity,* and only afterwards, by way of *selection,* will a style be born. Since we don't pretend at all to create a style (similar attempts of creation from nothing lead to results such as the "Liberty Style"); but rather to allow, from the constant use of rationality, from the perfect correspondence between the structure of the building and the purposes it serves, a style to be born through selection. We must succeed in this: to ennoble with indefinable and abstract perfection of pure *rhythm* the simple construction, which alone would not constitute beauty.

We said "by selection." This is surprising. We add: we must persuade ourselves of the necessity of creating *types,* a few *fundamental* types. This necessary, inevitable law encounters the greatest hostility, the most absolute incomprehension. But let us look behind ourselves. All the architecture which made the name of Rome glorious in the world was based on four or five types: the temple, the basilica, the circus, the rotunda, the cupola, and the bath. And all of its force stands in having maintained these schemes, repeating them in the farthest provinces, and perfecting them, exactly *by selection.* All this is very well-known, but no one seems to remember: *Rome built in series.*

And in Greece? The Parthenon is the greatest result, the greatest fruit of a single type chosen through the centuries. Note the distance between the doric of Aegina and the doric of the Acropolis. Thus, the basilica of the first Christian centuries had a single type, as did the Eastern church. Who cannot see in the Churches of Saints Sergio and Bacco the beginnings of Saint Sophia, and in this, in its turn, the origin of a type for the great mosques of Constantinople? And are not all the Tuscan and Umbrian houses of the Duecento and Trecento perhaps alike? And isn't the bare, already modern nobility of the Florentine *palazzi* of the Quattrocento of a single type?

Yet, the idea of a *house-type* disconcerts, gives rise to the most grotesque and absurd comments. One believes that making house-types, houses in series, means mechanizing them, building buildings that look like steamships or airplanes. What a deplorable misunderstanding! We have never thought of taking inspiration for architecture from the machine. Architecture must adhere to the new necessities, just as new machines are born from new necessities, and are perfected with time. The house will have its own new aesthetic, just as the airplane has its own aesthetic, but the house will not have the aesthetic of the airplane.

Too often we equate talent with facility, genius with talent; so, naturally, the concept of the house-type is not appealing to many people who have a cult of their own personality, which they suppose to be exceptional. They cannot adapt themselves to the new problems. We *must* persuade ourselves that at least for a while the new architecture will be made in part by *renunciation. We must have this courage. Architecture can no longer be individual.* In the coordinated effort to save it, to lead it back to the most rigid logic, to the direct derivation from the problems of our times—we must sacrifice our own personalities: and only through this temporary Standardization, through this fusion of all tendencies into one, can a new architecture, *truly ours,* be born. The history of architecture has known only a few geniuses only they had the right to create from nothing, following inspiration only.

In particular, then, our times have certain problems, greater problems, extremely urgent problems. We must follow them, and we, youth, are ready to follow them, ready to renounce our individuality for the creation of "types." To the elegant eclecticism of the individual we oppose the spirit of construction in series—a renunciation of individuality. It will be said that the new architecture will fare poorly; we should not confuse *simplicity* with poverty; it will be simple— perfecting simplicity is the *greatest* refinement.

Certainly the time is near when industrial buildings—factories, docks, silos—will have the same appearance throughout the world. Such internationalization is inevitable, and, what is more, if monotony results; it will not lack a grandiose sense. Other aspects of architecture, on the other hand, in spite of their absolute modernity, will keep *national* characteristics in every country, as is already happening.

Here, in particular, there exists a classical foundation. The spirit (not the forms, which is something different) of tradition is so profound in Italy that evidently, and almost mechanically, the new architecture will preserve a stamp which is typically *ours*. And this is already a great force, since tradition, as we said, does not disappear, but changes appearance. Note how certain factories can acquire a rhythm of Greek purity because, like the Parthenon, they are stripped of all that is superfluous and respond only to the character of necessity. In this sense, the Parthenon has mechanical value.

The new generation seems to proclaim an architectonic revolution, a seemingly total revolution. A desire for truth, logic, order, and Hellenic lucidity—here is the true character of the new spirit. Some of our predecessors, turning to the future, preached destruction in favor of the false new. Others, turning to the past, believed they were saving themselves with a return to the classical. We wish solely, exclusively, and *exactly* to belong to our time, and our art is to be that which the time requires. To have belonged to it—entirely with its good qualities and its defects—this will be our pride.

› Notes

1   Cf. "Il existe un esprit nouveau." Le Corbusier, *Vers une Architecture*, 1923.
2   We could also cite the perfect correspondence between music such as "Le Pacific n.31" by Honnegger, and literary extracts such as certain pages and descriptions by Cendrars in "Moravagine"; between the obsessive rhythm of "Prikaz" by Salmon and certain dizzying music, derived from that very slanderous "Jazz," which, too, is one of the characteristics of our time; so much for the analogies. And as for the influences of painters such as Marie Laurencin or Pruna had on composers like Aurig or Poulenc, in staging their works; or the influence of these new scene-paintings on the old Russian ballet, the last remainder of the orientalizing infatuations from before the War. Naturally, not all modern works are in the modern spirit; the surrealists signal a regression from this point of view, with the sort of neo-romanticism which is extremely noticeable in Soupault. Instead, the Radiguet phenomenon is an example of the new spirit.

8 August Perret

The modern museum (1929)

August Perret, 'Le musée moderne', *Mouseion*, vol. III, 9, December 1929. Bernard Champigneulle, *Perret*, Paris: Arts et Metiers, 1959, extract p. 155, translation by Julien Denis with the editors.

*   *   *

Look how we see, in the same Roman ruins, large sections of masonry where the mortar joints are jutting out from the brick face that has been eroded by the elements, while the mortar on the other hand, hardening continuously over time, has not been worn away.

There remains in the city of Carcassonne, some concrete lintels from the Middle Ages which are all still intact, whereas many of those in stone have fractured.

It is therefore to concrete and to reinforced cement concrete that we will have to recourse to, in order to constitute the framework of our Museum.

Our Museum would then be formed in sections of reinforced concrete, that is to say that it should be built of widely spaced posts supporting beams and slabs; it is the whole of this system that we call the framework.

The composition of this framework is very important as it is to a building what the skeleton is to an animal. Just as the rhythmic, balanced and symmetrical skeleton of an animal contains and supports the most varied and diversely placed organs, so the framework of our building must equally be composed, rhythmic, balanced, even symmetrical, and must be able to contain the most varied organs demanded by the programme.

In this is the very basis of Architecture. If the structure is not worthy of remaining apparent, the architect has badly fulfilled his mission.

Cladding and infill materials will be required to complete the framework but without concealing it, a beam should be evident where there is a beam and a post evident where there is a post.

These arrangements will save countless unpleasant surprises when comes the day where, following expansions, contractions and settlements the load-bearing elements assert their presence. Architecture is what makes beautiful ruins.

9 Carlo Enrico Rava

The mirror of rational architecture (1931)

Carlo Enrico Rava, 'Specchio dell'Architettura Razionale: Conclusione', *Domus*, November 1931, pp. 34–40, extract p. 40, translation by Stefania Boccaletti with the editors.

› IV CONCLUSION

*   *   *

The second accusation that was moved against us by some members of the 'intransigent' rationalist tendency was more serious. They in fact argued that, by pointing out certain gaps, inconsistencies and dangers inherent in what was implied, our criticism was not only unconstructive but also negative in highlighting the many weaknesses of rationalism. To these accusations we reply that it was our precise aim to discriminate between what was constructive and *useful* and what wrong-headed and dangerous, in guiding public opinion in order that they appreciate the real merits of Rationalism in *separating* those from vain and empty formulas. Overall, we believe that we have generally succeeded in the task of promoting healthier tendencies in our architecture, since we were sure in our opinion that Italian Rationalism already had a solid and strong enough constitution *not to fear* a 'remise en question' of its principles and characteristics. We were equally sure that there was nothing more *dangerous* than to continue to promote an ill-conceived solidarity in the name of which the more authoritative and sincere members of the Rationalist movement shared common ground with the many pseudo-rationalists – last-minute opportunists and recruits. In order to support a supposedly incontrovertible Rationalist dogma, they were in fact compelled to sanction, implicitly or deliberately, all the errors and incongruities that the many pseudo-Rationalists had introduced, greatly compromising the integrity of the movement. To those who reproached us for literally 'washing the dirty linen of Rationalism in public' we reply that such explicitness was not after all so soiled as to necessitate further 'private washing'.

It has been recently stated in writing that Rationalism in architecture is a 'historical fact' and it would be in vain to deny or attempt to repress it. We acknowledge that such a blatant truth had yet to be asserted, and so we also recognise, with pride, its exact relevance. We ourselves will never tire of repeatedly emphasising just how significant the Rationalist trend has been in bringing back to Italian architecture a degree of sincerity, seriousness, and logic that had been missing for near enough 100 years, and without which it is impossible for convincing architecture to be realised. However, we trust that the adjective 'historical' will allow Rationalist architects to recognise the value of the past as a warning against any complacency induced by the results already achieved.

Through this [editorial] column we are proud to have been the first to talk of a 'renaissance of the Mediterranean spirit' in contemporary architecture, and to proclaim its necessity in Italy. It has therefore given us considerable pride to note the influence of the manifesto for 'The Italian Exhibition of Rational Architecture' [Il Esposizione d'Architettura Rationale Italiana] which closes with the following words: 'Most importantly, it must be acknowledged that it is the Latin character of this architecture which defines itself as Mediterranean'. However, in that exhibition we did not see many examples of just such a 'Latin character' or 'Mediterranean spirit', to the point that we began to think that the proclamation in the manifesto was moved by some degree of opportunism. Nevertheless, we prefer to read that passage 'literally': that is for its *promise of evolution*; as a *commitment* to the future, and as an intent and prospect for an emergent Italian architecture.

One thing is still necessary, and actually essential, which is to declare once and for all that the term 'Rationalism' is nothing but a *word*, an inexact and in some ways ill-conceived definition which originally was not only a useful, but also a rather necessary, *label* which today cannot limit the horizon of opportunity nor preclude anyone's personal trajectory. The 'Rationalist impulse has already broadened its initially positive impact, and consequently exhausted its polemical role (to become a potential burden). Now, for this reason our development must not be hindered by adherence to theories and formulas from which we have already *absorbed the best*, and that we *no longer need* to subscribe to exactly.

Today it is no longer a question of whether to be 'Rationalists'; rather it is simply about being *Modern Italian Architects* each with their own free personality, each looking within themselves to find the most profound, sincere, *independent* expression of that sense of the 'Modernity' which makes us contemporary and proud of that status.

10 Piero Bottoni . . .

An architectural programme (1933)

Piero Bottoni et al., 'Un Programma d'Architettura', *Quadrante*, 1, May 1933, pp. 5–6, extract pp. 5–6, translation by Stefania Boccaletti with the editors.

*   *   *

Today it is urgently important to define our attitude towards:

1.   Clarification of the current situation in architecture.
2.   Elucidating the current confusion surrounding terms such as 'modern', 'rational' and 'C20th Architecture', as well as denouncing the self-appointed virtues of literally Neo-classical and 'culturalist' works.
3.   Collaborating with young, 'confident' architects who work within a more controlled and intransigent definition of rationality.
4.   Stating the importance of the co-existence of 'artistic' and 'moral' facts (particularly a 'moral conscience') as criteria for the individual/artist.
5.   Constituting, within the framework of European Rationalism, an Italian *tendenza*, one as direct and intransigent as that outlined in the polemical statements of 'Gruppo 7'.
6.   Defining the characteristics of the Italian Rationalist tendency. Stating both its 'Classical' and 'Mediterranean' characteristics (in terms of 'spirit', not forms or folklore) to contrast with the 'Nordism', the 'Neo-Baroque' and the 'arbitrary Romanticism', which each inspire distinct trends within the new European architecture.
7.   Opposing compromised foreign trends to support more consistently rationalist *tendenze* (Le Corbusier, Gropius, Mies van der Rohe).
8.   A balanced analysis of the most interesting European, and global, works [of architecture] without any false chauvinism or provincial prejudices. Revive and develop a programme of intellectual exchange.
9.   The dissemination of the most recent work of international congresses concerned with the implementation of contemporary architectural thinking (C.I.R.P.A.C.), through collaboration and contributing the revitalized Italian cultural discourse to mutual studies and research.

Architects: Piero Bottoni, Mario Cereghini, Luigi Figini, Guido Frette, Enrico A. Griffini, Piero Lingeri, Gino Pollini, Gian Luigi Banfi, Lodovico B. Di Belgioioso, Enrico Pressutti and Ernesto N. Rogers.

11 August Perret

Collective needs and architecture (1935)

Auguste Perret, 'Les besoins collectifs et l'architecture', *Encyclopédie Française*, November 1935. Christophe Laurent, Guy Lambert and Joseph Abram (ed.), *August Perret: anthologie des ecrits, conferences et entretiens*, Paris: Le Moniteur, 2006, extract pp. 273–274, translation by Julien Denis with the editors.

* * *

The links between architecture and collective needs can be considered from three standpoints, which are also those of the architect tackling a new project.

1. Architecture obeys certain *permanent laws* that govern – regardless of the era concerned – the stability and harmony of buildings.
2. Architecture makes use, in a given place and at a given time, of materials characterising that particular place and time. These materials, for the contemporary era, were described in the first part of this tome. Their use takes place according to *technical rules* that influence architecture and constitute a second set of laws acting upon it.
3. Architecture must satisfy the needs of the end-user. The individual or community who commissions an architect, imposes on him – in doing so – a certain *programme*. This programme, which varies according to the place, the times and the purpose, constitutes a third group of laws.

As such, among all arts, the art of constructing buildings is that most subject to material conditions, some of which are natural and permanent, and others transitory. The laws of stability, atmospheric variations (sunshine, rain, wind, dust, temperature differences), optical illusions, the universal and eternal significance of certain lines, the resistance and nature of materials, all impose permanent conditions. The cost of materials, the ease with which they can be worked, the purpose of the building, functions, regulations and fashion, all impose transitory requirements.

  The building will become less dated for being governed by natural and permanent conditions rather than by transient ones. The architect Ginain, author of the *Ecole de Médecine*, having obtained the commission for the Galliéra museum, exclaimed: 'At last! I will be able to do a building without use.' Behind its paradoxical wit, this observation implies that, freed from ephemeral conditions and without an explicit function (in this manner he understood the essence of the museum), governed only by natural and permanent conditions, the building in question would have a chance to endure over time. Others even went as far as to claim that architecture, being determined by use, is not an art and only achieves this status in confronting the commemorative monument or the mausoleum; even then, however, the choice, the disposition and the treatment of materials take precedence over use. The degree of usefulness is not a means to discriminate the art. 'The spirit, in order to testify, cannot do away with matter' (André Gide). Materials are to the architect what words are to the poet. What language and prosody are to the poet, the system of construction is to the architect. It is through the means of the system of construction that he fulfils permanent as well as momentary conditions.

12 Guiseppe Pagano and Guarniero Daniel

Rural architecture in Italy (1936)

Guiseppe Pagano and Guarniero Daniel, *Architettura Rurale Italiana*, *Quaderni della Triennale*, Milano: Ulrico Hoepli, September 1936, extract pp. 7–15, translation by the editors.

*   *   *

The history of architecture is almost exclusively concerned with stylistic identity, evidence of the art of building which, concerned with aesthetic value and its bias towards decorative forms, seems 'worthy' of a certain degree of attention. In the history of architecture we generally study a history of architectural taste epitomised in representative or important buildings: temples, churches or palaces. Technical considerations, relationship to the traditional formal canon, to economical influences or functional needs; which may have been significant in the evolution of these buildings; are of no particular interest to scholars or artists. When we look at style in architecture we are primarily interested in the 'how' and not in the 'why'. We accept it as a fact and explore creative genius as a manifestation of taste and freethinking, without any relationship to the practical conditions of constructive appearance. Given that the critical interest of architectural scholars is exclusively directed towards exemplary evidence of a particular period we tend to resist consideration of the practicality, which originated in attempts to overcome structural, economical and functional problems. However, we know that Doric architecture is an incongruous and aesthetically motivated application in stone of what was originally a logical and comprehensible structure made from timber. We know – more through intuition than through experience – that aesthetically pleasing representational form in architecture was [likely] inspired by a solution to a technical or functional imperative. But the relationship between the first and the last links of the chain [of influence] elude us, because we assume that evidence of intermediate solutions that served as precedents for 'elevated representation' has been lost in the historical record. However, we know that a form can outlast its practical *raison d'être*, and that habitually, a form, which arose out of a particular need can become an aesthetic habit or a decorative cipher (as the dead weight of tradition), but the majority of the researching fraternity refuse to look at architectural style with this in mind. But given the reaction to C19th academic formalism and the undercurrent of objective realism in the modern world, projecting the authority of reason against the ritualised rhetoric of the decorative: the moral habit of contemporary architects to subjugate their artistic fantasy to the laws of technology, function and economy without denying the aesthetic quality of their work; this desire to recognise and show that the relationships between functionality, technology, form and beauty are by no means inventions of our time, but have merely been rediscovered as the consequence of an ethical need for clarity and honesty; let us overcome any reluctance to present the historically documented evidence of the relationship between the 'high' architecture in the history books and the modest and straightforward constructions done in the spirit of an enlightened 'primitivism' [in order] to satisfy elemental needs. The attempt to put forward this evidence would, however, be doomed to failure if we restricted ourselves entirely to contemporary architecture and declined to use (the evidence of) naïve and primeval sources to validate our contention. Such a deferral does not correspond with practice. The parameters of architectural creation do not change where climate, lifestyles and economic conditions by and large remain the same; when construction is understood as a tool and is executed according to an instinctive as much as an archaic logic, architecture still yields the same built resolution. This incomparable encyclopaedia of constructive logic, through which we understand the creation of abstract form and its imaginative materialisation of the relationship of man to the ground and climate, to economy and technology, is openly manifest in our rural architecture. To investigate architecture under these premises is not only useful but also necessary in order to understand the causal relationships, which the study of style in architecture has led us to overlook. Rural architecture represents man's original and tangible success in gaining his livelihood from the ground; a success, which, while born out of necessity, also substantiated subsequent artistic developments. While the honeybee, under similar climatic conditions, always builds the same cell out of the same material, man has to adapt to more extreme environmental conditions. Consequently the sheltering instinct is manifest in analogue form whether in the Eskimo igloo, the straw hut or in the *trulli* of Southern Italy, which depending on agricultural viability and technical and economic parameters, take on more developed forms. It is a fact, however, that there has been, and still exists, a world of building where the house is not an aesthetic game, but a pure necessity, beyond display of wealth, the consequence of an effort achieved with minimal means. And with changes in agricultural practice (growing corn for example), the chain of gradual transition, and its accompanying economic and technical circumstances, has been broken. The first links (of the chain) may perhaps still survive in the straw barn, which serves Latium's farmers as a place of rest during harvest; a transitional phase between the stone *trulli* of Apulia and the shepherd's timber and straw huts retains a residual foothold in the hills of Liguria. Nevertheless one can attempt to logically reconstruct this sequence [of events]. And analysis of this extensive resource and trajectory of building, which has always existed as an inconspicuous 'style free' backdrop, can encourage us to rediscover the characteristic elements of honest building – clarity, logic and fitness – where before we could only see arcadia and folklore. It is like a cure with simple dishes for everyone who has grown tired of the confectionary art of Caryatids. We now have a measure of the distance between the commonplace and the real.

*   *   *

GUISEPPE PAGANO AND GUARNIERO DANIEL

13 Hans Schmidt

Architecture's relationship to typification (1956)

Hans Schmidt, 'Die Beziehung der Typisierung zur Architektur', from: Bruno Flierl (ed.), *Hans Schmidt – Beiträge zur Architektur 1924–1964*, Zürich: gta Verlag, 1993, extracts pp. 138–143, translation by the editors.

* * *

It is clear that industrial building methods must lead to strict rules for spatial organisation and three-dimensional expression – that is rules based on an unrelenting 'canon' of numbers and measurements which force us to exclude the momentary, the arbitrary, and the contingent.

But should this lead us to perceive industrial building as no more than a necessity forced on us, a restricting limitation which we can only moderate through external 'creative' factors which have not arisen from cause and effect? This would mean that that we had created a division between technology and art, which is alien to the nature of architecture, and that we would distinguish architects as either 'constructors' or 'decorators'. This would not only be unacceptable for architecture, but it would also be disastrous for the implementation of industrialisation.

It is therefore necessary to look closer at the relationship between architecture and typification.

* * *

› The typification of buildings

Industrial prefabrication and a relative standardisation of building elements is a step that is carried out in all highly industrialised countries today.

However, it is significant that all these steps, within the conditions of a market economy, could only be pursued to a certain point. In theory, which in this case reflects the conditions of practical economy, it is as Walter Gropius formulated the issue thirty years ago: industry is presumed to provide the [constructive] elements, but the architect retains the freedom to arrange an individual and complete design.

Typification of the building as an entity, seen allegedly as too restrictive, is rejected. But it is precisely this route, beyond the typification of building elements, which is taken by the Soviet Union. Does it really lead, as is feared by the architects in the West, to a restraint on architecture? Does it not rather demand that we introduce a new quality into architecture?

We will come back to this new quality in our conclusion, having for the time being to content ourselves with reference (as with building elements) to a principle that has been a substantial part of architectural practice in the past. We all know from experience that the characteristic beauty of old villages and towns is decisively based on the mass of dwellings which have been built as types, and that only public buildings were given the right to stand out through distinctive scale and richness of the architecture.

Of course we are dealing, in the first instance, with craft-driven forms of typification, permitting certain deviations. It is, however, characteristic that architecture's development quickly moved beyond this craft-based typification. With industrialisation the typical dwelling becomes an element of a self-conscious architectural order, or architectural intent. Until the middle of the C19th English building contractors (or developers) still built the English terraced house in the London suburbs as a unified type. For the Paris boulevards Haussmann prescribed a typical facade schema, which, together with a coherent use of stone contributed significantly to the city's beauty. What happened to this typification? For reasons beyond our brief, it almost entirely collapses and is replaced by a chaotic design culture in architecture, which has since overrun our villages, our exclusive residential districts and our cities.

We have thus no reason to regard the typification of buildings as a danger for architecture. On the contrary, through it we will rediscover the currently obscured path to [a contemporary] architecture.

› Typification and function

The typification of whole buildings for different uses inevitably causes a problem which becomes decisive but is also the most difficult problem of typification, that is the relationship between typification and the respective function of a building, its determination as a house, school, stable, workshop and so on.

We are therefore encountering certain contradictions. The striving for the least possible number of types is opposed by the multitude of determined uses. Bearing in mind building technology and economy we are compelled to conceive simple building organisms. However, the functional requirements our buildings have to accommodate are likely to be very complicated. Even flexible functions may be demanded, which would stand in contradiction to the more or less fixed form of a 'typical building'. In industrial buildings the demands of different production processes have to be considered. In housing we can help ourselves by taking account of the, in principle, normative use by a hypothetical 'average' family. For agricultural buildings their use depends in part on the still developing and contested forms of husbandry and mechanisation.

Admittedly we have little experience in the discipline of planning with types. The conventional individual planning of buildings, built on craft principles, allows the architect to respond to any special requirements. The idea of the expanding house and the 'free' plan, adaptable at wish, became the last word (in design). Architects have developed the distinctive art of freeing up and exploiting the largest possible plan area, in order to fulfil the demands of economy. When planning with types, this is, however, insufficient.

*   *   *

I think that we firstly, in the interest of planning with types and industrialisation, need to insist on the greatest possible typification of functions. We need to adopt this primarily because we need to return, in the interest of industrialisation, to the priority of the individual building itself, and to be precise, to a building that cannot be too clear, simple and generous enough, a building that excludes anything contingent, unique, spontaneous or untypical.

This emphasis is about reconstructing an architectural principle that was lost with the demise the C19th view of the typical. It was no coincidence that, in England during that period, identifying with a romantically tinted view of returning to a golden age of craft in building, they [architects] began to draw up plans for country houses according to a functional methodology, and a point was subsequently reached when the 'plan' was no longer part of the building [itself], but was seen as an independently functioning machine. The architects amongst you probably know the buildings and projects of the architect [Hans] Scharoun, in which the priority of function over the 'building' was pursued to its ultimate conclusion.

It is clear that with this logic [the relationship between] typification and industrialisation is impossible to resolve.

› Typification and architecture

*   *   *

The forces of industrial building privilege certain rules: of order, of number, of measurement and of formal expression. It is conceivable that the most straightforward result of thinking this way does not satisfy the architect as being beautiful 'at first sight'. And yet it is right to first move forward along these lines.

Is the Parthenon beautiful? It is said that it is – and yet we could recently hear in a lecture by Professor Tartakiewicz from Krakow, given at the Academy of Arts, that the builders of the Parthenon were not familiar with our ideal of aesthetic beauty. For them, art was an expression of the true, of the objective truth, derived from mathematical laws.

Let us address an epoch of architecture which under the remit of the French revolution endeavours to create one last great summation of architecture as a style. Describing the sensibility of this epoch Goethe wrote to Reimer: 'The classical is sober, modest, and represents a reality tinged with greatness.'

This is where I think we should begin.

Editors' note: Extracts from a speech given in 1956 at the founding celebrations of the '*Institut für Typung*' (Institute for Typification) at the '*Ministerium für Aufbau*' (Ministry for Construction), subsequently published in 'Typenprojektierung im zweiten Fünfjahresplan – Reden' (Type Development in the Second 5 Year Plan – Speeches), Berlin, 1956.

HANS SCHMIDT

The New City

14 Otto Wagner

Die Großstadt (1911)

Otto Wagner, *Die Grosstadt. Eine Studie über diese von Otto Wagner*, Vienna: Anton Schroll, 1911. English translation by A. D. F. Hamlin, *Architectural Record*, 31 (May 1912). Extracts here from: *Oppositions*, 17, 1979, pp. 99–116.

*   *   *

The considerations about to be presented apply to no one city, but to large cities in general, although there may be particular cities which stand out prominently by reason of their pressing need for the solution of the problems of future expansion as well as of the improvement of present conditions. What follows represents neither the radicalism of the iconoclast nor the wail of the traditionalist on the subject of city-planning, but proceeds from the fundamental assumption that the most important element in the solution of any such problem is the practical fulfillment of a definite purpose, and that art must impress its stamp upon whatever may result from the accomplishment of this purpose.

Since our manner of life, our activities and our technical and scientific achievements are different from what they were a thousand years ago or even a short time since, and are the results of constant development, art must give expression to the conditions of our own time. Art must therefore conform its city plan to the needs of the mankind of today.

Those favourite catchwords – "the art of the home," "co-operation in city-planning," "sentiment in city-planning," etc. – taken in the sense in which they are used by people who know and judge art from only textbooks are empty phrases to which such people cling because they are destitute of ideas on the real problem of the city plan. Only the true architect can distinguish between what is old and beautiful, and what is merely old; he will favour neither the wanton destruction of what is beautiful nor the copying of the antique; nor will he care for the much lauded "embellishment" of a city; all architectural extravagance is foreign to his nature.

Our democratic existence, in which the masses feel the pressure of the necessity for economy in their methods of living, and call for homes at once sanitary and cheap, has resulted in a certain uniformity in our dwelling houses. This tendency will therefore find expression in the plan of the future city. Individual dwellings of like cubical contents and plan are cheaper in first cost and rental price if combined in houses of many stories than in houses of few; the cost of the lot, of foundations, and of roof entering into account but once. And since the proverb "Time is money" is truer today than ever before, the increase in height of residential and office buildings in the city's center to seven or eight stories, indeed, to skyscrapers (if the city permits) is a natural development.

In any given city the number of dwelling houses must greatly exceed that of its public buildings; and their contiguous multiplication inevitably results in long and uniform block-facades. But our modern art has turned these to monumental account by the plotting of wide streets, and by the introduction of picturesque interruptions of their monotony is able to give them their full artistic effect. There can be no doubt when Art rightly handles such cases all talk about a "city-pattern" is beside the mark. This kind of talk is possible only when Art is left out of the question. Unfortunately the effort to avoid the uniformity of dwelling-house types which has resulted from practical and economic considerations, has led to an altogether objectionable and artistically worthless overloading of the exteriors of these utilitarian structure with purposeless features, meaningless projections, turrets, gables, columns, and ornament; although wide streets serve to mitigate somewhat the effect of these ungainly absurdities.

Quite as unjustifiable and as objectionable from an artistic viewpoint are intentional but unwarranted curves and irregularities in the layout of streets and squares, intended solely to produce artificially picturesque vistas. Every large city possesses of necessity a greater or smaller number of winding and irregular streets; but these have artistic warrant only when they result naturally from conditions of circulation, traffic, topography or the like.

The characteristic impression produced by a city results from its existing or inherent beauty and its potential beauty. The city's general "physiognomy" is the most important consideration in its plan. Upon it depends the success of the effort to make the first impression as pleasing as possible. This impression is furthermore dependent on the pulsating life of the city as a whole. With regard to this it must be remembered as a fundamental fact that the great majority of the community, including of course, visitors to the city (we are dealing now with the general mass) are quite ignorant of artistic matters. Therefore Art, if she would arouse the interest of and give satisfaction to the average man, must seize upon every opportunity that gives promise of producing a favorable impression. Industry, trade, fashion, taste, comfort, luxury, all provide media for artistic impression, and must all be availed of to attract the attention of the average man toward Art, so that he may be disposed to bestow favorable judgement upon works of art. The uninterrupted vista of a main thoroughfare flanked by fine stores displaying the artistic products of the city and of the country to the view of crowds hurrying by; other streets through which one may stroll for an outing and regale himself to the extent of his pocketbook; a sufficient number of good restaurants where one may find both satisfaction and relaxation; open squares where public monuments and buildings in artistic settings present themselves to the gaze of the beholder, and many other like factors not here enumerated – such are the things that give to a city its characteristic physiognomy. To these may be added an efficient system of transportation, a faultless street-cleaning department, living accommodations provided with every comfort and suited to every social grade – all these are conditioning factors of a favorable impression on the artistically indifferent average man. In the application of a criterion of excellence to these things beauty, that is, artistic quality, is the deciding factor; this alone makes it possible to produce a satisfactory first impression on citizens and stranger alike. Thus impressed, both citizen and stranger will be better disposed toward the city; less moved by a hypocritical pretense of art-interest to martyrize themselves "doing" the art treasures and museums of the town.

The more completely a city fulfills its practical ends, the better does it minister to the pleasures of its inhabitants; and the greater the part played by art in this ministry, the more beautiful the city. Neatness and scrupulous cleanliness go hand in hand with Art; city governments please take notice!

15 Le Corbusier

The city of tomorrow and its planning (1925)

Le Corbusier, *Urbanism*, Paris: Crès and Cie., 1925. English translation by Frederick Etchells, from Le Corbusier, *The City of Tomorrow and its Planning*, London: Rodker, 1929. Extracts here from: *Essential Le Corbusier: L'Esprit Nouveau Articles,* Oxford: Architectural Press, 1998, pp. 53 and 220–231.

› **IV Permanence**

*   *   *

The city is profoundly rooted in the realms of calculations. Engineers, nearly all of them, work for the city. And through them the necessary equipment for the city will come into being. This is the essential thing for that part of it which is utilitarian and consequently ephemeral.

But it is the city's business to make itself permanent; and this depends on considerations other than those of calculations.

And it is only Architecture which can give all the things which go *beyond* calculation.

*   *   *

› **XIII Hours of repose**

*   *   *

› *On repetition or mass production*

*   *   *

WE MUST BUILD ON A CLEAR SITE. *The city of today is dying because it is not constructed geometrically. To build on a clear site is to replace the "accidental" lay-out of the ground, the only one that exists to-day, by the formal lay-out. Otherwise nothing can save us. And the consequence of geometrical plans is Repetition and Mass-production.*

And as a consequence of repetition, the *standard* is created, and so perfection (the creation of types).

Repetition dominates everything. We are unable to produce industrially at normal prices without it; it is impossible to solve the housing problem without it. The builders' yard must become a workshop with a proper staff and machinery and specialized gangs. The vagaries of weather and seasons can then be ignored. "Building" must cut out its "off seasons."

Without making any claims in regard to their intrinsic value, we may honestly admit that the Plans I have put forward in support of the conception of my "cellular" system for dwellings anticipate the problem of mass-production. The classification which is inherent in it and the precise determining of the various functions can only result, after much experiment, in bringing about the realization of types which are genuinely *pure*. By breaking down first one thing and then another, every difficulty may be vanquished little by little and a functional and sane urban architecture will come into being.

If only our captains of industry would examine these plans they would see immense scope in these suggestions. Industry could then devote itself to "building," and the urban environment in which we work and rest would be transformed.

We must never, in our studies, lose sight of the purely human "cell," the cell which responds most perfectly to our physiological and sentimental needs. We must arrive at the "house machine," which must be both practical and emotionally satisfying and designed for a succession of tenants. The idea of the "old home" disappears, and with it local architecture, etc., for labour will shift about as needed, and must be ready to move, *bag and baggage*. The words 'bag and baggage' will do very well to express the kind—the 'type'—of furniture needed. Standardized houses with standardized furniture.

*   *   *

16 Ludwig Hilberseimer

Großstadtarchitektur (1927)

Ludwig Hilberseimer, *Großstadtarchitektur*, Stuttgart: Julius Hoffmann, 1927. Extract here from: Ludwig Hilberseimer, *Großstadtarchitektur*, reprint, Stuttgart: Julius Hoffmann, 1978, extract pp. 102–103, translation by the editors.

› Horizontal composition

The removal of walls and columns in the façade is emphasised through the horizontal layering of multi-storey building. The [nature of] horizontal composition, suppressed in a [typical] decorative system of pillars, has been totally ignored until now, but it is the main characteristic of a [contemporary] multi-storey building.

› Glass and steel [iron][1]

Together with reinforced concrete [ferroconcrete] the use of glass and steel as exclusive building materials is of far-reaching significance. Paul Scheerbart rightly recognised that glass offers completely new architectural possibilities. But his writings have led Expressionist architects to exploit glass construction for their own ends, a product of their anti-architectural and decorative imagination, ignoring the constructional parameters of building with glass and steel.

Since we are dealing here with new materials for the creation of space, [we] firstly need to investigate the possibilities of these material combinations in a purely experimental manner. Research will be needed in order to investigate how spatial perception will be affected by these [novel] material combinations and spatial constructs. Initially, this spatial quality will [continue to] affirm the physical properties and firmness of a stone wall rather than the glass wall supported on a steel frame of the equivalent structural stability. No material can be used other than according to its properties, however. Consequently a steel and glass building has to be treated in formally distinct terms to massive [load bearing] construction. In particular it is the relationship between light and transparent glazing that needs to be considered, since a glass building seems to absorb more light than it reflects.

The building without windows, or rather without openings, also requires a different constructive and dimensional composition from the traditional opening in a solid walled building. The specific ability to absorb colour and concurrently [exploit] the transparency of glass suggest possibilities, which exceed Scheerbart's supposedly utopian proposals.

In the meantime, however, we are as yet far from a systematic specification, logical observation and [constructive] manipulation of this new building material. Almost everyone concerned with glass and steel construction, has either overlooked or ignored the principles behind this new kind of building, seeing in it merely a novel means of decorative development.

› Colour

The element of colour in architecture has been treated with great indifference in the recent past. This general underestimation of colour was followed by its application in [a form of] Expressionism characterised by a hypertrophic and totally undisciplined manner. Colour was applied superficially on surfaces and buildings, without [any] organic connection to material and form, and without being 'characteristic' in any way. In architecture colour should never be used just for itself, but always and only as the 'colour of a material'. The colour spectrum of architecture is determined by the intrinsic colourfulness of a material, one of its [salient] characteristics. Thus colour as an element [of architecture] and colour's relationship to illumination (are of) great importance.

Homogeneity, consistency, intensity of light, speed of change, humidity and air temperature, are [all] aspects that unify the visual appearance of architecture in accordance with certain [physical] laws. The haze hovering over the city dulls the brilliance of colour. That is why the primary colour of all cities is an undefined grey, the [mute] colour of this atmosphere. And yet colourfulness can contribute significantly to the enhancement of the architectural intent. Saturated colour can unify and [the use of] multiple colours enliven elements of a composition. Individual buildings in themselves, but also associated buildings, can through [the use of] colour cohere more firmly, while three-dimensional form is heightened.

Accentuating parts of a building through colour; the coordination of separate elements with one another through [the application of] different colours, and the manifestation or support of a [constructed] hierarchy, or the direction of a prevailing view; are also possible. Colour should never be an added component, but one that is characteristic of the material concerned.

› Relationship to light

The relationship of building materials to light is extremely significant. Transparency and opacity; smoothness and dullness; the hardness and softness of material; sharp lines and edges, and transitions from additive to subtractive form, are decisive for the way that light dematerialises [form] and for degrees of light and shade, as they effect the nature of colour. All these determine the articulation [and condition] of materiality, and the relative independence of individual parts [of a building]. They are fundamentally important in dividing or unifying structural composition.

› General principles

The distinctive characteristic of an organism is revealed in its organs' embodiment of principal relationships. This generative principle is represented, in its commonality by the whole organism; in detail it only demonstrates its validity as an applicable case. Consequently, the difference between the metropolis (*Großstadt*) and other urban settlements has to be revealed in [the nature of] the individual building. Much as the metropolis is not a traditional town at a different scale, neither is a metropolitan building a dimensional translation of previous forms.

Under changed conditions, new ways of using buildings and different constructive and spatial needs and expectations, have led to unprecedented construction methods, and have produced accordingly new formal types [of building].

If the urban building is conceived as a [individual] cell within the 'organism' of the city and hence as part of a unit greater whole, then it has to exhibit fundamental architectural characteristics which are, through their nature, conditional on [the nature of] the city itself. Because the conditions affecting an earlier architecture no longer prevail, its means of expression cannot be retained. The decorative schema of the Renaissance cannot be transferred onto a tenement block, a department store or an office building, unless these building types are to lose their [constitutive] sense: a 'nonsense' like the one Ludwig Hoffmann has created for the new Berlin *Stadthaus*, results in a detrimental gloom in its offices. Any detail related to average room sizes becomes nonsense when the logic and intensity of intent cannot engage the whole building, where it is in reality [no more than] an intimate detail. Consequently the potential elaboration of details is necessarily restricted in *Großstadtarchitektur*. Essentially ornament becomes nonsense in this context. Everything [in design] is geared towards the definitive outline [of the building], and towards the determinant organisation of the plans. The [unprincipled] detail defers to decisive three-dimensional composition. All-important are the general massing [arrangement] and the application of proportional systems.

The necessity to create an often outrageously explicit and heterogeneous material mass, according to formal principles which are equally valid for each element, requires a reduction of architectural form to its most essential, necessary, general, and limited orthogonal basis: that is the generic aspect of any architecture. This where the architect's fundamental design skills: [namely] his sensitivity towards mass and proportion, and his ability to organise, become increasingly important. To shape mass form according to binding rules, while suppressing variety, is what Nietzsche (particularly) understood to be [the fundaments of] style. In the general (collective) case, the rule of law is emphatically respected, while the 'exception', on the contrary, is put aside; 'nuance' is deferred; 'measure' governs, and chaos is compelled to submit to form – that is a logical, unambiguous, mathematical, law.

› Note

1   Editors' note: in the G translation of 'Konstruktion und Form', which also became part of the book *Großstadtarchitektur*, reinforced concrete (*Eisenbeton*) is referred to as 'ferroconcrete', and steel (*Eisen*) as 'iron'. See also N 23 in this Reader.

17 CIAM / Le Corbusier

From the Athens Charter (1933)

CIAM *La Charte d'Athènes*, translation by Anthony Eardley as *The Athens Charter,* Jean Giraudoux (introduction), New York: Grossman, 1973, extracts pp. 47–48, 82 and 86.

> ## 1. Generalities

'City and region'

6. *Throughout history, specific circumstances have determined the characteristics of the city: military defense, scientific discoveries, successive administrations, and the progressive development of communications and means of transportation by land, water, rail, and air routes.*

History is inscribed in the layouts and in the architectures at cities. Surviving layouts and architectures constitute a guideline which, together with written and graphic documents, enables us to recreate the successive images of the past. The motivations that gave birth to the cities were varied in nature. Sometimes it was a defensive asset—and a rocky summit or a loop of a river saw the growth of a fortified village. Sometimes it was the intersection of two roads, a bridgehead, or an indentation in the coastline that determined the location of the first settlement. The city had an uncertain form, most frequently that of a circle or semicircle. When it was a center of colonization, it was organized like a camp built on axes at right angles and girdled by rectilinear stockades. Everything was disposed according to proportion, hierarchy, and convenience. The highroads set out from the gates of the enclosure and threaded indirectly to distant points. One can still recognize in city plans the original close-set nucleus of the early market town, the successive enclosing walls, and the directions of divergent routes. People crowded together within the walls and, according to the degree of their civilization, enjoyed a variable proportion of well-being. In one place, deeply human codes dictated the choice of dispositions while, in another, arbitrary constraints gave rise to flagrant injustices. Then the age of machinism arose. To an age-old measure that one would have thought immutable—the speed of man's walking pace—was added a new measure, in the course of evolution—the speed of mechanized vehicles.

7. *Hence the rationale governing the development of cities is subject to continual change.*

The growth or decrease of a population, the prosperity or decline of the city, the bursting of fortified walls that become stifling enclosures, the new means of communication that extend the area of exchange, the beneficial or harmful effects of a policy of choice or submission, the advent of machinism, all of this is just movement. With the progression of time, certain values become unquestionably engrained in the heritage of a group, be they of a city, a country, or humanity in general; decay, however, must eventually come to every aggregation of buildings and roads. Death overtakes works as well as living beings. Who is to discriminate between what should remain standing and what must disappear? The spirit of the city has been formed over the years; the simplest buildings have taken on an eternal value insofar as they symbolize the collective soul; they are the armature of a tradition which, without meaning to limit the magnitude of future progress, conditions the formation of the individual just as climate, geographical region, race, and custom do. Because it is a "microcosmic motherland," the city admits of a considerable moral value to which it is indissolubly attached.

'Traffic: observations'

57. *Magnificent layouts, intended for show, may once have constituted awkward obstacles to traffic flow, and they still do.*

What was admissible and even admirable in the days of horse-drawn carriages may now have become a source of constant disturbance. Certain avenues, which were conceived to ensure a monumental perspective crowned by a memorial or a public edifice, are a present cause of bottlenecks, of delays, and sometimes of danger. Such architectural compositions must be preserved from the invasion of mechanized vehicles, which they were not designed to accommodate and to whose speeds they can never be adapted. Traffic has now become a function of primary importance to urban life. It requires a carefully prepared program capable of providing whatever is needed to regularize its flow and to establish its indispensable outlets, thus doing away with traffic jams and the constant disturbance of which they are the cause.

'The historic heritage of cities'

65. *Architectural assets must be protected, whether found in isolated buildings or in urban aggregations.*

The life of a city is a continuous event that is expressed through the centuries by material works—layouts and building structures which form the city's personality, and from which its soul gradually emanates. They are precious witnesses of the past which will be respected, first for their historical or sentimental value, and second, because certain of them convey a plastic virtue in which the utmost intensity of human genius has been incorporated. They form a part of the human heritage, and whoever owns them or is entrusted with their protection has the responsibility and the obligation to do whatever he legitimately can to hand this noble heritage down intact to the centuries to come.

18 CIAM / Le Corbusier

The Athens Charter: conclusions (1933)

CIAM / Le Corbusier, 'Charter of Athens: tenets', Ulrich Conrads (ed.), *Programmes and Manifestoes on 20th-century Architecture*, London: Lund Humphries / Cambridge MA: MIT Press, 1970, extracts pp. 139, 140 and 141, translation by Michael Bullock.

* * *

77. *The keys to town planning are to be found in the four functions: housing, work, recreation (during leisure), and traffic.*

Town planning expresses the way of life of an age. Up to now it has attacked only one problem, that of traffic. It has confined itself to cutting avenues or laying down streets, thereby forming islands of buildings whose utilization is left to haphazard private enterprise. This is a narrow and inadequate view of its task. Town planning has four principal functions, namely: first, to provide the inhabitants with salubrious housing, that is to say, places in which space, fresh air, and sunshine are plentifully guaranteed; second, to organize workplaces so that, instead of being a painful thraldom, work will regain its character as a natural human activity; third, to set up the installations necessary for the good use of leisure, rendering it beneficial and productive; fourth, to establish links between these various organizations by means of a traffic network that facilitates movement from place to place while respecting the rights of all. These four functions, which are the four keys of town planning, cover an immense field, since town planning is the outcome of a way of thinking applied to public life by means of a technique of action.

78. *Planning will determine the structure of each of the sectors assigned to the four key functions and will fix their respective locations within the whole.*

Since the Congress of Athens, the four key functions of town planning demand special arrangements offering each of them the most favourable conditions for the development of its particular activity, in order that they may be manifested in all their fullness and bring order and classification into the usual conditions of life, work and culture. Town planning, by taking account of this need, will transform the face of cities, will break with the crushing constraint of practices that have lost their raison d'être and will open an inexhaustible field of action to creators. Each key function will have its own autonomy based on the circumstances arising out of climate, topography and customs; they will be considered as entities to which will be assigned territories and locations, for whose equipment and installation all the prodigious resources of modern technology will be mobilized. In this distribution, consideration will be given to the vital needs of the individual, not the interest or profit of any particular group. Town planning must guarantee individual liberty at the same time as it takes advantage of the benefits of collective action.

*   *   *

81. *The principle of urban and suburban traffic must be revised. A classification of available speeds must be drawn up. The reform of zoning that brings the key functions of the city into harmony will create between them natural links, which in turn will be reinforced by the establishment of a rational network of major thoroughfares.*

      Zoning that takes account of the key functions—housing, work, recreation—will bring order to the urban territory. Traffic, the fourth function, must have only one aim: to bring the other three usefully into communication. Great transformations are inevitable. The city and its region must be equipped with a network of roads exactly proportionate to the uses and purposes, and in conformity with the modern technology of transport. The means of travel must be classified and differentiated and for each of them a way must be created appropriate to the exact nature of the vehicles employed. Traffic thus regulated becomes a steady function that in no way interferes with the structure of housing or of workplaces.

*   *   *

83. *The city must be studied within the totality of its region of influence. A regional plan will replace the simple municipal plan. The limit of the agglomeration will coincide with the radius of its economic action.*

      The data of a town planning problem are given by the totality of the activities carried on not only in the town, but in the whole region of which it is the centre. The town's raison d'être must be sought and expressed in figures that will allow prediction of the stages of a plausible future development. The same work applied to the secondary agglomerations will provide a reading of the general situation. Allocations, restrictions, compensations can be decided that will assign to each town surrounded by its region its own particular character and destiny. Thus each one will take its place and its rank in the general economy of the country. The result will be a clear demarcation of the limits of the region. This is total town planning, capable of bringing balance to both the province and the country.

The Logic of Construction – Rationalization

19 Otto Wagner

Modern architecture (1896)

Otto Wagner, *Moderne Architektur* (1902 edition), translation by Harry Francis Mallgrave as *Modern Architecture*, Santa Monica CA: The Getty Centre, 1988, extracts pp. 77–80 and 91–95. Footnotes omitted.

› Style

*   *   *

In searching and groping for the right course, our age, far from expressing ourselves and our viewpoints, has sought salvation in mimicry instead of in new creations and natural improvements.

- The artist has been content to dissect the dead with a magnifying glass and lancet, instead of listening to the pulse of those who are living and relieving their pains.
- The perception that many architectural problems, such as churches, should appear the same today as centuries ago, whereas others should be of the most recent date, has produced great errors. Thus it happens that laymen and unfortunately also many architects are of the opinion that a parliament, for instance, may be in Greek style, but a telegraph office or a telephone exchange may not be built in Gothic, although they demand that a church be built in the latter style exactly. They forget in all of this just one thing, namely that the people who frequent these buildings are all equally modern, and that it is the custom neither to ride to the parliament bare-legged in an antique triumphal chariot, nor to approach a church or a city hall wearing a slit doublet.
- All errors that have and are being made in this regard are solely the artist's fault. The only excuse that can carry any weight is the earlier-cited haste in searching for the right course.
- The striving for a "painterly effect," for a harmony with the existing, has sprouted similarly strange flowers.
- In one of the most recent competitions for a city hall, the architects as well as the professional and nonprofessional jurors went to great pains to bring the proposed building into harmony

with the old "painterly" surroundings. They proceeded, as it were, from the method of theater decoration, yet never considered that the rebuilding of the city hall would have resulted in the renovation of all surrounding houses, so that in the end an "old" city hall would have been encircled by modern houses.

- In yet another competition for a city hall, fifty-two of the fifty-three entries—fifty-two I say—were designed in Gothic or Old German style.

- But the writer of these lines has discovered that the authorities in charge here were anything but Gothic or Old German men; they were smart, self-confident, modern Germans, and it was also these qualities that they wished to see expressed artistically in the appearance of the city hall.

- Artistic efforts that try to make imitations conform to existing buildings without taking into account other conditions (apart from revealing a certain impoverishment of the spirit and lack of self-confidence) cannot but make an impression similar to that of someone attending a modern ball in the costume of a past century, even rented for the occasion from a masquerade shop.

- This cannot possibly be the path that modern architecture has to take; otherwise all creative power would be denied it.

- ALL MODERN CREATIONS MUST CORRESPOND TO THE NEW MATERIALS AND DEMANDS OF THE PRESENT IF THEY ARE TO SUIT MODERN MAN; THEY MUST ILLUSTRATE OUR OWN BETTER, DEMOCRATIC, SELF-CONFIDENT, IDEAL NATURE AND TAKE INTO ACCOUNT MAN'S COLOSSAL TECHNICAL AND SCIENTIFIC ACHIEVEMENTS, AS WELL AS HIS THOROUGHLY PRACTICAL TENDENCY—THAT IS SURELY SELF-EVIDENT.

- What enormous work is thus reserved for modern art, and with what enthusiasm must we artists jump at the chance to show the world that we have grown equal to the task!

- If we take the right course, the recognition of man's innate ideal of beauty will be expressed honestly, quite of its own accord; the language of architecture will become understandable and the style representing us will be created.

- And there is more!

- We find ourselves in the midst of this movement. This frequent departure from the broad path of imitation and custom, this ideal striving toward truth in art, this longing for freedom— they are breaking through with enormous power, demolishing everything that obstructs their determined, triumphant advance.

- As always, art will have the power to show man his own ideal reflection.

- YET SO POWERFUL IS THE UPHEAVAL THAT WE CANNOT SPEAK OF A RENAISSANCE OF THE RENAISSANCE. A COMPLETELY NEW BIRTH, A NAISSANCE, HAS BEEN EMERGING FROM THIS MOVEMENT. UNLIKE EARLIER CIVILIZATIONS THAT HAD AVAILABLE ONLY SOME TRADITIONAL MOTIFS AND CONTACT WITH A FEW NEIGHBORING TRIBES, WE HAVE, AS A CONSEQUENCE OF OUR SOCIAL RELATIONS AND THROUGH THE POWER OF OUR MODERN ACHIEVEMENTS, ALL THE ABILITY AND KNOWLEDGE OF MAN AT OUR FREE DISPOSAL.

- THIS NEW STYLE, THE MODERN, IN ORDER TO REPRESENT US AND OUR TIME, MUST CLEARLY EXPRESS A DISTINCT CHANGE FROM PREVIOUS FEELING, AN

ALMOST COMPLETE DECLINE OF THE ROMANTIC, AND AN ALMOST ALL-ENCOMPASSING APPEARANCE OF REASON IN ALL OUR WORKS.

- THIS NASCENT STYLE, REPRESENTING US AND OUR TIME AND BUILT ON THE FOREGOING BASIS, NEEDS, LIKE ALL PRECEDING STYLES, TIME TO DEVELOP. YET OUR CENTURY WITH ITS RAPID PACE OF LIFE ALSO STRIVES TO ACHIEVE THIS GOAL MORE QUICKLY THAN EVER BEFORE, AND FOR THAT REASON THE WORLD, TO ITS OWN SURPRISE, WILL SOON ARRIVE THERE.
- Such views imply that to choose a style as a foundation for a modern architectural creation is out of the question; rather, the architect must try to create new forms or develop those forms that are most easily adapted to modern construction practices and needs, and that therefore best conform to truth.
- The architect may dip into the full repository of traditional forms, but he must never copy a selected form; he must adapt it to us and to the purpose by reshaping the form or by finding his intended effect from those produced by existing models.
- That this development, as already noted, can only take place gradually, that it needs the encouragement and assistance of our contemporaries, is surely obvious.
- Yet if one looks objectively at how things are stirring everywhere, how artists are struggling to shape new ideals of beauty, and if one surveys what has been accomplished up to now, then one must be convinced THAT TODAY THE CLEFT BETWEEN THE MODERN MOVEMENT AND THE RENAISSANCE IS ALREADY LARGER THAN THAT BETWEEN THE RENAISSANCE AND ANTIQUITY.

› Construction

* * *

The need and necessity for protection against inclement weather and against men and animals was certainly the first cause and the original purpose of building.

- In building itself lies the germ of every method of construction, whose development advances with the purpose.
- The creation of such work corresponds to the idea of pure utility. But it could not suffice; the sense of beauty dwelling within man called on art and made her the constant companion of building.
- Thus arose architecture!
- The decoration of huts and caves with flowers, boughs, trophies, weapons, and stone tablets certainly elicited the first feeling for imitation, and thus the first art, architecture, called into being her sisters, painting and sculpture.
- Their works are the independent creation of the beautiful.
- Need, purpose, construction, and idealism are therefore the primitive germs of artistic life. United in a single idea, they produce a kind of "necessity" in the origin and existence

of every work of art, and this is the meaning of the words "ARTIS SOLA DOMINA NECESSITAS."

- No less a person than Gottfried Semper first directed our attention to this truth (even if he unfortunately later deviated from it), and by that alone he quite clearly indicated the path that we must take.
- Need and construction keep equal pace with the aspirations of man, which art, majestically striding forward, cannot follow.
- A fear that the pure principle of utility will displace art therefore seems reasonable. Occasionally it has even led to a kind of struggle, founded on the erroneous belief that the differences between realism and idealism are irreconcilable.
- The error in this view lies in the assumption that utility can displace idealism completely and in the further inference that man can live without art; yet it is only to be supposed that utility and realism precede in order to prepare the deeds that art and idealism have to perform.

Since the beginning of art until today, this process, this development has remained the same. A glance at the past will show this clearly.

- The first human building form was the roof, the protective covering, surely a substitute for the lack of the cave. The roof preceded the supports, the wall, even the hearth. After the roof came the supports, artificially built of tree trunks and stones, and finally the wickerwork, the partition, the bearing wall.
- These building elements received further development in permanent settlements through the use of tools and natural circumstances. After an immeasurably long evolution, traditions (a continuous addition of new purposes and means of production) together with art (born of the human sense of beauty) gradually elevated the basic forms of supports, walls, and rafters to art-forms [*Kunstformen*].
- Only in such a way could art have arisen. There can scarcely be any doubt of the correctness of what I have said.
- Moreover, if one examines all the art-forms from historical periods, an almost unbroken series of gradual developments from the date of their CONSTRUCTIVE origin until today can easily be proven, notwithstanding all the stylistic epochs.

Logical thinking must therefore convince us that the following tenet is unshakable: "EVERY ARCHITECTURAL FORM HAS ARISEN IN CONSTRUCTION AND HAS SUCCESSIVELY BECOME AN ART-FORM."

This principle withstands all analyses and explains every art-form.

Earlier, in the chapter "Style" and just now, it was emphasized that art-forms undergo change. Apart from the fact that the form had to correspond to the ideal of beauty of each epoch, these changes arose because the mode of production, the material, the tools, the means available, and the needs were different, and further, forms came to fulfill different purposes in different places. 'IT IS THEREFORE CERTAIN THAT NEW PURPOSES MUST GIVE BIRTH

TO NEW METHODS OF CONSTRUCTION, AND BY THIS REASONING ALSO TO NEW FORMS.

- Our modern epoch has, like none earlier, produced the greatest number of such new methods of construction (one need only consider the success of iron).
- If today all of these forms have not yet developed into perfect art-forms, it is for the reason indicated earlier—namely, that utility first prepares these forms for art.
- It might again be emphasized that every shaping of form always proceeds slowly and imperceptibly.
- It is Semper's undisputed merit to have referred us to this postulate, to be sure in a somewhat exotic way, in his book *Der Stil*. Like Darwin, however, he lacked the courage to complete his theories from above and below and had to make do with a symbolism of construction, instead of naming construction itself as the primitive cell of architecture.

Construction always precedes, for no art-form can arise without it, and the task of art, which is to idealize the existing, is impossible without the existence of the object.

- Thus the formation of our very own art-forms, corresponding to modern construction, lies within ourselves; the possibility of creating them is offered and facilitated by the rich legacy that we have inherited.
- The useful result of this way of looking at things is very simple.
- "THE ARCHITECT ALWAYS HAS TO DEVELOP THE ART-FORM OUT OF CONSTRUCTION." Obviously the method of construction must fulfill its intended purpose.

Modern man immediately comprehended the enormous value of construction and assigned his most distinguished representatives to achieve its magnificent perfection.

- This field has therefore grown so vast that it has naturally led to the division of labor; thus we see today the separate specialties of bridge construction, railway construction, girder construction, and machine engineering continuing to develop with colossal speed.
- Yet the basic thought behind every construction is not to be sought in algebraic progressions and structural calculations but in a certain natural ingenuity—it is that which is invented.
- From this last point of view, however, construction enters the field of art; that is, the architect selects, specifies, perfects, or invents that method of construction that most naturally fits his image of what is to be created and best suits his nascent art-form.
- The means available and the purpose of the emerging object will always cause him to vacillate between the constraints of pure utility and artistic development; but with due consideration the influence of the architect or the engineer will be resolved.
- THE ENGINEER WHO DOES NOT CONSIDER THE NASCENT ART-FORM BUT ONLY THE STRUCTURAL CALCULATION AND THE EXPENSE WILL THEREFORE SPEAK A LANGUAGE UNSYMPATHETIC TO MAN, WHILE ON THE OTHER HAND, THE ARCHITECT'S MODE OF EXPRESSION WILL REMAIN UNINTELIGIBLE

IF IN THE CREATION OF THE ART-FORM HE DOES NOT START FROM CON-STRUCTION.

- Both are great errors. Since the engineer is seldom a born artist and the architect must train himself as a rule to be an engineer, it is safe to assume that art, or rather the architect, will in time succeed in extending his influence into the realm today occupied by the engineer so that here too legitimate aesthetic demands can be met in a satisfactory way.

- Thus the sequence mentioned at the start, of utility preparing the way and art developing what has begun, will come to pass in all cases and in time will put an end to the unsatisfactory work of the engineer.

- In order not to be misunderstood, it should be noted that there can be no question of the artist lowering the status of the engineer, if for no other reason than because the capabilities of both have never been combined in one individual in an outstanding way, and in fact cannot be combined. As the developing art-form is influenced by construction, so the latter is in turn influenced by many other factors that will be dealt with later.

- One of the most important of these that can be taken as a definite demand of our modern epoch may be discussed here. It concerns the time of production and the soundness usually dependent on it.

- A rather prevalent but, in part, totally false view is that our modern building methods, because they have been sharply accelerated, must also be unsound. The reason for this view is that speculation, which naturally has nothing to do with art and is even its greatest enemy, has a hand in building.

- If one examines our modern method of construction more closely, however, then one will easily be convinced that precisely the reverse is true, and that modern construction has set for itself the definite task of balancing, whenever possible, these two opposites: time of production and soundness. Modern construction in this regard has shown splendid results.

20 Adolf Behne

The modern functional building (1923)

Adolf Behne, *Der moderne Zweckbau*, Munich: Drei Masken-Verlag, 1926. Extracts here from: Adolf Behne, *The Modern Functional Building*, Santa Monica, CA: The Getty Centre for the History of Art and the Humanities, 1996, pp. 129–133, 137–139, and 143–146, translation by Michael Robinson. Notes omitted.

> ## III. No longer shaped space but designed reality

*   *   *

Functionalist deliberations are correct so long as they concern a specific matter, and they go wrong as soon as things have to fit together. It is correct to say that a single rectangular room is uneconomical, that a curve is a better biological transcription of real usable space. But if it is a matter of arranging several rooms together, the result is different. If several oval, circular, or curved rooms are put together, far more space is lost than in a group of rectangular rooms that fit together much better. The honeycomb can be cited once more as an example from nature. In individual organisms the single organs are certainly curved, but they fit snugly together because they are made of flexible, pliable material.

Häring and Scharoun sometimes choose different widths for their corridors, allowing them, like living arteries, to narrow, to shrink, in places where there is less traffic. This is all right provided that traffic always follows this same path until the death of the building, that the same conditions prevail as on the first day, in the same way as is the case for blood corpuscles in an organism. But it is wrong, and the functional becomes antifunctional as soon as the traffic finds different conditions—such as through a change of owner or when purpose alters traffic requirements— whereby it could be heaviest in precisely those places where the plan requires it to be lightest.

Thus in view of the fact that an individual item, even if it functions excellently in and for itself, and even if it is completely adapted to an infinitely manifold nature, is not adequate for society's living requirements, it indeed closes itself to them because it is exaggerated for the sake of uniqueness in space, time, and personality and is not open to duration, change, and multiplicity. In such a case it is questionable whether the mechanical structures of rectangularity are not socially more correct in functional terms!

Once more then: the deciding factor is the attitude toward society.

The human being stands between nature and society. He opts for human community and thus places himself in a certain state of tension with nature. He opts for nature and is in a certain state of tension with society.

Expressed differently, the human being bases his actions and work either on the fact, the awareness of human community and his membership in it, or on a feeling of unity with nature. As a creator he works from the whole to the individual or from the individual to the whole!

According to this, two clear types can be distinguished: at their extremes are the rationalist and the romantic.

In the context of architecture we have identified the consistent functionalist as representing one of these types, the romantic.

His opposite is the consistent rationalist who has congealed into formalism.

When van de Velde referred to the machine, he saw it as the neat, concise, modern, and elegant form.

When the functionalist refers to the machine, he sees it as the moving tool, the perfect approximation to an organism.

When the utilitarian refers to the machine, he sees it as an economic principle of saving work, power, and time.

When the rationalist refers to the machine, he sees it as the representative and patron of standardization and typification.

Let us now turn to the clear-thinking representative of the Western view, the Swiss Charles-Edouard Jeanneret (b. 1887), who has already been quoted several times. He is known as a purist painter and publisher of *L'esprit nouveau* in Paris and is better known as an architect under the pseudonym Le Corbusier-Saugnier, who worked for Peter Behrens for a short time. Le Corbusier adopts a position of absolute *Sachlichkeit*. Naturally he rejects the facade: "Architecture has nothing to do with styles. Louis XIV, XV, XVI, or Gothic are to architecture as the feather on a woman's head—occasionally pretty but not always, and never more than that." He admires the work of modern engineers. "Without pursuing an architectural idea, guided only by the conditions of functional calculations derived from the laws that govern the universe, and by the concept of a living organism, modern engineers have taken the fundamental elements and by putting them together according to firm rules, they have come close to great works of art and allow the work of the human hand to resonate with the universal order."

In a series of essays in *L'esprit nouveau*, "Des yeux qui ne voient pas" Le Corbusier contrasted types of modern motorcars, airplanes, etc., with conventional contemporary architecture and came to this result: "If problems of the dwelling and its layout were studied like a chassis, we should very soon see our houses transformed and improved. If houses were produced industrially, serially like a chassis, we would see unexpected forms, but they would be healthy, defensible forms, and an aesthetic would be formulated with surprising precision."

A house; protection against heat, cold, rain, thieves, the curious—a receptacle for light and sun. A certain number of compartments for cooking, work, intimate life. A room; a surface upon which one can move freely; a bed on which to stretch out; a chair for comfort and another for work; a table for work; drawers so that every object can quickly be put in its place. Number of rooms: one for cooking, one for eating, one for working, one for bathing, and one for sleeping. Such are the standards of a dwelling.

In order to arrive at a definition of a simple, clear, and defensible type for such "machines for living," Le Corbusier recommends the use of standards:

One has to set up a standard in order to face the problem of perfection. When a standard is established, competition immediately and violently comes into play. In order to win one has to do things better than one's rival, in every part, in the line of the whole, and in every detail. That is what all parties are compelled to: progress! The standard is a necessity. The standard is based on sure foundations, not arbitrariness, but with the certainty of intention and with a logic controlled by experiment. . . . The establishment of a standard means exhausting all practical and reasonable possibilities, deriving a type that will be recognized as appropriate to the maximum performance of functions, using minimal means, as little hand assembly as possible, and a minimum of materials: words, sounds, colors, forms.

This emphasis on the type, on the universally valid, the need for a norm is what makes Le Corbusier fundamentally different from the functionalists. The basis of his work is the primary awareness of belonging to human society. To be sure, functionalists will agree with many, perhaps all, of Le Corbusier's pronouncements but there then remains the distinction that what is heterogeneous for them is autogenous for Le Corbusier, to use Paul Tillich's terminology *(Das System der Wissenschaften nach Gegenständen und Methoden)*.

A recurring and vigorously emphasized aspect of Le Corbusier's approach is the importance of the floor plan, because it is the floor plan that primarily contains the social element of building.

"Mass and surface are determined by the plan. The plan is the generator. All the worse for those people with no imagination."

The whole structure rises on a foundation and develops according to a rule drawn on the ground in the floor plan. Good forms, variety of form, unity of a geometric nature, communication of harmonies—that is architecture. The plan is the basis. Without a plan there can be no greatness of invention and of expression, no rhythm, no volume, no coherence. Without a plan we have only the sensation intolerable to man of formlessness, misery, disorder, and arbitrariness. The plan demands the most active invention. At the same time it demands the strictest discipline. The plan is the determining factor for the whole. It is the decisive moment. A plan is not a pretty thing to draw, like a Madonna's face. It is a severe abstraction, nothing but dry mathematics for the eye. But the work of the mathematician remains one of the highest activities of the human mind, The unity of the law is the law of the good floor plan—a simple, infinitely variable law.

What is already clear in these statements by Le Corbusier is his social view of architecture. His thinking moves from the whole to details, that is, for him the fundamental element is order, which is inseparable from any overview, whereas architecture can just as logically be directed toward expression, at the point where it creates and forms a single object, an individual body, something that exists for itself. Even an architect concerned with expression will, of course, draw plans and will not underestimate how very important they are, but it is right that we should hear a paean of praise to the plan from an architect who makes the totality his starting point. The plan is the element that fits the structure into the floor, the universal; it is the union of the enduring base with the earth common to all. But the elevation is the more individual element, the differentiating factor. A plan belongs to the world of the horizontal, an elevation to the world of the vertical.

The plan conveys, in the most compressed form possible, the order and overview of the building; the elevation conveys the construction. It is therefore not surprising that someone who lays such emphasis upon the plan should emphatically underline the element of order. "Architecture is art in the highest sense—mathematical order." "More and more, constructions and machines can be represented in proportions and in a play of volumes and materials; many of them are true works of art as they contain number—that is order."

Order—universal validity—rejection of all subjective elements in building, rejection of precisely that movement that van de Velde called "dramatic". The cathedral is not a plastic work of art, it is a drama: a struggle against the law of gravity, concern with the sphere of emotions. For this reason we search in it for complementary values of a subjective nature beyond the plastic element." If order is to be visible in built space it needs elementary primary forms. For the architect concerned with expression, such demands do not exist: what is most irregular can at the same time be most expressive. Le Corbusier works with clear, recurring, unambiguously comprehensible masses: "Cube, cone, cylinder, sphere, and pyramid are the great primary forms that light reveals to advantage. They give us a clear and tangible image without ambiguity. For this reason these forms are beautiful forms, the most beautiful forms." "If the fundamentals of architecture are sphere, cone, and cylinder (one thinks of Cézanne's statement), as creators and emphasizers of form, they are purely geometrical by nature. But geometry frightens today's architect." The first European architect to recognize the positive role of geometry for architecture would seem to have been Berlage, who praised geometrical form as early as his Zurich lectures of 1907. It stands above the all too personal and often ugly character of the idiosyncratic because it is "not individual and essentially always beautiful in itself."

Something that is very important to our case now emerges, justifying and explaining the extent to which we have followed Le Corbusier's pronouncements: whereas an architect who is concerned with the individual work, and is therefore looking for expression, always places the demands of purpose clearly in the foreground and consequently stresses construction, the architect proceeding from the whole, and thus concerned with order, will stress an element that has no fundamental significance for functionalists—play! Functionalists want to make their buildings into tools, but rationalists (and this is surprising at first) are equally determined to see them as toys!

Expression isolates, is always serious by nature, and in attempting to overcome its seriousness does not transcend the half-measures of the grotesque.

The overview may well be able to be lighthearted. Play requires community, order, rules.

* * *

Nothing is more self-evident than that a rationalist should stress form. Form is nothing more than the consequence of establishing a relationship between human beings. For the isolated and unique figure in nature there is no problem of form. Individuals, even individuals in nature, are free. The problem of form arises when an overview is demanded. Form is the prerequisite under which an overview becomes possible. Form is an eminently social matter. Anyone who recognizes the right of society recognizes the right of form.

If humanity were just a sum of individuals, it would probably be possible to see the house as a pure tool, as purely functional. Anyone who sees a form in humanity, a pattern articulated in time and space, approaches the house with formal requirements, in which case "formal" is not to be confused with "decorative."

If every building is part of a built whole, then it recognizes from its aesthetic and formal requirements certain universally valid rules, rules that do not arise from its individual functional character [*Zweckcharakter*] but from the requirements of this whole. For here in the social sphere after all, must lie the primeval elements of the aesthetic (Guyau: Art is tenderness). A one sided fulfillment of function [*Zweckerfüllung*] leads to anarchy. Where a building is perceived as part of a whole, the character of a toy is added to the character of a tool, the absolute to the relative element.

The concept of "form" does not deal with accessories, decoration, taste, or style (from Gothic to Biedermeier) but with the consequences arising from a building's ability to be an enduring structure. The functionalist prefers to exaggerate the purpose to the point of making it unique and momentary (a house for each function!) but the rationalist takes the purpose broadly and generally as readiness for many cases, simply because he gives thought to the enduring qualities of buildings, which perhaps see many generations with changing requirements and therefore cannot live without leeway. The rationalist is no more indifferent to purpose than the functionalist. Although he does not have the perspective of the Baroque genius opposing purpose, he avoids the tyrannical rule of purpose. As the functionalist looks for the greatest possible adaptation to the most specialized purpose, so the rationalist looks for the most appropriate solution for many cases. The former wants what is absolutely fitting and unique for the particular case; the latter wants what is most fitting for general need, the norm. The former is all for adaptation, relation, formlessness growing from selflessness, and mimicry; the latter is also for personal will, self consideration, play, and form.

There is no doubt that the West leads in its determination to see architecture as a whole and from a social point of view. I quote from a programmatic essay by Victor Bourgeois for the Brussels magazine *Sept arts:* "Since the building is inseparable from its neighbor and since a street extends into another street, all powerful architecture tends to style, that is to say, a superior collective equilibrium." The following passage explains how personal and psychological work comes to be rejected: "A modern architect who is compelled to build today on any street in Brussels is almost insolent with regard to his art if he realizes an interesting building—what progress is this if this hostile architecture becomes an indifferent architecture."

In Western Europe the feeling is not that an architect should work in a special, original, and personal style (which he had best protect from irritations by official patent). Here conspicuous work is considered bad eo ipso—simply because it is conspicuous: "A home must be made a measure of man" (Malespine) and "Originality is, moreover, a form of insubordination" (Georges Linze). From this point of view it is understandable when Roland Holst emphatically points Dutch artists toward "the correction that the romantic always and under all circumstances signifies" (*Architektura,* February 1924).

It is not surprising that Le Corbusier addresses the problems of the modern metropolis, for these accord with the basic thrust of rationalism, that is, working from an awareness of community, moving from the whole to the individual. (It is precisely by this means that form emerges since form is correspondence, and tact comes from *tangere* = to touch.) In his *Principes fondamentaux d'urbanisme moderne,* Le Corbusier maintains the clarity of his rationalism throughout, but at the same time demonstrates that the consistent rationalist gets stuck in just the same cul-de-sac as the consistent functionalist. Functionalism may court the danger of exaggerating to the point of becoming grotesque, but rationalism courts the danger of reducing everything to the schematic.

It is quite logical that the individual aiming at expression will arrive at moving curves with maximum fluidity, fulfilling every function, and will therefore see concrete as a plastic mass that can be modelled. Contrast this with R. van t'Hoff: "Only with ferroconcrete are the horizontal and vertical adaptations consistent" (*De Stijl* 2, no. 5). The rationalist who is inclined toward an overview likewise emphasizes straight lines and right angles. "Why," asks Scharoun, "must everything be straight, when the straight line is produced only by the environment?" Le Corbusier might reply: "Precisely because nothing can remain isolated, because we all stand within an environment, everything must be straight and the curve is individualistic lack of discipline."

There is no question that only the straight line and right angle can be the basis of the modern creation, which seeks to eliminate arbitrariness and rejects all anthropomorphic curves – and yet it would be wrong to turn the straight line and right angle into a dogma or rigid principle. The modern metropolis sketched by Le Corbusier, which in fact hardly touches upon many problems, is certainly consistently straight-lined and right-angled down to the last detail, but it can be so only because and for as long as it remains on paper. Here Le Corbusier can certainly decree: "The curve—that's paralysis:" but if he were to realize his plan and did not find a field as flat as a silver platter, he would be forced by every bend in a river or by every hill to depart from the rigid straight lines and strict right angles; otherwise one could say, "This straight line is senility," and thus the functionalist would be justified.

Le Corbusier's city plan shows fairly clearly the dangers of a consistent rationalism: form becomes an overbearing, life constraining, stifling mask, and the result is no longer the integration into a living whole but an academic division that turns play into a show. And then it is time again to emphasize purpose and underline function to lead the way to recovery and reflection.

*   *   *

If we return to the building, we can say that its concrete form is a compromise between individual (function) and society (form). In its pure development this compromise is inhibited by "expression" and soul. Its pure form is living equilibrium, realization of a behavior that plays to many sides, open and yet determined. We may join Theo van Doesburg in calling it "formless" provided that we do not confuse "formless" [*formlos*] with "shapeless" [*gestaltlos*]. Closed form in the sense of a "figure" is today no longer a satisfying element in art, either in architecture or in other fields. A drive toward the final fusion breaks the bounds of closed form (in painting this was done by Cubism) and tries to achieve pure relationships, spatial tensions that are never arbitrarily limited. "Art is equilibrium achieved by evaluation of all parts" (Schwitters). "Proportion" is the interpenetration of "function" and "form," that is, a plastics of proportion replaces a morphoplastics (Piet Mondrian). "As long as design uses any form, it is impossible to shape pure proportionalities. For this reason the new design has liberated itself from all creation of form" (Piet Mondrian).

The younger generation of German architects insists on strict *Sachlichkeit*. Miës van der Rohe explains: "We reject all aesthetic speculation, all doctrine, and all formalism. Let form be shaped by the nature of the task, using the means of our time. That is our work." Otto Wagner had already insisted on the same thing in a very similar formulation.

The necessary and only sound approach is to reject aesthetic speculation, formalism, and doctrine, but it seems to us quite a frequent error to make this rejection from an anti-aesthetic point of view, even if we inveigh against the aestheticism of aesthetes one hundred times a day. Rejecting aesthetic demands (which is not the same as aesthetic speculation) would be to saw off the branch on which one sits. As long as individual objects are being dealt with, the fulfillment of purpose may suffice to create a healthy form. But if we accept the demands of a monumental architecture, that is, of an architectural whole, the bringing together of forms – even genuinely sound ones – does not suffice. The demand for unity is through and through an elementary aesthetic or artistic demand, and to assume that all strictly *sachlich* works "in themselves" would form a unity, even if they were developed in a vacuum, is to draw a false conclusion. The task is not merely an overview of new buildings but also an overview of their landscape or urban environment.

> House, human being, sun, and landscape form a complex of mutual relationships. Just as the individual form gets its face and body organically from these relationships, so, for the sake of the overall idea, must a housing complex, as an overall urban composition of a complicated organism, fulfill more and various environmental demands in order to absorb, integrate, and subordinate the personality of individual organisms converted to something impersonal. Only when they are all conjoined do the parts attain the validity and meaning each intends. The types that result from such architectural tasks are not a necessary evil of an anxious economy; they are a necessity of life in terms of what a housing complex demands and means and what the individual objects, considered within the same framework must be namely an organic unit.
>
> (Richard Döcker, *Volkswohnung*, 10 July 1923)

We should not abandon this demand because we are prejudiced – rightly! – against previous romantic methods of doing it justice. The demand itself remains as long as we do not abandon the full claim of design. A bridge over a river is not just a utilitarian problem but also a town planning problem, that is, the demand to insert its mass into the movement of the bank, into the rhythm of the streets and squares, by means other than formal nonsense and naturalistic mimicry is completely an artistic-aesthetic one. One can deny these demands only by including under the concept of utility the consideration of the optical and logical, of the perceptually correct. But then one has done nothing more than give aesthetic demands another name. In fact, according to utilitarian dogmatists, there is a double demand: the accord with *sachlich*-constructional demands and the accord with demands arising from the nature of our organs of perception. And it is precisely these that we call aesthetic demands in the pure, original sense of the word (αισθάνομαι = I perceive). We do not doubt for a moment that these demands, just as much as *sachlich*-constructional ones, belong to the realm of human reason; these demands are not mystical and arbitrary nor are they in any way satisfied by that.

To care whether and if things relate to one another is under no circumstances a matter of utility. But if we abandon the demand for unity, we can no longer speak well of design. The problem is not solved by the fact that hitherto people have always tried to create unity in an emotional or romantic fashion, using only the values and realities of the landscape. We have to solve it on the basis of reason.

We find that German architecture is somewhat inclined to devote itself to an extreme that changes fairly frequently and then gives way to the opposite extreme – the consequence of inner uncertainty. It is all too rarely recognized that the aim should be to stabilize the strong dynamic tensions that living architecture must absorb in order not to become aesthetic, and this certainly includes tensions of extreme revolutionary power and force, the kind demanded by Selinski's essay.

It is erroneous to think that dynamism can only be expressed in the elevation, in the animated "form" [*Form*]: instead, it is to a great degree a matter of the floor plan. And it is just as erroneous to believe that structural requirements are assured by a quadrature of the plan, which often enough remains a drawing-board ornament. In contrast Mendelsohn says: "Architecture establishes the conditions of its animated masses from its own laws: the dynamic condition, movement of space (seen in outline as its linear element), the rhythmic condition, the relationship of masses (seen in elevation as its surface projection), and the structural condition or balance of movement (seen in plan and section as their structural elements)."

We find a clear and secure attitude in recent Dutch architecture as well as in recent Czech architecture, which is getting under way with surprising élan.

Theo van Doesberg, editor of *De Stijl*, stresses the double function of building: "Function from the perspective of practice; proportionality from the perspective of art." Function and play. "Intentional artistic design and utilitarian constructivism combine to produce complete equilibrium" (*De Stijl* 6, nos. 6–7). Political realism and confidence of this kind spare Dutch architecture from swinging from extreme to extreme between opposing dogmas; it allows it the possibility of coping with all the dynamic tensions of our time openly and freely, without abandoning the demand for monumentality; it allows Dutch architecture the possibility of steady development.

Under the pressure of circumstances and through the expansion of aesthetic insight, it is only now that an architecture shaped by and through itself seems possible, an architecture in which the other arts will not be applied and thus subordinated but one that will work organically together with the other arts; it makes possible an architecture that from the beginning experiences beauty in its constructional functions, that is, an architecture that through the tension of its proportions raises the construction itself above its material necessity to aesthetic form.

(J. J. P. Oud)

21 Mies van der Rohe

Office building (1923)

Mies van der Rohe, 'Office Building', *G: Material zur elementaren Gestaltung,* 1, 1923. English facsimile edition: Detlef Mertins and Michael W. Jennings (ed.), *G: An Avant-garde Journal of Art, Architecture, Design, and Film 1923–1926*, Los Angeles, CA: Getty Publications, 2010, extract p. 103, translation by Steven Lindberg with Margareta Ingrid Christian.

We reject   { every aesthetic speculation,
             { every doctrine,
             { and every formalism

The art of building is the will of our time captured in space. Living. Changing. New.

Not yesterday, not tomorrow, only today can be formed. Only this practice of building gives form.

Create the form from the nature of the task with the means of our time.

That is our task.

› OFFICE BUILDING

The office building is a place of work of organisation of clarity of economy.

Bright, wide working spaces, clearly laid out, undivided, subdivided only according to the organism of the firm. Maximum effect with minimum expenditure of means.

The materials are concrete iron glass.

Ferroconcrete buildings are by nature skeleton buildings. Neither baked goods nor armored towers. Supporting girder construction; a nonsupporting wall. Hence, skin and bone buildings.

The most efficient organisation of work places determined the depth of the space, which is 16 meters. A dual-shaft frame spanning 8 meters, with a console on each side that projects 4 meters, was determined to be the most economical principle for the construction. The trusses are spaced 5 meters apart. This girder system supports the ceiling panel, which at the end of the cantilever arm is angled up vertically to form an external skin and a backing wall for the shelves that were moved from the interior into the exterior walls for the sake of clarity. Above the 2-meter high shelves lies a continuous band of windows that reaches to the ceiling.

22 Mies van der Rohe

Building (1923)

Mies van der Rohe, 'Bauen', *G: Material zur elementaren Gestaltung*, 2, 1923. English facsimile edition: Detlef Mertins and Michael W. Jennings (ed.), *G: An Avant-garde Journal of Art, Architecture, Design, and Film 1923–1926*, Los Angeles, CA: Getty Publications, 2010, extract p. 105, translation by Steven Lindberg with Margareta Ingrid Christian.

BUILDING

We know no formal problems, only building problems.

Form is not the goal but the result of our work

There is no form in itself [*an sich*].

The truly formed thing is conditioned, grown together with the task. Indeed, it is the
   most elemental expression of the solution of that task.

Form as goal is formalism; and we respect that. Nor do we strive for a style.

The will to style is also formalistic.

We have other concerns.

Out task is precisely to liberate building activity from the aesthetic specialisation of
   developers and to make it once again the only thing it should be, namely,

BUILDING

The introduction of ferroconcrete as a building material for residential construction has been attempted several times. Usually, however, in an insufficient manner. The advantages of this material were not exploited and its disadvantages were not overcome. By rounding the corners of the house and those of the individual rooms, one imagined that the material had been paid its due. Round corners are entirely inconsequential for concrete, however, and they are not even very simple to produce. Naturally it is not enough to translate the brick house into ferroconcrete. – In my view, the main advantage of ferroconcrete lies in the possibility for great economy in the use of materials. To make this possible for a residence, one must concentrate the bearing and supporting forces in just a few points in the building. The disadvantages of ferroconcrete are its limited effectiveness as insulation and its noise conductivity. It is thus necessary to provide additional insulation as protection against outside temperatures. The simplest way to address the unfortunate effect of conducting noise is, in my view, to do away with everything that produces noise. I am thinking here of rubber floors, sliding windows and doors, and similar measures — but also of spaciousness in the floor plan. — Ferroconcrete must be implemented with the overall installation laid out as precisely as possible; in this respect, the architect still has everything to learn from the engineer who designs ships. In brick construction, it is possible if not exactly sensible, to turn the plumbers and heating specialists loose on the house as soon as the roof is finished: in no time at all, the house, which has been barely erected, will be transformed into a ruin. Such an approach is impossible with ferroconcrete construction. Here only disciplined work can achieve its ends.

The model illustrated above demonstrates an attempt to approach the problem of the ferroconcrete residence. The main living quarters are supported by a four-shaft girder system. This constructional system is surrounded by a thin ferroconcrete skin. This skin forms not only the walls but the roof. The roof inclines slightly away from the exterior walls toward the center. The channel that is formed by having each half of the roof incline permits the simplest drainage system imaginable. This eliminates the plumbers work entirely. I cut openings out of the walls at points where they would permit views and light the rooms.

23 Ludwig Hilberseimer

Construction and form (1924)

Ludwig Hilberseimer, 'Konstruktion und Form', *G: Material zur elementaren Gestaltung,* 3, 1924. English facsimile edition: Detlef Mertins and Michael W. Jennings (ed.), *G: An Avant-garde Journal of Art, Architecture, Design, and Film 1923–1926,* Los Angeles, CA: Getty Publications, 2010, extract pp. 126–128, translation by Steven Lindberg with Margareta Ingrid Christian.[1]

Identity of construction and form is an indispensable precondition for any architecture. At first, the two seem to be opposed. But precisely their combination, their unity, is the basis of architecture. Construction and material are the material preconditions of architectural form-creation. They stand in constant correlation. Thus Greek architecture is based on the alternation of horizontals and verticals that is required by stone construction. It perfectly develops the possibilities of ashlar, while preserving the unity of the material. A Greek temple is a perfect work of engineering in stone. Through the construction of arches and vaults, the Romans significantly enriched the simple alternation of horizontals and verticals, although they abandoned the unity of the material. By dividing the whole into constructional parts, filling, and facing, they established the composite building style that has remained characteristic to the present day: namely, one that uses ashlar to frame openings and to cover storey breaks. By superimposing several floors, structured by column orders, the usual horizontal division of multistoried buildings emerged. It is a principle that was not violated until Michelangelo. He was the first to combine several floors under a single order. The purely decorative function of architectural forms derived from antiquity may be traced back to this time. They increasingly lost their function as constructional divisions. They became utter mockups: the architecture of the nineteenth century!

*　*　*

It was only with the architecture of the large city and its new building tasks that the necessity of new constructions and materials became inevitable. The only materials that can be used in the architecture of the large city are those that maximize the use of space and combine a heightened resistance to wear and weathering with maximum firmness. Iron, concrete, and ferroconcrete are the building materials that permit the new types of constructions demanded by a large city:

constructions to cover wide spaces, the greatest possible stratification of stories, and jutting horizontal projections.

Iron and ferroconcrete are building materials that impose relatively few limits on the architect's imagination. We are not referring to their ductility, their ability to overcome all material restrictions by casting, but rather their consequences for construction, the possibility to produce a completely homogenous building, the combination of supporting and supported parts, the enabling of clear limitations on proportion, and the elimination of the need for any enclosure or coverage structuring.

The possibilities of iron and ferroconcrete construction overcome the old support and load system, which allowed only for a building from bottom to top and one behind the facade. Both methods also enable one to build toward the front, to project out beyond the piers. They enable a complete separation into supporting and supported parts. A transformation of the building into a bearing skeleton and nonbearing walls that merely surround and separate. This not only results in new technical and material problems but above all in a new architectural problem. A complete alteration of the seemingly firm static appearance of the building.

*   *   *

These new constructions allow for a consequential design of commercial buildings according to their necessity and conditionality. The clarity of the layout and its possibility for change, as well as the maximized light supply, determine the meaning and form of this type of building. Whereas the essential features of, say, Alfred Messel's Berlin commercial buildings rely on the layout and the construction of Renaissance palaces, Hans Pölzig's building in Breslau attempts to use the possibilities of a new kind of construction. Thus, in reminiscence of the wood construction of the Middle Ages, he had the floors project out above one another, achieving an essential structural change to the building.

Erich Mendelson addressed the same problem while working on an extension of the Mosse publishing house in Berlin. Not directly, but indirectly. Circumscribing it symbolically, as it were. By having certain floors project out diagonally to the side, he tries to express his independence from the falling vertical.

Miës van der Rohe was the first to recognize the latest design possibilities of the new constructional ideas, and, in his design for an office building, he found the architectural solution for them. His construction is based on a two-shaft framing system with console projections on both sides. At the end of the cantilever arm, the cover plate is bent up vertically to form the exterior skin, which also serves as the back wall for the racks that have been moved for practical reasons from the interior to the exterior walls. Above these racks, there is a band of windows that extends up to the ceiling and stretches horizontally, uninterrupted, around the building. Without walls or piers on the facade. Thus the horizontal layering of the multistory house is dynamically accentuated. The dominant horizontal combined with the lack of piers on the facade completely changes the structural character of the building, and the lack of piers creates an architecture of floating lightness.

The layout and structure of this office building are of an uncommon clarity. It corresponds to the aims perfectly. It is shaped out of the essence of the task, using the means of our time. The constructional function is conceived as architecture. The formal structure developed from the constructional idea. Construction and form have become one: clear, logical, simple, unambiguous, and regular.

The architecture is the identity of construction and form. Today building is done decoratively only. Beton and reinforced beton give the fantasy of the architect new possibilities and problems. The uptodate architecture is the realisation of those possibilities.[2]

› Notes

1   Editors' note: 'Konstruktion und Form' eventually became part of the book *Großstadtarchitektur* by Hilberseimer. See N 16 in this Reader.
2   Editors' note: this statement was repeated in French and Russian in the original.

24 Le Corbusier and Pierre Jeanneret

Five points towards a new architecture (1926)

Le Corbusier and Pierre Jeanneret, *Almanach de l'Architecture moderne*, Paris, 1926. English translation by Michael Bullock, from: Ulrich Conrads (ed.), *Programmes and Manifestoes on 20th-century Architecture*, London: Lund Humphries / Cambridge MA: MIT Press, 1970, extract pp. 99–101.

The theoretical considerations set out below are based on many years of practical experience on building sites.

Theory demands concise formulation.

The following points in no way relate to aesthetic fantasies or a striving for fashionable effects, but concern architectural facts that imply an entirely new kind of building, from the dwelling house to palatial edifices.

1. **The supports.** To solve a problem scientifically means in the first place to distinguish between its elements. Hence in the case of a building a distinction can immediately be made between the supporting and the non-supporting elements. The earlier foundations, on which the building rested without a mathematical check, are replaced by individual foundations and the walls by individual supports. Both supports and support foundations are precisely calculated according to the burdens they are called upon to carry. These supports are spaced out at specific, equal intervals, with no thought for the interior arrangement of the building. They rise directly from the floor to 3, 4, 6, etc. metres and elevate the ground floor. The rooms are thereby removed from the dampness of the soil; they have light and air; the building plot is left to the garden, which consequently passes under the house. The same area is also gained on the flat roof.

2. **The roof gardens.** The flat roof demands in the first place systematic utilization for domestic purposes: roof terrace, roof garden. On the other hand, the reinforced concrete demands protection against changing temperatures. Over-activity on the part of the reinforced concrete is prevented by the maintenance of a constant humidity on the roof concrete. The roof terrace satisfies bath demands (a rain-dampened layer of sand covered with concrete slabs with lawns in the interstices; the earth of the flowerbeds in direct contact with the layer of sand). In this way the rain water will flow off extremely slowly. Waste pipes in

the interior of the building. Thus a latent humidity will remain continually on the roof skin. The roof gardens will display highly luxuriant vegetation. Shrubs and even small trees up to 3 or 4 metres tall can be planted. In this way the roof garden will become the most favoured place in the building. In general, roof gardens mean to a city the recovery of all the built-up area.

3. **The free designing of the ground-plan.** The support system carries the intermediate ceilings and rises up to the roof. The interior walls may be placed wherever required, each floor being entirely independent of the rest. There are no longer any supporting walls but only membranes of any thickness required. The result of this is absolute freedom in designing the ground-plan; that is to say, free utilization of the available means, which makes it easy to offset the rather high cost of reinforced concrete construction.

4. **The horizontal window.** Together with the intermediate ceilings the supports form rectangular openings in the façade through which light and air enter copiously. The window extends from support to support and thus becomes a horizontal window. Stilted vertical windows consequently disappear, as do unpleasant mullions. In this way, rooms are equably lit from wall to wall. Experiments have shown that a room thus lit has an eight times stronger illumination than the same room lit by vertical windows with the same window area.

   The whole history of architecture revolves exclusively around the wall apertures. Through use of the horizontal window reinforced concrete suddenly provides the possibility of maximum illumination.

5. **Free design of the façade.** By projecting the floor beyond the supporting pillars, like a balcony all round the building, the whole façade is extended beyond the supporting construction. It thereby loses its supportive quality and the windows may be extended to any length at will, without any direct relationship to the interior division. A window may just as well be 10 metres long for a dwelling house as 200 metres for a palatial building (our design for the League of Nations building in Geneva). The façade may thus be designed freely.

The five essential points set out above represent a fundamentally new aesthetic. Nothing is left to us of the architecture of past epochs, just as we can no longer derive any benefit from the literary and historical teaching given in schools.

› Constructional considerations

Building construction is the purposeful and consistent combination of building elements.

Industries and technological undertakings are being established to deal with the production of these elements.

Serial manufacture enables these elements to be made precise, cheap and good. They can be produced in advance in any number required.

Industries will see to the completion and uninterrupted perfecting of the elements.

Thus the architect has at his disposal a box of building units. His architectural talent can operate freely. It alone, through the building programme, determines his architecture.

The age of the architects is coming.

25 Mies van der Rohe

Remarks on my block of flats (1927)

Mies van der Rohe, 'Concerning my block',[1] *Bau und Wohnung*, Stuttgart: Deutscher Werkbund, 1927, pp. 77, from: Tim and Charlotte Benton (ed.), *Form and Function*, London: Crosby Lockwood Staples/OUP, 1975, p. 156.

In the building of rented apartment blocks today, economic considerations demand a rationalisation and standardisation of construction. But, on the other hand, the increasing variety of our housing needs demands the greatest freedom of methods of utilisation. In the future it will be necessary to satisfy both these tendencies. For this, skeleton construction is the most suitable system. It permits rational manufacture while leaving free the organisation of interior space. If one limits oneself to designing only the kitchen and bathroom as permanent rooms, on account of their installations, and if one resolves to divide up the remaining living space with movable walls, then I believe that by these means we will be able to satisfy every reasonable requirement.

› Note

1   Editors' note: apartment block at the *Weissenhofsiedlung* in Stuttgart.

26 CIAM (Congrès Internationaux d'Architecture Moderne)

La Sarraz Declaration (1928)

CIAM, 'Declaration of La Sarraz', *i10* (Amsterdam), 14, 1928. English translation by Michael Bullock, from: Ulrich Conrads (ed.), *Programmes and Manifestoes on 20th-century Architecture*, London: Lund Humphries/Cambridge MA: MIT Press, 1970, extract pp. 109–112.

* * *

> ## I. General economic system

1. The idea of modern architecture includes the link between the phenomenon of architecture and that of the general economic system.
2. The idea of 'economic efficiency' does not imply production furnishing maximum commercial profit, but production demanding a minimum working effort.
3. The need for maximum economic efficiency is the inevitable result of the impoverished state of the general economy.
4. The most efficient method of production is that which arises from rationalization and standardization. Rationalization and standardization act directly on working methods both in modern architecture (conception) and in the building industry (realization).
5. Rationalization and standardization react in a threefold manner:
    (a) they demand of architecture conceptions leading to simplification of working methods on the site and in the factory;
    (b) they mean for building firms a reduction in the skilled labour force; they lead to the employment of less specialized labour working under the direction of highly skilled technicians;
    (c) they expect from the consumer (that is to say the customer who orders the house in which he will live) a revision of his demands in the direction of a readjustment to the new conditions of social life. Such a revision will be manifested in the reduction of certain individual needs henceforth devoid of real justification; the benefits of this reduction will foster the maximum satisfaction of the needs of the greatest number, which are at present restricted.

6. Following the dissolution of the guilds, the collapse of the class of skilled craftsmen is an accomplished fact. The inescapable consequence of the development of the machine has led to industrial methods of production different from and often opposed to those of the craftsmen. Until recently, thanks to the teaching of the academies, the architectural conception has been inspired chiefly by the methods of craftsmen and not by the new industrial methods. This contradiction explains the profound disorganization of the art of building.

7. It is urgently necessary for architecture, abandoning the outmoded conceptions connected with the class of craftsmen, henceforth to rely upon the present realities of industrial technology, even though such an attitude must perforce lead to products fundamentally different from those of past epochs.

› II. Town planning

1. Town planning is the organization of the functions of collective life; it extends over both the urban agglomerations and the countryside. Town planning is the organization of life in all regions.

    Urbanization cannot be conditioned by the claims of a pre-existent aestheticism: its essence is of a functional order.

2. This order includes three functions: (a) dwelling, (b) producing, (c) relaxation (the maintenance of the species). Its essential objects are: (a) division of the soil, (b) organization of traffic, (c) legislation.

3. The relationships between the inhabited areas, the cultivated areas (including sports) and the traffic areas are dictated by the economic and social environment. The fixing of population densities establishes the indispensable classification.

    The chaotic division of land, resulting from sales, speculations, inheritances, must be abolished by a collective and methodical land policy.

    This redistribution of the land, the indispensable preliminary basis for any town planning, must include the just division between the owners and the community of the *unearned increment* resulting from works of joint interest.

4. Traffic control must take in all the functions of collective life. The growing intensity of these vital functions, always checked against a reading of statistics, demonstrates the supreme importance of the traffic phenomenon.

5. Present-day technical facilities, which are constantly growing, are the very key to town planning. They imply and offer a total transformation of existing legislation; this transformation must run parallel with technical progress.

› III. Architecture and public opinion

1. It is essential today for architects to exercise an influence on public opinion by informing the public of the fundamentals of the new architecture. Through the baneful effects of academic

teaching, opinion has strayed into an erroneous conception of the dwelling. The true problems of the dwelling have been pushed back behind entirely artificial sentimental conceptions. The problem of the house is not posed.

Clients, whose demands are motivated by numerous factors that have nothing to do with the real problem of housing, are generally very bad at formulating their wishes. Opinion has gone astray. Thus the architect satisfies the normal prerequisites of housing only poorly. This inefficiency involves the country in an immense expense that is a total loss. The tradition is created of the expensive house, the building of which deprives a large part of the population of healthy living quarters.

2. Through educational work carried out in schools, a body of fundamental truths could be established forming the basis for a domestic science (for example: the general economy of the dwelling, the principles of property and its moral significance, the effects of sunlight, the ill effects of darkness, essential hygiene, rationalization of household economics, the use of mechanical devices in domestic life, etc.).

3. The effect of such an education would be to bring up generations with a healthy and rational conception of the house. These generations (the architect's future clients) would be capable of correctly stating the problems of housing.

*   *   *

27 Mies van der Rohe

What would concrete, what would steel be without mirror glass (1933)

Mies van der Rohe, 'What would concrete, what would steel be without mirror glass', unpublished prospectus, Verein Deutscher Spiegelglas-Fabriken, 13 March 1933. English translation by Mark Jarzombek, from: Fritz Neumeyer, *The Artless Word: Mies van der Rohe on the building art*, Cambridge MA: MIT, 1991, extract p. 314.

The space-toppling power of both would be undermined, yes, even canceled; would remain empty promise. The glass skin, the glass walls alone permit the skeleton structure its unambiguous constructive appearance and secure its architectonic possibilities. Not only in the large functional structures. Although there, on the basis of function and necessity, a development sets in that needs no more justification, the full unfolding of which, however, will not occur there but in the realm of residential buildings. Here, in greater freedom without immediate obligation to narrow functionality, the artistic value of these technical means could be proven.

They are genuine building elements and the instruments of a new building art. They permit a measure of freedom in spatial composition that we will not relinquish any more. Only now can we articulate space freely, open it up and connect it to the landscape. Now it becomes clear again what a wall is, what an opening, what is floor and what ceiling. Simplicity of construction, clarity of tectonic means, and purity of material reflect the luminosity of original beauty.

28 Giuseppe Pagano

Structure and architecture (1935)

Giuseppe Pagano, 'Struttura ed architettura', *Dopo Sant'Elia*, Milan: Editoriale Domus, 1935, extracts, pp. 97, 98–99, 99, 101, 103, 104, 105, 112, 114 and 118–119, translation by Stefania Boccaletti with the editors.

* * *

An opinion that often surfaces in the discourse of both Modern Architecture's architects and critics is that the process of the revision of architectural values can be explained through the development of construction techniques. In other words, we witness a polarisation of the general turmoil towards the regeneration of architecture – as well as civil society at large – focused purely on technical facts: standardisation, concrete, industrialisation of the building site, the structural frame and off-site prefabrication, etc. This constitutes a brutal relation between spirit and matter, where the technical component is the necessary and sufficient condition for aesthetic determination. If this was true, we would irreconcilably confuse the natural hierarchy between things and ideas, premises and conclusions – we would decisively choose 'parts', 'manners', and 'forms', forgetting the fundamental value of the 'whole', of a 'synthesis' or of a material 'substance'. We would turn aesthetic discussion on beauty and ugliness into a purely economic conversation; we would introduce unilateral and inappropriate criteria to determine the nature of spatial and architectural 'harmony', and we would finally choose the needs of the 'body' over those of the 'spirit'.

* * *

Before delving into the specific aesthetic problem of the structural frame, a fundamental fact about the evolution of Modern Architecture must be grasped. It is clearly essential to understand that changes of taste precede the introduction of any new technique. In fact, even without the introduction of concrete and the ongoing progress made by the construction industry, architecture – as an art and not business – would naturally incline towards the civil values to which the whole of society aspires; a consequence of questions of morality, profound spiritual inclinations and the eternal law which demands from the arts the expression of the ideals of the contemporary world.

What are these ideals? What is the moral core from which Modern Architecture springs? What is the hidden voice compelling and guiding architects throughout civil society? Essentially there is a new sense of honesty, a new sincerity emerging, which translates into identification with the contemporary world, and also a profound yet feisty and stubborn feeling for simplicity and clarity. In other words a 'rhetoric of simplicity'.

Reason! The demon of reason invoked by the men of refined artistic sensibility! Reason is necessary in order to explain the principle of aesthetic honesty since moral intuition is only ineffective where misapprehensions have become deeply engrained over a long period. To defend such faith in truth, sincerity and clarity we marshal reason, science, and technique.

* * *

We consider that a construction becomes 'architecture' when it detaches itself from boorish utilitarian concerns (through its specific attributes) and, most importantly, retains decorative character. In other words, there is a hierarchy expressed in the forms [employed], and a 'differentiation' in genre similar, for instance, to that between poetry and fiction.

* * *

Figurative arts such as painting and sculpture are distinct from architecture for differing reasons: the aesthetic factor is predominant and decisive, since they draw inspiration from nature which is 'external' to the artist and exists independently from their decision to reproduce, interpret, or symbolise it. Whereas for both these arts there is a 'truth' from which to compare a language of forms and colours, architecture does not have an absolute reference to 'imitate' (the colours of a sunset or the silhouette of a human figure). The architectural construct, as a formal expression, is purely geometrical, abstract, interiorised, and detached from any possibility of 'external imitation'. However, [the nature of] this artifice, which is more abstract than any other human language, has been invented by human society to provide for its own needs. Why do we build? This is not, then, to imitate nature, nor for superfluous amusement or as a spiritual exercise. Construction is born out of necessity. Architecture is a service. The starting point remains strictly and rigorously utilitarian: we define space to protect ourselves from the cold and inclement elements.

* * *

'Usefulness' serves a practical function defined in time and space; 'abstraction' requires a deep sincerity and emancipation from 'verism' and cultural influences of an academic or scholarly kind; 'coherence' identifies with a spiritual unity and a unity of language, adhering to the moral, economic, social, technical conditions of the ambient environment from which they emerge.

* * *

GIUSEPPE PAGANO

In order to aspire to fundamental truths and understand architecture as a social mission, it is necessary to move beyond the decorative shell and go to the heart of tradition, to violate personal vanity and consider the issue of contemporary taste as an issue of content. It is not about a 'new Rationalist academia' but rather a 'new constructive reality'.

*   *   *

Is there an aesthetic of the structural frame? When we said that taste and artistic 'fantasy' precede technical implementation, we also implicitly said that we cannot entertain artistic creativity without making use of the vocabulary provided by contemporary techniques. In other words, modern technology is not a sufficient and necessary condition to generate an artwork; nonetheless, it is also clear that our creative imagination cannot ignore the developments of contemporary technology.

*   *   *

The material revolution introduced by frame construction in contrast to load-bearing walls is revealed in the nature of the structural diagram. In fact the introduction of a tectonic skeleton impacts on structural analysis since it adds 'forces' other than the solely gravitational. It breaks the relationship between architrave and column; it also breaks the continuity with which stresses are distributed, and therefore radically transforms how structural members rest on and support each other as well as the expression of the cantilever or suspension. By utilising concrete to build frame structures, the principles of statics adhere to those employed in nature, be it the human body or the leaf of a tree. A structural frame in steel extends these concepts as it opens up new possibilities of expression: for instance, thinner columns, lightness, rapid assembly, [explicit] control, absence of shuttering, strength in tension, exceptional capacity to cope with high sheer and compression stresses, as well as a playful potential to extend, add, change, and deform the structural cage without weakening it. Its apotheosis is the skyscraper.

However, in order for 'modern' eye to become accustomed to and appreciative of steel structures: their interplay of tension and compression (*tiranti e di puntoni*), so minimal yet resistant with such a high strength; we have surely not only to see them as engineering structures, but also infused with explicit artistic potential.

*   *   *

When the 'spirit of steel' is complemented by that of 'welding' — a dynamic which deletes and destroys all the received expectations of the architect who thought in terms of gravity and masonry — new horizons are created in the realm of architectural fantasy, the constraints of statics loosen up, and the poetry of space is enriched by these hard won developments. Techniques overcome many antique limitations almost setting aside entirely the constraints of weight, the laws of gravity, and the value of materials. The dream of many precursors – from Wright to Sant'Elia – has become reality. Techniques manifest lyric qualities and provide architects with new forms of an 'elegance of the absolute' and the pleasures of arduousness.

The offices of *Procuratie* in San Marco miraculously anticipate certain ideas, constituting on two levels an uninterrupted row of ninety windows alternated with a slim column. Now, with the same logic, in setting back the structural frame and cantilevering the external wall, we can achieve what to the very rational builder of the *Procuratie* must have naturally represented an ideal solution: doing away with the all the [intermediate] window supports. Medieval town halls; those in Monza and Milan are typical; were articulated on two floors with an open ground level accessible to the public. The same principles can be achieved with minimum thicknesses thanks to steel, and are now advocated by Le Corbusier for aesthetic and urbanistic reasons. The balcony that – like the older bow-window – used to cantilever out over the twenty centuries old Pompeian alley, now becomes the cluster of residential units proposed in Fiorini's tensile structure thanks to steel resolving elements in tension. Everything is an evolution, and even in more apparently daring ideas one can find a link to the past! To trace a genealogical tree of this kind is neither offensive nor pointless, it actually teaches us to make use of tradition as a springboard towards the future. However, those who mistake any reference to tradition as the means to cowardly fall back onto the past betray the legacy of Italian art history as they seek to bolster timid technological progress with aesthetically superseded forms. When one thinks along these lines and a sincere exchange between contemporary art and techniques is lacking, the results are ridiculous museums shaped like ships eventually to be superseded by the 'Conte di Savoia' [Count of Savoia], 'Victoria' or 'Neptunia'.[1] When architecture is denied the right of belonging to its own time, scientific knowledge is deprived of its intellectual breath and [contemporary architecture] is compelled to plagiarise 'foreign' imitations. When one wants to deviate from the absolute laws of artistic morality and seeks to dominate, insinuating a second-hand patriotism imbued with folklore (mainly because of a lack of personal integrity), one also voluntarily excludes oneself from the canons of art history.

For these spiritual and universal reasons also, and not only for the many others suggested by economy, safety, utilitarian convenience and rapidity of construction – one has to become familiar with structural frames. They manifest a message that is not just economical or technical: they speak the inevitable aesthetic language of tomorrow's buildings.

› Note

1   Editors' note: famous Italian cruise liners of the time.

29 Walter Gropius

The new architecture and the Bauhaus (1935)

Walter Gropius, *The New Architecture and the Bauhaus*, London: Faber and Faber, 1935, extracts, pp. 30–38 and 111–112, translation by P. Morton Shand.

› Standardization

The elementary impulse of all national economy proceeds from the desire to meet the needs of the community at less cost and effort by the improvement of its productive organizations. This has led progressively to mechanization, specialized division of labour, and rationalization: seemingly irrevocable steps in industrial evolution which have the same implications for building as for every other branch of organized production. Were mechanization an end in itself it would be an unmitigated calamity, robbing life of half its fulness and variety by stunting men and women into sub-human, robot-like automatons. (Here we touch the deeper causality of the dogged resistance of the old civilization of handicrafts to the new world-order of the machine.) But in the last resort mechanization can have only one object: to abolish the individual's physical toil of providing himself with the necessities of existence in order that hand and brain may be set free for some higher order of activity.

Our age has initiated a rationalization of industry based on the kind of working partnership between manual and mechanical production we call standardization which is already having direct repercussions on building. There can be no doubt that the systematic application of standardization to housing would effect enormous economies—so enormous, indeed, that it is impossible to estimate their extent at present.

Standardization is not an impediment to the development of civilization, but, on the contrary, one of its immediate prerequisites. A standard may be defined as that simplified practical exemplar of anything in general use which embodies a fusion of the best of its anterior forms—a fusion preceded by the elimination of the personal content of their designers and all otherwise ungeneric or non-essential features. Such an impersonal standard is called a 'norm' a word derived from a carpenter's square.

The fear that individuality will be crushed out by the growing 'tyranny' of standardization is the sort of myth which cannot sustain the briefest examination. In all great epochs of history the existence of standards—that is the conscious adoption of type-forms—has been the criterion of a polite and well-ordered society; for it is a commonplace that repetition of the same things for the same purposes exercises a settling and civilizing influence on men's minds.

As the basic cellular unit of that larger unit the street, the dwelling-house represents a typical group-organism. The uniformity of the cells whose multiplication by streets forms the still larger unit of the city therefore calls for formal expression. Diversity in their sizes provides the necessary modicum of variation, which in turn promotes natural competition between dissimilar types developing side by side. The most admired cities of the past are conclusive proof that the reiteration of 'typical' (i.e. typified) buildings notably enhances civic dignity and coherence. As a maturer and more final model than any of the individual prototypes merged in it, an accepted standard is always a formal common denominator of a whole period. The unification of architectural components would have the salutary effect of imparting that homogeneous character to our towns which is the distinguishing mark of a superior urban culture. A prudent limitation of variety to a few standard types of buildings increases their quality and decreases their cost; thereby raising the social level of the population as a whole. Proper respect for tradition will find a truer echo in these than in the miscellaneous solutions of an often arbitrary and aloof individualism because the greater communal utility of the former embodies a deeper architectural significance. The concentration of essential qualities in standard types presupposes methods of unprecedented industrial potentiality, which entail capital outlay on a scale that can only be justified by mass-production.

*   *   *

› Structural instruction

*   *   *

No one who has explored the sources of the movement I have called the New Architecture can possibly subscribe to the claim that it is based on an anti-traditional obsession for mechanistic technique *qua* mechanistic technique, which blindly seeks to destroy all deeper national loyalties and is doomed to lead to the deification of pure materialism. The laws by which it seeks to restrict arbitrary caprice are the fruit of a most thorough and conscientious series of investigations. In these I am proud to have taken a share. And I may add in parenthesis that I belong to a Prussian family of architects in which the tradition of Schinkel—the contemporary as well as the 'opposite number' of your own Soane was part of our heritage. This in itself helps to convince me that my conception of the role of the New Architecture is nowhere and in no sense in opposition to 'Tradition' properly so called. 'Respect for Tradition' does not mean the complacent tolerance of elements which have been a matter of fortuitous chance or of individual eccentricity; nor does it mean the acceptance of domination by bygone aesthetic forms. It means, and always has meant, the preservation of essentials in the process of striving to get at what lies at the back of all materials and every technique, by giving semblance to the one with the intelligent aid of the other.

Industrial Production
and the Collective

30 Le Corbusier

Mass produced buildings (1924)

Le Corbusier, 'Mass produced buildings', *L'Almanach d'Architecture*, Paris, 1924, pp. 102–103. English translation: Tim and Charlotte Benton (ed.), *Form and Function*, London: Crosby Lockwood Staples/Open University Press, 1975, extracts pp. 134 and 135.

*   *   *

Mass production demands a search for standards. Standards lead to perfection.

When it is decided to make 100,000 items, that item is examined very closely, that one must meet 100, or 1000 requirements, which are the requirements of 100, 1000 or 100,000 individuals. If the requirements of 100,000 individuals are satisfied, it can be said that the human constants have been met and that a being has been created *which is like a son to Man*. The sole underlying principle of art must be the deep satisfaction of human needs. What else is our folklore which has survived over the centuries, if not a focus on the human scale of profoundly unanimous feelings, expressed in forms which have a truly universal effect upon all men? When 100,000 people have formed an opinion about a single issue, then a choice has been made, a positive judgement has been formed and perfection is attained. A standard is the result of a process of selection.

But there is another reason for the enduring quality and beauty of the standard. To create a standard you must satisfy completely economic criteria. You must find the exact, and not the approximate solution. And precision is the essence of beauty. Beauty consists of emotive interactions and only very precise constituents can interact. Economy is the fundamental principle of beauty. Economy is the most elevated sense of the word.

Now, economy in the most brutal sense of the word dictates the methods of mass production. When I make a single object, the wastage of materials, effort and time does not matter. Multiplied by 100,000, such wastage becomes unacceptable. At that moment economy in the brutal, materialistic sense, becomes economy in the most elevated sense.

*   *   *

Little by little this new spirit is forming. The greatest crisis of the present day stems from the conflict between our new situation and our way of thinking which is retarded by adherence to traditional practices and beliefs.

There are positive signs that, faced with the new facts, we are forming a new spirit and approaching harmony; the signs are clear: the demise of the decorative arts, the arrival of a purified, intense, concentrated art, with a strongly poetic content (modern art; cubism in particular is an early example); slowly, construction sites will adapt to industrialisation; the introduction of mechanisation in construction work will lead to the general acceptance of *standard elements;* even the design of houses will alter, under the sway of the new economics; the standard elements will provide unity of detail, and unity of detail is an indispensable requirement of architectural beauty. Then our towns will lose that appearance of chaos which blights them at the moment. Order will reign and new networks of streets, more immense and with a wealth of architectural solutions will present us with magnificent sights.

Thanks to the machine, to the identification of what is typical, to the process of selection, to the establishment of a standard, a style will assert itself. That order which the poet seeks by looking back to past eras, will reign once again; the poet must look forward, holding in his hand a ball of shining steel as a symbol of perfection henceforth attainable; he must be the advocate of order, and must bring to the new order of things, his spirit in its quest for harmony. New patterns will be established; the style of our time . . .

31 Mies van der Rohe

Industrial building (1924)

Mies van der Rohe, 'Industrielles Bauen', *G: Material zur elementaren Gestaltung,* 3, 1924. English facsimile edition: Detlef Mertins and Michael W. Jennings (ed.), *G: An Avant-garde Journal of Art, Architecture, Design, and Film 1923–1926*, Los Angeles, CA: Getty Publications, 2010, pp. 120–122, translation by Steven Lindberg with Margareta Ingrid Christian.

Until recently, the need to industrialize the building trade was disputed by nearly all the groups involved, and I view it as progress that this question is now being discussed by a fairly large group, even if only a few are actually persuaded. Advancing industrialization would also have taken hold of the building trades, without any concern for antiquated opinions and emotional values, had not special circumstances obstructed its path. I view the industrialization of the building trade as the key problem of building in our time. If we achieve this industrialization, then the social, economic, technical, and even artistic questions can be resolved easily. The question of how to carry out this industrialization can perhaps be answered by trying to determine what has been blocking its path until now. The assumption that backward business practices are the cause is inaccurate. They are not the cause but the effect of a state of affairs, and they are not at all in conflict with the nature of the old building economy. The attempt to establish new business practices has been made repeatedly, but it has only addressed those aspects of the building trade that permit industrialization. In addition, the assembly line character of today's building has, no doubt, been overestimated. It has been applied almost exclusively in large hall structures for industry and agriculture, and indeed it was companies using iron construction that were the first to produce ready-to-assemble construction parts in their factories. Recently, the lumber industry has also sought to produce its construction parts by industrial means in order to turn building into a process of pure assembly. With almost every other kind of building, the entire building shell and large parts of the interior construction have been executed in the same way from time immemorial, and their character is derived purely from the crafts. This character can be changed neither by economic forms nor by work methods, and it is precisely what guarantees the livelihood of small businesses. The use of larger and other stone formats can of course save material and labor costs, as the new building methods have demonstrated, but that in no way alters the craft character of building. It should be noted, moreover, that brick masonry has undeniable advantages over these new building methods. The point is not so much to rationalize the working methods used thus far, as to fundamentally reshape the building trade as a whole.

As long as we use essentially the same materials, the character of building will not change, and, as I have already mentioned, this character ultimately determines business practices. The industrialization of the building trade is a question of materials. Consequently, a call for a new building material is its first precondition. Our technology must and will succeed in inventing a new building material that can be produced technically and processed industrially; one that is solid, weather-resistant, and sound- and heat-proof. It will have to be a light material, which not only permits industrial processes but demands them. The industrial production of all parts can only be truly rationalized during the process of manufacture. Then the work at the building site will be exclusively one of assemblage, and it will be reduced in time to an unsuspected degree. That, in turn, will significantly reduce the costs of building. In addition, the new architectural efforts will also find their true tasks. I am convinced that the building trade, in the form it has existed hitherto, will be destroyed. However, anyone who might regret that the house of the future will no longer be produced by craftsmen should recall that the automobile is no longer built by wheelwrights either.

The industrialisation of construction depends upon materials. Anyone expecting to reach the industrialisation of construction only through the active and contemporary form of organisation is wrong.[1]

1   Editors' note: this statement was repeated in French and Russian in the original.

32 Mart Stam

Collective design (1924)

Mart Stam, 'Kollektive Gestaltung', *ABC: Beiträge zum Bauen*, 1 (first series), 1924. Reprint: *ABC: Beiträge zum Bauen Contributions on Building 1924–1928*, Werner Möller (ed.), Baden, CH: Verlag Lars Müller, 1993, 'Commentary' p. 10, translation by Catherine Schelbert.

The struggle for survival is becoming more and more acute, and the supreme, united efforts of all peoples are required as never before. Production, the main issue in this struggle, is intimately bound up with the steadily increasing populations of the world; the path of the future is a progressive economy, i.e. better exploitation of materials and greater production in less time. Production is to be understood above all as the manufacture of foodstuffs, and further, of utensils and shelter – the house.

To ensure speedy and profitable labor, the engineer organizes the mechanical forces and, with the help of science, seeks to maximize efficiency, to discover the most economic combinations of effort in all areas. In this organizational task, artists must stand side by side with engineers. In addition to a scientific knowledge of materials and their economic demands, the former must dispose of an inner insight, an awareness of the pure, elemental value of materials.

The engineer for his part will invest his rational powers in improving the system of production down to the finest details; he will construct his machines with ever greater consistency and expediency. On the other hand, he will create new technical potential for public and domestic life. As this work progresses, the scientific achievements of each generation will in turn serve as points of departure for the studies and developments of the next. In this way, the machine, the entire process of production, the technical universe will approach greater and greater perfection through the support of research conducted by thousands of brains.

Next to the engineer, who is rationally concerned with the properties of materials, with their scientific application and with the discovery of new modes of application through the combination of new properties – next to the engineer stands the artist.

The artist must acquire knowledge, must master scientific facts, but after that he must understand the materials, he must understand the larger organic context that redeems all things from their status as isolated objects, thus placing them in and subordinating them to the totality of laws that dominate the cosmos.

Artists must discover in each object the essence of these laws in order to acquire the ability to organize things even better than the engineer. They will find the most elemental expression for the essence of the task at hand, the expression of the task itself, formed by means of suitable materials in their most suitable form.

Thus design will emerge that is removed from any formalistic tendency, that is not born of a particular artist's disposition or the fantastic inspiration of the moment but is instead solidly based on the general, the absolute.

Thus design will emerge that turns to collective means for every form of expression.

The engineer and the artist should be able to build on what their comrades have succeeded in bringing about before them –

Thus development will be possible.

33 Walter Gropius

Principles of Bauhaus production [Dessau] (1926)

Walter Gropius, 'Principles of Bauhaus production [Dessau]', Ulrich Conrads (ed.), *Programmes and Manifestoes on 20th-century Architecture*, London: Lund Humphries/Cambridge MA: MIT Press, 1970, extract p. 96, translated by Michael Bullock.

*   *   *

The creation of standard types for all practical commodities of everyday use is a social necessity.

On the whole, the necessities of life are the same for the majority of people. The home and its furnishings are mass consumer goods, and their design is more a matter of reason than a matter of passion. The machine – capable of producing standardized products – is an effective device, which, by means of mechanical aids – steam and electricity – can free the individual from working manually for the satisfaction of his daily needs and can provide him with mass-produced products that are cheaper and better than those manufactured by hand. There is no danger that standardization will force a choice upon the individual, since, due to natural competition, the number of available types of each object will always be ample to provide the individual with a choice of design that suits him best.

The Bauhaus workshops are essentially laboratories in which prototypes of products suitable for mass production and typical of our time are carefully developed and constantly improved.

In these laboratories the Bauhaus wants to train a new kind of collaborator for industry and the crafts, who has an equal command of both technology and form.

To reach the objective of creating a set of standard prototypes which meet all the demands of economy, technology and form, requires the selection of the best, most versatile, and most thoroughly educated men who are well grounded in workshop experience and who are imbued with an exact knowledge of the design elements of form and mechanics and their underlying laws.

34 Hannes Meyer

The new world (1926)

Hannes Meyer, 'Die Neue Welt', *DasWerk*, vol. 13, 7, 1926, pp. 205–224. English translation from: Tim and Charlotte Benton (ed.), *Form and Function*, London: Crosby Lockwood Staples/OUP, 1975, extracts pp. 107–108.

*   *   *

Each age demands its own form. It is our mission to give our new world a new shape with the means of today. But our knowledge of the past is a burden that weighs upon us, and inherent in our advanced education are impediments tragically barring our new paths. The unqualified affirmation of the present age presupposes the ruthless denial of the past. The ancient institutions of the old – the classical grammar schools and the academies – are growing obsolete. The municipal theatres and the museums are deserted. The jittery helplessness of applied arts is proverbial. In their place, unburdened by classical airs and graces, by an artistic confusion of ideas or the trimmings of applied art, the witnesses of a new era are arising: industrial fairs, grain silos, music halls, airports, office chairs, standard goods. All these things are the product of a formula: function multiplied by economics. They are not works of art. Art is composition, purpose is function. The composition of a dock seems to us a nonsensical idea, but the composition of a town plan, a block of flats . . .? Building is a technical not an aesthetic process, artistic composition does not rhyme with the function of a house matched to its purpose. Ideally and in its elementary design our house is a living machine. Retention of heat, insulation, natural and artificial lighting, hygiene, weather protection, car maintenance, cooking, radio, maximum possible relief for the housewife, sexual and family life, etc. are the determining lines of force. The house is their component. (Snugness and prestige are not leitmotifs of the dwelling house: the first resides in the human heart and not in the Persian carpet, the second in the attitude of the house-owner and not on the wall of the room!) Today we have new building materials at our disposal for building a house: aluminium and duralium in plates, rods and bars, Euböolith, Ruberoid, Torfoleum, Eternit, rolled glass, Triplex sheets, reinforced concrete, glass bricks, faience, steel frames, concrete frame slabs and pillars, Trolite, Galalith, Cellon, Goudron, Ripolin, indanthrene paints, etc. We organise these building elements into a constructive unity in accordance with the purpose of the building and economic principles. Architecture has ceased to be an agency continuing the growth of tradition or an embodiment of emotion.

Individual form, building mass, natural colour of material and surface texture come into being automatically and this functional conception of building in all its aspects leads to pure construction. Pure construction is the characteristic feature of the new world of forms. Constructive form is not peculiar to any country; it is cosmopolitan and the expression of an international philosophy of building. Internationality is a prerogative of our time.

*　　*　　*

In Esperanto we construct a supranational language according to the law of least resistance in standard shorthand, a script with no tradition. The constructive mode of thought is most urgently needed in town planning. Unless we approach problems of town planning with the same impartiality as the factory engineer, we shall throttle the social life of the modern city through monument worship and uncritically accepted ideas about street axes and viewing points. The city is the most complex biological agglomeration, and it must be consciously regulated and constructively shaped by man. The demands we make on life today are all of the same nature depending on social stratification. The surest sign of true community is the satisfaction of the same needs by the same means. The upshot of such a collective demand is the standard product. The folding chair, roll-top desk, light bulb, bath tub and portable gramophone are typical standard products manufactured internationally and showing a uniform design. They are apparatus in the mechanisation of our daily life. They are manufactured in quantity as a mass-produced article, as a mass-produced device, as a mass-produced structural element, as a mass-produced house. The standard mental product is called a 'hit'. Because of the standardisation of his needs as regards housing, food and mental sustenance, the semi-nomad of our modern productive system has the benefit of freedom of movement, economic simplification and relaxation, all of which are vitally important to him. The degree of our standardisation is an index of our communal productive system.

35 Hannes Meyer

Building (1928)

Hannes Meyer, 'Bauen', *Zeitschrift für Gestaltung* (Bauhaus Dessau), vol. 2, 4, 1928. English translation by Michael Bullock, from: Ulrich Conrads (ed.), *Programmes and Manifestoes on 20th-century Architecture*, London: Lund Humphries/Cambridge MA: MIT Press, 1970, pp. 117–120.

building

all things in this world are a product of the formula: (function times economy).

all these things are, therefore, not works of art:

all art is composition and, hence, is unsuited to achieve goals.

all life is function and is therefore unartistic.

the idea of the 'composition of a harbour' is hilarious!

but how is a town plan designed? or a plan of a dwelling? composition or function? art or life?

building is a biological process. building is not an aesthetic process.

in its design the new dwelling becomes not only a 'machine for living', but also a biological apparatus serving the needs of body and mind.

the new age provides new building materials for the new way of building houses:

reinforced concrete	aluminium	ripolin
synthetic rubber	euböolith	viscose
synthetic leather	plywood	asbestos concrete
porous concrete	hard rubber	bitumen
woodmetal	torfoleum	canvas
wire-mesh glass	silicon steel	asbestos
pressed cork	cold glue	acetone
synthetic resin	cellular concrete	casein
synthetic horn	rolled glass	trolite
synthetic wood	xelotect	tombac

we organize these building materials into a constructive whole based on economic principles, thus the individual shape, the body of the structure, the colour of the material and the surface texture evolve by themselves and are determined by life. (snugness and prestige are not leitmotifs for dwelling construction.) (the first depends on the human heart and not on the walls of a room . . . (the second manifests itself in the manner of the host and not by his persian carpet!)

architecture as 'an emotional act of the artist' has no justification.
architecture as 'a continuation of the traditions of building' means being carried along by the history of architecture.
this functional, biological interpretation of architecture as giving shape to the functions of life, logically leads to pure construction: this world of constructive forms knows no native country. it is the expression of an international attitude in architecture. internationality is a privilege of the period.
pure construction is the basis and the characteristic of the new world of forms.

1. sex life	5. personal hygiene	9. cooking
2. sleeping habits	6. weather protection	10. heating
3. pets	7. hygiene in the home	11. exposure to the sun
4. gardening	8. car maintenance	12. service

these are the only motives when building a house. we examine the daily routine of everyone who lives in the house and this gives us the function-diagram for the father, the mother, the child, the baby and the other occupants. we explore the relationships of the house and its occupants to the world outside: postman, passer-by, visitor, neighbour, burglar, chimney-sweep, washerwoman, policeman, doctor, charwoman, playmate, gas inspector, tradesman, nurse, and messenger boy, we explore the relationships of human beings and animals to the garden, and the interrelationships between human beings, pets, and domestic insects, we determine the annual fluctuations in the temperature of the ground and from that calculate the heat loss of the floor and the resulting depth required for the foundation blocks, the geological nature of the soil informs us about its capillary capability and determines whether water will naturally drain away or whether drains are required. we calculate the angle of the sun's incidence during the course of the year according to the latitude of the site. with that information we determine the size of the shadow cast by the house on the garden and the amount of sun admitted by the window into the bedroom. we estimate the amount of daylight available for interior working areas. we compare the heat conductivity of the outside walls with the humidity of the air outside the house. we already know about the circulation of air in a heated room, the visual and acoustical relationships to neighbouring dwellings are most carefully considered. knowing the atavistic inclinations of the future inhabitants with respect to the kind of wood finish we can offer, we select the interior finish for the standardized, prefabricated dwelling accordingly: marble-grained pine, austere poplar, exotic okumé or silky maple. colour to us is merely a means for intentional psychological influence or a means of orientation, colour is never a false copy of various kinds of material. we loathe variegated colour, we consider paint to be a protective coating. where we think colour to be psychically indispensable, we include in our calculation the amount of light reflection it offers. we avoid using a purely white finish on the house. we consider the body of the house to be an accumulator of the sun's warmth . . .

the new house is a prefabricated building for site assembly; as such it is an industrial product and the work of a variety of specialists: economists, statisticians, hygienists, climatologists, industrial engineers, standardization experts, heating engineers . . . and the architect? . . . he was an artist and now becomes a specialist in organization!

the new house is a social enterprise, it frees the building industry from partial seasonal unemployment and from the odium of unemployment relief work. by rationalized housekeeping methods it saves the housewife from household slavery, and by rationalized gardening methods it protects the householder from the dilettantism of the small gardener. it is primarily a social enterprise because it is – like every government standard – the standardized, industrial product of a nameless community of inventors.

the new housing project as a whole is to be the ultimate aim of public welfare and as such is an intentionally organized, public-spirited project in which collective and individual energies are merged in a public-spiritedness based on an integral, co-operative foundation. the modernness of such an estate does not consist of a flat roof and a horizontal-vertical arrangement of the façade, but rather of its direct relationship to human existence. in it we have given thoughtful consideration to the tensions of the individual, the sexes, the neighbourhood and the community, as well as to geophysical relationships.

building	is the deliberate organization of the processes of life.
building	as a technical process is therefore only one part of the whole process. the functional diagram and the economic programme are the determining principles of the building project.
building	is no longer an individual task for the realization of architectural ambitions.
building	is the communal effort of craftsmen and inventors. only he who, as a master in the working community of others, masters life itself . . . is a master builder.
building	then grows from being an individual affair of individuals (promoted by unemployment and the housing shortage) into a collective affair of the whole nation.
building	**is nothing but organization: social, technical, economic, psychological organization.**

Rationalism in Retrospect

36 Reyner Banham

Theory and design in the first machine age (1960)

Reyner Banham, *Theory and Design in the First Machine Age*, London: Architectural Press, 1960, extracts pp. 306–308, 311 and 320.

› Germany: the encyclopaedics

*   *   *

Its title, *Beton als Gestalter*,[1] gives a false impression of it, and suggests that it belongs to a current of thought which was becoming increasingly prevalent at this time, tending to interpret the International Style in purely Rationalist terms, as the product of the materials and techniques employed. Lissitsky may well have started this tendency in German-speaking circles, for Hannes Meyer who took it into the Bauhaus had come under his influence, and it is noteworthy that the young Italian architects who formed the like-thinking *Movimento Italiano per l'Architettura Razionale* had also come under Constructivist influence. It is also noteworthy that they were not anti-Traditionalists, and this neo-Rationalist movement in general found considerable reinforcement in the past, as in such studies of the nineteenth century as Giedion's *Bauen in Frankreich*, which will be discussed later.

But Berlin played no great part in this development, which was largely the work of 'provincials' from Switzerland, Italy, and the Anglo-Saxon countries. Though Berlin writers had plenty to say about the new materials at this time their tone was not Rationalistic. Thus in *Glas im Bau und als Gebrauchsgegenstand*, Artur Korn, whose architecture at this time had taken a very tough, almost *G*, quality, nevertheless writes of glass in an almost poetic tone, laying particular stress on its aesthetic qualities. Indeed, his book begins with an almost Scheerbartian apotheosis of mediaeval stained glass, and then goes on

> Nothing has been lost of the riches of those earlier creations, but it has been reworked in new materials for new functions. A new world of glass has been opened that concedes nothing to the windows of the Gothic world in beauty.

But we have secured a great advance over them . . . in making an independent glass skin. No more wall and window, even though the window might be the dominant part— this window is the wall itself, this wall is itself the window.

And therewith a development is consummated, something absolutely new over and above all that the past can show: the denial of the outer wall that for thousands of years had to be made of solid materials—stone, wood or something similar. In this new dispensation the outer wall no longer makes itself visible.

The interior spatial depths, the form-giving structural frame are in evidence, appearing through the glass wall which itself is only hinted at, only barely to be appreciated through reflected light, distortion and mirror effects.

And therewith appears the truly unique quality of glass compared to all materials hitherto in use: It is there and it is not there.

It is the great mystery membrane, delicate and strong at the same time.

The words 'there and not there' are to be interpreted in more than one sense, for he cites examples of transparency (the Bauhaus), reflectivity (Mies's glass towers) and of the use of non-reflecting glass as an invisible barrier against the weather (a shop designed by himself and his partner Konrad Weitzmann). But his attitude, if poetically inclined, remains practical: he does not philosophise.

Hilberseimer does; and the introduction to *Beton als Gestalter* is a reflective essay on the relationship of architecture as an art to science and technology. His opening paragraph rejects at once both the Rationalist determinism of the nineteenth century and the science-as-spiritualisation of *de Stijl*

The scientific spirit of the nineteenth century had for its ultimate goal the conquest of the forces of nature. The rapid perfection of scientific methods of research and their technical aids led in every field to unexpected results and caused, for a whole epoch, an over-estimation of the possibilities of technology. The dangers that lurked here for the *Geisteswissenschaften,* through the connection of material conclusions with immaterial conceptions—these dangers can fortunately be avoided with the disciplines grouped as 'Technology'. The discoveries and inventions in this province can be compared directly with reality, and be corrected accordingly

This separation of the spiritual sciences from physical science and technology is remarkable for the time at which it was written, but—since he clearly includes aesthetics among the spiritual sciences—it also involves him in some rather perilous reasoning. Having defined the relationship of technique and architecture thus

. . . that technique is never more than a means for the art of building, that technique and art are profoundly different.

after having praised engineers for perfecting concrete construction unrestricted by aesthetic preconceptions and free from nostalgia for things outside their technique.

he is in a strong position in discussing the quality of buildings where conscious aesthetic intention is apparent, but badly placed where it is not. Thus, he is well placed to castigate Auguste Perret and Martin Elsässer for dressing up their concrete in period style, or Rietveld who is blamed for indulging in *Konstruktivismus* and *artistisches Spiel,* those who disguise the economical aims of reinforced concrete construction with gratuitous mass, and even Gottfried Semper

who wished to hear of iron used only to increase the tensile strength of mass construction

and not as a visible architectural element in its own right.

But he is badly placed to evaluate a class of buildings that have had peculiar standing in the eyes of Modernists ever since Muthesius—engineering structures.

If we categorise constructions and projects conceived in the spirit of reinforced concrete construction as architecture, then the aesthetic rules connected with and derived from stone building will no longer serve. For a new sense of space has become effective, a new relationship of support and load that has radically affected the optical aspect of buildings.

Out of mental convenience all this has been given out as 'Neue Sachlichkeit' or simply technology, without, to be sure, anyone having any standards for where technique leaves off and creativity begins. Certainly, purely technical construction is still not architecture, but even in the field of so-called technological building it would still be difficult to draw a line between the creative and the uncreative. And besides, many of these buildings are of an astonishing architectonic quality, powerful originality and primitive architectural feeling.

He offers no solution to this dilemma, except possibly a marginal reference to the concept of *Einheit Von Aussen-und Innenbau* as a key to the new architecture, but his closing paragraph suggests that he has little faith in any deductive formulation of rules of judgement.

Aristotle justly observed that art runs ahead of its theories. The creator is intuitive—the work comes spontaneously from his hands according to its own rules. All science, all research, all perception cannot replace the naive certainty of the artist. The new therefore can be judged neither by the old rules nor by these deduced rules . . .

Such reasonable doubt, anti-Rationalist but not irrational, seems not to have been shared by those who, in the same two or three years sought to fix the position of the Modern Movement in history. Either they did not recognise the emergence of a specifically new architecture, and gave blanket treatment to all Twentieth century architecture, progressive or otherwise. Or, alternatively, they recognised a new architecture, but saw it as a continuation of the Rationalist tradition of the previous century. The first attitude made it possible to bring Modern architecture within the scope of existing series of art-historical publications—three volumes of the *Blauen Bücher* edited by Walter Müller-Wulckow and dealing with Factories, Housing, and Public Buildings respectively, put Modern German architecture into an established semi-popular series of picture-books, while Gustav Platz's compendious *Die Baukunst der neuesten Zeit* elevated it to the level of the Propyläen-Verlag, and thus to the highest levels of commercial art-historical publishing.

Works that recognised the emergence of a new architecture but linked it back exclusively to restricted aspects of the nineteenth century also appeared at both the popular and specialist levels. The most influential of the former class was undoubtedly Bruno Taut's *Modern Architecture*, which appeared in a German edition as *Die Neue Baukunst in Europa und Amerika* in the same year (1929).

* * *

While, clearly, Giedion's terms of reference did not necessarily require him to recognise every beginning, and while he has subsequently repaired the omission in his later book *Space Time and Architecture*, the absence of the theoretical and aesthetic 'débris' from *Bauen in Frankreich* has given most of its readers the impression that the International Style is directly descended from the *Grands Constructeurs* of the nineteenth century, and is purely Rational and Functional in its approach. Such an idea was sympathetic to many architects at the time, and it was of particular usefulness to apologists of the style in Anglo-Saxon countries where, despite the efforts of Geoffrey Scott, firmly established Ruskinian prejudices made argument from moral, rather than aesthetic grounds, more effective. Yet, by a fortunate historical irony, when men in those countries set out to train young architects in the supposedly Functionalist disciplines of the new architecture, the only pedagogic textbook available to them, the book that made the Bauhaus method available to the world, was almost exactly opposite in bias, was sophisticated on just those subjects where Giedion was naïve, and by a further historical irony, was the work of the typographer of *Bauen in Frankreich,* Moholy-Nagy.

* * *

> ### Conclusion: functionalism and technology

By the middle of the Thirties it was already common practice to use the word *Functionalism,* as a blanket term for the progressive architecture of the Twenties and its canon of approved forerunners that had been set by writers like Sigfried Giedion. Yet, leaving the shortlived *G* episode in Berlin on one side, it is doubtful if the ideas implicit in Functionalism—let alone the word itself—were ever significantly present in the minds of any of the influential architects of the period. Scholiasts may care to dispute the exact date on which this misleading word was first used as the label for the International Style, but there is little doubt that the first consequential use was in Alberto Sartoris's book *Gli Elementi dell'architettura Funzionale,* which appeared in Milan in 1932. Responsibility for the term is laid on Le Corbusier's shoulders—the work was originally to have been called *Architettura Razionale*, or something similar, but, in a letter which is reprinted as a preface to the book, Le Corbusier wrote

> The title of your book is limited: it is a real fault to be constrained to put the word *Rational* on one side of the barricade, and leave only the word *Academic* to be put on the other. Instead of Rational say *Functional*. . . .

Most critics of the Thirties were perfectly happy to make this substitution of words, but not of ideas, and *Functional* has, almost without exception been interpreted in the limited sense that Le Corbusier attributed to *Rational,* a tendency which culminated in the revival of a nineteenth-century determinism such as both Le Corbusier and Gropius had rejected . . .

› Note

1   Julius Vischer and Ludwig Hilberseimer, *Beton als Gestalter*, Stuttgart: Julius Hoffmann, 1928.

37 Hans Schmidt

Modular co-ordination in architecture (1964)

Hans Schmidt, 'Modularkoordination in der Architektur', from: Bruno Flierl (ed.), *Hans Schmidt – Beiträge zur Architektur 1924–1964*, Zürich: gta Verlag, 1993, extracts pp. 182–187, translation by the editors.

*   *   *

It is plausible [to assert] that a purely intuitive 'architecture of the contingent' is incompatible both with a unified geometric system and also, similarly, with industrial mass production. Many architects and architectural theoreticians thus consequently draw the conclusion that in the future we will have to speak of an architecture of 'creative freedom' on the one hand and of a 'non-architecture' epitomised by mass-production on the other. Industrial mass production in the form of 'catalogue architecture' would therefore ultimately lead to the end of architecture. Can we agree with such a conclusion?

We have to start from the assumption of the principle of unity: of function, building technology, economy and architecture. If we maintain this principle, it becomes absurd to visualise the end of architecture simply because one of these [aspects], in our case building technology, is fundamentally changing.

We have to look at the particular technological, economic and social aspects of mass production. Consider the immense need for flats, schools and hospitals, which is caused by the rapid growth of our global population, or the large stock of existing, aged and compromised houses, which we need to replace with new buildings. These demands can only be fulfilled through a radical increase in building production utilising the methods of industrialisation. With this in mind, not only the technical and social aspects, but also the aesthetic dimension of architecture changes significantly.

According to the critique proposed by the enemies of 'catalogue-architecture', an architecture that in the first instance stems from technical, economical and social necessities should lose its intrinsic character (as architecture).

The historical experience of traditional towns and villages manifests 'an architecture of the people' arising from harsh necessities and realised with restricted means. Today we not only admire Greek temples and Gothic cathedrals, but also this modest architecture (of the masses) for its beauty. But we have also experienced over (almost) one hundred years the development of an architecture which had forgotten that 'necessity is the master (teacher) of the arts'. The fatal consequences of this architecture of abundance, of the exceptional, of 'individual' freedom, are well established. Should we continue to pursue the same spectacle, if only with a changed décor?

Today we are speaking of a 'turning point' in architecture. Such a point of transition also demands new concepts and methods in the artistic realm. Among the issues dominating today's discussions regarding industrial building, the question of monotony is a central focus. Every [system of] mass production based on extensive standardisation imposes a certain level of uniformity on its products. But it would be wrong in the first instance to blame the system of modular coordination for this.

Uniformity evolves only through [the fact of] the large number of identical elements, which a range based on modular coordination (the 'catalogue') makes available to the architect. But a variation of these elements is, within the frame of modular coordination, perfectly possible. We have already seen, in considering the question of technical developments, that there is no limit to the development of elements with regard to materials and construction. But [similarly] a variation and an expansion of the aesthetic range is also perfectly possible.

The task of architects will be to find the right balance between the potential variability of elements and the unity of the building. One premise, however, is indispensable. Architects must have the requisite influence on the mass production of elements, and on their aesthetic quality. They will need to become a determining influence in collaboration about the 'catalogue'. Architecture will otherwise turn into a [no more than a free market] Bazaar.

We speak of monotony not only with regard to individual buildings, but more particularly with urban design in mind. But this question was addressed in the 'mass' construction of cities during the last century. It is consequently not necessarily a typical trait of industrialised building.

As a remedy against monotony in urban planning today we generally see a desire to create the greatest possible variation in the architecture, in the scale, and in the arrangement of buildings. As a result in many cases we find residential areas lacking urbanity and running the danger, in seeking the greatest possible diversity, of a new form of monotony, namely disorder and anarchy.

In the end, the question of monotony is not an aesthetic problem, but one of society. The most famous cities of the past demonstrate the artistic potential of uniformity. The Rue de Rivoli in Paris; Bedford Square in London and the frontage of St Mark's Square in Venice, were erected in an absolutely 'uniform' architecture. The Paris we know and love regulated the architecture of its Boulevards in the form of a singular and uniform pattern of building. Why don't we speak of monotony there?

In all these cases their uniformity has a particular artistic sense motivation? The buildings, Streets and Squares form the city as a social organisation. What we would otherwise perceive as being monotonous is transformed to manifest an inherently artistic quality.

If we understand the art of urban design in its social sense, in being 'of society', the conditions of industrial building will not hinder the task of the urban designer, rather they will support it.

In summary:

Modular coordination represents a geometrical system of order, which enables the uniform mass production of standardised, versatile and interchangeable building elements.

Modular coordination acquires a sense of validation in relationship to the construction of a procedurally uniform and coordinated building industry. The appropriateness and the scale of its implementation depend on a country's prevailing economic conditions.

The relationship between modular coordination and architecture arise from the development of industrial building and mass production. New attitudes and methods become necessary which initiate changes in the practice of architects and urban designers as well as in the social and aesthetic character of their design work.

Editors' note: extracts from a contribution to a colloquium at the TU Delft.

38 Vittorio Gregotti

The fine red thread of Italian rationalism (1978)

Vittorio Gregotti, 'Il filo rosso del razionalismo italiano', *Casabella*, 440/441, 1978, extracts pp. 31–34, translation by M. L. O'S, from the 'Translations and digests' supplement.

It was from Rogers that my generation learned to re-examine history as a theoretical problem. They did this with a rather special concentration, arriving at either a type of diachronic neurosis which tries to follow every flex and change in historical transformation itself, or else obsessed with ideological and general judgement, to counterbalance the gap brought about by the conditions of architectural production between the conservation of its identity and historical reality.

This obsession probably represents, apart from many differences, a possible element of identification for Italian architecture with regard to international debate, and beginning from this obsession, I should here like to pay homage to Rogers's thought and try to establish some possible line of continuity between a part of my generation's architectural production during recent years and the architecture of the Italian rationalist movement of the '30's, which found in "Casabella", if not its entire representation, its most rigorous voice.

* * *

I remember the maquette of that extraordinary project for the new Academy of Brera building designed by Figini, Pollini, Lingeri and Terragni in 1933. I spoke to Pollini, who proudly explained how, in spite of the clean cut of the prismatic plant, they had arranged the parallelepiped so that not even one tree had to be chopped down. I remember what I thought at that time: Goodness! In the heart of the historical centre of Milan, a few metres from the Brera Museum building, the only pre-existing value that they intend to measure themselves against is the tree, which is the precise negation of the historic value of the pre-existing condition.

But of course, thinking about it later, this reasoning of mine was vague and superficial, because the pre-existent was there, right in front of me, completely absorbed by the project, by its ability to specify unambiguously and qualify the spirit of the place and the historical situation. This is done by means of a very fine linguistic skid which defines that project as extremely recognisable with respect to the language of the epoch's international rationalism, even though the authors themselves were not completely aware of it, even though they felt deeply that the internationalist front was the modern front.

Thinking about it, this skid is common to and characteristic of, for better or for worse, the best things pertaining to Italian rationalism. It seems that these things pivot around a mysterious but unitary centre which make them recognisable within the context of the modern movement.

What then is the secret of this identity? It is certainly connected to some idealistic and political ambiguity, and perhaps to a certain contamination with the language of its direct cultural enemies. There is then a double mystery around Italian rationalism: on the one hand its stylistic (horrible word, but apt enough) identity, and on the other the reasons for our present interest in the contradictoriness of its component elements.

*   *   *

All of these projects have some element of coherence: the system of spatial indication is founded upon two linguistically noted instruments, the lattice frame and the screen, but offered as a hypothesis more than as an ordained system; the hypothesis is always specific, never proposed as a final solution: it is the moral duty of clarity without the elimination of risk, acceptance of the fear of emptiness and ambiguity. The tension basically comes from this: it is principally [a contrary], minority tension, the conscious presence of something essential which escapes us, and which is always beyond the ordained.

Building control is always very clearly proposed and defined in a real or virtual way, within precise perspective limits. The questioning originates internally: emptiness, denied symmetries, interruption of the proposed rhythm, articulated appearance of a series of internal plans which propose the principle defence as a reference to the exception. Here then is an un-clarified matter: the treatment of space in a certain way presupposes space itself as an existing and specific data and proposes a creative reasoning upon it.

*   *   *

No, we are not dealing only with an interest in history, but with the form which this interest takes, the form of the defence at any cost of the identity of architecture.

A defence against production relationships as they are at the moment, against the neo-positivist myth of the world game, against graceful, communicative, natural, demagogically participative or formalistically modern architecture, a defence also against the realistic-managerial politics of the institutions; an identity which must be defended today even against academia, from escape [from] the concrete and substantial difficulties of architecture which cannot be confused with illustration nor coincide with design.

A neo-rationalist language then? No, a design of reason, but touched with the awareness of the limits of reason, of the ambiguities and uncertainties which form its width and depth, and which has at the same time the indispensable sidelong glance of its morality.

39 Dennis Doordan

Building modern Italy (1988)

Dennis P. Doordan, *Building Modern Italy: Italian Architecture, 1914–1936*, New York: Princeton Architectural Press, 1988, extracts pp. 51–52 and 73–74.

› Rationalism

*   *   *

The ideas presented in the *Rassegna italiana* articles were absolutely fundamental for the development of Italian Rationalist architecture. As we shall see in later chapters, Gruppo 7's manifesto was repeatedly cited in the following years as a critical document in the formation of new architectural attitudes in Italy. On a number of crucial points, however, the manifesto was frustratingly vague. Although Gruppo 7 emphasized the importance of *type* in Rational design, precisely what they understood by *type* is not clear. At times it seems the group conceived of typologies according to the purpose served by a building (temple, basilica, factory, warehouse, etc.). Elsewhere in the manifesto it appears that material or structural, not programmatic, considerations determined a *type* (stone, concrete, steel, trabeated, arcuated, etc.). Although Gruppo 7 severely criticized contemporary architectural education, their proposals for revising the curriculum dealt primarily with the selection of appropriate architectural models for analysis during the first year's course. In its survey of the international scene in architecture, the group passed some questionable judgments on contemporary developments.

Despite Gruppo 7's desire to distinguish its platform from those advanced by Futurist and Novecento architects, a careful analysis of the Rationalists' position as outlined in the four *Rassegna italiana* articles reveals that they did owe a debt to their predecessors. From the Futurists, they inherited the belief that the conventions of the past were inadequate to meet the challenges of the present. The Rationalists committed themselves to forging a contemporary architectural identity. From the Novecento architects, they accepted the premise that a respect for tradition and a commitment to modernity need not be incompatible positions as long as the architects understood each term correctly. Their own efforts to comprehend as objectively as possible such terms as modernity and tradition reveal the Rationalists to be more realistic than the Futurists and more radical than the Novecento architects.

The Rationalists owed a debt to their transalpine contemporaries as well. The members of Gruppo 7 eagerly devoured any information they could obtain regarding developments in the rest of Europe. Returning from the Paris Fair of 1925, the Futurist Fortunato Depero made available copies of Le Corbusier's *Vers une architecture* as well as catalogs and publications describing the fair's Soviet, Polish, Czech, French, Austrian, and Danish contributions to his longtime friends, and former students Luigi Figini and Gino Pollini, now members of Gruppo 7.[1] Gruppo 7's rhetorical appeal to the "spirito nuovo" echoes Le Corbusier's use of the phrase "*L'Esprit Nouveau:*" Strong parallels also exist between some of the themes discussed in the Rationalist manifesto and progressive architectural theory in Germany. Gruppo 7's discussion of architecture as the expression of the spirit of the age and of the importance of the renunciation of individualism in favor of disciplined team work inevitably brings to mind the similar pronouncements of Walter Gropius and Ludwig Mies van der Rohe on the same subject.

Obviously the Rationalists belonged to the broad European movement involved with the modernization of architectural theory and practice and, equally clearly, the Italians attempted to delineate their own distinctive conception of modern architecture. The desire to explain the complex relationship between Rationalism and contemporary progressive ideologies and to define as precisely as possible their own understanding of terms such as modernity and tradition accounts for the great length of the Rationalist manifesto.

Italian critics tend to express reservations regarding certain aspects of the Rationalist manifesto. They cite the equivocal nature of the relationship between internationalist and nationalist principles as a weak point in the definition of Italian Rationalism. Gruppo 7's development of an architecture with recognizable national characteristics has been interpreted as an obstacle to the effective modernization of Italian architectural practice. The architectural critic Edoardo Persico was one of the first to identify this interest in a national spirit as inimical to the affirmation of a truly modern architecture. In 1933, Persico wrote:

> The greatest obstacle to the integral affirmation of rationalism in Italy was the inability
> of its theoreticians to pose rigorously the problem of the antithesis between national and
> European taste.[2]

Persico's negative assessment, ironic in light of his own contribution to the 1936 Milan Triennale, has been repeated and amplified in much of the post-1945 literature on Italian architecture.[3]

Despite its flaws, the Rationalist manifesto remains an impressive document. The criticisms of Gruppo 7's chauvinism and its avowed interest in a distinctive national identity within the context of progressive European design reflects the narrowness of the interpretive framework often used to discuss modern architecture. In retrospect, Gruppo 7's belief that the principles of functionalism need not preclude the development of an architecture with national characteristics is one of the more intriguing aspects of the Rationalist program. Even if it failed to resolve every issue raised by its framers, the Rationalist manifesto should be recognized as an ambitious proposal for a far reaching revision of the then current way of thinking about architecture in Italy. Gruppo 7 correctly identified most of the major issues which dominated the discussion of architecture in Italy for the next fifteen years: functionalism, rationalized typologies, contemporary aesthetics, respect for tradition, and the role of the individual architect.[4] The sophistication of their argument for the modernization of architectural theory and practice deserves special note in light of the fact that the authors were seven young architectural students with virtually no experience as designers or as polemicists. They would soon gain experience as both.

*   *   *

› The first exhibition of rationalist architecture

*   *   *

Piacentini found the Rationalist formula inadequate for Italy, both technically and aesthetically. He viewed the functionalist credo of the Rationalists as too simplistic and climatically inappropriate; extensive glazing and ribbon windows were feasible in northern Europe, he felt, but the intensity of the Mediterranean sun argued against such devices in Italy. The lack of moldings, pediments, and cornices invited disaster, Piacentini warned, because water would inevitably seep in along the roof line and around windows and destroy first the plaster and then the wall itself. Piacentini's final criticism involved the importance of hierarchy in architecture, an importance, he felt, the Rationalists did not appreciate. He argued that a typological hierarchy existed in architecture and that what was appropriate for certain types, such as factories or commercial buildings, was inappropriate for others, like monumental civic or religious buildings. The Rationalists had not yet developed, in his opinion, an architectural formula subtle and rich enough to accommodate the range of architectural expression necessary in a big city.[5]

In an interview, Alberto Sartoris recalled an anecdote which illustrates Piacentini's ability to pursue seemingly contradictory goals simultaneously. Following the La Sarraz conference of modern architects in 1928, and while formulating his negative critique of the emerging Rationalist movement in Italy, Piacentini apparently applied for membership in the new C.I.A.M.

> We received many telegrams of solidarity from the architects of the "other side" who would have liked to obtain membership . . . The Chief Architect of the city of Geneva, a famous French academician, and our own Piacentini, among others, all wrote to us . . . Everyone received the same reply: congresso—riservato—architetti—moderni.[6]

In May 1929, Adalberto Libera, speaking on behalf of the Rationalists, finally replied to Piacentini's criticisms in an article in *Rassegna italiana*. Libera took a conciliatory tone in his reply; he began by suggesting that Piacentini had misunderstood the Rationalists' position on certain key points and, in particular, their interpretation of the word "rational." Rationalism, Libera explained, depended upon a dualistic conception of architecture. In addition to the traditional, Crocian understanding of architecture as a form of artistic expression springing from the creative intuition of the artist-architect, specific material circumstances conditioned architectural expression. Thus architectural evaluation required the development of a set of criteria that take into account techno-structural as well as aesthetic factors. The Rationalists never meant to deny the importance of aesthetic values, according to Libera, nor did they wish to confine architecture to the material concerns of structure and technique. Rather, they wanted to expand the architect's horizons; they wanted to integrate the aesthetic and the technical aspects of architecture to a far greater degree than was customary in Italy at that time. A building that satisfied the economic and technical aspects of a program without expressing the new spirit of the modern age, however, was not a "Rationalist" building in Libera's opinion, nor was a building that expressed a modern aesthetic sensibility alone, without satisfying programmatic requirements, worthy to be called a "Rationalist" building.

For us the coexistence and the perfect connection of the two elements, materiality and spirituality, is evident and fundamental.[7]

Piacentini had expressed the fear that modern buildings would be out of character in the historic fabric of Italian cities. Libera concluded his reply by claiming that the urban scene was, itself, the product of a long series of juxtapositions of the old and the new, and that Rationalist architecture would take its place among other architectural styles the way the baroque, the Renaissance, and the Gothic had each, in their time, assumed their positions among the monuments of earlier eras.

> Notes

1 Bruno Passamani, *Fortunato Depero* (Rovereto: 1981), 297, note 14; Passamani corrects Carlo Belli's assertions [Origini e sviluppo del Gruppo 7," *La Casa 6* (1959)] regarding when the Rationalists first acquired Le Corbusier's *Vers une architecture*.

2 Edoardo Persico, "Gli architetti italiani," *L'Italia letteraria* (August 6, 1933), in *Edoardo Persico: Scritti d'architettura (1927/1935)*, ed. Guilia Veronesi (Florence: 1968), 65.

3 Cesare De Seta, *La cultura architettonica in Italia tra le due guerre:* (Bari: 1972), 194; Bruno Zevi, *Storia dell'architettura moderna,* 5th ed. (Turin: 1975), 183.

4 Two issues of great importance during the 1930s which are not discussed in the *Rassegna italiana* articles are 1) the proper relationship between architectural and political ideologies, and 2) the effect on building of the economic policy of autarky.

5 Piacentini continued his attack on the functional basis of progressive architecture in a second article, published in November 1928; see: Marcello Piacentini, "Problemi reali piu che razionalismo preconcetto," *Architettura e arti decorative* 7 (November 1928), in *Cennamo 1*, 132–136.

6 Claudio Scale, interview with Alberto Sartoris (October 19, 1974), in "Il movimento moderno torinese nella critica attuale ed in quella coeva," Tesi di Laurea (Politecnico di Torino: 1973–74), 130–131.

7 Adalberto Libera, "Discussioni *artistiche* del razionalismo in architettura." *Rassegna italiana* (May 1929). in *Cennamo 1, 138.*

40 Richard Etlin

Modernism in Italian architecture, 1890–1940 (1991)

Richard Etlin, *Modernism in Italian Architecture, 1890–1940*, Cambridge MA/London: MIT Press, 1991, extracts pp. 235–236 and 237–238.

› The birth of Italian rationalism

*   *   *

Polemical rationalism

What was "rationalism"? At the onset of the period under consideration in this book, Anatole de Baudot, former student and follower of Viollet-le-Duc, gave a clear definition that would serve the purposes of the later Italian Rationalists as well. Responding to critics who were misrepresenting the word, de Baudot explained that rationalism compels the artist to adhere to "the principle of sincerity." Reason "leads the artist to develop his aesthetic from the system of construction selected according to available materials and resources, as well as the conditions and needs that he must satisfy."[1] The essential features of this definition could later be found in Walter Gropius's explanation of the basis for the new architecture given in the preface to *Internationale Architektur*, a book to which the Gruppo 7 referred at least as much as to *Vers une architecture*. Today, affirmed Gropius, there is a new architectural form "that does not find its reason for being from within itself, but rather it springs from the way of building, from the function that it must fulfill."[2] In the Italian translation of this essay published in Fillia's *La nuoua architettura* (1931), the text continued, "Hence the expression 'functional architecture.'"[3] This dual imperative of satisfying programmatic needs and deriving architectural form in response to the constructive system furnished the basis for the Gruppo 7's adoption of the word "rationalism." "The new architecture, the true architecture," explained these young Milanese architects, "must result from a strict adherence to logic, to rationality. A rigid constructivism must give the rules. The new architectural forms must receive their aesthetic value only from the character of *necessity,* and only then, through a process of *selection,* will a style be born." The mistake of Art Nouveau, or "il 'liberty,'" as the Gruppo 7 called it, was precisely the attempt "to create a style . . . from nothing." A new style could develop only "from the constant use of rationality, from the perfect correspondence of the building's structure to its scope."[4]

* * *

The polemical use of the word *rationalism* in the years preceding the Gruppo 7's manifesto was largely associated with avant-garde commercial or industrial architecture. Looking in 1912 at "the steel skeleton as the new element of construction" in modern American buildings, the architect G. Albert Lansburgh, for example, defined *rationalism* in essentially the same terms that would mark its polemical use in the 1920s: "Rationalism is the formation of ideas, produced by reasoning and depending alone upon logic for its support. Rationalism in architecture is the logical expression of a correct and practical solution and depends also upon correctness in the aesthetic requirements of the design and correctness in the methods of their construction."[5]

Similarly, in an article published in *Architettura e Arti Decorative* (February 1924), the German architect Erwin Gutkind reported on the "Estetica tecnica nelle moderne costruzioni tedesche" (technological aesthetic in modern German buildings) to Italian readers with an argument that would be echoed in the Gruppo 7's articles. Writing about factories, office buildings, power plants, and other utilitarian structures, with illustrations from the architecture of Walter Gropius and Adolph Meyer, Mies van der Rohe, Peter Behrens, and Otto Banning, Gutkind explained:

> The concept that animates all of these constructions derives from a pure rationalistic process that does not admit any hesitations, but rather that compels with the extreme logic of creating all at once. The details of the union of the individual parts result from the contrast between the masses, further reinforced by the gradation of colors and not through the introduction of cornices that are only decorative and that in their essence have no reason to exist.[6]

In their discussion of the same and similar industrial buildings by Walter Gropius, Kosina, Erich Mendelsohn, Arthur Korn, and Hans and Wassili Luckhardt, all pictured in Gropius's *Internationale Architektur*, the Gruppo 7 described the new aesthetic in much the same terms as had Gutkind. These German architects, explained the young Italian Rationalists, had in their industrial buildings achieved "the essence of pure rationality" by "applying the spirit of necessity and an extreme constructive sincerity" to produce "an ultimate manner truly close to logical perfection." Using the phrase *estetica tecnica* found in both the title and the editors' introduction to Gutkind's article, the Gruppo 7 declared that this German architecture had created an "estetica tecnica ultramoderna" (ultramodern technological aesthetic).[7]

In a later account of the origins of the Gruppo 7, Agnoldomenico Pica, who had been both a Rationalist architect and a chronicler of Italian Rationalism in the 1930s, explained that Carlo Enrico Rava had "proposed the label for the new architecture: Rationalism. The term derives from the German *Sachlichkeit:* it was not a perfect translation, nor was it free of ambiguity and imprecision, but it was to be successful."[8] By 1926, however, there was no need to seek an imperfect translation for *Sachlichkeit,* for the word *rational* had become a common attribute used by Italian critics and architects to characterize progressive developments elsewhere in the West. The article on current developments in Germany by Erwin Gutkind published in the November 1923 issue of *Architettura e Arti Decorative* had called for *una edilizia razionale* based on the "economical and rational use of materials."[9] In 1924 the architect Gaetano Minnucci, who would become co-organizer of the First Italian Exposition of Rational Architecture (1928), had identified one of the four tendencies in modern Dutch architecture as *razionalista*.[10] Its first major realization was Hendrik Petrus Berlage's Stock Exchange (Amsterdam, 1897–1903), which Minnucci described as exhibiting an "organic and rational architectural composition that immediately impresses the observer." A primary lesson of Berlage's architecture was "to obtain the decoration only rationally from the constructive elements themselves: here was one of the bases of modern architecture."[11] Roberto Papini, in reporting on the 1925 Paris exposition for *Architettura e Arti Decorative* had affirmed:

> Modern European architecture has these essential characteristics: a tendency toward the rational, the expression of structure, a free movement of masses, the emancipation from academic canons, an adherence to purely geometric forms, an independence from conventional proportions, and the maximum parsimony in ornamentation.[12]

Similarly, in the summer of 1926 Minnucci defined the "international characteristics" of contemporary modern architecture in this same journal as "mathematical, strong, rational, and strongly logical."[13] In selecting *rationalism* as their credo, the Gruppo 7 focused on what was commonly recognized as the defining feature of a new Western architecture.

Notes

1 A. de Baudot, "Le Rationalisme en architecture. Sa part dans le passé. Comparaison des édifices anciens et modernes. Edifices religieux," *Encyclopédie d'Architecture* (1888–89), 145.

2 W. Gropius, "Vorwart," *Internationale Architektur* (1925, 2nd rev. ed.), 6.

3 W. Gropius, "L'archirettura funzionale," in Fillia, *La nuova architettura* (1931), 30.

4 Il Gruppo 7, "Architettura," 852 [Editors' note – see Etlin, note 2, p. 626: Il Gruppo 7 (Ubaldo Castagnoli, Luigi Figini, Guido Frette, Sebastiano Larco, Gino Pollini, Carlo Enrico Rava, and Giuseppe Terragni), "Architettura," *Rassegna Italiana* 18 (December 1926), 849–54, and reprinted in *Il Tevere* (January 11, 1927); "Architettura (II). Gli stranieri," *Rassegna Italiana* 19 (February 1927), 129–37; "Architettura (III). Impreparazione–incomprensione–pregiudizi," *Rassegna Italiana* 19 (March 1927), 247–52; "Architettura–IV. Una nuova epoca arcaica," *Rassegna Italiana* 19 (May 1927), 467–72. For English translations with commentary by Ellen R. Shapiro, see *Oppositions* no. 6 (1976), 86–102; no.12 (1978), 88–105. For brief discussion of *Rassegna Italiana* and its editor who published these essays, see C. Belli, Il volto del secolo. *La prima cellula dell'architettura razionalista italiana* (1988), 19.]

5 G. A. Lansburgh, "Rationalism of the Twentieth Century: Architecture," *The Western Architect* (June 1912), 65, 67.

6 E. Gutkind, "Estetica tecnica nelle moderne costruzioni tedesche," *Architettura e Arti Decorative* 3 (February 1924), 276. For Gutkind's own modern architecture, see A. Korn, *Glass in Modern Architecture* (1929; 1967 English tr.; 1969 reprint), 74–75, 77.

7 Il Gruppo 7, "Architettura (II)," 133 [see note 4].

8 Pica, "Il 'Gruppo 7'," 145 [Editors' note – see Etlin, note 36, p. 628: A. Pica, "Il 'Gruppo 7' e la polemica razionalista," in *La Casa* no. 6 (1959), 146]. More recently Carlo Belli has written that it was "[Alberto] Sartoris who, it appears, was the first to coin, with Carlo Enrico Rava, the word *razionale* (and this must have been in the summer of '26)" (Belli, *Il volto del secolo*, 54).

9 E. G[utkind], "Notizie dalla Germania," *Architettura e Arti Decorative* 3 (November 1923), 140.

10 G. Minnucci, "Moderna architettura olandese," *Architettura e Arti Decorative* 3 (July 1924), 494: "cubista, espressionista, romantica e razionalista."

11 Ibid., 494, 498.

12 R. Papini, "Le arti a Parigi nel 1925. Primo: l'architettura," *Architettura e Arti Decorative* 5 (January 1926), 208.

13 G. Minnucci, "L'architettura e l'estetica delgi edifici industriali," *Architettura e Arti Decorative* 5 (July-August 1926), 488, 490.

41 Michelangelo Sabatino

The politics of *mediterraneità* in Italian modernist architecture (2010)

Michelangelo Sabatino, 'The Politics of *Mediterraneità* in Italian Modernist Architecture', from: Jean-Francois Lejeune and Michelangelo Sabatino (eds), *Modern Architecture and the Mediterranean: Vernacular Dialogues and Contested Identities*, London/New York: Routledge, 2010, extracts pp. 42–44 and 44–45.

› Rationalism, *Mediterraneità*, and the vernacular

From the late 1920s, architects in Italy used the term "Rationalism" to describe a movement in modern architecture that prioritized functional or technical requirements as well as spiritual qualities having to do with tradition and identity. Between 1928 when the first exhibition of Rationalist architecture was promoted by the *Movimento Italiano per l'Architettura Razionale* (MIAR), and 1931, the year of the second and final exhibition of the Rationalism group, debates raged over the agenda and validity of the movement with respect to the Fascist political agenda.[1] Adalberto Libera defended it against critics who accused the Rationalists of "internationalism" at the expense of nationalist ideals, asserting that,

> It might seem that Rationalism in architecture is synonymous with internationalism. However, even though qualities associated with commonly accepted international standards regarding technology, comfort, and culture are intrinsically part of Rationalism, those associated with nationalism like climate and ethics will also continue to exist alongside these.[2]

Although the critic Edoardo Persico endorsed Rationalism as a broader, European phenomenon, he criticized Italian Rationalists for their opportunism and what he perceived as ethical compromise with the nationalistic and self-aggrandizing agenda of the Fascist regime. Persico viewed *Romanità* or Roman-ness with the same disdain as *Mediterraneità*:

> Italian Rationalism is unable to absorb the lesson of European architecture because it lacks the faith necessary to do so. And so, moving from the dubious "Europeanism" of

early "Rationalism", the Italians moved, with cold calculation regarding practical circumstances, from the "Roman" and the "Mediterranean", right down to the recent endorsement of corporative architecture.[3]

Shortly before this statement was published, Alberto Sartoris employed the terms "modern," "functional," and "rational" almost interchangeably in the introduction to his 1932 survey of functional architecture.[4] He defined Rationalism in this way:

> In contrast to what one might expect, European Rationalism is not only about mechanics, statics, or dynamism. It is also about sculptural ideas that reflect timeless desires for lyricism and spirituality that can easily be fulfilled within the framework of Rationalism.[5]

For Sartoris, Rationalism was grounded in a complex attitude toward design, one that embraced spiritual, lyrical as well as practical concerns. Just a year before Sartoris's book appeared, Giuseppe Pagano and co-authors of a plan for Via Roma in Turin proclaimed that "the architecture of the new street should be rational but even more than that, it should be resolutely modern."[6]

From the extreme right wing, Ardengo Soffici lashed out at the Rationalists with vitriol:

> Architectural Rationalism, not unlike other pseudo-artistic expressions, is of German and Anglo-Saxon derivation, and thus Protestant. Rationalism and everything that resembles it is nothing other than an expression of aggression on the part of northerners and Protestants against Rome and Latin-ness.[7]

At the heart of this debate between North and South and scrambling to defend Rationalism from nationalistic attacks, like those perpetrated by Soffici, the authors of the *"programma"* published in the first issue of *Quadrante* (whose editors were Pier Maria Bardi and Massimo Bontempelli) managed to promote the "intransigent Rationalism" of Le Corbusier, Walter Gropius, and Mies van der Rohe, while defending classicism and its roots in southern *Mediterreaneità*.[8]

At this point of the essay it is essential to underline that during those same years the concept of the Mediterranean was fast expanding beyond the classical heritage to include the vernacular tradition. And although classicism's impact on core issues of twentieth-century Italian architecture and urbanism has been thoroughly examined, the equally important contribution of the vernacular has been in fact overlooked. In particular, the role that vernacular architecture played toward shaping Rationalism and the evolving concept of *Mediterraneità* has been little studied,[9] whereas the rhetorical and representational power associated with classical architecture has preoccupied historians anxious to deconstruct the difficult relationship between architecture and politics in Italy.[10] Unlike the vernacular, which has only been recognized as a category by historians for less than a century (in spite of its importance in the works of major figures such as Sebastiano Serlio, Andrea Palladio, and Karl Friedrich Schinkel), classicism consolidated its meanings in theory as well as practice over centuries in parallel with the rise of the profession of architecture.[11]

*   *   *

During the charged years between the two World Wars when Fascism dominated the Italian political sphere, Rationalist architects who embraced *Mediterraneità* did so in contrast to narrow nationalist agendas espoused by some members of Mussolini's regime. The transnational cultural heritage of the Mediterranean basin is characterized by "many voices" and architectural traditions, and as such offered Rationalist architects a wide cultural horizon on which to forge their brand of Mediterranean modernism.[12] Before the rise of nation states in the nineteenth century and the reconfiguration of the European geopolitical landscape, the Mediterranean basin was the theatre of successive empires, from Roman to Ottoman, each of which attempted to consolidate (typically more coercively than voluntarily) highly diverse traditions. The monumental as well as the vernacular buildings of Greco-Roman antiquity across a region extending west as far as Portugal, east as far as Turkey, and south as far as Africa inspired Italian Rationalists as diverse as Giuseppe Pagano and the *Gruppo Sette,* seven architects who banded together in 1926 just out of school to promote a modern architecture that creatively embraced tradition and tempered the universal qualities of the machine with the poetic qualities of context and culture.[13]

Although Italian Rationalist architects and their contemporaries throughout the Mediterranean region embraced tradition, with the inevitable "misprisions" that operative uses of the past risk, they rejected the mere imitation of historical styles promoted by exponents of the Fascist regime in the name of a chauvinistic Italianess or *Italianità.* Just as the Amsterdam School, Alvar Aalto, the German Expressionists and other modernist movements across Europe sought ways to combine traditional materials and building technologies with modern ones, and embraced both figuration and abstraction, the Rationalists approached traditional forms with a progressive agenda. Unlike their conservative counterparts in Italy and elsewhere, they looked to tradition as a source of invention, neither slavishly imitating it nor resisting progress in the name of past glories. In a bid to win Mussolini over to a modernist aesthetic, the militant critic Pier Maria Bardi assailed historicist architects as *"culturalisti"* with his *Tavolo delgi orrori* or Panel of Horrors, a montage of historicist buildings realized in Italy.[14]

› Notes

1 See the anthology by Giorgio Ciucci, Francesco Dal Co (eds.), *Architettura italiana del '900–Atlante*, Milan, Electa, 1993. In particular see chapter 2, "Razionalismo architettonico e impegno politico fra arte e urbanistica," pp. 97–123. For an English translation of "The Rationalist Manifesto" presented to Mussolini on the inauguration day of the Second Exposition of Rationalist Architecture in Rome see Bruno Zevi, "Gruppo 7: the Rise and Fall of Italian Rationalism" in *Architectural Design* 51 1/2, 1981, pp. 40–43.
2 Adalberto Libera, "Arte e razionalismo," in *La rassegna italiana*, March 1928, pp. 232–236. Republished in Luciano Patetta (ed.), L'Architettura in Italia 1919–1943. *Le polemiche*, Milan, Clup, 1972, pp. 149–151
3 Edoardo Persico, "Punto ed a capo per l'architettura" in *Domus*, November, 1934. Republished in Giulia Veronesi (ed.). *Edoardo Persico Scritti d'architettura* (1927/1935), Florence, Vallecchi editore, 1968, pp. 153–168 Cited in Bruno Zevi, "The Italian Rationalists" in Dennis Sharp (ed.), *The Rationalists – Theory and Design in the Modern Movement*, London, Architectural Press. 1978, pp. 118–129.
4 Alberto Sartoris, *Gli elementi dell'architettura funzionale*, Milan, Hoepli, 1932.
5 Reprinted in Giorgio Ciucci, Francesco Dal Co (eds.), *Architettura italiana del '900 – Atlante*, pp. 114–116
6 Giuseppe Pagano Pogatschnig, Gino Levi Montalcini, Umberto Cuzzi, Ottorino Aloisio, and Ettore Sottsass, "La Via Roma di Torino," *Per Vendere*, June, 1931., republished in Cesare De Seta (ed.), *Pagano – Architettura e città durante il fascismo*, Bari and Rome, Laterza, 1990, pp. 217–233.

7　Ardengo Soffici, "Bandiera gialla," *Il Selvaggio*, May 30, 1931

8　Piero Bootoni, Mario Cereghini, Luigi Figini, Gino Frette, Enrico Griffini, Piero Lingeri, Gino Pollini, Gian Luigi Banfi, Ludovico de Belgiojoso, Enrico Peressutti, and Ernesto N. Rogers, " Un programma d'architettura," in *Quadrante*, May, 1933, 1. Republished in Luciano Patetta (ed.), *L'Architettura in Italia* 1919–1943, pp. 227–229

9　An exception is found with Richard A. Etlin, *Modernism in Italian Architecture, 1890–1940*, Cambridge, The MIT Press, 1991: see chapter "A Modern Vernacular Architecture", pp. 129–161.

10　For an overview of classicism in Italian architecture see: Giorgio Ciucci, "Italian Architecture during the Fascist Period: Classicism between Neoclassicism and Rationalism: The Many Souls of the Classical," in *Harvard Architectural Review* 5, 1987, pp. 76–87.

11　This issue is addressed in depth in the introduction of my forthcoming book: Michelangelo Sabatino, *Pride in Modesty; Modernist Architecture and the Vernacular Tradition in Italy*, Toronto and Buffalo, University of Toronto Press, 2010.

12　On Ferrand Braudel's observation of "many voices," see Iain Chambers, *Mediterranean Crossings. The Politics of an Interrupted Modernity*, Durham, NC, and London, Duke University Press, 2008, pp. 1–22.

13　For an overview of the Mediterranean's complex history see David Abulafia (ed.), *The Mediterranean in History*, London, Thames and Hudson, 2003.

14　Bardi first used the expression "*culturisti*" to refer to nineteenth-century architects: Pier Maria Bardi, Rapporto sull'Architetturra (per Mussolini), Rome, Critica fascista, 1931. The term is echoed in Sigfried Giedion, "Situation de l'architecture contemporaine en Italie," in *Cahiers d'art* 9–10, 1931, pp. 442–449.

42 Pier Vittorio Aureli

Architecture for barbarians—Ludwig Hilberseimer
and the rise of the generic city (2011)

Pier Vittorio Aureli, 'Architecture for Barbarians—Ludwig Hilberseimer and the Rise of the Generic City', *AA Files 63*, 2011, extract pp. 4–5.

*   *   *

Within the history of architecture there is no more drastic representation of the generic ethos of capitalistic production and the urban consequences of economic reasoning than the work of Ludwig Hilberseimer (1885–1967). It is worth stating from the outset, however, that here the term representation is introduced paradoxically. Indeed, as Schmitt has led us to believe, the fundamental principle of economic mastery is to exclude any convincing process of representation. At the core of his project, Hilberseimer saw the reduction of architecture and the arts to their immanent generic properties not just as the mechanical consequence of the ethos of capitalistic production, but as a potentially proactive attempt to provide an aesthetic, a pedagogical value and a social form—that is, to contain such an ethos. As such, his work—encompassing not just his designs but his articles and books—fundamentally represents (in all senses of the word) the industrial metropolis precisely because it removes any depiction that is not the most generic. On numerous occasions Hilberseimer stated that the general and the typical constitute the only architectural criteria in the modern metropolis. This statement, however, should not be understood as a polemical plea for functional simplicity and the standardisation of material components. Rather, his argument was rooted in a much more profound understanding of the physical and cultural form of the metropolis. Over the following pages I would like to reconstruct Hilberseimer's understanding of the capitalistic metropolis by embracing the totality of its project (rather than through the entirety of his projects—an archival undertaking that is desperately required, given the scarce literature available on such a key protagonist of twentieth-century architecture). And so the totality of Hilberseimer's project is evoked here by reinterpreting its theoretical premises as they were manifested during the German period of his work, and in light of today's awareness that the generic is no longer the epiphany of a new urban reality but the accomplished condition of our civilisation.

The term generic comes from the Greek *genus,* meaning 'race', 'kind' or 'species', and from the verbs 'generating' and 'producing'. It refers to an undifferentiated common quality that appears prior to that of the individual. Generic is thus both what is common and what is coming-into-being, what is potential. It is for this reason that the generic is a fundamental category of capitalist production. If capitalism is first of all the management of production, and not simply production *per se,* then what is at stake is not only what is being produced but also the very potential for production (as much as what allows that potential—that is, the circulation of consumption, or even the social in its most disguised aspect).

The process by which the generic becomes an explicit attribute of capitalistic production is the process of abstraction. In the *Grundrisse* Karl Marx describes abstraction as both a method of political economy and a concrete reality that permeates the ethos of capitalism. According to Marx abstraction is a positive thing, a concrete reality. Categories such as labour and production are abstract because they do not refer to one particular moment of their manifestation but instead constitute general frameworks that determine economic relations. For Marx abstractions such as 'labour in general' express the ethos of a society in which individuals move easily from one job to another, indifferent to the kind of work they do. In this way, the most simple abstraction—labour as a generic faculty—stripped of its artisan-like character, becomes the most advanced means of capital. As Francesco Marullo has demonstrated, the more work is reduced to its generic essence as labour *sans phrase,* the more the spatial apparatus that is meant to extract surplus value from labour embodies the barest condition of possibility. This minimal condition is what in architecture we call the *typical plan,* a reduction of architecture to its most essential, universal structural system, and the figure that postulates the indifference of the building structure towards its spatial and distributive organisation. Such a plan serves the purpose of making the subject's experience of place as if simultaneous with other places. This is made possible through a spatial organisation that implies interaction rather than self-sufficiency, which in turn allows for the coexistence of qualitatively different elements within an overall 'collage-like-totality'.[1] Infinitely reproducible, by virtue of its simple layout and indifference towards any context, the typical plan became the architectural apparatus of the factory—the place of work *par excellence.* And just as labour itself is a generic and ubiquitous condition informing all aspects of social life, then the apparatus of the typical plan soon spread out from the factory to underpin the whole building system of the city. As I will argue over the following pages, the spatial logic of typical plan is what constitutes Hilberseimer's (and Mies's) idea of architecture.

Großstadt Architektur (1927), Hilberseimer's most important book, can be understood as one of the very few attempts to theorise the city in relation to its role as a concentration of capital and workers. Though many of its examples and case studies were already outdated by the time Hilberseimer moved to the United States in the late 1930s, the premise of the book in many ways indicates the meaning and direction of all of Hilberseimer's work. The book itself is organised into ten chapters. The first two are devoted to the reality of the *Großstadt* as an unprecedented urban formation driven by capital, while the last section details a general idea of architecture conceived in response to this new urban condition. The chapters in between can be understood as an atlas of the most important programmes for the new capitalist city, addressing, in succession, housing, commercial building, skyscrapers, galleries and theatres, stations and airports, industrial buildings and, finally, the differences between traditional artisanal construction techniques and the contemporary building industry.

Though *Großstadt Architektur* is essentially a city planning manual, each programme is illustrated by a careful selection of projects—built and unbuilt—that Hilberseimer presents as exemplary for the modern metropolis. The selection is rather eclectic in terms of its style and language, ranging from Le Corbusier's Ville Contemporaine to Adolf Loos's terraced houses, from Frank Lloyd Wright's Lexington Terraces to Anton Brenner's apartment block in Rauchfangkehrergasse, from Mies van der Rohe's 1923 design for an office building to Henry van der Velde's Werkbund theatre. But nevertheless there is a common thread running throughout: notably, the appropriateness of the buildings to their programmatic and structural purpose. Compared to Le Corbusier's *Vers une architecture,* published four years earlier, Hilberseimer's book is not so much a manifesto for a new architecture as a realist compendium of architectural solutions for the problems then confronting the metropolis. The ordering of the chapters and the selection of the various projects reflect an attempt to illustrate the most obvious typologies of the totalising space of industrial production, encompassing not only industrial buildings such as factories but also housing, offices and theatres. In this way, implicit to the study is a critique of the existing city focused not on its purpose but in how such purpose had not been answered by an adequate project. For Hilberseimer the *new* city—the *Großstadt*—requires an overall structural, economic and spatial plan that goes beyond the scale of the traditional city. For this reason, he places great emphasis on both the problem of the individual cell (or room or apartment) and on traffic circulation, since it is precisely by linking these two extreme scales that it becomes possible to define the strategic scale of the urban project.

Above all Hilberseimer argued that the *Großstadt* was the product of economic development and the natural consequence of modern industry. Accordingly, the modern metropolis was fundamentally different from the traditional city, which had never experienced industrial production on such a massive and totalising scale. What is interesting about this claim is that in making it Hilberseimer broke with the tradition of urban theorists like Joseph Stübben, Reinhard Baumeister and Camillo Sitte, who all emphasised the continuity of urban design, from the modern period all the way back to antiquity. There was, however, one important, perhaps unlikely, precedent for Hilberseimer's conception of the modern metropolis as distinct from anything that had come before it: Otto Wagner's ideas about planning. Despite the obvious disparities in their architectural styles, the similarity of their approach to the city is striking. Only in their politics do the two architects really diverge.

In 1911 Wagner had published his own pamphlet—significantly also titled *Die Großstadt*— devoted to the three main aspects of urban design: the cityscape, the planning of the city and the economic foundations of the modern metropolis.[2] With this small book Wagner attacked a kind of palliative approach to urban design, and one based on historical precedents and a purely morphological approach to the city—an approach that reached its apogee with Sitte's *Der Stadtbau* (1889).[3] Instead, Wagner advocated a 'realist' attitude and an urban model that would take into account not only the large-scale form of the metropolis, but also its social and economic structures. Before Hilberseimer, Wagner was therefore the very first architect to view the city as the result of economic processes, and whose form needed to be radically re-imagined. He recognised, for example, that the city's fundamental asset was no longer the building, but rather the dynamism of the traffic systems whose logic shaped the urban form. Another innovative aspect of Wagner's project for the city was his emphasis on economic management. The city, he argued, offered a kind of investment opportunity where, as in Haussmann's Paris, expenditure on public spaces could be recouped from the appreciation of private land values.[4] As a result, Wagner attempted to subsume the individuality of the building into a predefined planning principle. This approach had already been anticipated by Wagner's plan for greater Vienna in 1893, which proposed an unlimited expansion of the city fuelled by the concentration of capital. This *Großstadt* was to be divided by radial roads into distinct districts, each containing between 100,000 and 150,000 inhabitants. Residential and public facilities were distributed uniformly throughout with a generic gridiron; the effect of which was that apart from its central monumental axis, this *Großstadt* was read only as an infinite carpet of urbanisation formed by anonymous buildings, blocks and streets—an anonymity of urban form made explicit by the economic and managerial condition of the city. Anticipating Schmitt's scepticism about the possibility of representing an economic process, Wagner seems to suggest that the impact of urban economics reduces the city to a nondescript place of human association where the sole design principles are to manage traffic circulation and structure financial investment.

Editors' note: some footnotes have been omitted.

> ## Notes

1   Christian Norberg-Schultz, 'Free Plan and Open Form', *Places*, no 2, 1983, p 5.
2   Otto Wagner, Die Großstadt: Eine Studie über diese von Otto Wagner (Vienna: Anton Scholl, 1911).
3   Camillo Sitte, *Der Stadtbau nach seinen kuunstlerischen Grundsätzen. Ein Beitrag zur Lösung moderner Fragen der Architektur und monumentaler Plastik unter besonderer Beziehung auf Wien* (Vienna: 1909).
4   August Sarnitz, 'Realism Versus Verniedlichung: The Design of the Great City', in Harry Francis Mallgrave (ed), *Otto Wagner: Reflections on the Raiment of Modernity* (Santa Monica, CA: Getty Center, 1988), pp 85–112.

43 David Rifkind

'Everything in the state, nothing against the state':
corporative urbanism and Rationalist architecture in fascist Italy' (2012)

David Rifkind, *Planning Perspectives*, vol. 27, 1, 2012, extract pp. 55–60. Only selected notes included.

› CIAM and corporativist urbanism

Among *Quadrante's* significant contributions to the discourse of urbanism was the journal's attempt to synthesize CIAM planning principles with the economic concerns of fascist corporativism. Their advocacy of CIAM's methods distinguished them from their Italian peers, while their enthusiastic allegiance to fascism made them unique among CIAM's predominantly leftist membership. At the heart of the CIAM-corporativist hybrid was a conceptual affinity between the international organization's concern with organizing urban space according to programmatic function and the regime's interest in coordinating each sector of the national economy to maximize efficiencies. Both hinged on the efficient distribution of populations or industries under a powerful central authority.

The scale of construction described by CIAM and corporativist urbanism required a strong central authority, which the *Quadrante* circle believed they had found in Mussolini. By the time they launched the journal and began sketching the outlines of the 'corporativist city', the first two cities in the reclaimed Pontine marshes were underway, and contemporary propaganda made it clear that their rapid and uncompromising construction was made possible by the singular authority of the Italian dictator. *Quadrante* enthusiastically repeated these claims, and used them to justify their call for state agencies to use broad powers to appropriate, plan and rebuild large expanses of land. The *Quadrante* circle also lauded Mussolini's ability to suppress the 'private interests' which undermined collective action and were 'the primary cause of urban disorder', a concern that also appeared in the Athens Charter's later published form.

CIAM was deeply concerned with the ability of architecture and urban planning to promote the physical and mental health of the populace. The architects and planners of the *Quadrante* circle alloyed this desire to foster salubrity through better building practices with the fascist regime's rhetorical promotion of virility, athleticism, martial prowess and fertility, and thus emphasized the role of parks, sports facilities and parade grounds in their city plans. They also modified CIAM's policy positions on working-class residential districts to reflect the anxieties of the national government and local housing agencies about increasing the birth rate and lowering the spread of communicable diseases. Thus, *Quadrante's* writers stressed the benefits of design practices that fostered improved hygiene, yet were anything but sterile.

Towards this end, Piero Bottoni and Enrico Agostino Griffini designed and promoted rationalized, functional kitchens and baths in Italy, and led the effort to replace dated, dusty furniture with modern, functional, hygienic furnishings in workers' housing. They and their *Quadrante* colleagues conceptualized the integral relationships between furnishings, dwellings, architecture, landscape and urbanism. The journal thus reported on advances in technologies, ranging from appliances and lighting to transportation and sanitation, as part of its discussion of urban planning.

Rationalist writers like Rogers, Bottoni and Griffini did not discuss the role of architecture in terms of social control, but the geometry of their plans facilitated surveillance and management of housing district residents. Bottoni justified the preference for slab, rather than courtyard, housing blocks in terms of public health, writing, 'modern urbanism tends towards the abolition of the closed block house for reasons of hygiene, insolation and ventilation'.[1] Yet in contrast to the courtyards of traditional Italian apartment buildings, which shield their inhabitants from the gaze of passers-by, the open spaces between the 'blocco aperto' (open block) slabs of places like Giuseppe Terragni and Alberto Sartoris's Rebbio district were easily monitored from the surrounding streets. The broad avenues and streets advocated by CIAM were intended to facilitate easy travel between residence and workplace, but in the Italian context they can also be seen to enable the rapid deployment of troops and police forces in unruly districts.

While CIAM had discussed the importance of collective action at length, especially at the fourth congress in 1933, the organization did not grant collectivity the same status as Bottoni and the Rationalists of the *Quadrante* circle. For Le Corbusier and his colleagues, collective action constituted one end of a spectrum (whose opposite pole was individual freedom) that comprised the full range of human activity, however vaguely defined. For the *Quadrante* circle, Rationalist architecture and urbanism aspired to foster a mass identity on the part of the citizenry, in accord with the fascist regime's insistence on obedience and sacrifice. Terragni, in particular, oriented public spaces towards buildings representative of the regime's authority (such as the casa del fascio or local fascist party headquarters) in his urban schemes, in order to stress the individual citizen's duty to his fellows and to the state.

Bottoni's, Terragni's and BBPR's political uses of archaeology and historic preservation also distinguished their planning concerns from those of other CIAM planners, for whom the protection of historical monuments served cultural, but not ideological, purposes. Bottoni related the protection of historical monuments to the preservation of the urban 'landscape' (*paesaggio*), which included streets, piazze, gardens, rivers, canals, bridges and 'isolated buildings'. In the master plans for Verona and Como, Bottoni placed great importance on the preservation of Italy's cultural heritage. These gestures served the ideological function of legitimizing the fascist regime by visibly connecting its public works to those of the Roman Empire. While much of Bottoni's writing tends towards a universality suggesting applicability outside Italy, his concern with archaeology focused entirely on Italian, and specifically Roman, examples.[2] Bottoni looked towards the Roman heritage of Italian cities and underlined the political importance of these ruins at a time when government propaganda favoured allusions to the country's imperial past. His concern with the sites of collective life in the Italian city similarly drew fascist politics into contemporary urban planning, as the *Quadrante* architects emphasized the concrete ways in which architecture and urbanism could promote the regime's efforts at enforcing social discipline.

› The Italian involvement in CIAM

Architects associated with *Quadrante* represented Italy at each CIAM meeting, beginning with the first congress in 1928. The two subsequent congresses dealt with housing, increasing the scale of investigation from the individual dwelling (1929) to the residential neighbourhood (1930),[3] and setting the stage for the IV CIAM theme of 'The Functional City' in 1933.

The fourth CIAM meeting established city planning as an integral concern of modern architecture. Catalan architect Josep Lluis Sert, who attended as a recent architecture graduate, wrote 40 years later, 'previous Congresses had discussed housing in relation to modern technology and housing developments, which naturally brought them to the conclusion that these subjects were part of the larger complexes – the city and the urban regions'.[4] Another participant, Swiss architect Alfred Roth, later summarized the position that emerged from the IV CIAM:

> All the architectural, technical, economic and social tasks find their synthesis in town planning extended to regional and national planning. The object of modern town-planning is the organized distribution of the municipal domain into dwelling, working and business zones, the creation of sufficient green surfaces and recreation grounds, the proper distribution of the social institutions and the regulation of the traffic problems.[5]

The *Quadrante* architects comprised the entire Italian delegation to the IV CIAM. In preparation for the congress, they worked prodigiously: 5 of the 33 urban analyses presented on board the *Patris* were of Italian cities. The Italian delegates' lengthy response to the CIAM questionnaire distributed during the voyage is one of only two that survive, thanks to its publication in *Quadrante*. As was the case with most members, the *Quadrante* architects demonstrated their enthusiasm for CIAM by funding their participation in the congress out of their own pockets.

The Italian group initially proposed examining four cities. Como, Genoa, Milan and Rome were chosen to represent specific urban typologies: tourist destinations, ports, industrial centres and political capitals, respectively. The group selected Luigi Vietti to study Genoa, Gaetano Minnucci to analyse Rome and Bottoni and Pollini to examine Milan. After consulting Terragni about the project in March 1933, Bottoni decided to substitute studies of Verona and Littoria for that of Milan.

The choice of Verona and Littoria allowed Bottoni and his colleagues to juxtapose planning strategies appropriate to cities of archaeological significance against those built *ex novo*. Littoria, the first of the new towns built as part of the Pontine marsh reclamation south of Rome, was one of only two new towns examined by the CIAM conferees. Bottoni had studied Verona and its Roman remains in great detail the previous year while preparing an entry to the competition for the city's master plan. His scheme served as a model for preserving urban historic centres while rationalizing the city's transportation infrastructure and expanding its commercial, industrial and residential districts. Before the 1933 CIAM meeting, Bottoni and Terragni had discussed at length the problem of selectively preserving monuments and other elements of Verona's historic fabric in the context of modern urbanism, and these deliberations greatly informed the design of their 1934 CM8 plan for Como. Terragni's CIAM 'analysis' of Como included proposals for relocating the city's industries and new housing districts throughout the surrounding area, all of which later appeared in the CM8 plan.

Quadrante dedicated its fifth issue (September 1933) to the IV CIAM. Bottoni edited the issue, which included documentary texts by himself, Bardi and Pollini, as well as articles by Le Corbusier and Fernand Léger. *Quadrante* provided the most comprehensive treatment of the congress in the Italian press.

Quadrante 5 published the analyses of Como, prepared by Terragni, and of Littoria and Verona, produced by Bottoni, Figini, Griffini and Pollini. The studies, following the CIAM format, examined cities according to three themes: zoning (distinguishing between residential and industrial districts, and identifying parks and parkways), circulation and the 'city's zone of influence', which related the first two analyses to the city's regional context.[6] Each theme was depicted on a separate plate. Bottoni discussed the goals of this approach and its relevance to urban planning in an accompanying article, 'Analisi di una citta', as did Bardi in his 'Cronaca di viaggio'.[7] Three years later, Terragni's lengthy essay on the Casa del Fascio in Como revealed the lasting importance of these analyses. The architect discussed how his study of Como in the context of regional development prompted him to design the building as the cornerstone of a 'centre of political representation' facing the Duomo at the edge of the walled city.[8]

The immediate influence of the 1933 CIAM meeting on the *Quadrante* circle architects can be seen in the differences between their responses to the master plan competition for Verona (1932) and those for Pavia (1933) and Como (1934). The Verona project, designed by a team of seven led by Bottoni and Griffini, preserved the historic urban fabric of the city (especially its Roman-era remains) while replacing unsanitary neighbourhoods with new, salubrious housing districts. Yet the project did not separate residential and commercial areas, as CIAM prescribed. The first Italian master plans to do so were the Pavia and Como master plan competition entries.

While the Pavia project (described at length below) demonstrated the Italians' quick adoption of program-specific zoning, the Como scheme showed the full influence of CIAM's analytical, planning and representational techniques. A team of eight designers led by Terragni and Bottoni prepared the project under the rubric CM8 (for Como Milano 8). Using rigorous statistical analysis and employing standardized isotype graphics common to CIAM, the project diagnosed problems arising from, and proposed solutions to facilitate, the city's growing population and expanding industries. The CM8 team identified the expression of collective interests as one way the modern city could embody the values, and engage the economic planning, of the corporative fascist state. The large teams who prepared the Verona, Pavia and Como competition entries affirmed the importance of collectivity through their commitment to professional collaboration, and thus fulfilled a CIAM principle shared by the Gruppo 7 (the first group of Italian Rationalists), MIAR (the national organization formed to promote Rationalism in 1930) and *Quadrante*, as well as fascist corporativism itself. Corporativist urbanism extended these collectivist and collaborative impulses into the programming of everyday life, in which every aspect of the citizenry's existence – from the home to the workplace and beyond – was assigned its proper place.

› Notes

1   Piero Bottoni, *Urbanistica*. Milan: Ulrico Hoepli Editore, 1938, 47.
2   Ibid., 86–9.
3   Terragni joined Pollini and Bottoni on the Italian delegation to the fourth congress in 1933, which Bardi attended in his role as a journalist. Bardi, 'Viaggio di architetti in Grecia', *Quadrante* 5 (September 1933): 1.
4   Josep Lluis Sert, foreword to Le Corbusier, *The Athens Charter*. Translated by Anthony Eardley. New York: Grossman Publishers, 1973, viii. On the IV CIAM, see also Josep Lluis Sert, *Can Our Cities Survive?* (Cambridge: Harvard University Press, 1942).
5   Alfred Roth, *The New Architecture* (Zurich: Dr. H. Girsberger, 1940), 9.
6   Giorgio Ciucci, Giuseppe Terragni: Opera Completa. Milan: Electa, 1996, 415–7. Plate 1, zonizzazione, of Terragni's analysis of Como appeared in *Quadrante* 5 (September 1933): 45. All three plates are conserved at the CIAM archives in Zurich, and are reproduced in Ciucci.
7   Piero Bottoni, 'Analisi di una città' *Quadrante* 5 (September 1933): 39–41. Pietro Maria Bardi, 'Cronaca di viaggio', 5.
8   Giuseppe Terragni, 'La costruzione della Casa del Fascio di Como', *Quadrante* 35/36 (October 1936): 16. Terragni's relazione also refers to the CM8 plan for Como.

Addendum

Nicholas Bullock

Architecture, rationalism and reconstruction: the example of France 1945–55

With the end of the war in 1945, the scale of destruction across Europe demanded that reconstruction be carried out using new ways of building. For all the major combatant nations, the loss of skilled manpower, the shortage of resources generally and particularly of traditional building materials meant that a return to established ways of building would not be possible in the short term. At a time when the need to rebuild shattered cities, to re-house the homeless and to restart Europe's war-torn economy was most acute, new forms of construction and new materials would have to replace traditional ways of building. For those who believed that architectural form was intimately connected to the materials and the means of construction, the consequences for architecture were challenging.

Many radical architects had hoped that the war like the housing shortages of the inter-war years would privilege the widespread adoption of a new architecture able to exploit the potential of new materials and ways of building.[1] But by the end of the war as the development of non-traditional construction became government policy, the preoccupations of many who spoke for the New Architecture had moved on. The first post-war meetings of CIAM focused on lofty cultural and symbolic questions, on the role of architecture in rebuilding the social and democratic values and institutions of post-war Europe.[2] Discussion turned around issues such as the 'New Monumentality' and the social and cultural importance of the 'Heart of the City', not around the utilitarian and technical agenda of reconstruction.

How the discussion of these issues was reconciled with the immediate priorities of reconstruction, with the needs of housing, health and education, varied from country to country.[3] In Germany, for example, faced with the need to establish an architectural identity for the new republic and to address the huge task of rebuilding shattered cities, the architects of reconstruction favoured a return to the Neues Bauen. In northern Italy reconstruction would provide the first opportunities for a revival of the rationalist values of the 1930s, but in Rome it prompted instead an interest in an 'organic' architecture more akin to Sweden's 'new empiricism'. France, with a long tradition of celebrating the identity and the achievements of the state through architecture, provides an accessible example to illustrate the way in which the architecture of reconstruction had to balance symbolic concerns with utilitarian priorities. How would the architecture of reconstruction express the values of a new post-Liberation France, remote from the humiliation of defeat and the shadow of occupation, while answering the desperate need to make good the destruction of the war?

> Reconstruction and the industrialisation of building

Invaded in 1940, bombed by the allies and then subjected to the campaign of liberation that swept across the country, the spread and the scale of destruction was much greater and more widespread than in 1918.[4] By 1945, France had, for example, lost 40 per cent of its rail network and around 20 per cent of all dwellings. In cities like Le Havre, one of France's foremost *ville martyres,* allied bombing and the battle to liberate the city and the port left over 5,000 civilians dead, the centre devastated, and 40,000 homeless and in urgent need of re-housing. With an economy stripped of resources during the German occupation and ruined by war, how were towns like Le Havre to be rebuilt?

The building industry's ability to respond to these challenges had been weakened by the war and its manpower reduced to around half its pre-war total.[5] Moreover, this reduced workforce was scattered across a large number of small firms, most employing 5 or fewer workers, which further reduced its efficiency. The war years also changed the industry in other ways, favouring public works at the expense of conventional building. Wartime pressures, particularly German demands for fortifications and other large scale construction projects, had sharpened still further the pre-war contrast between the small scale, essentially artisan operations of traditional building firms, and the large well-equipped contractors, backed with extensive capital resources who dominated the world of major public works contracts.[6]

It is against this background that we must understand the urgency of the arguments made for transforming the building industry. There was general agreement that there was far too much for the traditional artisan sector to do. Rebuilding war-damaged buildings would absorb most of those with traditional skills and the supply of traditional materials. Thus the only way to increase the supply of new building, particularly housing, so central to the modernisation of France, was to explore new ways of building that would increase the volume of production and by-pass the bottleneck of traditional methods of construction. For many the most plausible way to achieve this was to tap the interest and the skills, developed during the war, of the large public works contractors. A few radical voices even suggested seeking the involvement of firms from outside the building industry who had experience of industrialised methods of production.

> From the industrialisation of building to a rational architecture

Closely associated with this discussion about the future of the building industry was the debate about architecture, reconstruction and the modernisation of France. Widely covered in the architectural press by journals from the most progressive to the most conservative, the debate had a particular relevance as the newly formed Ministry of Reconstruction and Urbanism (MRU) raised its sights from the most immediate tasks of reconstruction to the larger task of transforming the fabric of French towns and cities to meet the challenges of post-war modernisation.[7] Though the first minister at MRU, Raoul Dautry, proclaimed himself agnostic on questions of architectural style – a stance maintained publicly by his successors – he arrived with a reputation as a technocrat and for operating in a 'top down' manner with policy set in Paris. What course would MRU set not just for reconstruction but the longer-term modernisation of France?

Over the first post-war years, debate about architecture and the industrialisation of the building industry was generally framed in terms of two rival approaches to the construction of housing, seen as being the highest priority for France's second national plan after the renewal of the economy during the first. On the one hand were the radicals, led by Marcel Lods and Jean Prouvé and supported by progressive architectural journals like *L'Architecture d'Aujourd'hui* and *Techniques et Architecture*, who drew on both the modernist tradition of the pre-war years and recent American and British experience and pressed for a radical programme of reform.[8] On the other were the voices of the mainstream, writing in more established journals such as *L'Architecture Française* or *Construction Moderne*, who favoured a continuation of the cautious pragmatism of the Vichy years.

On this side stood many of architects and engineers who had been engaged in the day-to-day tasks of rebuilding after 1940, of clearing rubble, of finding shelter for the homeless, of fending off the increasingly insistent demands of the Germans for manpower and materials. Short of most building materials they had turned back to a French tradition of building with small pre-cast concrete components, well-established since the turn of the century which, in the interests of maximum economy, they combined with a draconian programme of standardisation. For this group the practical advantages of continuing this wartime strategy must have seemed reassuringly sane.

One of the principal spokesmen for this view was Pol Abraham whose reconstruction work in Orleans was one of the few projects started before the Liberation.[9] Known for his pre-war work with complex masonry and concrete structures, a number of them vaulted, he was a self-professed follower of Viollet-le-Duc and spoke for many who had struggled to develop an architecture for reconstruction under the Vichy regime. The difficulties of transport, whether by road or rail, forced architects to adopt an almost pre-industrial reliance on local materials that, combined with Vichy's 'back to the land' ideology, gave new relevance to the development of a regional architecture. Studies, such as 'Chantier 1425', sponsored by the regime, produced a flowering of interest in local traditions of building and attracted the interest of many progressive architects, including those who had worked with Le Corbusier before the war, who saw – as had Viollet-le-Duc before them – in regional architecture a model for a rational architecture particularly suited to wartime conditions.[10]

In his book *Architecture préfabriquée* (1946), Abraham opposed the idea of any extension of industrialisation to the production of major elements or whole buildings, arguing instead for the rationalisation of traditional building.[11] His book opens with a clear differentiation between the artisanal processes of building and the controlled world of industrial mass-production: 'Terminology – you build a house; but you assemble a lorry'.[12] However, if the construction of a building could not be industrialised, this did not mean, he argued, that the building industry could 'ignore the factory' as nearly all building materials, tools and mechanical plant were produced by highly developed industries. What was needed in his view was to extend this industrial capacity to the mass-production of standardised components in order to increase the productivity of the industry.

This mainstream view was vigorously opposed by the younger and more radical architects led by Lods and Prouvé. They saw this approach as tainted by its Vichy origins, a product of working in the shadow of defeat. It seemed to suggest too ready an acceptance of limited resources, of the rolling back of the modernisation of the inter-war years, of the devastated state of French industry, too obvious an acquiescence in the reactionary values of Vichy. Instead, their vision of a new modernity drew inspiration both from the technological fascinations of the pre-war avant-garde, now up-dated and recast by the experience of the war, and from the extraordinary mechanised might of America and the allies.

In place of mainstream caution, they argued that the current shortages and difficulties of the immediate post-war period were but a temporary interruption of the natural evolution of the building industry away from traditional methods to new forms of construction appropriate for an industrialised society. To the objections of the pragmatists that this vision was irrelevant

NICHOLAS BULLOCK

to current conditions in France and no more plausible than the machinist fantasies of the pre-war years, the modernisers argued that far from accepting Abraham's distinction between building a house and assembling a lorry, the urgent demands of reconstruction required a radical rethinking of how to produce housing. If, in the special conditions of wartime, industry could mass-produce everything from Liberty ships to bombers then the peacetime production of something as simple as a house should be straightforward. The problem of the house needed to be rethought in terms of the manufacture of products like the Jeeps not in the traditional terms of the building industry.[13]

This group could point to a number of successful applications of this approach: before the war, with his partner Beaudoin, Lods had worked with Prouvé on buildings such as the covered market at Clichy (1936–39) and the small but elegant Aéroclub at Buc of 1935.[14] Even in the difficult conditions following the Liberation there had been successes. Developing ideas on which he had been working for the French Air Force before the war, and which he had taken further during the occupation, Prouvé was asked in the spring of 1945 by MRU to produce 800 emergency housing units for Lorraine.[15] Despite the shortages of materials, particularly steel, and transport, Prouvé and his sub-contractors were able to deliver and erect over a six-month period 450 emergency dwellings, erected on site using factory-produced components. By the late summer of 1945, Prouvé had high hopes that his ideas might be taken up on a larger scale by MRU. At last it appeared that the possibility of producing houses by means of full industrialisation was at hand. All that was now necessary for success was to win those in command at MRU to the cause.

› 'Heavy' versus lightweight models of industrialised building

To explore the potential of these two approaches MRU organised from early in 1946 a series of competitions to test in practice the claims made for different forms of construction. MRU's first attempt to promote non-traditional ways of building was the construction of 56 individual houses, rather than flats, in Noisy-le-Sec, a railway suburb to the east of Paris.[16] Submissions were invited not just from France but from abroad in an attempt to draw on wartime experiments with non-traditional construction in countries like Sweden, the UK and the USA. Though the majority of houses were French and built of precast concrete, a small number were of lightweight construction. Comparison between the different forms of construction was difficult and the results inconclusive but what did emerge was highly damaging to the cause of lightweight construction. There were two lightweight houses from France: a steel house by Chemineau and Mirabaud abandoned before completion and Prouvé's house that took longer to build and was far more expensive than its 'heavy' competitors. Worse, the houses from the US, with its long tradition of lightweight timber panel construction, were dismissed by critics and the French public as being built of little more than cardboard and quite unsuitable for France.

The next major competition, in 1949 for 200 dwellings at Villeneuve-Saint-Georges, a railway suburb to the south of Paris, was for flats not houses thus favouring 'heavy' construction.[17] Not only was the basis for the comparisons of cost and construction times to be firmer but a more active attempt was made to engage the interest of large public works contractors. Each entry had to be made by a team consisting of architect, engineer and contractor with submissions to include full costings and a detailed programme of construction. The winning 12 storey tower blocks appeared to confirm the view that prefabricated 'heavy' construction for serial production could be significantly cheaper and quicker than traditional forms of building.

However, the culmination of MRU's first programme of competitions was the attempt to demonstrate the benefits of reducing unit costs by building a still larger development – this time of 800 dwellings – at the Cité Rotterdam in Strasbourg. The winning project, by Beaudoin and the contractors Boussiron, combined an imaginative site layout around a generous open space with the rigorous rationalisation of detailed design to speed production and pare costs to a minimum. Finished on time and on budget, MRU claimed it was 20 per cent below the cost of traditional construction and presented it as a triumphal vindication of its policy of promoting industrialised building.

This well-publicised success set the pattern for a number of even larger experimental projects during the 1950s: the building of '4,000 dwellings for the Paris region' on six sites around Paris and the nationwide programme for the *Secteur Industrialisé*.[18] Prototypes for a long-term programme of 'Construction' rather than 'Reconstruction', they were the models for the surge of large housing developments built from the mid 1950s that were to change the suburbs of so many large French cities. Their forms were presented in the architectural press as a clear product of a rational approach to construction and a successful collaboration between the engineer, the contractor and the architect, the very qualities that Viollet-le-Duc claimed to see in the work of the medieval mason/architect.

The triumph of 'heavy' prefabrication did not mean the end of Lods and Prouvé's hopes of developing a lightweight industrialised architecture. In the immediate post-war years their ambitions were shipwrecked by the absence of materials like steel and the architectural importance of housing which with its cellular nature of mass-housing was so much better suited to masonry or concrete construction. Even Lods was compelled by the logic of materials and structure to work with 'heavy' prefabrication. His project for Sotteville-les-Rouens, originally intended (like the Cité de la Muette at Drancy) to be built with a steel frame had to be built using a reinforced concrete frame and his major housing projects of the 1950s – the 4,000 dwellings for Paris that he built as head of a 'college' of architects and the 800 dwellings at Marly les Grandes Terres – made exemplary use of the pre-cast concrete components.[19]

But by the early 1950s Prouvé was assembling a number of buildings that exemplified in the most elegant and sophisticated form what an architecture of lightweight assembly might be like.[20] The building for the Centenary of Aluminium, the delicate pump room at Evian and the curtain wall for the Fédébat Building are a reminder of a pre-war tradition of building exemplified by Beaudoin and Lods' little flying club and their market hall at Clichy. They anticipate the technical sophistication of buildings like Raymond Lopez's office building for the Consigne d'allocations familiales inspired by Lever House and other buildings that French architects had seen when they visited the USA under the auspices of the Marshall aid programme.[21] By the end of the first post-war decade, an architecture of lightweight assembly was to be seen in France alongside the architecture of 'heavy' prefabrication.

> ## Conclusion: Perret and his students at Le Havre

The widely published photographs of 'industrialised' building, the Cité Rotterdam under construction with the panel casting factory at the foot of the travelling cranes or the taut, unclad steel frame of the CAF against the backdrop of the Eiffel Tower, were reminders of the parallels between the architecture of the first post-war decade and the heroic engineering so admired by the pioneers of the new architecture. They were a visual rejoinder to Le Corbusier's opening paragraphs in *Vers une architecture*: by the mid 1950s the architect could legitimately claim to be working as rationally and economically as the engineer.

But could the work of these architects – working with the new forms of building – claim to have achieved an architecture that exemplified a new visual order capable of addressing larger questions such as the relationship between past and present, so central to the larger debates about France's post-Liberation condition? Much of the architecture of the first postwar decade was necessarily utilitarian, much – disparaged as *le style MRU* – was uninspired.[22] But occasionally contemporaries saw in the rebuilding of France's towns and cities an architecture that went beyond the utilitarian and the economical to engage with larger architectural themes. The most widely recognised was not le Corbusier's Unité d'habitation but the work of Auguste Perret and the team of ex-students, the Atelier du Havre, responsible for the reconstruction of Le Havre.[23]

The 'structural classicism' of Le Havre's reconstruction was rooted in Perret's rationalist beliefs, developed since the turn of the century, in the centrality of construction as a determinant of architectural form.[24] In the widespread use of the techniques of prefabrication and pre-stressing for both the apartment blocks and for the major public buildings, the reconstruction of Le Havre shared the priorities of rationality and economy with the major housing projects like the Cité Rotterdam.

But the architectural vocabulary of Perret's Le Havre was explicitly rooted in the classical tradition, anticipating the way that a later generation of Neo-rationalists, Rossi, Aymonino or Krier, would again turn to classicism as a source of architectural authority. Perret's contemporaries read the architecture of Le Havre as entirely appropriate for the port city whose rebuilding was key to regenerating the national economy. It stood for a continuation into the present of an illustrious architectural past that had celebrated the great achievements of the French state, be it under Louis XIV or Napoleon. With its use of modern construction to realise a formal vocabulary of frame and infill, Perret's architecture answered perfectly the ambiguities of a reconstruction called upon to privilege both the ties of the past and the promise of the future. The monumental qualities of Le Havre's town hall, set at the end of main north–south axis, the *cardo maximus*, leading down to the port was widely publicised – and welcomed – as an emblem of the new France, modernising and forward looking but still in touch with the great traditions of her past.

> Notes

1 Jean Louis Cohen, *Architecture in Uniform*, CCA, New Haven and London: Yale University Press, 2011, chapter 4.
2 Eric Mumford, *CIAM Discourse on the Urbanism, 1928–1960*, Cambridge MA: MIT Press, 2000.
3 For an international summary of approaches to reconstruction see Carlo Olmi (ed.), 'The Reconstruction in Europe after World War II', *Rassegna*, 54, 1993.
4 Danièle Voldman, *La reconstruction des villes françaises de 1950 à 1954, histoire d'une politique*, Paris: L'Harmattan, 1997.
5 Ibid., chapters 3 and 11.
6 Yvan Delemontey, *Le béton assemble, prefabriquer la France de l'après–guerre (1940–1955)*, Ph.D. dissertation Université de Paris 8 and Université de Genève 2009.
7 Voldman, *La reconstruction des villes françaises de 1950 à 1954*, see note 4, chapter 4.
8 The radicals included André Sive, Lionel Mirabaud, Jean Chemineau, Henri Prouvé and the engineer Vladimir Bodiansky and were supported by Eugène Claudius-Petit, the future Minister of Reconstruction et Urbanisme and a long-term supporter of modern architecture; see Benoit Pouvreau, *Un politique en architecture, Eugène Claudius-Petit (1907–1989)*, Paris: Le Moniteur, 2004, chapter 7.
9 For example, Pol Abraham, 'Orleans, Une expérience de préfabrication', *Technique et Architecture*, 6, 7–8, 1946, pp. 312–319; Pol Abraham, 'L'Industrialisation du bâtiment', *L'Architecture Française*, 58–59, 1946, pp. 77–79.

10 For the scope of Chantier 1425 see Guy Pison, 'L'enquête rurale du Chantier 1425', *Techniques et Architecture*, 3, 11–12, pp. 561–76.

11 Pol Abraham, *Architecture préfabriquée*, Paris: Dunod, 1946.

12 Ibid, p. 1.

13 This opposing view was given generous coverage by *L'Architecture d'Aujourd'hui* and *Techniques et Architecture*: Marcel Lods, 'L'Industrialisation du Bâtiment', *L'Architecture d'Aujour'hui*, 1945, 1, pp. 29–30 and the special number of *L'Architecture d'Aujourd'hui*, 1946, 4, devoted to the subject of prefabrication.

14 This pre-war work was given new coverage in 1946, *L'Architecture d'Aujourd'hui*, 4, 1946, pp. 10–12.

15 Prouvé's work in Lorraine was reported in *L'Architecture d'Aujourd'hui*, I, 1945, 2 (July–August), pp. 76–77 and again the following year in the same journal, II, 1946, 4 (January), pp. 19–28.

16 Nicholas Bullock, 'You assemble a Lorry, but you build a House, Noisy-le-Sec and the French Debate on Industrialised Building 1944–49', *Construction History*, 22, spring 2007, pp. 75–96.

17 Nicholas Bullock, 'Developing prototypes for France's mass housing programme 1949–53', *Planning Perspectives*, 22, January 2007, pp. 5–28.

18 Nicholas Bullock, '4,000 dwellings from a Paris factory, Le Procédé Camus and State sponsorship of industrialised housing in the late 1950s', *ARQ*, 13, 1, 2009, pp. 59–72, and Nicholas Bullock, '20,000 dwellings a month for forty years, France's industrialised housing sector in the 1950s', *Construction History*, 23, 2008, pp. 56–76.

19 For work of Marcel Lods see Pieter Uyttenhove, *Marcel Lods, Action, Architecture, Histoire*, Lagrasse: Verdier, 2009.

20 Peter Sulzer, *Jean Prouvé: oeuvre complete: vol. 4, 1944–1954*, Basel: Birkhäuser, 2005.

21 Giulia Marino, *Un monument controversé: la Caisse d'allocations familiales à Paris, 1953–2008,* Paris: Picard, 2009.

22 Joseph Abram, *L'architecture modern en France, du chaos à la croissance, 1940–1966*, Paris: Picard, 1997, chapter 2.

23 Le Corbusier's Unité d'habitation was championed principally by *L'Architecture d'Aujourd'hui* whereas Perret's work was published by journals across the spectrum.

24 Roberto Gargiani, *Auguste Perret 1874–1954: teoria e opere*, Milano: Electa, 1993.

DOCUMENTS TWO
1960–1990

Henk Engel

The Neo-Rationalist perspective

If the term 'architects of reason' has any meaning, I believe it must relate to the experience in architecture (and hence in building, the city, its assessment in the light of history and so on) that specifically led to an analysis and construction of architecture in rational terms, in other words making use of techniques peculiar to reason.[1]

Precisely because of the special significance of the analytical choice in this case, in the openly stated purpose of arriving at criteria of certainty and of expressing constant and general elements, precisely because of this characteristic coincidence of analysis and design in a common cognitive goal, architecture is seen here as a construction, in other words as a procedure that follows a logical series of choices.[2]

Giorgio Grassi, *La costruzione logica dell'architettura*

› The presence of the past

The return to rationalism in architecture after the Second World War grew out of the discussions concerning a new impetus for Modern Architecture in the 1950s and 1960s. Early on, the debate was most lively in CIAM and in architectural journals in Britain and Italy, especially *The Architectural Review* and *Casabella Continuità*. The role of 'monumentality', the future of 'historic city centres', the question of 'regional traditions' – in short, the relationship of modern architecture to history – became the main topic of the debate and would eventually strike at the very roots of the discourse of modernity in architecture.[3] By the end of the 1970s a complete shift in the assessment of Modern Architecture had taken place, exemplified by the precarious concept of Postmodernism. Modern Architecture had ended up as a historical footnote.

In this process of transformation – brought about by architects, critics and historians alike – Neo-Rationalism had its own particular place. It is important to remember that, when Charles Jencks borrowed the concept of Postmodernism from the field of literary criticism in 1977, he specifically excluded Neo-Rationalism.[4] In *The Language of Post-Modern Architecture* (1977), Jencks aimed at a radical eclecticism, in contrast to the purism of Aldo Rossi's housing at Gallaratese in Milan (1969–1970).[5] Although Heinrich Klotz, in *The History of Postmodern Architecture*, proposed a broader scope for the concept, he too made a clear distinction between the stylistic pluralism of American architects like Robert Venturi and Charles Moore and the return to rationalism of Aldo Rossi and Oswald Mathias Ungers; the two key developments in the emergence of Postmodernism (American and European).[6] Nevertheless, during the 1970s a growing international dialogue emerged, and in 1980, curated by Paolo Portoghesi, the two extremes collaborated in the ironic setting of the *Strada Novissima* at *The Presence of the Past*, the first International Exhibition of Architecture at the Venice Biennale.[7] Now at the apex of his international fame, Aldo Rossi was a significant presence with his Teatro del Mondo and the entrance to the exhibition site. Back in 1964, a bridge and outdoor exhibition spaces at the Thirteenth Milan Triennale had foreshadowed his subsequent metaphysical architecture. *The Architecture of the City* was published in 1966, and, as he wrote later, it was a book whose time had clearly come.[8]

Neo-Rationalism had been launched in the international arena at the International Section on Architecture of the Fifteenth Milan Triennale (1973). Under Rossi's direction, the exhibition highlighted the work of a group of young Italian architect teachers within the broader context of modern architecture. *Architettura Razionale*, the book published to mark the exhibition, was received as a manifesto of Neo-Rationalist architecture.[9] Among the many designs illustrating the aspirations for a 'new architecture', Rossi's designs for the urban square in Segrate, the Gallaratese housing project and the school in Fagnano Olona were best qualified to represent the intentions stated by Massimo Scolari in 'The New Architecture and the Avant-Garde'.[10]

1973 can be seen as the turning point in Aldo Rossi's career; yet, at the same time, the perspective of Neo-Rationalism was changing. For Rossi the exhibition was an opportunity to present the work of the *Tendenza* as a continuation of the rationalist approach in modern architecture, in contrast to expressionist trends. A broad spectrum of similar endeavours outside Italy was represented by the work of Ungers, Martin, Stirling, the Krier brothers and the New York Five.[11] Even work by Robert Venturi was present at the exhibition, although it was not included in the book. This was the background to the (academic) profile of the Italian *Tendenza*. Beyond Italy, the Kriers gave Neo-Rationalism a more radical outlook. The tone of the prevailing discourse changed from critical reflection to outright declamation.

In 1975 Rob Krier's *Urban Space*[12] was published and the exhibition *Rational Architecture* was organised in London by his younger brother Leon. The book *Rational–Architecture–Rationnelle 1978* followed.[13] Rob had studied in Munich and worked with Ungers in the mid-1960s on *Grünzug-Süd* in Cologne, his first exemplary urban project involving morphological urban analysis. Meanwhile, in 1969, Leon had moved from the University of Stuttgart to work for James Stirling.

Out of key with Rossi's and Ungers' initial work, public space became the main focus of Neo-Rationalism. Urban morphological analysis had created a critical distance from the new discipline of territorial planning, underpinning the claim of autonomy for the architectural project.[14] The Kriers, however, aimed at the total dissolution of 'late capitalist' planning and the resurrection of 'urban design' in the spirit of Camillo Sitte's 'art of building cities': 'The revolutionary element of the new architecture does not lie in its form but in the model of its social use, in its coherency, in the reconstruction of the public realm.' Neo-Rationalism, in their view, was to be seen as 'a critical attempt at the *Reconstruction of the European City*'.[15]

This shift in focus, towards restrictive rules for urban design, had serious consequences. Any suggestion of continuity with 'the Rationalism of the 1920s' was denied, just as earlier with *Team 10*. CIAM and especially Le Corbusier's *Ville Radieuse* were blamed for providing the 'architectural model' for the destruction of inner cities and for the bleak suburbs built after the Second World War. This position was restated at the end of the 1970s in various publications such as Castex, Depaule and Panerai's *Formes urbaines: de l'îlot à la barre* (1977 – Urban Forms: The Death and Life of the Urban Block – see note 16), and Rowe and Koetter's Contextualist manifesto *Collage City* (1978).

These publications basically aimed to replace one 'architectural model' with another, and did so with the same kind of propaganda and apocalyptic perspective on the development of 'the city', which they shared with Le Corbusier.[16] The *Tendenza*, on the contrary, specifically set out to break this coercive hegemony in architectural practice and education.

› The project of the *Tendenza*

Rossi's work as a scholar and an artist is crucial to an understanding of Neo-Rationalism, but the shift in perspective after the Milan exhibition makes it difficult to reconstruct the initial 'academic and didactic project' of the *Tendenza*. As his international reputation grew, Rossi's discourse became increasingly personal, something that was confirmed in the publication of *A Scientific Autobiography* by Oppositions Books in 1981.[17] The American edition of *The Architecture of the City* followed. Peter Eisenman, the editor (and director of the New York IAUS) noted that its relevance lay not so much in the actual book as in 'the Rossi that this book anticipates;' accordingly, the book, 'notwithstanding its attempt to place itself within a certain "scientific" writing about the city, is a very personal text.'[18]

In reviewing the project of the *Tendenza*, and Neo-Rationalism in general, exactly this 'attempt to place itself within a certain "scientific" writing' is important. As Scolari argued, the aim of the *Tendenza* was nothing less than a refounding of architecture as a discipline and an attempt to instigate 'a new design method, rational and transmittable'.[19] For Scolari, the success and the failure of the *Tendenza* were very much connected with Rossi's career. Clearly, *The Architecture of the City*'s raison d'être lay in the academic world of architectural education and research.[20]

This consensus, however, 'turned into the most undesired but also most expectable results: formal imitation.' According to Scolari, 'imitative processes are not particularly reproachable; major schools adopted it, and successfully too. But in the case of the Tendenza this was not a conscious didactic decision, but the result of a difficult personal poetics.'[21]

The Architecture of the City was based on the typological and morphological studies of the city of Padua and Rossi's series of lectures at the *Istituto Universitario di Architettura di Venezia* to mark Carlo Aymonino's appointment as professor in 1963.[22] Together with Aldo Rossi and Costantino Dardi, Aymonino developed a theory in which building typology, his field of study, was related to the morphological study of the city.[23] Until then, these two areas of study had been examined separately. Aymonino's 'team' formulated a logical relationship between the two: 'Each of these two disciplines studies a class of homogeneous facts. However, the building types that are realised are in fact the buildings of which the city is made up.'[24]

Although only an initial synthetic result of the work done in Venice, *The Architecture of the City* displayed no small ambition in paving the way for the development of a 'science of the city'.[25] Venturi's *Complexity and Contradiction in Architecture* was published the same year; and, just as Rossi's book was crucial to the formation of European Neo-Rationalism, so Venturi's book was to American Post-Modernism.[26] Although both books have been viewed as criticisms of Modern Architecture, their approach is quite different. Venturi's book opens with a direct attack on 'the puritanically moral language of orthodox modern architecture', a comment which reveals how this European phenomenon was introduced into the US under the banner of a style: the International Style.[27]

Rossi and the *Tendenza* chose as their key concept not 'style' but 'the architecture of the city', just as had O. M. Ungers, and later the Kriers and the French research group at the Versailles School. This focus on the city, considered the prerogative of Neo-Rationalism, was in fact shared by inter-war Rationalism. CIAM in particular had made the city central to their architectural agenda, so that the discipline became subservient to economic and social planning processes. In the Italy of the early 1960s this again became a serious issue in the debate on territorial planning.[28]

At the tenth congress of the National Institute of Urban Planning in 1965, the Venice-based researchers turned against the prevailing obsession 'with the problem of "the whole": the overall master plan of the city. In their view, architecture and urbanism had lost all sense of the singular intervention'.[29] Immediate needs, political requirements and urban affairs as a whole are naturally the basis for every development process; however, its tangible reality depends on the moment of formalisation, on the concept and design of the work.

The Architecture of the City was conceived against this background. In the preface to the second edition, published in 1969, Rossi confirms that the main purpose of the book is 'to focus on the meaning of the individual project by analysing the way in which it becomes an urban fact'.[30] The theories of the Modern Movement have a major place both in his book and, even more so, in Giorgio Grassi's *La costruzione logica dell'architettura* (The Logical Construction of Architecture). Taking account of the legacy of architecture as an autonomous force determining the form of the city, modern architecture is seen as just one episode among others, and its moral and political claims beyond the Heroic Period are abandoned.

The ideological impact of the two fundamental town-planning models in modern architecture – the English Garden City and Le Corbusier's *Ville Radieuse* – on the city as a whole is of little importance. What counts is their real impact on cities.[31] As competing forms of typological criticism, closely related to 'the social question' and housing in particular, both models are firmly rooted in the history and fabric of the European city. Consequently, *The Architecture of the City* paid particular attention to individual instances, mainly in central Europe: Vienna, Berlin, Hamburg and Frankfurt am Main.

The modern architecture built in these cities between the wars was a specific manifestation of municipal strategies to tackle the speculative practice of the *Mietskasernen* (rented housing blocks). Linked to political struggles, such projects should be analysed as specific transformations of the architectural fabric.[32] To Rossi, they confirmed a general rule of urban growth and change, expressed in the notion of 'the city of parts'. This stated that the architecture of a city cannot be reduced to a single fixed model.[33] Over time, the city incorporates successive projects, which, as *faits accomplis*, become the context for subsequent works.[34]

Postulating 'a science of the city' as Rossi did – that is a science of its construction over time confirmed in processes of transformation and conditions of permanence – challenges the ideological legacy of Modern Architecture and concentrates on the architectural syntax of individual interventions. This science of the city was also instrumental in overcoming the dominant role of art history in modern architectural criticism.

› The analogous city

The leitmotif of the 1973 Milan exhibition was a panoramic *capriccio*, a scenic view of an imaginary city, painted by Arduino Cantafora. It was the first visual representation of the concept of the 'analogous city'. The painting shows Rossi's designs in the select company of the Roman Pantheon, the Tower of Pisa, two of Boullée's projects, Antolini's design for the Foro Bonaparte in Milan, a small pyramid by Friedrich Weinbrenner in Karlsruhe and the *Mole Antonelliana* in Turin. They share this fictional urban space with buildings by Behrens, Poelzig,

Loos, Mies van der Rohe and Terragni, with slabs from Ludwig Hilberseimer's Vertical City appearing in the background.

The programmatic significance of the painting becomes evident when compared with the scenic view of the central area in Le Corbusier's *Ville Contemporaine* (1922 – The Contemporary City). Instead of a pastoral landscape with glazed skyscrapers, Cantafora's painting places the 'new architecture' amid a jumble of works from the past. In the context of the exhibition, 'Rational Architecture', now as previously, can evidently only be based on the tangible experience of architecture in history.

Rossi introduced his concept of 'the analogous city' following publication of *The Architecture of the City*. His focus shifted from urban analysis to design theory; 'Architecture for Museums', a lecture given in 1966, is a key text. It shows how design as an individual activity, with an inherent subjectivity, can be conceptualised in relation to architecture as a collective entity – its own history as laid down in cities and their monuments, as well as in unbuilt designs, treatises and manuals.

'The creation of a design theory is the first objective of an architectural school before all other types of research' Rossi argues, emphasising that a design theory must be seen as part of a theory of architecture: 'To talk about a theory of design I have to say first what I think architecture is. I shall give some definitions of the term "architecture"; I shall then go on to say by which criteria architectural design should be inspired, and what are its relations with architectural history. I shall end by saying what I consider to be the essential terminology of architecture, the city, history, the monument'.[35]

This was precisely the subject matter of *The Architecture of the City*, but the relationship between design and urban analysis is not discussed directly. In 1965 Rossi became professor at the *Politecnico* in Milan where, together with Giorgio Grassi and his staff, a new research group was formed (continuing until he was dismissed in 1971). Two key essays by Rossi from this period are his 'Introduction to Boullée' (1968) and 'L'architettura della ragione come architettura di tendenza' (1969), in which he introduced the concept of 'analogy'.[36] The studies by other members of the Milan group, however, are equally interesting, above all Giorgio Grassi's *La costruzione logica dell'architettura* (1967).[37] In his introductions to new editions of *The Architecture of the City*, Rossi repeatedly refers to the newly developed notions of 'the analogous city' and 'the logical structure of architecture'.

Significantly, the research group's joint publication *Urban Analyses and Architectural Design* (1970) included two crucial essays by Rossi and Grassi, focused on the question 'How can architectural analysis be seen as part of design?'[38] In 'The Goal of Our Research' Rossi states: 'What we look for in the study of the city is the attempt to put together an "analogous city", a series of elements linked together in the urban and territorial context, to form the basis for the new city. The analogous city uses places and monuments whose meanings are derived from history with which it identifies itself while it defines its form.'[39] In 'Analysis and Design' Grassi investigates this methodology in further depth.

By implication, in this rational approach the selection and classification of architectural elements was envisaged as part of a logical structure, demonstrating their value in the formal syntax of the architectural project. Logical structure lent itself to analytical judgment, its bond with reality secured by virtue of convention. In this sense, the new foundation of architecture envisaged by the *Tendenza* was not simply a return to 'origins' or 'archetypes'. It viewed the operative rules of architecture as a cognitive process, which provided the only basis for speculative design. Structured as 'a genealogy of references', 'the analogous city' would bridge the gap between analysis and architectural design, between the collective corpus of architecture and individual action.[40]

In his concise formulation of the *Tendenza*, Massimo Scolari defines their project first and foremost as a process of *clarification*:[41]

> For the *Tendenza*, architecture is a cognitive process that in and of itself, in the acknowledgement of its own autonomy, is today necessitating a refounding of the discipline; that refuses interdisciplinary solutions to its own crisis; that does not pursue and immerse itself in political, economic, sociological, and technological events only to mask its own creative and formal sterility, but rather desires to understand them so as to be able to intervene in them with lucidity – not to determine them, but not to be subordinate to them either.[42]

Besides its appeal to the rationalist tradition in architecture, the rationalism of the *Tendenza* was informed by the philosophy of science of the Vienna School, providing an antidote to the pervasive influence of Benedetto Croce in Italian culture. Grassi's reference to Rudolf Carnap's *Der logische Aufbau der Welt* (1928, translated into English in 1967 as *The Logical Structure of the World*) in his book *La costruzione logica dell'architettura* confirmed this polemical link.[43] Special attention should be given to the Marxist philosopher Ludovico Geymonat who introduced 'New Rationalism' in Italy.[44] Geymonat argued that 'scientific work' confounded any uniform methodology, and that consequently philosophical rationalism could only analyse the historical formation of different kinds of knowledge, and clarify their assumptions.[45]

› Structure and event

The publication of *Architettura Razionale* in 1973 can be seen as the end of the period of Milanese influence. Scolari's 'The New Architecture and the Avant-Garde' was not only a statement of doctrine, but also a precise distancing from contemporary neo-avant-garde tendencies (Archigram and the Florence-based groups Superstudio and Archizoom). In his view, the legacy of Modern Architecture left the younger generation a fundamental choice: prolonging the utopia of the avant-garde, or refounding the discipline of architecture. In contrast to the revived utopianism of the neo-avant-garde, the *Tendenza* chose the latter, initiating a rigorous reflection on the 'competence' of architecture, its limits and its unique capacity to act as a form of knowledge specific to the field of architecture and urban planning.[46]

Given this perspective, the *Tendenza* should be placed within the wider field of academic studies in architecture and urban planning during the 1960s and 1970s. Subsumed into the category of Postmodernism, its position has been blurred, and further clarification has been impeded by Aymonino's, Rossi's and Grassi's manner of writing. Unlike much contemporary discourse, especially in the field of architecture, theirs was seldom straightforwardly polemical. Concerned to maintain narrative continuity with previous architectural research and to acknowledge related efforts in other disciplines, they address a wide range of academic studies, and a thorough knowledge of other disciplines is necessary if their argument is to be fully understood.

Here we can do no more than briefly reflect on the *Tendenza* as 'an academic and didactic project'. Only from this perspective can the (apparent) criticism of Modern Architecture within the movement be asserted (even today). The central problems the *Tendenza* confronted were the 'scientific' claims of modern architecture and their post-war impact on architectural education. Since these were identified with the concept of Functionalism, Logical Empiricism became the guardian of scientific respectability in the field of architecture and urban planning, and a serious challenge to the traditional conception of the study of design and architectural form.

In this context, Neo-rationalism can be seen as a reflection on what was left to the competence of architecture given the growing number of specialist empirical sciences that invaded its domain. Two publications from the early 1960s reflected this trend: Kevin Lynch's *The Image of the City* (1960) addressed environmental perception and Christopher Alexander's *Notes on the Synthesis of Form* (1964) design methodology.[47] The former became the main focus of Rossi's critique in *The Architecture of the City*, just as the latter became Grassi's in *La costruzione logica dell'architettura*.[48]

To arrive at a descriptive method appropriate to the conception of the city as the primary context of architectural practice, and of an understanding of architecture itself, Rossi chose a radical disciplinary approach. He defined architecture as the art and science of building the city, and the city in terms of that discipline. In *The Architecture of the City*, Rossi proposed the urban artefact as the focus of research in architecture and attempted to define the concepts with which to describe its physical form and mechanisms of transformation.

Here the role of O. M. Ungers in the emergence of Neo-Rationalism is important, not simply because Ungers influenced younger architects as varied as the Kriers, Koolhaas and Kollhoff, but because his early polemical statements recall the developing discourse of the *Tendenza*. Although Klotz ranks Ungers alongside Rossi as a leading proponent of Neo-Rationalism, this relationship has not been fully explained.

It is widely believed that the *Tendenza*'s approach to architecture and the city was based on Saverio Muratori's urban analysis.[49] This seems highly questionable, however, since Muratori was seen as rather conservative by the younger generation.[50] *Casabella* in 1960 was the first international journal to publish Ungers' work, with an introduction by Aldo Rossi.[51] Ungers's 'Towards a New Architecture' (1960) and his notes on the *Neue Stadt* housing project in Cologne (1963)[52] present key notions that were to form the basis for Rossi's *The Architecture of the City*: 'the city as a work of art'; 'the analogy of the house and the city'; 'the concept of *genius loci*' and, most important, 'the city of parts'.

Comparison of these short texts and Rossi's detailed book reveals significant differences with respect to these concepts, which are generally taken for granted in the discourse of Neo-Rationalism: morphology and typology. Whereas morphology is central to Ungers's argument, linked via Herman Sörgel to the German concept of *Kunstwissenschaft* (history and theory of art);[53] this term is absent from Rossi's text. In contrast, Rossi pursued the concept of type, defined by Quatremère de Quincy as a regulating principle established prior to decisions about form and its constitution.[54]

Finally, we should be cautious about linking the *Tendenza*'s attitude towards analysis and design to the Structuralism found in other disciplines at the time. Rossi did refer directly to Saussure's structural linguistics and Lévi-Strauss' *Tristes Tropiques*,[55] while Scolari pointed to the relevance of Shklovsky and Russian Formalism for an understanding of the *Tendenza*'s design techniques. Rossi himself, however, stated clearly that he did not envisage 'a systematic development of a programme of this type'. Rather, his main interest was in the 'historical problems and methods of describing urban artefacts' and 'the identification of the principal forces at play' in the formation and development of the city.[56]

Saussure's *Course in General Linguistics* presents both a 'synchronic' and a 'diachronic' understanding of language. The former views language as a static system of signs, which has informed structural analysis in other disciplines in terms of the general 'science' of semiotics.[57] Diachronic analysis studies the evolution of language discussed at length in Saussure's *Course* (but this had little impact on the practice of semiotics).[58] It is here, however, that we find the concept of 'analogy', which for Rossi became the key to an understanding of the relationship between the individual architectural project and the architecture of the city.[59]

According to Saussure, 'analogy' belongs to the normal functioning of language, playing an active role in its preservation as a collective sign system and acting as its evolutionary 'creative force'. Although speaking is a rule-based practice, words and sentences are in fact created anew in every individual act of speech.[60] Innovations result from changes in the practice of speaking, i.e. 'the general activity that singles out units for subsequent use'.[61] Every act of speech involves different associative series, and 'analogical innovations' can be seen 'as symptoms of changes in interpretation'.

In this sense every architectural project may be understood as 'an event'. If I understand him correctly, Giorgio Grassi takes this a step further. Logical analysis can clarify the potential rules of the game, but the rule as norm, as principle, shows itself only in the act of design.[62] Perhaps it is only in making this clear distinction between analysis and design that it is justified to speak (now) of a new rationalism in architecture.

› Notes

Editors' note: particular thanks to Kevin Cook for his rigorous help with translation, editing and referencing of parts of this text.

1   G. Grassi, *La costruzione logica dell'architettura*, Turin: Umberto Allemandi & C., 1998, pp. 24–25.
2   Ibid., p. 15.
3   Eric Mumford, *The CIAM Discourse on Urbanism, 1928–1960*, Cambridge MA/London: MIT Press, 2000. See also Henk Engel, 'Team X revisited', *OverHolland* 5, Amsterdam: SUN, 2007, 115–126.
4   Ihab Hassan, 'The Question of Postmodernism', *Performing Arts Journal* 16, 1981.
5   Charles Jencks, *The Language of Post-Modern Architecture*, London: Academy Editions, 1977, p. 20.
6   Heinrich Klotz, *The History of Postmodern Architecture*, Cambridge MA/London: MIT Press, 1988, pp. 210–213.
7   G. Borsano (ed.) *The Presence of the Past*, Venice: Electa, 1980.
8   Aldo Rossi, *The Architecture of the City*, Cambridge MA: Opposition Books/MIT Press, 1982 (first published in Italian as Aldo Rossi, *L'architettura della citta*, Padua: Marsilio, 1966).
9   E. Bonfanti, R. Bonicalzi, A. Rossi, M. Scolari and D. Vitale, *Architettura Razionale*, Milan: Franco Angeli, 1973; *Controspazio* V, 6 (December 1973), special issue on *La Sezione Internazionale di Architettura della XV Triennale*.
10 Massimo Scolari, 'Avanguardia e nuova architettura', in E. Bonfanti, R. Bonicalzi, A. Rossi, M. Scolari and D. Vitale, *Architettura Razionale*, Milan (Franco Angeli), 1977, pp. 153–187 (article published in English as 'The New Architecture and the Avant-Garde', in K. Michael Hays (ed.) *Architecture Theory Since 1968*, Cambridge MA: MIT Press, 1998).
11 Eisenman, Graves, Gwathmey, Hejduk and Meier.
12 Rob Krier, *Urban Space*, London: Academy Editions, 1979 (first published in German as *Stadtraum in Theorie und Praxis*, Stuttgart: Karl Krämer Verlag, 1975).
13 Leon Krier et al., *Rational–Architecture–Rationnelle 1978*, Brussels: Archives d'Architecture Moderne, 1978.
14 Aldo Rossi, E. Mattioni, G. Polesello and L. Semerani, 'Città e territorio negli aspetti funzionali e figurativi della pianificazione continua', in *Atti del X Congresso INU, Trieste, 14–16. 10. 65*, included in Aldo Rossi, *Scritti scelti sull'architettura e la città, 1956–1972*, Milan: Clup, 1978, p. 297. This position was first stated in 1962 by Gianugo Polesello, Aldo Rossi and Luca Meda in *Locomotivo 2*, their competition entry for the business centre of Turin, published in: *Casabella Continuità* 278, August 1963, pp. 48–51. See also Aldo Rossi, 'Nuovi problemi', in *Casabella Continuità* 264, June 1962, pp. 3–6, English digest, pp. V/VI (published in English in *Ekistics* 87, 1963), and Carlo Aymonino, *La città territorio: un esperiménto didàttico*, Bari: 1964.
15 Leon Krier, 'The Reconstruction of the City', in *Rational–Architecture–Rationnelle 1978*, pp. 38–42.
16 For the 'architectural model' concept, see Philippe Panerai, Jean Castex, Jean-Charles Depaule and Ivor Samuels, *Urban Forms: The death and life of the urban block*, Oxford: Architectural Press, 2004, pp. 134–136

(originally published in French as Panerai, Castex and Depaule, *Formes urbaines: de l'îlot à la barre*, Paris: Dunod, 1977).

17   Henk Engel, 'Aldo Rossi, The Architecture of the City', a review of the Dutch edition in *The Architectural Annual 2001–2002*, Rotterdam: (010), 2003, pp. 18–22. See also Umberto Barbieri, François Claessens and Henk Engel, 'Giorgio Grassi en Tendenza gezien vanuit Nederland', afterword to Giorgio Grassi, *De logische constructie van de architectuur* (the Dutch translation of *La costruzione logica dell'architettura*), Nijmegen: SUN, 1997, pp. 212–228.

18   Rossi,*The Architecture of the City* (see note 8), pp. vii/11.

19   Scolari, 'Avanguardia e nuova architettura', see note 10, p. 162 and p. 170.

20   Carlo Aymonino, 'Facoltà di Tendenza?', in *Casabella Continuità* 287 (May 1964), p. 11, English translation p. IX; Daniele Vitali, 'Presentazione di alcuni progetti', in E. Bonfanti et al., *Architettura Razionale* (see note 9), pp. 253–265. See also *Controspazio* IV, 5–6 (March–June 1972) and *Controspazio* V, 1 (June 1973).

21   Massimo Scolari, '*Impegno tipologico*/The Typological Commitment', in *Casabella* 509–510, special issue entitled *I terreni della tipologia*/The Grounds of Typology, 1985, pp. 42–45.

22   The series of lectures was published in *Aspetti e problemi della tipologia edilizia: documenti del corso di 'Caratteri distributivi degli edifici', anno accademico 1963/64*, Venice: CLUVA, 1964; *La formazione del concetto di tipologia edilizia: atti del corso di 'Caratteri distributivi degli edifici', anno accademico 1964/65*, Venice: CLUVA, 1965; *Rapporti tra morfologia urbana e tipologia edilizia: atti del corso di 'Caratteri distributivi degli edifici', anno accademico 1965/66*, Venice: CLUVA, 1966.

23   Carlo Aymonino, 'Über Aldo Rossi', in *Aldo Rossi, Die Suche nach dem Glück: frühe Zeichnungen und Entwürfe*, Munich: Prestel, 2003, pp. 21–25.

24   Aldo Rossi, 'Considerazioni sulla morfologia urbana e la tipologia edilizia', in *Aspetti e problemi della tipologia edilizia: documenti del corso di 'Caratteri distributivi degli edifici', anno accademico 1963/64*, Venice: CLUVA, 1964, republished in Aldo Rossi, *Scritti scelti sull'architettura e la città 1956–1972*, Milan: Clup, 1975, p. 209.

25   'Introduction: Urban Artifacts and a Theory of the City', in Rossi, *The Architecture of the City* (see note 8), pp. 20–27. The studies of the city of Padua were only completed and published in 1970, with remarkable essays by both Aymonino and Rossi: Carlo Aymonino, 'Lo studio dei fenomeni urbani' and Aldo Rossi, 'Caratteri urbani delle città venete'.

26   Robert Venturi, *Complexity and Contradiction in Architecture*, New York: The Museum of Modern Art, 1966.

27   Ibid., p. 22; Henry-Russell Hitchcock and Philip Johnson, *The International Style: Architecture since 1922*, New York: Norton & Co., 1932. For more on the distortions resulting from this *tour de force*, see R. Sierksma, 'INDRUKwekkend: over het codificeren van regels in de architectuur; ook wel: een alternatieve lezing van *The International Style* (1932)', in *OASE Tijdschrift voor architectuur* 42, 1995, 61–86.

28   Manfredo Tafuri, *History of Italian Architecture, 1944–1985*, Cambridge MA/London: MIT Press, 1989 (originally published in Italian as *Storia dell'architettura italiana, 1944–1985*, Turin: Einaudi, 1982).

29   Rossi at al., 'Città e territorio' (see note 14).

30   Rossi, *The Architecture of the City* (see note 8), p. 165 (revised translation by the author).

31   Ibid., pp. 82–86.

32   Ibid., pp. 72–82. See also Giorgio Grassi, 'Introduzione a L. Hilberseimer', in L. Hilberseimer, *Un'idea di piano*, Padua: Marsilio, 1967; Giorgio Grassi, '*Das Neue Frankfurt* et l'architecture du nouveau Frankfurt', in *Texte zur Architektur*, Zürich: Eidgenössische Technische Hochschule, 1973.

33   Rossi, *The Architecture of the City*, p. 64.

34   Aldo Rossi et al., 'Città e territorio' (see note 14), p. 297.

35   Aldo Rossi, 'Architecture for museums', in J. O'Regan (ed.) *Aldo Rossi*, London: Architectural Design, Dublin: Gandon Editions, 1983, pp. 14–25. Published in Italian as 'Architettura per i musei' in Rossi, *Scritti scelti* (see note 14).

36   Aldo Rossi, 'Introduction to "*Architecture, essai sur l'art*"', *UCLA Architecture Journal* 2, 1989, 40–49. Aldo Rossi, 'L'architettura della ragione come architettura di tendenza', a contribution to the catalogue of the *Illuminismo e architettura del '700 veneto* exhibition, Castelfranco Veneto, 31–8 / 9–11 1969. Both texts are also included in Rossi, *Scritti scelti* (see note 14), pp. 346–364 and pp. 370–378.

37   Grassi, *La costruzione logica* (see note 1).

38   Giorgio Grassi, 'Il rapporto analisi progetto', in Gruppo di ricerca diretta da Aldo Rossi, *L'analisi urbana e la progettazione: contributi al dibattito e al lavoro di gruppo nell'anno accademico 1968/1969*, Milano: Clup, 1970. Also in Giorgio Grassi, *L'architettura come mestiere e altri scritti*, Milan: Franco Angeli, 1989, p. 52.

39 Aldo Rossi, 'L'obiettivo della nostra ricerca', in Gruppo di ricerca diretta da Aldo Rossi, *L'analisi urbana* (see note 38), p. 20. Translation taken from Micha Bandini, 'Aldo Rossi', in *A+U Architecture and Urbanism* 11, 1982, p. 20.

40 Massimo Scolari, 'Avanguardia e nuova architettura' (see note 10), pp. 182–184. In the first edition of *Architettura Razionale* a second book by Aldo Rossi was announced: *La città analoga*. Rossi's *I quaderni azzurri 1968–1992* gives a fair indication of how the initial plan to write this book changed over time and finally resulted in the publication (in English) of Aldo Rossi, *A Scientific Autobiography*, Cambridge MA: Oppositions Books/MIT Press, 1981.

41 Scolari, ibid., p. 160.

42 Ibid., p. 162.

43 Rudolf Carnap, *The Logical Structure of the World: Pseudoproblems in Philosophy*, Berkeley CA: University of California Press, 1967.

44 Ludovico Geymonat, *Saggi di filosofia neorazionalistica*, Turin: Einaudi, 1953.

45 Ibid., p. 24.

46 Scolari, 'Avanguardia e nuova architettura' (see note 10), pp. 155–158. For a recent evaluation of the *Tendenza* and the Florence-based groups, see Pier Vittorio Aureli, *The Project of Autonomy: Politics and Architecture within and against Capitalism*, New York: Princeton Architectural Press, 2008.

47 Kevin Lynch, *The Image of the City*, Cambridge MA: Harvard University Press, 1960; Christopher Alexander, *Notes on the Synthesis of Form*, Cambridge MA: Harvard University Press, 1964.

48 Rossi, *The Architecture of the City* (see note 8), pp. 112–114; Grassi, *La costruzione logica dell'architettura* (see note 1), pp. 208–212.

49 Saverio Muratori, *Studi per una operante storia urbana di Venezia*, Rome, 1959. For the further development of the theory and method of Muratorian urban analysis, see Gianfranco Caniggia and Gian Luigi Maffei, *Architectural Composition and Building Typology: Interpreting Basic Building*, Florence: Alinea Editrice, 200 (first published in Italian as *Composizione architettonica e tipologia edilizia: lettura dell'edilizia di base*, Venice: Marsilio, 1979).

50 Giorgio Ciuci, 'Gli anni della formazione/The formative years', in *Casabella* 619–620 (January–February 1995), special issue on Manfredo Tafuri, p. 21.

51 Aldo Rossi, 'Un giovane architetto tedesco: Oswald Mathias Ungers', in *Casabella Continuità* 244 (October 1960), pp. 22–35, English translation p. VI.

52 R. Gieselmann and O. M. Ungers, 'Towards a New Architecture', in U. Conrads, *Programmes and Manifestoes on 20th-century Architecture*, London: Lund Humphries, 1970, pp. 165–166, and O. M. Ungers, 'Zum Projekt "Neue Stadt" in Köln', *Werk* 7, 1963, 281–284, partly translated as 'The City as a work of Art', in J. Ockman (ed.), *Architecture Culture 1943–1968: A Documentary Anthology,* New York: Rizzoli, 1993, pp. 362–364.

53 Ungers, ibid. and H. Sörgel, *Einführung in die Architektur-Ästhetik: Prolegomena zu einer Theorie der Baukunst,* Munich, Piloty & Loehle, 1918.

54 Rossi, *The Architecture of the City* (see note 8), pp. 35–41, with reference to G. C. Argan, 'Sul concetto di tipologia aritettonica'.

55 Ibid., pp. 22–23 and 33–34.

56 Rossi, *The Architecture of the City* (see note 8), p. 23.

57 Umberto Eco, *Opera aperta*, Milan: Valentino Bompiani, 1962 (published in English as *The Open Work*, Cambridge MA: Harvard University Press, 1989); Umberto Eco, *La struttura assenta,* Milan: Valentino Bompiani, 1968.

58 Perry Meisel, Haun Saussy, 'Saussure and his context', introduction to the newly published English translation of *Cours de linguistique générale* (1916) by David Baskin, in Ferdinand de Saussure, *Course in General Linguistics*, New York: Columbia University Press, 2011, pp. XV–XLVIII.

59 Vittorio Savi, *L'architettura di Aldo Rossi*, Milan: Franco Angeli, 1976, pp. 107–108.

60 Ferdinand de Saussure, see note 58, pp. 171–173.

61 Ibid., p. 166.

62 Grassi, *La costruzione logica dell'architettura* (see note 1), pp. 97–125.

Neo-rationalism: Type and Typology

44 Giulio Carlo Argan

Architecture and ideology (1957)

Carlo Giulio Argan, 'Architettura e ideologia', *Zodiac*, 1, 1957, pp. 47–52, extract of English translation, pp. 261–263.

Why has there been so much talk about "setting aside rationalism"; why have some even felt a need to uproot it, as if it were some kind of peril hanging over our culture; why have even its earliest and only approximate premises been challenged, as they have been in Cesare Brandi's recent book *Eliante*? True, those premises were already outdated, not only in the formal concreteness of factual works, but even in the statements made by the leading figures of the movement: Brandi himself, after having pointed out how programs conceived from a pre-dominantly practical and technical point of view preclude any artistic merit, is later obliged to restate his condemnation by pointing out the abstractness and utopianism of the selfsame utilitarianism. It is a fact, then, that an extremely penetrating and sensitive critic like Brandi felt a need to dig up those old and much more than outdated premises; and that contemporary architects cannot help adopting "rationalism" as a point of reference, of departure, or term of comparison, or dialectical position, as if the artistic movement which arose at the beginning of this century and matured in Europe between the two wars implied the appeal to a principle or was to be regarded as a law or condition to any kind of architecture. This was a new classicism, then, or rather a total anticlassicism; but for this very reason absolute and apodictic: in fact, what is now happening to rationalism happened to classicism, which hardly ever constituted a precise formal system but for a long time influenced the work of artists as a particular way of approaching the problems of art.

The "rational" architectural approach may be the opposite of the classical, but "rationalism" certainly has something in common with classicism: how else can we explain that quality of "rationalism" the incongruence of which would be easily noticed if we only realized that periods of philosophical rationalism were marked by a fundamentally classical architecture, contriving to reflect in their structure the rationalistic qualities of a nature obeying constant and therefore objectively knowable laws. It is quite true that classicism and rationalism equally admit the geometrical basis of constructive form; but while classicist theorcticians consider geometry as a natural form *par excellence,* or rather as the very principle of every natural form, "rationalist" theoreticians consider it a constitutionally unnatural form, and, if anything, representative of the logical structure of the mind, or the mind itself separated, as it were, from its own quality of consciousness.

It is not enough to claim that "rationalist" architects are interested not in nature, but in society; this undoubtedly correct position must be followed by an examination of the attitude assumed toward society, beginning with the statement that such an attitude cannot in any case be considered analogous to that adopted by "classicists" toward nature. Carrying to the extreme the criticism of "rationalism," we might say that the limit (or the *felix culpa* of the Illuminists) of that approach lay in its not having carried to their extreme consequences the antinomy between nature and society, or having attributed to society a logical structure, and observance of constant laws, not unlike those which classical theoreticians recognized and exalted in nature. In an age in which the triumphs of scientific and technological research offered apparently unlimited opportunities for man's control of nature, many men (and not only architects) evidently believed that society could be transformed by processes analogous to those by which matter and natural form were being transformed. The mistake would have been unpardonable if "rationalism" had aimed, like classicism, at a gnostic end, the merely objective knowledge of certain constant laws of reality—the laws of society, in this case—rather than those of nature. Aiming, as they did, at acting on a given social situation and at profoundly changing it, we can no longer speak of objective error, nor even of abstractness and utopianism. It would be much nearer the truth to speak of "ideology"; and this is also shown in the fact that very soon theoreticians sought to replace the clearly improper term "rational" with the more technically exact term "functional," or "international," which is more in keeping with its ideological, or even "democratic" (it was Wright himself who suggested it), assumptions, which clearly allude to political thought and content.

› Rationalism and radicalism

As for the leading figures of the "rationalist" movement, none of them ever displayed the speculative balance and the sure grasp of reality which are the typical qualities of the truly great rationalist; but neither did they pose as social reformers, prophets of a perfectly arranged, perfectly orchestrated social future moving to an eternally unvaried rhythm. This ideal of what society ought to be conceals an uneasiness at the thought of what really is; it is more a psychological compensation than a positive program; it can only be deplored that for so long society has been living on these psychological compensations, has been obliged to imagine its own well-being as something which belongs to the beyond, to paradise. Gropius is a tortured man living with vivid pain the crisis which World War I (not to mention World War II) did not resolve but rather created; Le Corbusier reacts to the situation with the paradoxical eruptiveness and capricious excitement of a Picasso—he is the first to discover that as soon as they are found the terse forms of "rationalism" change at sight into myths, idols, fetishes; Mies van der Rohe soars at great and rarefied intellectual heights, but he has experienced the dizziness of looking at the abyss below. What about the Italians? Persico finds "rationalism" a pretext for an indirect criticism, the breaking forth of suppressed political sentiments; for Pagano it is the lever with which he absurdly seeks to reverse a situation; for Terragni it is the basis of a will to poetry which the viciousness of our crude times threatened to suffocate. I believe these examples should be sufficient to show that the architectural movement dominant between the two wars was not in any way connected to a rationalist system (of which, moreover, there are no traces in other fields of culture) but to a glaring problem of human behavior, to a bitter political struggle; and in this sense it has such an advanced position, such an active role that one wonders whether this architecture had not been better defined "radical" rather than "rational." Seen in the historical perspective of the twenties and thirties it becomes, in fact, a rather important aspect of that kind of middle-class reformism which, as eighteenth-century liberalism became more radical, came into contact with the ideological themes and political action of socialism, accepting many of its claims, but also offering itself as an alternative to the growing revolutionary thrust of the working class.

45 Giulio Carlo Argan

On the typology of architecture (1962)

Giulio Carlo Argan, 'Sul Concetto di tipologia architettonica', from: Karl Oettinger and Mohammed Rassem (eds), *Festschrift für Hans Sedlmayr*, Munich: C.H. Beck, 1962. Extract here from: *Architectural Design*, vol. 33, 12, 1963, pp. 564–565, translation by Joseph Rykwert.

*   *   *

Most modern critics who depend ultimately on some form of idealistic philosophy would deny that an architectural typology could in any way be valid. They are right in so far as it would be absurd to maintain that the formal value of a circular temple is increased as it approaches an ideal "type" of circular temple. Such an ideal "type" is only an abstraction; so it is inconceivable that an architectural "type" could be proposed as a standard by which the individual work of art could be valued. On the other hand it cannot be denied that architectural typologies have been formulated and passed down in theoretical treatises and the work of famous architects. It is therefore legitimate to postulate the question of typology as a function both of the historical process of architecture and also of the thinking and working processes of individual architects.

There is an obvious analogy between architectural typology and iconography: typology may not be a determining factor of the creative process, but it is always in evidence much as iconography is in figurative arts, though its presence is not always obvious. How does an architectural "type" appear? Those critics who would admit that types have a certain importance are those who explain architectural forms in relation to a symbolism or to a ritual pattern connected with them. This kind of criticism has not resolved (and cannot resolve) a crucial problem: does symbolic content exist before the creation of the "type" and determine it—or is it just a subsequent deduction? This question of precedence is, however, not decisive where it is considered in the context of an historical process; when symbolic content precedes the "type" and determines it, this content is only transmitted in connection with certain architectural forms; in the same way when the reverse happens, the succession of forms transmits the symbolic content in a more or less conscious manner. There are cases in which symbolic content is sought for consciously as a link to an ancient formal tradition; such a procedure may become an important consideration by virtue of its historical and aesthetic function. Two test cases of a conscious linking of architectural form with ideological content are those of the symbolism of centralized religious building of the Renaissance studied by [Rudolf] Wittkower; and that of a Baroque architectural allegory studied by [Hans] Sedlmayr.

Quatremère de Quincy gives a precise definition of an architectural "type" in his historical dictionary. The word "type," he says, does not present so much an image of something to be copied or imitated exactly as the idea of an element which should itself serve as a rule for the model . . .

> the model understood as part of the practical execution of art is an object which should be imitated for what it is the "type" on the other hand is something in relation to which different people may conceive works of art having no obvious resemblance to each other. All is exact and defined in the model; in the "type" everything is more or less vague. The imitation of "types" therefore has nothing about it which defies the operation of sentiment and intelligence. . . .

The notion of the vagueness or generality of the "type" which cannot therefore directly affect the design of buildings or their formal quality, also explains its generation, the way in which a "type" is formed. It is never formulated *a priori* but always deduced from a series of instances. So the "type" of a circular temple is never identifiable with this or that circular temple (even if one definite building, in this case the Pantheon, may have had and continues to have a particular importance) but is always the result of the confrontation and fusion of all circular temples. The birth of a "type" is therefore dependent on the existence of a series of buildings having between them an obvious formal and functional analogy. In other words, when a "type" is determined in the practice or theory of architecture, it already has an existence as an answer to a complex of ideological, religious, or practical demands which arise in a given historical condition of whatever culture.

In the process of comparing and superimposing individual forms so as to determine the "type," particular characteristics of each individual building are eliminated and only those remain which are common to every unit of the series. The "type" therefore, is formed through a process of reducing a complex of formal variants to a common root form. If the "type" is produced through such a process of regression, the root form which is then found cannot be taken as an analogue to something as neutral as a structural grid. It has to be understood as the interior structure of a form or as a principle which contains the possibility of infinite formal variation and further structural modification of the "type" itself. It is not, in fact, necessary to demonstrate that if the final form of a building is a variant of a "type" deduced from a preceding formal series, the addition of another variant to the series will necessarily determine a more or less considerable change of the whole "type."

Two salient facts show that the formative process of a typology is not just a classifying or statistical process but one carried out for definite formal ends. Firstly: typological series do not arise only in relation to the physical functions of buildings but are tied to their configuration. The fundamental "type" of the circular shrine for instance, is independent of the functions, sometimes complex, which such buildings must fulfill. It was only in the second half of the nineteenth century that an attempt was made to set up a typology based on the order of physical functions (typical plans for hospitals, hotels, schools, banks, etc.) which, however, has not produced any important formal results. Historical "types," such as centrally planned or longitudinal temples, or those resulting from a combination of the two plans, are not intended to satisfy contingent, practical requirements; they are meant to deal with more profound problems which—at least within the limits of any given society—are thought fundamental and constant; it is, therefore, essential to lay claim to all the experience matured in the past in order to be able to conceive forms in such a way that they will continue to be thought valid in the future. However much a "type" may allow of variation, the ideological content of forms has a constant base, though this may—indeed should—assume a particular accent or character at any particular time. Secondly, although an infinite number of classes and sub-classes of "types" may be formulated, formal architectural typologies will always fall into three main categories; the first concerned with a complete configuration of buildings, the second with major structural elements and the third with decorative elements. Examples of the first category are centrally or longitudinally planned buildings; of the second, flat or domed roofs, traviated or arcuated systems; and of the third, orders of columns, ornamental details, etc. Now, it is clear that a classification so constituted follows the succession of the architect's working process (plan, structural system, surface treatment) and that it is intended to provide a typological guide for the architect to follow in the process of conceiving a building. So that the working out of every architectural project has this typological aspect; whether it is that the architect consciously follows the "type" or wants to depart from it; or even in the sense that every building is an attempt to produce another "type."

But if the "type" is a schema or grid and the schema inevitably embodies a moment of rigidity or inertia, the presence of such a schema needs to be explained in the context of an artist's creative process. This leads one back naturally to the general problem of the relation between artistic creation and historical experience, since it is from historical experience that the "type" is always deduced. What requires further explanation, however, is the proposition that at least a part of that historical experience presents itself to an architect who is designing a building in the form of a typological grid. The "type," so Quatremère de Quincy has said, is an "object" but "vague or indistinct"; it is not definite form but a schema or the outline of a form: it also carries a residue of the experience of forms already accomplished in projects or buildings, but all that makes for their specific formal and artistic value is discarded. More precisely in the "type" they are deprived of their character and of their true quality as forms; by sublimation into a "type" they assume the indefinite value of an image or a sign. Through this reduction of preceding works of art to a "type," the artist frees himself from being conditioned by a definite historical form, and neutralizes the past. He assumes that what is past is absolute and therefore no longer capable of developing. Accepting Quatremère de Quincy's definition, one might say that the "type" arises at the moment at which the art of the past no longer appears to a working artist as a conditioning model.

The choice of a model implies a value judgment: a recognition that a certain definite work of art is perfect and has to be imitated. When such a work of art re-assumes the schematic and indistinct nature of a "type," the individual action of the artist is no longer bound to a value judgment; the "type" is accepted but not "imitated" which means that the repetition of the "type" excludes the operation of that kind of creative process which is known as mimesis. In fact, the acceptance of the "type" implies the suspension of historical judgment and is therefore negative;

although also "intentioned," directed to the formulation of a new kind of value in as much as it demands of the artist—in its very negativity—a new formal determination.

It is true that the assumption of a "type" as a starting point for the architect's working process does not exhaust his involvement with historical data: it does not stop him from assuming or rejecting definite buildings as models.

Bramante's tempietto of San Pietro in Montorio is a classic instance of such a process; it obviously depends on a "type": the peripteral circular temple described by Vitruvius (Book IV, Chapter X) which integrates the abstraction of the "type" through historical "models" (for instance, the temple of Sybil at Tivoli), and so appears to claim for itself the status of both model and "type." Indeed it is characteristic of Bramantesque classicism to aspire to a syncretic union of ideal antiquity (which is essentially "typical") and of historical antiquity which has a status of a formal model. An instance of a diametrically opposed attitude is that of neoclassical architects who assume classical architectural typology, not classical architectures, as a model so that the movement produces works which are merely three-dimensional transcriptions of "type." If the concept of typology could in some way be brought back to that of "techtonics" as recently defined by Cesare Brandi *(Eliante o della archa, 1956),* one might say that typology is a notional base on which formal development of the artist must inevitably rest.

It will, therefore, be clear that the position of the artist vis-à-vis history has two aspects, the aspect of typology and that of formal definition. That of typology is not problematic: the artist assumes certain data, taking as a premise of all his work a group of common notions, or a heritage of images with all their more or less explicit content and their ideological overtones. This aspect may be compared to the iconographic and compositional treatment of themes in figurative art. The aspect of formal definition, on the other hand, implies a reference to definite formal values of the past on which the artist explicitly arrives at a judgment. This judgment, however, must itself imply a typology since, whenever a value judgment on given works of art is passed, a judgment must also be passed about the way in which the artist, in creating them, had dealt with the relevant typological scheme.

The question of the value of architectural typology has recently been examined by Sergio Bettini *(Zodiac* no. 5) and by G. K. König *(Lezioni del Corso di Plastica,* Florence: Editrice Universitaria, 1961). In these writings the opinion prevails that an architectural "type" must be treated as a schema of spatial articulation which has been formed in response to a totality of practical and ideological demands. From this one might deduce that the formal invention which overcomes the "type" is a response to immediate demands in reference to which the "type" had lost any real value. A recourse to the "type" would therefore occur when the immediate demand which the artist is called to answer has its roots in the past. A significant instance is provided by the comparison between modern religious and industrial architecture. Industrial architecture which deals with altogether new demands has created new "types" which have, in many cases, great importance for the later development of architecture. Religious architecture which answers demands rooted in the past has resulted in typological repetition (artistically valueless) or in attempts at freeing the artist of all typological precedent (as, for instance, Le Corbusier at Ronchamp). These have led to the proposing of counter-types, mostly ephemeral or unacceptable—there are few instances of modern developments of historical "types."

The conclusion must be that the typological and the inventive aspect of the creative process are continuous and interlaced—the inventive aspect being merely that of dealing with the demands of the actual historical situation by criticizing and overcoming past solutions deposited and synthesized schematically in the "type."

46 Giorgio Grassi

The question of style (1969)

Giorgio Grassi, 'Architettura e razionalismo', Istituto di Composizione Architettonica, Facoltà di Architettura del Politechnico di Milano, N 80, 1969/70, pp. 115–154 extract 'Stilo', translation by Stefania Boccaletti with the editors.

› 2. The question of style

The debate that took place within the Modern Movement about the term 'style' was quite extensive and articulate; while other topics that presented themselves as equally important quickly became mere pretexts for breaking down otherwise promising relationships between different yet often complementary personalities, for instance between Gropius and Theo van Doesburg. Gropius always refused to associate the Bauhaus with the term *style* and somehow (in a fairly unique manner, explained by power and influence) Gropius's voice became invariably, and *tout court,* the official voice of the Modern Movement. The term *style* suffered the same fate as equally *unfortunate* terms during this period (like *classicism*, *monumentality*, etc., which since then have endured authentic and lengthy ostracism), engendering suspicion and rejection, as if the use of those terminologies was in itself proof of a residual link with the past. A choice in principle adopted by almost everyone, but also a strategic choice, a confrontational choice in the fight against academicism which still held strong, a choice against historicism and the last manifestations of eclecticism.

However, the most important avant-garde movements (*De Stijl*, the Constructivists, etc.), if their statements and manifestos are not read too literally, do search for a style that adheres to the canonic meaning of the term; they are in fact seeking a unitary language and common methodology, a new collective language for the arts; in other words, they are searching for a language capable of bringing architecture once again to an equivalent status with the other arts.

It is important to recognize that this ultimate goal will tend to lead architecture, given different modes of expression (or different levels of freedom of expression), to constantly pursue, occasionally in a pathetic manner, the most diverse experiments and provocations.

In using this term [style], the avant-garde movements don't refer to any specific framework or group, because their intentions and programmes have to epitomize a *new style* and furthermore a style at one remove from precedents, without debts nor nostalgia. [It has to be] a revolutionary style that makes no compromise with history, which can start afresh but that nonetheless is a *Stijl* in the classical sense; in other words, a recognizable and unitary style.

Oud's longstanding militancy within Van Doesburg's movement should be understood in relation to this goal, as Oud himself stated in *Mein Weg in 'De Stijl'*:

> Even when I abandoned De Stijl because I didn't agree that with the assertion of a formal rule over a willingness to form (formal purpose), it didn't mean that I wanted to give up all the ideas I had pursued at the very beginning. My contention was, and still is, a universal architecture, a Stijl.

But for Oud, as indeed for Loos, Hilberseimer and Mies, the search for a new style was generated from the need to critically review the totality of historical experience, rather than by a juxta-position of formal and programmatic historical aspects. This stemmed from an interest, concrete and realistic, to view history with a renewed awareness (compared to C19th historicism and contemporary eclecticism); in other words, to perceive the historical roots of their work, reviewing its link with everyday life in a perceptive objectivity, open to historical change. The position of Oud, Hilberseimer and Mies, is richer and more self aware than that expressed in the parameters of the various programs and proclamations signed by De Stijl, 'G' and De 8. And in my opinion, this is one of the more significant lessons that we can now draw from the experience of the Modern Movement as a whole.

Because clearly it is not possible to talk about *style* as an agenda without taking into account temporality and the problem of continuity and duration (in other words the problem of the relationship *pre* and *post-priori*), that is to say, precisely, without a relationship with history. Because the concept of a *style* assumes cohesive means and objectives and is an experience that occurs over time measured by its resistance to time, it is also identified with stability and conservation. However, with regard to the use of the word *style* in the *anti-historicist* programme of the Modern Movement, this was proclaimed as an expedient choice dictated by temporary objectives; that these objectives, because strategic and of the moment, were always connected to a suggestive *slogan* whether about *style* or *anti-style*, does not make much difference. *Style* and *anti-style*; avant-garde and the Bauhaus; *style* and its antithesis; Loos, Tessenow or Oud's rationalism and classicism in search of a new expressiveness, and the romantic empiricism and experimentalism of architects such as Poelzig, Mendelsohn, the Tauts, the Luckhardts, Häring and Scharoun, just to mention the most interesting.

The rationalist choice, concerned to identify the permanent elements of this architecture, leads [us] instead to the consideration of those architectural forms that are beyond history, so to speak; and it aims at two objectives: 1) The isolation of classical forms (to be more precise, the elements of permanence); and 2) The transformation of classical forms into a historically determined and representative formal language. This epitomizes what is meant by *style* in this case, style as the basis for an operative programme. As mentioned previously, Oud refers to *style* as a *willingness to form*; in other words the intent to endow the permanent elements of architecture with historically appropriate form, and in this sense he refers to a *universal architecture*, an architecture that changes over time in continuity with what preceded it. This conception of a universal architecture informs an ongoing search into the general terms of architecture (that is elements which are repeated), capable of unifying different experiences far apart in time, but which concurrently make it historically appropriate that the same form is repeated over time. It is that choice that allows form to belong unequivocally to its own time.

By *style* we mean the architectural expression of forms given a simultaneous place in history *and* in their own time. Universal architecture: that is a programme for architecture diametrically opposed to the *International Style* (one cornerstone of the Modern Movement, and its characteristic *slogan*), an architecture supported by (architectural) history rather than established only in the present. Architecture becomes fundamentally about the 'reconstruction' viewed through the lens of the present of the reality represented by the history of architecture; a form of reconstruction specific and unique to architectural form.

This mode of understanding and general application, in the course of history, determines a *period*, or a group, a tendency, or a *school* etc., but it can also be the trajectory of an individual or single experience. For instance, if we consider the work of an artist, or an architect such as Mies van der Rohe, and analyse it in its totality, as a singular body of work (as it actually is), what stands out is a progressive development of a specific reality, the construction of a personal world of form (Mies's formal universe), and then the characteristics of this formal position become much clearer. The argument is further clarified if we refer to painting and to exhibitions like the comprehensive monographic display of Mantegna's work in Mantua a few years ago (or the current exhibition in Milan on de Chirico). In these instances the entire work of an artist is laid out identically on the wall to be confronted directly and in an ordered sequence that obliterates the actual chronology of production as well as any other forms of 'distancing' between the individual works. From the simultaneous presence of all the works (which bear evidence of, and present an interpretation of, the epoch in which they were actually produced) what emerges with great clarity is the construction of a defined reality, a particular and unique world created by this lengthy process. This [personal] worldview only partially reflects the culture in which it was established, on the contrary it is immediately clear that the author is only concerned to show us a partial aspect of its reality, the one that is pertinent to the completion of his work. It is also characteristic that this aspect is something whose existence is understood unselfconsciously or simply intuited, which we also acknowledge, but only in this particular instance of its specific manifestation and form. This is in fact the expression of a *style*, which allows us to appreciate things from a specific *point of view*, a common perspective. On the walls of a museum another piece of theatre also unfolds, that of the connections formed over time between other experiences which share an objective with the work, that is, which constitute the spectacle of history (whether this is the history of architecture or painting makes no difference) of which only a partial aspect is displayed, one that can be contained in a single experience, fragment, or incomplete (contingent) 'history', but which nevertheless is able to show us the potential and versatility of a specific 'art', here expressed in great depth but along a single path. Such a trajectory is determined by a fully defined and recognizable *idea of architecture* (or painting – again there is no difference), in the idealization and construction of a particular reality, that is again the product of an *idea of architecture* which results in the most comprehensive and general definition of *style*, as both an operational and methodological choice in its broadest sense.

* * *

In any case we cannot talk about an architecture, which transmits, expresses, and represents, an idea of the world, without running the danger of that resting on a series of debased assumptions. This is evident in Arnold Hauser's book the *Social History of Art*, a book, by the way, that if not read as a definitive and exhaustive social analysis of artistic experience but rather as one of several possible vantage points from which social life and art are seen to constitute communal experience, would still retain the originality and depth of its methodological perspective. If we were to exclude the stance taken by *ingenuous symbolism*, so to speak, that is all architectural production which aims to link ideas and forms by explicitly and directly using symbolic or allegorical forms (such as the *architecture parlante* of Ledoux), we could confidently affirm that what architecture expresses through its forms is never an idea of the world, but rather, an idea of its role as part of that world, in relationship to that world, as a critical assessment of itself in relationship to the world that is. And that is what Boullée's fantastic drawings are communicating in their representation of architectures which are visionary and concrete at the same time, and which in their theatrical evocation of other architectures (equally mythical and visionary), are simply attempting to establish a direct relationship, in the most *natural* and at the same time most emphatic way, with the general ideas that inspire them. The difference between Ledoux and Boullée lies in this: while they both have in mind a radically new world, the manifestation of a utopia, reference to these general ideas is, in Ledoux's case transmitted through the use of elementary symbols, the most clear and immediate, even extra-architectural symbols, so long as they are explicit; and with Boullée this is produced exclusively through architecture, through its experience and evocative character, in the authority and persuasion of immortal forms of architecture.

Nevertheless, despite everything, despite its apparent autonomy, the specificity of its task, the singularity and uniqueness of its expression over time, architecture still remains one of the ways, one of the most relevant, to approach an idea of the world that comes before any expressive response (precisely because of the social nature of architecture and because it is first of all a collective work). It can be said that the permanent forms of architecture have been always identified with general ideas to which they have been consistently linked, even if the reasons for that are almost always to be found outside logic and are no longer grounded (just as this has always been an aspiration during periods of notable stability in architecture, that is during moments of unquestionable stylistic unity).

One might ask how evident, if still recognizable, this relationship is nowadays between form and general ideas (which certainly in the past has never been a problem), and how does this relationship remain implicit, permanently imprinted into the forms that manifest it? In general, I believe that this relationship is one of the elements of permanence in architecture, as discussed earlier; but at the same time I believe it is not a direct relationship, it has never been a direct one, not even during its original formation; the proof comes from the 'great' historical movements and singular periods of stylistic unity in architecture. For example, what a Greek temple communicates is certainly not the idea of a direct relationship to its forms, its architecture, or to the elements of its decoration. The more we go back in time, the more the relationship between forms and ideas seems to concern only the most general objectives; beyond these are increasingly separate and autonomous paths; the more different objectives coincide (until they merge) then the more their connections and the modes of expression remain divergent and autonomous. On the one hand there is religiosity and the problem of knowledge in the Greek world, and on the other the Greek temple without tangential relationships, without general or even more specific references; two different worlds essentially. In reality I believe that what unifies forms and ideas, to the point of making them identical, is always and only their common goal, and this is just because that goal is predominantly of an ethical nature. It is about collective choice and the construction of a communal point of view: it is a vote for the future, it expresses a hope and a promise, in itself (with all the possible consequences, including periodically an escape route ahead: the romantic rationale of the avant-garde).

Rationalist thought considers architecture to have a particular perspective, one of several possible ways of comprehending reality, and a world in itself, one having a progressive attitude towards the future. This is how we have to understand referring to ethics in this context, which has both to do with an ethical view of the world as well as of the 'forms' to be found in it. Once again, what is at stake are historical issues: the meaning of forms (with its ethical implications), that is their historical meaning as this has developed over time, as well as their variable and contingent meaning acquired every time they are deployed in the design process. The relation between ideas and the meaning of forms (social, human or ethical) slowly develops over time to become intrinsic to a series of conventions: that is the way we read and employ certain forms to evoke predetermined ideas identified with a number of forms whose meaning is consensual. Forms can consequently have a two-fold reading: on the one hand a persistent meaning evoking general ideas, and on the other a fundamentally tautological character with regard to their internal history and original meaning. For a long period, the design of architecture has not primarily referred to general ideas but, rather, to the persistent forms these have taken, so much so that these forms have become designated to convey these ideas. In other words, this is what we mean when we speak of tautology in architecture as a way to comprehend, interpret, and utilize architectural forms.

Though schematic in its delineation, we could say that Rationalist thought elaborates an *idea of architecture* (both historically and as a design method) as a *heraldic world* in which life and architecture converse with each other only to recognize their mutual inability to directly influence one another. Architecture is defined as a parallel reality, and to make architecture means entering this reality, acting within its own terms entirely, otherwise its very own *raison d'être* will be lost. So, the heraldic world of architecture expresses the same ethical tension which we demand and encounter in our daily life; a tension that has no other way to manifest itself but through its designated forms.

I believe that since classic European thought has made clear that there is a conscious and necessary relationship with the historical experience, this awareness has taken place within the limits circumscribing artistic experience (with regard to the complexities of life). These limits are not reductive since on the contrary they define the boundaries of a parallel and equally expansive field of activity. In this sense the 'world' of architecture is no longer a mediation between forms and life in relationship to predetermined ethical issues and in a way external to its own 'experience', but rather a world that represents an 'ethic' in its own right in demonstrating a manner of communication, illustrative and propositional, that is in first instance critical (in the sense that it confronts and exposes) and at the same time expresses the elements of this critique. In other words it takes an ethical stance in the decision to measure itself against the world through a choice of expression, fundamentally ethical in itself because it directly relates to life. On the other hand, is this not the manner and objective of Oud's critique of Functionalism as a practice, mutated from a means to an end (a scandal, this so-called betrayal by Oud)? But what is this choice if it is not one of a profoundly ethical nature?

47 Massimo Scolari

The new architecture and the avantgarde (1973)

Massimo Scolari, 'Avanguardia e nuova architettura', Massimo Scolari et al., *XV Triennale*, Milan: Franco Angeli, 1973. From: K Michael Hays (ed.), *Architecture Theory since 1968*, Cambridge Massachusetts, MIT Press, 2000, extracts, pp. 131–134 and 137–139, translation by Stephen Sartarelli.

* * *

For the Tendenza, architecture is a cognitive process that in and of itself, in the acknowledgment of its own autonomy, is today necessitating a refounding of the discipline; that refuses interdisciplinary solutions to its own crisis; that does not pursue and immerse itself in political, economic, social, and technological events only to mask its own creative and formal sterility, but rather desires to understand them so as to be able to intervene in them with lucidity—not to determine them, but not to be subordinate to them either.

This cultural position, which has its roots in the legacy of the modern movement as handed down by such masters as Giuseppe Samonà and Ludovico Quaroni, defines itself negatively, opposing what Nino Dardi calls the "*Picturesque International*," which, in accordance with optico-perceptual evaluations, "brings together the secondary derivatives of expressionism and constructivism—Sacripanti's proposals and Moshe Safdie's associations, Michelucci's plasticisms and Scharoun's huts, Archigram's pop architecture, Candilis' inlaid plates, Venturi's geometrisms, Frei Otto's structures, Paolo Soleri's anamorphisms, Gunnar Bikerts's constructions, St. Florian's space capsules—and inevitably reduce the experience of architecture to a series of formal preconceptions in which the apparent freedom of the gesture is actually a limitation to unmotivated choices."[1]

Yet the Tendenza's recognition of a heritage in the modern movement does not mean mechanically absorbing it: the Tendenza accepts all history as *event*, as a "pile of simulacra," and perceives "our architectural culture as a static twilight bathing all forms, all styles, in an equal light."[2]

In this sense, one cannot recognize the Tendenza in the general principles "around which modern architecture has come to be developed, according to the content-oriented and ethical interpretation of it provided by Giulio Carlo Argan: (1) the priority of urban planning over architectural planning; (2) a maximum of economy in the use of the terrain and construction, for the purpose of resolving, if only at the level of a *minimum of existence*, the problem of housing; (3) the rigorous rationality of the architectural forms, which are seen as logical deductions (effects) from objective needs (causes); (4) the systematic use of industrial technology, standardization, mass prefabrication—that is, the progressive industrialization of the production of things having to do with everyday life (industrial design): (5) the conception of architecture and industrial production as factors conditioning the progress and the democratic education of the community."[3] The gap between, as Montale puts it, "the roaring thirties and the rattling fifties," prompt the new generations to look critically on the legacy of the modern movement, particularly on its choice of antihistoricism.

In this way, the book of architectural history, next to the universal drafting device, can become a real image for representing a new critical attitude and a new relationship with history, which for some has actually become the painful stuff of planning, if not the project itself.

The discussion of history thus assumes, for some of the most representative architects, a veritable unit of measure, not only for evaluating mutual differences, but also for calculating the individual *heretical distances* separating contemporaries from the modern movement.

Sigfried Giedion, recapitulating the architectural development of the 1920s in eight points, foregrounded, in the architect of the "third generation," a very strong relationship with the past. It might therefore be interesting to gauge the extent of this relationship in the work of Italian architects. But given the occasion for this essay, we would do well to limit ourselves to certain significant positions as examined by the Tendenza.

Manfredo Tafuri, one of the liveliest architectural historians in Italy, is, on this subject, at least as categorically defensive in his position as Bruno Zevi. Tafuri unequivocally asserts that "even today, we are obliged to recognize history not as a great reservoir of codified values, but as a vast collection of utopias, failures and betrayals." On the subject of its new instrumentalization. Tafuri's judgment leaves no way out: "As a tool of planning, history is sterile; all it can offer are solutions already taken for granted."

Tafuri, though an architect, is an excellent historian—that is, an architect who has chosen history as his field of autobiographical research. And he has done so with such dramatic, trenchant emphasis that in him, the historian's mask has taken on the dignity of the face. In a certain sense Tafuri can be considered one of the most passionate "planners" of the Tendenza, since the relationship to history, though "forbidden" in the designed architecture that he personally does not practice, contains a well-defined project, entirely thought out but no less important or suggestive than those that are "only" designed: a kind of meta-project that extends to all the architecture that is thought, designed and written.

One could say paradoxically that Tafuri is the Italian architect most "dripping with history." In fact Tafuri, who in Venice has succeeded in creating an important, aristocratic school of historians, does not claim *tout court* the death of architecture, as is commonly believed.

In a recent updating of an essay of his,[4] he partially withdrew the apocalyptic prophecy born of the complex cauldron of 1968. The drama of architecture today, for Tafuri, is that of "seeing ourselves forced to turn back to 'pure architecture,' an instance of form devoid of utopia, a sublime uselessness in the best of cases. Yet to the mystified attempts to dress architecture in ideological clothing, we shall always prefer," says Tafuri, "the sincerity of those who have the courage to speak of that silent, unrealizable purity." The reference to the planned and written work of Aldo Rossi is quite explicit here.

Aldo Rossi has the merit of having succeeded in lucidly formulating a Tendenza position which, in the Italian debate, constitutes, if not the only one, at least the most precise, and the one most pregnant with possible developments.

In defining the architecture of Aldo Rossi, the relationship to history is quite useful: "Roman monuments," says Rossi, "Renaissance palaces, castles, Gothic cathedrals, constitute architecture. They are part of its construction. As such they shall always return, not only and not so much as history and memory, but as elements of planning."[5] With a new kind of "operative critique," which Tafuri defines as "typological critique," Rossi assumes history as an uninterrupted event to be studied and explored, to be drawn and written; a world pregnant with magical evocations and inscrutable correspondences.

In planning, Rossi looks to history with an attitude that we shall define as *laconic*. As Ezio Bonfanti acutely noted in his fine essay on Rossi, we find ourselves "before an architecture that underscores its own sectionality and the existence of a limited number of elements"; and "the fact of using finished parts, veritable architectures, as elements, is the very precise choice of an architecture."[6]

By other routes, somewhat more tortuous and twisting, we find the relationship to history in the architectures of an "enlightened" professional such as Vittorio Gregotti.

His very situation as a mannerist compels him to look at history but not to touch it; the anxiety of contemporaneity, consumed in the lacerating convulsions of professional compromise, requires novelty, mutation; every imitation is closely watched. "History," says Gregotti, "presents itself . . . as a curious tool, the knowledge of which is indispensable; but once this is attained, it is not directly usable. It is a kind of corridor through which one must pass in order to gain access, but which teaches us nothing about the art of walking."[7]

Unlike Rossi, who composes *parts* and *pieces* of history without preclusions of time, Gregotti seems more ready to assume history by grasping its possible *variations*, digging out and eroding its most recent and sedimented layers, as in a refined *collage* using fragments with which we are already familiar.

History, for Gregotti, is above all the history of the modern movement, analyzed with the impatience of the gaze more than with the calm of the collector. Gregotti constructs contemporary ambiguity and complexity through complex erosions of form. He starts with the tautological and crystalline, at the very point, that is, where Rossi's project ends.

The true essence of comparison, most useful in tracing the paths of the new architecture, is thus to be found between simplicity and complication, between evocation and description, between the possibilities of the *type* and the repeatability of the *model*.

* * *

In 1963 Francesco Tentori (editor-in-chief of *Casabella-Continuità*, under the direction of E. N. Rogers) presented a group of architects from Milan, Udine, and Trieste, who had joined together in an association under the name of "Incontri del Biliardo" (The Billiard Encounters).[8]

The group—which was actually very heterogeneous (A. Rossi, N. Dardi, V. Gregotti, C. Pellegrini, P. L. Crosta, G. U. Polesello, F. Tentori, G. Canella , E. Mattoni, etc.)—revolved around Rogers's *Casabella* and presented itself in the Italian debate with a profoundly critical attitude toward the 1950s, which had been "a distressing example, for architects, of the Italian path to *arrivisme*."

In subsequent years, many of them made significant contributions as professors (in Milan and Venice) and as the central figures of the most important architectural competitions (the Administrative Center of Turin, the Reconstruction of the Teatro Paganini at Parma, etc.). What they had in common was a militant critical engagement, aimed at calling into question, in the praxis of planning as in university teaching, the entire "doctrine" of the modern movement. This engagement succeeded in bringing the discipline, through the measure of politics, into a broader confrontation with the realities of the whole country, using "the written page not as occasional, detached activity, but as an expression fully consistent and commensurable with the planned work, almost the extension of a single cognitive process."[9]

On the occasion of his survey, Nino Dardi underscored, in the prospects for renewal, the need for a "reinvention of the architectural organisms," proposing the recuperation of certain fundamental moments in modern architecture. Guido Canella, like Vittorio Gregotti already active professionally, posited the need for "overturning the conventional relationship between abstraction and reality, where in the name of reality we are accustomed to accepting the brutal conditioning of an improvident, rapacious society, labeling all radical alternatives as abstract, and where what prove to be abstract are those propositions . . . in which one achieves an effective view of the essential politico-cultural themes of our age that await decisive revolutions."[10]

In more or less explicit ways, the common perspective was that of *architecture as a cognitive problem*, whether specifically as the "conscious call to the city on the part of the most recent modern architecture" (Canella) or as an autobiographical or personal matter (Rossi).

Already at that time, the work of Aldo Rossi (based on studies in Lombard neoclassicism, in Antonelli, Ledoux, Loos, and Le Corbusier, and in the urban morphology and building typologies of Milan) appeared to be the leanest, the most linear, unbendingly aiming at a process of essentialization. "In my projects," said Rossi, "or in what I write, I seek to focus on a rigid world, with few objects, a world already established in its givens. . . . A position of this sort denies, and is unaware of, the whole process of redemptive attribution that the modern movement wanted to impute, as both attitude and formal result, to architecture and art. For this reason I personally—not polemically, but because the problem has a different dimension for me—have never distinguished between modern and non-modern architecture, with the understanding that it is simply a question of making a choice between certain types of models."

And on the subject of urbanism and the city, Rossi continued: "I wonder, and have wondered from the start, what urbanism really is. For now I am unable to see it as anything other than a morphological problem whose field of study is the cities and, in part, other territories. The description of the city's forms, and thus the invention—that is, the new formulation—of these forms, can help us to know and understand something extremely useful."[11]

Yet beyond the individual declarations that we have presented here, what "markings," what "pedigree" precedes the majority of these architects?

For many, Ernesto N. Rogers was an invaluable reference point. Director of one of the most prestigious international architectural reviews (*Casabella Continuità* from 1953 to 1963), Rogers at the time was the only Italian architect with any international stature.

A friend of Gropius, Wright, and Le Corbusier and an active member of the CIAM, he brought the method and maieutic system of Gropius to his magazine and later to the architecture faculty of Milan (1953). His profound commitment to civil society and democracy, together with his acute syncretic intelligence, found in teaching a particularly congenial field of action. His editorials and lectures serve as the central argument for the most advanced sector of Italian architectural culture.

In the classroom, in particular, Rogers shaped the best of the latest generation. His lectures on the problems of the modern movement, on Wright, Behrens, van de Velde, Pagano, and Terragni, on democratic commitment in the university, remain exemplary; as does his slogan— *the utopia of reality*—utopia as "the teleological charge that projects the present into the possible future," and reality as the reasonable surpassing of contingent boundaries."[12]

Equally important is the second reference point, represented by the "culture" and irrepressible action of Giuseppe Samonà. Author of a book of fundamental importance to Italian architectural culture,[13] he was the outstanding dean, professor, and teacher of that miraculous creation that since 1945 has been the Istituto Universitario di Architettura di Venezia.

Alongside these two masters, an unusual and in some ways unique role was played by the "urbanist" Ludovico Quaroni, who, together with the typological studies of Saverio Muratori,[14] the formal rigor of Luigi Moretti and the solitary civic engagement of Mario Ridolfi, constitutes the most incisive point of reference that the Roman school has to offer to the "Incontri del Biliardo."

Here one could extend the "genealogical" picture of this group by discussing the refinement of Ignazio Gardella and the subtle poetics of Franco Albini rather than the rationalism of Piero Bottoni, but I shall resist this nevertheless tempting prospect in order to limit this brief portrait to the essential.

It should suffice to add that the "Incontri del Biliardo" have had increasing difficulty taking place, and that personal affairs and the passage of time have gradually led some away, pushed others to the background, and brought still others to the foreground.

The internal struggles at *Casabella*, followed by the liquidation of the "Rogers staff," eventually shattered that syncretism that had already begun to crack with the polemics over neoliberty and the departure of Vittorio Gregotti in 1961.

This is a good point at which to make an observation. The scattering of the group into various university sites (Rossi, first to Venice and then Milan, Canella to Milan, Aymonino to Venice, Gregotti to Palermo) slowly led to the eclipse of their genealogical references, due to the emphasis of the different directions of their research. Thus when speaking today of the Tendenza, we can no longer include Gregotti's research on the *environment* or Canella's studies of the "consolidation and integration of several functions," and scarcely, and only because of the common theoretical foundations, can we liken the research of Carlo Aymonino and Aldo Rossi, though they are now clearly differentiated from each other on the planning level.

The "scuola di Rossi" in Milan, for example, became widespread. One could say that the numerous thesis projects appearing in architectural reviews[15] and exhibition catalogues starting in

1967 bear witness to an unusual consistency and homogeneity that acquires the dignity of "contribution," freeing itself from the formal mimesis of the epigone. Moreover, from his array of assistants have come some theoretical and planning contributions of great value: one need only mention Giorgio Grassi's book[16] and his didactic role first as Rossi's assistant in Milan and later as professor in the department of architecture at the University of Pescara.

It is therefore necessary to realize that the Tendenza has by now achieved an unquestionable presence and authority thanks to the precision of its forms and to the clarity of its principles. From Aldo Rossi's book[17] to the contributions of Giorgio Grassi and Carlo Aymonino,[18] to the work of *diffusion* conducted after 1969 by a few editors of *Controspazio* (up to the dissolution of the Milanese editorial staff in 1973), the Tendenza succeeded in providing a real alternative to the facile utopias, to the abstraction of "revolutionary" discourse, and to geometrical research as an end in itself, and in finally confronting the sovereignty of the most accredited Italian professionalism in the field (Gio Ponti, P. L. Nervi).

An early attempt to historicize the Tendenza was made in Vittorio Gregotti's book.[19] In defining the three new orientations of Italian architecture, Gregotti individuated the Tendenza in the orientations present in Milan and Venice. Its "center of attention [lies] in the relationship between urban typology and morphology and especially in that aspect which defines the idea of architecture as testimony and persistence. This follows a line of reasoning that through the notion of monument tends to link the neoclassical architects of the French Revolution with the example of Loos and one side of Le Corbusier, and manages (via the most rigorously objective German rationalists such as Hannes Mayer and Klein) to include as well one aspect of Kahn."

This attitude, which Tafuri defined more precisely as one of "typological critique," contrasts with the other two singled out by Gregotti (the "environmentally" oriented one, and that concerning "methods" of planning).

From Gregotti's description emerge a number of elements that constitute some, if not all, of the principles to which one may legitimately link the concept of Tendenza: the strict relationship to history, the predominance of urban studies, the relation between building typology and urban morphology, monumentality, and the importance of form.

* * *

› Notes

1 Dardi, *Il gioco sapiente, tendenze della nuova architettura* (Padua: Marsilio, 1971), p. 21.
2 F. Tentori, "D'où venons-nous? Qui sommes-nous? Où allons-nous?" in *Aspetti dell'arte contemporanea*, catalogue of the exhibition at L'Aquila, July 28–October 6, 1963 (Rome: Edizioni dell' Ateneo, 1963), pp. 264–265.
3 Argan, *Arte moderna*, pp. 324–325.
4 Manfredo Tafuri, "Per una critica dell'ideologia architettonica," *Contropiano* 1 (1969); now updated in *Progetto e utopia* (Bari: Laterza, 1973).
5 A. Rossi, letter to F. Tentori in Tentori, "D'où venons-nous?"
6 E. Bonfanti, "Elementi e costruzione-note sull'architettura di Aldo Rossi," *Controspazio* 8–9 (1970).
7 V. Gregotti, *Il territorio dell'architettura* (Milan: Feitrinelli, 1966), p. 133.
8 Tentori, "D'où venons-nous?"

9   Ibid.

10 Ibid.

11 Ibid

12 E. N. Rogers, "Utopia della realtà," *Casabella* 259 (1962).

13 G. Samonà, *L'urbanistica e l'avvenire della città negli stati europei* (Bari: Laterza, 1959).

14 On the role played by S. Muratori in the founding of urban science, see M. Scolari, "Un contributo per la fondazione di una scienza urbana," *Controspazio* 7–8 (1971).

15 See the special issue of *Controspazio*, no. 5–6 (1972), devoted to planning research in university architecture departments in Italy

16 G. Grassi, *La costruzione logica dell'architettura* (Padua: Marsilio, 1967).

17 A. Rossi, *L'architettura della città* (Padua: Marsilio, 1966).

18 C. Aymonino, *Origini e sviluppo della città moderna* (Padua: Marsilio, 1971); see also C. Aymonino, A. Rossi, et al., La città di Padova (Rome: Officina, 1970).

19 Gregotti, *Orientamenti nuovi.*

48 Anthony Vidler

The third typology (1978)

Anthony Vidler, 'The third typology', from: *Rational Architecture Rationelle*, Bruxelles: AAM Editions—Archives d'Architecture Moderne, 1978, pp. 28–32.

From the middle of the eighteenth century two dominant typologies have served to legitimize the production of architecture: The first, returned architecture to its natural origins—a model of primitive shelter—seen not simply as historical explanation of the derivation of the orders but as a guiding principle, equivalent to that proposed by Newton for the physical universe. The second, emerging as a result of the Industrial Revolution, assimilated architecture to the world of machine production, finding the essential nature of a building to reside in the artificial world of engines. Laugier's primitive hut and Bentham's Panopticon stand at the beginning of the modern era as the paradigms of these two typologies.

Both these typologies were firm in their belief that rational science and later, technological production, embodied the most progressive forms of the age, and that the mission of architecture was to conform to and perhaps even master these forms as the agent of material progress.

With the current re-appraisal of the idea of progress, and with this, the critique of the Modern Movement ideology of productivism, architects have turned to a vision of the primal past of architecture—its constructive and formal bases as evinced in the pre-industrial city. Once again the issue of typology is raised in architecture, not this time with a need to search outside the practice for legitimation in science or technology, but with a sense that within architecture itself resides a unique and particular mode of production and explanation. From Aldo Rossi's transformations of the formal structure and institutional types of eighteenth century urbanism, to the sketches of Leon Krier that recall the "primitive" types of shelter imagined by the eighteenth century philosophes, rapidly multiplying examples suggest the emergence of a new, third typology.

We might characterize the fundamental attribute of this third typology as an espousal, not of an abstract nature, not of a technological utopia, but rather of the traditional city as the locus of its concern. The city, that is, provides the material for classification and the forms of its artifacts over time provide the basis for recomposition. This third typology, like the first two, is clearly based on reason, classification, and a sense of the public in architecture; unlike the first two, however, it proposes no panacaea, no ultimate apotheosis of man in architecture, no positivistic escatology.

The small rustic hut is the model upon which all the wonders of architecture have been conceived; in drawing nearer in practice to the simplicities of this first model essential faults are avoided and true perfection is attained. The pieces of wood raised vertically give us the idea of columns. The horizontal pieces that surmount them give us the idea of entablatures. Finally, the inclined pieces that form the roof, give us the idea of pediments. This all the masters of the art have recognized.

(M.A. Laugier, 1755)

The first typology, which ultimately saw architecture as imitative of the fundamental order of Nature itself, allied the primitive rusticity of the hut to an ideal of perfect geometry, revealed by Newton as the guiding principle of physics. Thus, Laugier depicted the four trees, types of the first columns, standing in a perfect square; the branches laid across in the form of beams, perfectly horizontal, and the boughs bent over to form the roof as a triangle, the type of pediment. These elements of architecture, derived from the elements of nature, formed an unbreakable chain and were interrelated according to fixed principles: if the tree column was joined in this way to the bower/hut, then the city itself, agglomeration of huts, was likewise susceptible to the principle of natural origin. Laugier spoke of the city—or rather the existing, unplanned and chaotic reality of Paris—as a forest. The forest/city was to be tamed, brought into rational order by means of the gardener's art: the ideal city of the late eighteenth century was thereby imaged on the garden; the type of the urbanist was Le Nôtre, who would cut and prune an unruly nature according to the geometrical line of its true underlying order.

The idea of the elements of architecture referring in some way to their natural origin was, of course, immediately extensible in the idea of each specific kind of building representing its "species" so to speak, in the same way as each member of the animal kingdom. At first the criteria applied to differentiate building types were bound up with recognition, with individual physiognomy, as in the classification systems of Buffon and Linnaeus. Thus, the external affect of the building was to announce clearly its general species, and its specific subspecies. Later this analogy was transformed by the functional and constitutional classification of the early nineteenth century (Cuvier), whereby the inner-structure of beings, their constitutional form, was seen as the criterion for grouping them in types.

Following this analogy, those whose task it was to design the new types of public and private buildings emerging as needs in the early nineteenth century began to talk of the plan and sectional distribution in the same terms as the constitutional organization of species; axes and vertebrae became virtually synonymous. This reflected a basic shift in the metaphor of natural architecture, from a vegetal (tree/hut) to an animal analogy. This shift paralleled the rise of the new schools of medicine and the birth of clinical surgery.

Despite the overt disgust that Durand showed toward Laugier—laughing at the idea of doing without walls—it was Durand, professor at the Polytechnique, who brought together these twin streams of organic typology into a lexicon of architectural practice that enabled the architect, at least, to dispense with analogy altogether and concentrate on the business of construction. The medium of this fusion was the graph paper grid which assembled on the same level the basic elements of construction, according to the inductively derived rules of composition for the taxonomy of different building types resulting in the endless combinations and permutations, monumental and utilitarian. In his *Receuil* he established that the natural history of architecture resides so to speak in its own history, a parallel development to real nature. In his *Lessons* he described how new types might be constructed on the same principles. When this awareness was applied in the next decades to the structural rationalism inherited from Laugier the result was the organic theory of Gothic "skeletal" structure developed by Viollet-le-Duc. The operation of the romantics on classic theory was simply at one level to substitute the Cathedral for the Temple as the formal and later the social type of all architecture.

> II

The French language has provided the useful definition. thanks to the double sense of the word type. A deformation of meaning has led to the equivalence in popular language: a man = a type; and from the point that the type becomes a man, we grasp the possibility of a considerable extension of the type. Because the man-type is a complex form of a unique physical type, to which can be applied a sufficient standardization. According to the same rules one will establish for this physical type an equipment of standard habitation: doors, windows, stairs, the heights of rooms, etc.

(Le Corbusier, 1927)

The second typology, which substituted for the classical trinity of commodity, firmness and delight, a dialectic of means and ends joined by the criteria of economy, looked upon architecture as simply a matter of technique. The remarkable new machines subject to the laws of functional precision were thus paradigms of efficiency as they worked in the raw materials of production: architecture, once subjected to similar laws, might well work with similar effectiveness on its unruly contents—the users. The efficient machines of architecture might be sited in the country-side, very much like the early steam engines of Newcomen and Watt, or inserted in the fabric of the city, like the water pumps and later the factory furnaces. Centralized within their own operative realm, hermetically sealed by virtue of their autonomy as complete processes, these engines—the prisons, hospitals, poor houses—needed little in the way of accommodation save a clear space and a high wall. Their impact on the form of the city as a whole was at first minimal.

The second typology of modern architecture emerged toward the end of the nineteenth century, after the takeoff of the Second Industrial Revolution; it grew out of the need to confront the question of mass-production, and more particularly the mass-production of machines by machines. The effect of this transformation in production was to give the illusion of another nature, the nature of the machine and its artificially reproduced world.

In this second typology, architecture was now equivalent to the range of mass-production objects, subject themselves to a quasi-Darwinian law of the selection of the fittest. The pyramid of production from the smallest tool to the most complex machine was now seen as analogous to the link between the column, the house and the city. Various attempts were made to blend the old typology with the new in order to provide a more satisfactory answer to the question of specifically architectonic form: the primary geometries of the Newtonian generation were now adduced for their evident qualities of economy, modernity and purity. They were, it was thought, appropriate for machine tooling.

Equally, theoreticians with a classical bias, like Hermann Muthesius stressed the equivalence of ancient types—the temple—and the new ones—the object of manufacture—in order to stabilize, or "culturalize" the new machine world. A latent neoclassicism suffused the theories of typology at the beginning of the contemporary epoch, born of the need to justify the new in the face of the old. The classical world once again acted as a "primal past" wherein the utopia of the present might find its nostalgic roots.

Not until the aftermath of the First World War was this thrown off, at least in the most advanced theories—articulated with more and more directness by Le Corbusier and Walter Gropius. A vision of Taylorized production, of a world ruled by the iron law of Ford supplanted the spuriously golden dream of neoclassicism. Buildings were to be no more and no less than machines themselves, serving and molding the needs of man according to economic criteria. The image of the city at this point changed radically: the forest/park of Laugier was made triumphant in the hygienist utopia of a city completely absorbed by its greenery. The natural analogy of the Enlightenment, originally brought forward to control the messy reality of the city, was now extended to refer to the control of entire nature. In the redeeming park the silent building-machines of the new garden of production virtually disappeared behind a sea of verdure. Architecture, in this final apotheosis of mechanical progress, was consumed by the very process it sought to control for its own ends. With it, the city, as artifact and polis disappeared as well.

In the first two typologies of modern architecture we can identify a common base, resting on the need to legitimize architecture as a "natural" phenomenon and a development of the natural analogy that corresponded very directly to the development of production itself. Both typologies were in some way bound up with the attempts of architecture to endow itself with value by means of an appeal to natural science or production, and instrumental power by means of an assimilation of the forms of these two complementary domains to itself. The "utopia" of architecture as "project" might be progressive in its ends, or nostalgic in its dreams, but at heart it was founded on this premise: that the shape of environment, might, like nature herself, affect and hereby control the individual and collective relations of men.

> III

In the first two typologies, architecture, made by man, was being compared and legitimized by another "nature" outside itself. In the third typology, as exemplified in the work of the new Rationalists, however, there is no such attempt at validation. Columns, houses, and urban spaces, while linked in an unbreakable chain of continuity, refer only to their own nature as architectural elements, and their geometries are neither naturalistic nor technical but essentially architectural.

ANTHONY VIDLER

It is clear that the nature referred to in these recent designs is no more nor less than the nature of the city itself, emptied of specific social content from any particular time and allowed to speak simply of its own formal condition.

This concept of the city as the site of a new typology is evidently born of a desire to stress the continuity of form and history against the fragmentation produced by the elemental, institutional, and mechanistic typologies of the recent past. The city is considered as a whole, its past and present revealed in its physical structure. It is in itself and of itself a new typology. This typology is not built up out of separate elements, nor assembled out of objects classified according to use, social ideology, or technical characteristics: it stands complete and ready to be decomposed into fragments. These fragments do not reinvent institutional type-forms nor repeat past typological forms: they are selected and reassembled according to criteria derived from three levels of meaning—the first, inherited from the ascribed means of the past existence of the forms; the second, derived from the specific fragment and its boundaries, and often crossing between previous types; the third, proposed by a recomposition of these fragments in a new context.

Such an "ontology of the city" is in the face of the modernist utopia, indeed radical. It denies all the social utopian and progressively positivist definitions of architecture for the last two hundred years. No longer is architecture a realm that has to relate to a hypothesized "society" in order to be conceived and understood; no longer does "architecture write history" in the sense of particularizing a specific social condition in a specific time or place. The need to speak of nature of function, of social mores—of anything, that is, beyond the nature of architectural form itself— is removed. At this point, as Victor Hugo realized so presciently in the 1830s, communication through the printed work, and lately through the mass media has apparently released architecture from the role of "social book" into its own autonomous and specialized domain.

This does not, of course, necessarily mean that architecture in this sense no longer performs any function, no longer satisfies any need beyond the whim of an "art for art's sake" designer, but simply that the principal conditions for the invention of object and environments do not necessarily have to include a unitary statement of fit between form and use. Here it is that the adoption of the city as the site for the identification of the architectural typology has been seen as crucial. In the accumulated experience of the city, its public spaces and institutional forms, a typology can be understood that defies a one-to-one reading of function, but which at the same time ensures a relation at another level to a continuing tradition of city life. The distinguishing characteristic of the new ontology beyond its specifically formal aspect is that the city polis, as opposed to the single column, the hut-house, or the useful machine, is and always has been political in its essence. The fragmentation and recomposition of its spatial and institutional forms thereby can never be separated from their received and newly constituted political implications.

When typical forms are selected from the past of a city, they do not come, however dismembered, deprived of their original political and social meaning. The original sense of the form, the layers of accrued implication deposited by time and human experience cannot be lightly brushed away and certainly it is not the intention of the new Rationalists to disinfect their types in this way. Rather, the carried meanings of these types may be used to provide a key to their newly invested meanings. The technique or rather the fundamental compositional method suggested by the Rationalists is the transformation of selected types—partial or whole—into entirely new entities that draw their communicative power and potential criteria from the understanding of this transformation. The City Hall project for Trieste by Aldo Rossi, for example, has been rightly understood to refer, among other evocations in its complex form, to the image of a late eighteenth century prison. In the period of the first formalization of this type, as Piranesi demonstrated, it was possible to see in *prison* a powerfully comprehensive image of the dilemma of society itself, poised between a disintegrating religious faith and a materialist reason. Now, Rossi, in ascribing to the city hall (itself a recognizable type in the nineteenth century) the affect of prison, attains a new level of signification, which evidently is a reference to the ambiguous condition of civic government. In the formulation, the two types are not merged: indeed, city hall has been replaced by open arcade standing in contradiction on prison. The dialectic is clear as a fable: the society that understands the reference to prison will still have need of the reminder, while at the very point that the image finally loses all meaning, the society will either have become entirely prison, or, perhaps, its opposite. The metaphoric opposition deployed in this example can be traced in many of Rossi's schemes and in the work of the Rationalists as a whole, not only in institutional form but also in the spaces of the city.

This new typology is explicitly critical of the Modern Movement; it utilizes the clarity of the eighteenth century city to rebuke the fragmentation, decentralization, and formal disintegration introduced into contemporary urban life by the zoning techniques and technological advances of the twenties. While the Modern Movement found its Hell in the closed, cramped, and insalubrious quarters of the old industrial cities, and its Eden in the uninterrupted sea of sunlit space filled with greenery—a city became a garden—the new typology as a critique of modern urbanism raises the continuous fabric, the clear distinction between public and private marked by the walls of street and square, to the level of principle. Its nightmare is the isolated building set in an undifferentiated park. The heroes of this new typology are therefore not among the nostalgic, anti-city utopians of the nineteenth century nor even among the critics of industrial and technical progress of the twentieth, but rather among those who, as the professional servants of urban life, have directed their design skills to solving the questions of avenue, arcade, street and square, park and house, institution and equipment in a continuous typology of elements that together coheres with past fabric and present intervention to make one comprehensible experience of the city. For this typology, there is no clear set of rules for the transformations and their objects, nor any polemically defined set of historical precedents. Nor, perhaps, should there be; the continued vitality of this architectural practice rests in its essential engagement with the precise demands of the present and not in any holistic mythicization of the past. It refuses any "nostalgia" in its evocations of history, except to give its restorations sharper focus; it refuses all unitary descriptions of the social meaning of form, recognizing the specious quality of any single ascription of social order to an architectural order; it finally refuses all eclecticism, resolutely filtering its "quotations" through the lens of a modernist aesthetic. In this sense, it is an entirely modern movement, and one that places its faith in the essentially public nature of all architecture, as against the increasingly private and narcissistic visions of the last decade. In this it is distinguished from those latter-day romanticisms that have also pretended to the throne of post-modernism—"townscape", "strip-city" and "collage-city"—that in reality proposed no more than the endless reduplication of the flowers of bourgeois high culture under the guise of the painterly or the populist. In the work of the new Rationalists, the city and its typology are reasserted as the only possible bases for the restoration of a critical role to public architecture otherwise assassinated by the apparently endless cycle of production and consumption.

49 Bernard Huet

Small manifesto (1978)

Bernard Huet, 'Small manifesto', from: *Rational Architecture Rationelle*, Bruxelles: AAM Editions—
Archives d'Architecture Moderne, 1978, p. 54.

› Small manifesto

1. Historically Architecture has been created at the beginning of the XVth century in Italy by the rising bourgeoisie, for its own use. If Architecture had a beginning, it could well have an end.
2. As the ideological function of Architecture has now lost its initial urgency, it is logical that the bourgeoisie concedes a marginal role to Architecture for the formulation of its environment.
3. This must not necessarily mean that Architecture will disappear. On the contrary, Architecture might in this way gain a certain autonomy in relation to the goals to whose attainment it was originally instaured.
4. Although Architecture is done by a group of intellectuals organised in a profession, its exercise is not the sole privilege of architects. The profession is therefore not necessary to the survival of Architecture.
5. We will not try here to define Architecture. We will designate as "architectural" all the built objects which through history have entered the field of Architecture.
6. However, Architecture as conscious or "poetic" intellectual production, is to be distinguished from construction. To paraphrase B. Brecht "its sole justification being the pleasure which it confers" knowing "that the sciences and the arts have one thing in common, in that they exist to make men's life more easy: the sciences in helping their needs, the arts in diverting them".[1]
7. We refuse the erronous alternatives which sanction the opposition between the Arts and Industry, Architecture and urbanism, city and territory. The solution consists in a correct discipline in the dialectical relationship of productive forces, architectural typology and urban morphology.
8. We reject all qualitative distinction between "modern" Architecture and Architecture which would not be modern. A neo-gothic edifice built in 1975 is Modern in the measure where it is situated within the contemporary relations of production.

9. There exists no PROGRESS in architecture, neither in the functional, constructional nor the esthetical field, for the very reason that the architectural TECHNIQUE has to correspond to an architectural TENDENCY which in turn has to be part of a correct political TENDENCY. [2]

10. For that reason we refuse a sterile debate on form and content which would throw us back to an impossible situation of AVANT-GARDE.

11. Architecture can no longer be "natural" nor universal. Architecture must be historicised, it has to become an integral part of the dialectics of transformation of the social relationships.

12. To found a new critique of Architecture one has to ask oneself with W. Benjamin "Instead of asking: what is the position of a work IN RELATION to the conditions of production of an era? Does it agree with them, is it reactionary or does it aspire to transform them, is it revolutionary? Instead of this question, or rather before this question, I want to ask another one . . . I would like to ask: what is its place WITHIN these same conditions?". [3]

> Notes

1   B. Brecht: Petit Organon pour le théâtre – L'Arche 1970.
2   W. Benjamin: L'Auteur comme producteur, in Essais sur B. Brecht – Maspero 1969.
3   Op. Cit.

50 Gianfranco Caniggia and Gian Luigi Maffei

Introduction: motives and propositions (1979)

Gianfranco Caniggia and Gian Luigi Maffei, *Interpreting Basic Building,* Firenze: Alinea Editrice, 2001, extract pp. 51–55, translation by Susan Jane Fraser.

*   *   *

› Building type

The term building type was used in the past and still is today to indicate any group of buildings with some characteristics, or a series of characteristics, in common.

In this sense it was adopted by past manuals, grouping together buildings with a certain function in common (schools, dwellings, hospitals, prisons or the like) or, less generally, buildings with a similar structural-distributive plan (e.g. baptisteries with a central plan) or, more pertinently, it was used with enlightened attempts at systematizing buildings when the need arose to connect the term to a system of constants, unitarily characterizing buildings with the same purpose and similar architectural characteristics. However, this was done *a posteriori* and analytically, taking these unitary characteristics and grouping them into "types" in order to catalogue existing building or control buildings still to be built by regulations without basically raising the issue of the whys and wherefores of the real, not purely logical, existence of these "types". In other words, if we see that two or more houses have similar characteristics, we label them together and say that these houses belong to the same "building type". Let us examine an example: if in Florence walking around the routes of S. Frediano or Santa Croce I see many buildings that appear to be different until I take every detail and each individual characteristic into account. However, I immediately note that, apart from some outstanding buildings (noblemen's palaces, churches etc.), the majority of buildings are used as dwellings and largely behave similarly, sometimes to the extent that there are only superficial differences between one house and another. If I retrieve the elements that I recognize as being similar in a unitary definition, I obtain a statistically derived "building type": in other words, I see numerous buildings existing of two dwelling stories placed on top of a ground floor, with two windows per story and with a large door, and a small door on the ground floor. I also see that buildings of the kind are built close to one another to form a row of similar houses along a whole route, generally featuring vertical perpendicular structures in the front usually placed on the edge of the route and facing it; at the back is an uncovered area exclusively for their own individual use. I label these characteristics together under the name of "row houses". This means that I acknowledged the existence of such a type *a posteriori,* i.e. I noted its physical existence, and I produced a logical diagram out of it and classified this diagram as a "row house". It is clear that this wording arises from its opposite: if I invent such a term and recognize the existence of a "row house", it already means that I implicitly admit at least two things: the existence of houses that are not row houses, which I will have labelled differently, and the existence of buildings that are not houses. Furthermore, I admit to having seen buildings that are not houses and called them, for instance, churches, palaces and convents. Therefore, I classified building in districts examined through an "*a posteriori analysis*".

Let us now see what happens when I ask myself why types exist or, in other words, when I objectively raise the issue of how much the conceptual logic is produced only in my mind or how much in the authentic physical existence of these "building types". Let us try to solve this problem using the logical-deductive tools appropriate to critical moments: for instance we shall ask ourselves whether several houses are similar because they used the same plan or because they are by the same builder or builders belonging to the same school or whether the houses look the same because of the previous enforcement of a building regulation, law or edict. [. . .] Our logic runs aground when faced with evidence that similar houses, from which we "statistically" derived a building type "row house", are produced in such a way because their builders would not have been capable of producing them differently. Actually, as each house corresponds to the house concept in force at the time in which each of them was built, Tom, Dick or Harry's house – by virtue of the fact that they were produced nearby and more or less the same time – have exactly the same cultural background, focusing on "building one's house". In other words, they used the same house concept that similarly formed in their three minds. The concept summed up all the appearances that the houses took on once built prior to the three houses themselves physically existing because prevalent spontaneous consciousness guided that "house concept" to correspond during that era and in that cultural precise era. This mental plan that is responsible for the resemblance between the end products which, using our critical consciousness, we now call, verify and label as building type.

[. . .]

If, instead of San Frediano or Santa Croce, we examine any recently built aggregate on the outskirts of Florence and we go to Novoli, Sesto or Rifredi, it is easy to find that three adjoining houses are similar in appearance: the first has "strip" windows crossing the whole façade; the second has tall, narrow windows from the ceiling to the floor and in the third windows vary in measure and position, mixed with overhanging balconies or receding loggias. The first house seems to be made of only beams while pillars move backwards from their casing line, and the second appears to consist of only pillars, projecting from their casing itself, while beams do not appear. The third has a continuous wall, or so it appears; a fourth could be a curtain wall and looks as though it were a single window, with no sign of how it is supported. The best part is that each of these houses continues to be an inhabited "house", therefore legitimizing it, given that in its own way it stands up and is useful to someone and that these houses all belong to the same historic moment and to the same cultural area. Therefore, we can only refer to what we said before: what appears in these houses is a result of product personalization due to individual choices from a vast repertoire. However, these choices only relatively affect product use. Some degree of continuity is guaranteed not by those choices, but by what various builders did not choose and by what has remained in their working, predetermined prior to their choices themselves, by what continues to be the vestige of "spontaneous consciousness", "house concept" and, therefore, intrinsically current "building type".

Therefore, type exists and is not logical fiction; type exists and is a product of past and present spontaneous consciousness. However, it is likewise true that talking about type and reviving it is a result of critical consciousness. If we were to ask a 15th Century mason what he was building at the time – if he was building a three-story row house with two windows per floor, five meters wide and twelve meters deep – he would have no idea of what we were talking about because he simply intends to "build a house" and not a "building type", which we distinguish by comparing it to other types.

Thus type can have a critical formulation, derived by *a posteriori* analysis; however, it inevitably owes its existence to being an "a priori synthesis". That is to say, it exists in the builder's mind before producing a house and is not a prefiguration of one or several aspects of the building but of all of them together: a real organism, bringing the whole house to life before it exists physically. Through our critical work which brings us to recognize a building type, we basically go through the formation of buildings until a moment before they come into being when they only exist conceptually in their producers' minds, with all their historicity, namely belonging to a moment in time and fixed place.

Type is, therefore, the conception of the building produced: it is total projection – initially conceptual, when it comes into being, and then logical, when we examine it, of existing building, shaped according to the "house concept" that exists in the builder's mind at spontaneous consciousness level and is in force in a given historic moment, resulting from the succession of "house concepts" that developed before that moment in history. Overall "type components" can be summed up as three building characteristics in the well-known Vitruvian triad: *firmitas, utilitas, venustas* (firmness, commodity, delight) or rather, *ratio firmitatis, ratio utilitatis, ratio venustaris.* This is an important specification because it stresses the meaning of distinction, reasserting its fundamental unity. It is a single *ratio,* a single overall reason in three concurrent aspects. In modern language we could call it the global rationality of the structure (i.e. a house's way of standing upright), inseparable from the demand that it be used according to an integrated global distribution rationality (i.e. the use made of a house); these are both inseparable from global rationality of readability (i.e. of how this house makes itself understood by onlookers or by its inhabitants and manages to transmit its uprightness and working procedures).

› Typological process

Type cognition necessitates another further definition, typological process. If we examine several historical building types in the same cultural area, we perceive progressive differentiation among them, more marked in very old buildings and less so in more recent buildings.

GIANFRANCO CANIGGIA AND GIAN LUIGI MAFFEI

14th Century builders built their houses according to type and the house concept at the time; 15th Century builders built their houses according to the concept and type in force during their era. Therefore, it is easy to find a scalar mutation of the building type depending on the era. Albeit within the same definition, "row houses" vary according to their date of building; it is easy to note how in order to be used in the 15th Century, 14th Century row houses tend to follow the trends. This means that every era attributes a different meaning to the "house concept" producing different houses. However, differences apart, we can see a phenomenon of striking continuity, easy to read from the differences between similar products. In this way, 14th Century row houses will have certain characteristics in common with 15th and 12th Century row houses, demonstrating a gradual change in buildings produced before and after a certain era.

The mechanics of change are most greatly affected by progressive variations in existing buildings, widespread – albeit limited – adaptation of existing building to make it apt to the continuous pursuit between formation and transformation processes of buildings and parallel process changes in needs. In actual fact, the contribution of widespread changes can only be read at prolonged intervals, comparing a new order to its previous version.

* * *

51 Ignasi Sola-Morales

Neo-rationalism and figuration (1984)

Ignasi Sola-Morales, 'Neo-Rationalism and Figuration', *Architectural Design*, vol. 54, 5/6, 1984, pp. 15–19.

› The modern movement reconsidered

In Italy the term rationalism acquired renewed prestige during the sixties. A body of doctrines and a repertoire of works matured exactly during the years when the dissolution of modern architecture—whose origins lay precisely in the rationalism of the historical avant-garde of the twenties—became abundantly clear.[1]

By 1973, when Aldo Rossi organised the architectural section of the Milan Triennale, the neo-rationalist doctrine had been fully formulated. The movement had an expressly public status not simply as regards cultural politics but moreover in connection to its theoretical position.[2]

The intellectual milieu that nurtured those ideas was to be found in three circles. Of these, the Milanese circle was the most clearly formulated, no doubt due to the irrefutable presence of Ernesto N. Rogers and the group around *Casabella-Continuità*. The second circle was that of the Venice School of Architecture: under the guidance of Giuseppe Samonà, its director for many years, the school stressed the importance of relating architecture to the city. The third was the circle of Ludovico Quaroni whose compromise with the architecture of the Modern Movement did not make him lose sight of the limitations of modern architecture and of the need for its revision.

Rogers, Samonà, Quaroni and their respective circles in the cities of Milan, Venice and Rome formed the framework within which it was possible to find young architects who had not taken part in the struggle for the institutionalisation of the Modern Movement. Such young architects had not been involved in the chaotic race of the fifties for economic development nor had they witnessed the gradual decline of the principles of the Modern Movement as they were turned into instruments of property speculation and of the destruction of the city. Moreover, since the sixties represented a definitive trivialisation of the functional, technological and social principles of the Modern Movement, it was left to a group of young architects to demand that such principles be reappraised. They had both a yearning for the lost purity of the Modern Movement and an interest in restating the theoretical foundations of architectural design. This deliberate self-criticism that young architects made of their own tradition generated a voluminous critical literature: the history of the Modern Movement itself was now the object of a relentless debate aiming at reinterpreting modern Architecture's ultimate significance. Furthermore, they set out to formulate theoretically both the specific tools of architectural discourse and those general, logical and rational methods that would support architectural design practice.

Ultimately the task of re-establishing foundations began in the sixties with Aldo Rossi, Carlo Aymonino, Guido Canella, Manfredo Tafuri, Emilio Bonfanti, Giorgio Grassi, Giorgio Polesello, Luciano Semerani, Nino Dardi, Vittorio Gregotti, and others, and was marked at its core by a moral drive. The majority of these architects drew their criticism of Christian Democratic policies of architecture and urbanism from the political positions of the left which they occupied. They rejected conventional professionalism because of the commercial vulgarity to which it had reduced Italian architecture and design (for though acclaimed worldwide, Italian design had reduced the images of the Modern Movement into *kitsch*) and the immorality of its urban policies which were based on consumerism and destruction.[3]

› Historical standpoint

The neo-rationalists began their critical revision of modern architecture with a historical reading. That was a task they could not and did not want to avoid; their masters had bequeathed them a taste for history. That was contrary to the mainstream of the Modern Movement which had shed its interest for architectural history. In Italy, however, the love for architectural history had never ceased; if anything it had gained impetus from the studies of the work of the protagonists of the Modern Movement. The issues of *Casabella* on Wright, Loos, Oud, and those analysing contemporary work carried out by architects in their home towns were very popular at the time. In this way *Casabella* contributed to the discovery of secondary Modernist architects and thus to the formulation of a dialectically conceived history of the Modern Movement. The Modern Movement was no longer to be thought of as the monolithic tradition set out by the Giedion-Pevsner-Zevi lineage, but as an interplay of tendencies in face of which it became necessary to be critical and discerning.

To reconsider modern history meant, at the time, to propose as models certain names against others—Oud against De Stijl, Terragni against Futurism, Asplund against Nordic Organicism. But all these 'discoveries', the polemical value of which was accompanied by a hesitant definition of a new taste, were but the first step in an investigation of the historical origins of rationalism. The historical reappraisal of architecture, beyond the narrow limits of the Modernist avant-gardes, became necessary. Tafuri looked for the origins of the modern architect in Brunelleschi's Renaissance, while Aldo Rossi became fascinated with the architecture of the Enlightenment as the most genuine manifestation of the rationality with which modern culture built its cities.[4]

The appeal that the architecture of the Enlightenment exerted on the young neo-rationalists was not grounded simply on its historical aura. Rather, it was a real source of theoretical, ideological and formal inspiration. Kaufman's influence was decisive in this respect.[5] To understand the formal innovations of the Modernist avant-garde as a continuation of the 'break' that Enlightenment architecture had initiated was to add to the latter's figurative values certain ethical resonances. By analogy, therefore, a neo-rationalist 'genuine avant-garde' was to stand against the trivialised versions of fifties' and sixties' Modernism as Neoclassical purism had stood against the trivialisations of nineteenth-century historicism.

Italian neo-rationalists also showed renewed interest in the treatises and manuals of architectural history, thus illustrating a salient tendency to find models and references in the past that would be capable of clarifying present problems. Giorgio Grassi showed special interest in Le Muet, Viollet-le-Duc, Tessenow, Hilberseimer, while Aldo Rossi focused on Boullée, Palladio and Loos. Yet another common development in such historical studies was Rossi's re-statement of the universal principles of architecture. At the time Rossi had an interest in the architecture and urbanism of the socialist countries. Since the mid-sixties, the influence of Aymonino in the University of Venice and its *Gruppo Architettura,* as well as the knowledge and publication of works from the German Democratic Republic, the Soviet Union, Czechoslovakia, Yugoslavia and Poland had the great value of challenging the dominant architectural and urban models of European capitalism. This European socialist model—itself an offspring of the Modern Movement—was influenced by socialist policies and saw the ideal of collective values as the main objective in the construction of the city.[6]

› Critique of architecture

The comprehensive critique launched by the neo-rationalists did not stop itself simply in historical reappraisal but moved on to formulating methods of analysis and design which were to have a powerful influence on the development of architecture. The design process itself was to be subjected to rigorous analysis so that whimsical architectural forms would be eliminated. In years past, too much personal licence and calls to creativity and inventiveness had dominated the architectural panorama. Such an approach had undermined the confidence in general principles. The 'international picturesque', as Nino Dardi has called it, was no longer acceptable and against its intuitionist whims the solidity of a general method would have to be opposed. The will to avoid the pitfalls of idealism and a renewed interest in the social sciences were procedures used against voluntarism or ideological constructions.

The neo-rationalists of the sixties found in structuralism the necessary theoretical tools for their own method of architectural analysis. Structuralism (as for example in the work of Lévi-Strauss) studies social facts—say kinship relations—both as independent objects and as systems of differential relationships. 'Object' and 'difference' are the key notions in structuralism; its descriptive and analytical categories are supported by the nexus of relationships that the researcher can find in the material he studies.[7] The neo-rationalists, distancing themselves from semioticist temptations, felt the need to act in a similar way within the field of architecture. There is certainly a parallel between the structuralist methodology of the social sciences of that period and the analytical tools developed by Italian neo-rationalists in their search for the objective foundations of design.[8] From this point of view, the recognition of the autonomous architectural object entailed a fundamental epistemological change. The notion of environment, so characteristic of the picturesque tradition, was now of no interest: the city as 'constructed fact' was the referent from which analysis should proceed. Aldo Rossi's seminal text of these years, *L'architettura della città,* put forward a 'théorie d'ensemble' which established the analytical methods of neo-rationalism.[9] The physical reality of the city became the point of departure, the material datum of every analysis, and the context within which any architectural work was to be judged irrespective of its scale, functional or stylistic characteristics. To recognise the city as the fundamental architectural reference meant to efface all boundaries between architecture and urban design. Every physical intervention was now to be measured against the physical and constructed reality of the city.

This realisation that the city is a necessary referential datum entailed a break with the Taylorist logic of the production line that characterised the Modern Movement. Against the linear design process of the Modern Movement (ie, from the industrial element, to the building, to the city) neo-rationalism proposed the techniques of topography/cartography and typification.

With the techniques of topography/cartography one can describe the actual condition of the city or its parts, and it is possible to carry out analytical operations based on the objective data and accurate dimensions provided. Topography describes the site and the physical structure of the settlements upon which the city is founded. It tells us about the material conditions upon which architecture operates. Cartography describes the intervention—the architectural activity—upon the physical site, showing us the form created from the moment these interventions take place. The morphological analysis of the city and its architecture cannot be explained by conditions other than those of its own form. No reference, therefore, is necessary to the 'life' of its inhabitants, to its 'society', to its 'style' or 'culture', to all those phenomena which do not have a material counterpart discernible through topography and cartography.

Furthermore, due to the importance of description, it would now be necessary to develop a discourse which would be, above all, about the differences of forms: thus a renewed interest in taxonomy and formal typification is established. Description would now mean the description of relationships; above all the description of a structure of *formal* relationships.

The same line of enquiry leads to the typological understanding of architecture. By using the notion of type (taken from the academic tradition) Rossi found a way to describe architecture in relation to its physical conditions and by means of descriptive categories that do not depend on the 'idealist' concepts of style and character. Building types are formal constants that permit the classification, recognition and description of buildings of all periods and places. These formal constants act as containers that reduce the complexity of architectural appearances to their most outstanding physical characteristics.

Through the notion of type one is able to understand architectural form as a system that describes the logic of its own formation; a system that describes the transformations of the elements of a certain formal repertoire. The notion of type permits also the study of the city's relations of production as well as its formal developments or ruptures. Ultimately, the city's physical structure and that of its buildings can be related in an analytical whole.

› Reductivism

The architecture that evolves from such theoretical premises has evident reductivist characteristics. The Modern Movement perpetrated a romantic conception of art, and for Gropius, Adolf Behne or Le Corbusier, modern architecture had to unite the whole human environment into one organised and poetic impulse.

By contrast, an almost puritanical austerity characterised neo-rationalist architectural theory. Interest lay only in the physical and structural expression of architectural and urban forms. Architecture was to emerge out of a highly intellectualised and abstract procedure. In the search for a new foundation, rational architecture resorted neither to criteria of other practical fields, nor to the images found in the technical and artificial world of the modern city.[10] An enormous difficulty now became apparent: how does one make the transition from analysis to design? How can analytical procedures provide something more than information about the site, the urban structure or the possible formal repertoire; how can something more than factual information be found? Analysis seems to offer only a clear and orderly description according to certain dominant criteria but it gives no clues as to the process of design.

Though loathe to admit it, neo-rationalists encounter at the project state the need to take a step into the unknown. This is an intuitive moment for which the analytical process cannot generate an intentionality: this cannot arise from the repertoire of urban typologies. Due to the reductivism of its morphological repertoires, the analytical method, no doubt, tends to reduce the available alternatives to a minimum. The city and its architecture are seen as the articulation of a few permanent and immutable elements—certainly with an almost metaphysical sense—which offer a complete compositional range of design possibilities. But even so, the moment of free choice, the moment of decision that guides from the analytical stage to the project cannot be eliminated. Perhaps in an attempt to minimise subjective risks, neo-rationalist theory does not deal with this stage in a conscious way. In my opinion, this point of crucial ambiguity surreptitiously introduces a component of freedom or chance into an otherwise rigorous intellectual method.

If the avant-garde of modern architecture aspired to individual freedom that was manifested in subjectivism and experimentalism,[11] neo-rationalism chooses to operate within the field of necessity. The debate between necessity and innovation reintroduces an old dispute: the dispute between a theory of imitation versus a theory of invention. Neo-rationalism seeks to defend itself from the formal arbitrariness of the modern avant-garde by resorting to the imitation that architecture necessarily makes of itself. A traditionalist component—or, if one prefers—a self-reflective one is thus introduced. Architecture does not invent since its repertoire has always existed. Its elements have always been the same and they appear always inside the peculiar 'nature' which is the tradition of architecture. In a manner similar to the academic tradition but with a more radical and elemental procedure. Neo-rationalism defines its design possibilities within the discipline of Architecture. It is this body of accumulated knowledge that defines its rules and the repertoire of its possible references, establishing, in this way, a framework for all design decisions.[12]

Perhaps the connection between academicism and neo-rationalism might seem at first paradoxical. And yet, the neo-rationalism of the sixties and seventies cannot be understood without reference to its most conspicuous predecessors: the rationalists of the Enlightenment and the tradition of the mimetic conception of architecture during the nineteenth century.

In its purest expression the notion of imitation considers that the contents of architecture cannot be invented by the architect in each project; such content is viable only insofar as it refers to architecture itself, to its tradition, so that it can be construed as a meta-language, a self-referring operation whereby architecture speaks of itself, presents itself anew and in this renewed representation performs the basic aesthetic action of imitating its own doings. It is no longer nature, generically considered, which is the object of imitation but rather a pre-existing sector of the real world which serves as a reference for architectural discourse. Consequently, the foundations of neo-rationalism lie in its conception of the architectural project, the limits of which are already established by architectural tradition and whose field of action is logically framed by the constant return of types, plans, and basic elements: all synchronically understood as permanent and immutable, rooted in tradition and history.

› Figuration

One must now analyse how it is that the neo-rationalist problem of formal figuration (which lacks a general and explicit solution) is resolved in specific cases.

The comparison of the work of two architects—Aldo Rossi and Giorgio Grassi—may indicate two radically different solutions to the problem of figuration. These two architects (who collaborated for some years and who had much in common) clearly exemplify the positions analysed in this essay. In both cases their work shows the reductivism previously referred to. The influence of structuralism is clear in both cases, and their interest in history can be interpreted as a form of remembrance of a permanent architectural heritage, the diversity and fundamental logical unity of which constitutes the precise context within which architecture had, is, and will continue to manifest itself. But though they share a common position on several theoretical points, their architecture is different.

Aldo Rossi, in addressing the problem of figuration, proposes a subjective criterion. Analysis and the systematic and rational method do not encompass the design process in its totality. There is a final point in this process which is governed by subjective intuition. '*There is no art that is not autobiographical*', writes Rossi in his 'Introduction to Boullée'.[13] To propose an autobiographical condition of architecture might appear to contradict what has gone before. But this is not the case.

Rossi's architecture mediates the break between the objective and the poetic discourse inherent in modern culture. Between reason and desire there exists a gap that can be bridged only by means of analogy: an analogy that is hesitant, painful and fragile to the extent that it is personal, mythical and contingent.[14] It should not surprise us that recently Rossi explained his work as an autobiography. Putting aside the *esprit de systéme* of his projects and writings of previous years, he decided to stress the most subjective aspects that ultimately make up the figures of his work.[15] In his drawings, relationships and displacements are established surrealistically, no longer explicable by reference to a logical system but intelligible only to a Freudian consciousness, for it is in the uncontrolled interaction of biographical events that the net of associations which structures our behaviour is built up. If the memory of a coffee pot or the recollection of the landscapes of childhood could be brought forward at the time of designing a theatre or a students' residence, Rossi's methodological discourse ends up by becoming a celibate machine, not unlike the way in which surrealism conceives of the confrontation between desire and impotence.[16]

The surreal and therefore illogical component, dreamed rather than materially manifested, is for Rossi the plausible explanation for his figurative options. The solution might appear surprising; but not if we remember that it was precisely the surrealist tradition which maintained the most committed critical stance against the Modern Movement and that it is surrealism that has given the best expression to the futility of modern reason. With this leap into the unknown Aldo Rossi, with the greatest anguish but also lucidity, points simultaneously to the necessity and impossibility of the neo-rationalist project.

By contrast, in Giorgio Grassi the problem of figuration addresses different issues. Grassi refuses the subjective approach and his work becomes a spirited research for an objective foundation of his formal decisions. Perhaps it is Grassi who sets out the problem of figuration with the greatest rigour precisely due to the lack of an objective solution which he does not want to relinquish in any case.

There are two approaches in Grassi: that of anonymous architecture and that of the objectivity of construction. In the last thirty or forty years, Grassi has written the most salient and inspired texts on the lessons to be learned from anonymous architecture. His analysis of rural buildings, of the Gothic one-family house, of the housing schemes of the Modern Movement, all seem to point towards the same end: the encounter between an objectively defined, socially acceptable figuration and the architecture of the house. In Grassi's work the collective social condition of architecture is not simply reaffirmed but becomes instead the very foundation of his convictions. Only through their social legitimacy can architectural forms become plausible.[17] Building types and compositional elements—few and schematically reduced to their most essential features—are acceptable only if one can find in them a verification of their efficacy and social acceptance. These types and elements have material validity only in their constructive logic and in the historical experience that legitimises their functions. Grassi's figuration, which reflects his demanding social ethics, tends towards anonymity, towards a dissolution of the subject in a collectivity that is more willed than existing, and which assures the authenticity of his references.

Where Rossi dwelt on contradiction and duality and eventually employed a personal poetic which freed him from the requirements he had imposed upon himself, Grassi, on the contrary, espouses a millenial tendency, a utopian projection towards a socially and technically coherent space which, though in reality exists only in fragments, is now made absolute and becomes eventually the basis of his work.

Contradiction and utopia, dualism and monism are, in the end, the opposite attitudes that guide these two architects in their search for solutions to the obscure problem of figuration. The problem of realism again reappears as an open, unresolved question. At the same time, the experience of both architects demonstrates in different ways but with equal intensity that the neo-rationalist project is an insoluble question.

› Notes

1 Cf. *Teoria della progettazione architettonica,* Dedalo, Bari, 1968. Also see texts by Canella, Coppa, Gregotti, Rossi, A. Samonà, Scimemi, Semerani and Tafuri in a publication bearing the same title and comprising of lectures delivered in a symposium in 1966. Formerly published under the title *Aspetti e problemi della tipologia edilizia,* Venice. During the academic year 1963–1964, the neo-rationalist methodology had already been initiated in a systematic way.

2 The book *Architettura razionale,* Franco Angeli, Milan, 1973, constitutes the catalogue of the architectural sections of the Milan Triennale. The term *Tendenza* was then coined by Massimo Scolari. The connection that exists between Italian neo-rationalism and that of the 'New York Five' marks both the moment of the movement's consolidation and of its eclectic diffusion in the seventies.

3 The Italian design boom is exemplified by the exhibition organised by the M.O.M.A. of New York, 1972, entitled *Italy: The New Domestic Landscape.* From the fifties onwards it is the socially committed Italian cinema that deals with the themes of urban devastation and property speculation.

4 See Manfredo Tafuri, *Teorie e storie dell'architettura,* Laterza, Bari, 1968. Also, Aldo Rossi, 'Introduzione a Boullée' in *Saggio sul'arte ,* Padua, 1967.

5 See Aldo Rossi, 'Emil Kaufmann e l'architettura del'illuminismo' in *Casabella Continuità,* No 222, 1958.

6 See 'Gruppo Architettura' *Quaderni di Documentazioni,* Nos 1 and 2, Venice, 1971 and 1973, including texts by Aymonino, Babri, Lena, Polesello, Semerani, Burelli, Billa and others. Also the references to the architecture of socialist countries in the book *Architettura rationale, op. cit.,* note 2.

7 See Gilles Deleuze, *L'écriture et la différence,* Ed. Minuit, Paris, 1967.

8 The references by Aldo Rossi to the work of Lévi-Strauss are frequent and explicit in many of his writings.

9 See Also Rossi, *L'Architettura della città,* Marsilio, Padua, 1966.

10 See Xavier Rubet de Ventós 'El funcionamiento como puritanismo' in the book *La estética y sus herejias,* Anagrama, Barcelona, 1974.

11 See Giorgio Grassi, 'Arquitectura, realidad y vanguardia', in the records of *Primer Simposio de Arquitectura y Ciudad: Vanguardia y Continuidad,* Valencia, 1980.

12 See Giorgio Grassi 'Il rapporto analisi-projetto', in *L'analisi urbana e la progetazzione architettonica,* School of Architecture, Milan Polytechnic, contributions to the Academic Year 1968–69, CLUP, Milan, 1970.

13 See Aldo Rossi, 'Introduzzione a Boullée', *op. cit.,* note 4.

14 Manfredo Tafuri 'L'architecture dans le boudoir', in *La sfera e il labirinto: Avanguardie e architettura da Piranesi agli anni 70,* Einaudi, Turin, 1980.

15 See Aldo Rossi, *Scientific Autobiography;* Rizzoli, New York, 1982.

16 See A.A.V.V., *Junggesellenmaschinen—Les machines célibataires,* Alfieri, Venice, 1975.

17 See Giorgio Grassi, *La costruzione logica dell'architettura,* Marsilio, Padua, 1967.

52 Werner Oechslin

Premises for the resumption of the discussion of typology (1986)

Werner Oechslin, 'Premises for the resumption of the discussion of typology', *Assemblage*, 1, 1986, extracts pp. 37–46 and 50–52.

The discussion of typology was at the front ranks in architectural circles in the 1960s and early 1970s, but has lately fallen back to the second eschelon. The "post-modern" now takes all the headlines instead. But this shift in current events is not at all a matter of replacement. The increasing réclame in architecture, on the contrary, has tended to favor superficial methods of study, methods for the most part oriented toward the outer appearance, the superficial image of architecture. The discussion of architecture at present suffers especially from these ills, and as a result a deeper understanding of typology is hardly thinkable. What survives of such an understanding outside of a restricted circle of initiates seems to have long since been reduced to a trivial conception of typology. The misunderstanding stubbornly endures that typology is a matter of classifying forms and functions as simply and unequivocally as possible. This banalized understanding of a conception so rich in tradition and so important in intellectual history joins forces with what is furthered and practiced as "economic functionalism." Standardization and typification have long since occurred in this sphere but not toward an ideal reduction of the architectural design process to its universal foundations, not even for the purpose of guaranteeing light and air, but rather for the sake of increasing productivity. As we know, this economic functionalism has led neither to more dwelling space nor to a more livable environment and, even more than in other parts of the field, it has been oriented toward the no longer profoundly examined laws of production (and of the producers).

This also indicates how explosive the discussion of typology is in its possible, and in part already historically proven, consequences. It is also clear how great a disservice is done by those architectural critics who allow this trivial understanding to persist undisturbed. One voice should be cited here that has spoken out systematically, polemically, and often scornfully against virtually every tendency toward any degree of profundity since the moment renewed discussion of "rationalism" began. It is representative of those "misunderstandings" that come of rejecting a deeper analysis. Bruno Zevi makes the inexcusable mistake of basing his evaluation of the concept of typology on that purely diagnostic and trivial form of types determined entirely by function. Instead of correcting such a one-sided and inappropriate use of the concept of typology, he questions the usefulness of the concept itself. On the basis of these functionally based uses of the concept, he decides that it is unsatisfactory. What is then proposed in opposition to the possibility of such theoretical models forgoes any and all reflection on the relationship between artistic individuality and artistic convention—a matter which has kept the discussion of the theory of art in suspense for centuries. Instead, one reads in Zevi statements delivered with an unsurpassable arrogance, such as: art is anti-typological; every architectural creation is necessarily an individual interpretation by the artist; individual style is more decisive in the shaping of a work of art than the type. It is as if he wanted to overlook the impact of the Palladian villa or of Schinkel's Old Museum!

* * *

Nevertheless, in discussions of typology architects, particularly in Italy, have taken seriously the distinction between type and model, for example, and an attempt has been made to bring theory back to the practice of design in an intelligent manner. Distinct positions have been taken and defended and can be individually characterized. The names of Aldo Rossi, Giorgio Grassi, and Carlo Aymonino come to mind.

The reference point for the Italian discussion of typology has always been Quatremère de Quincy's article "Type,"[1] which has since become famous. It was first published in 1825 in the third volume of the *Encyclopédie méthodique*. G. C. Argan deserves the credit for taking up and disseminating this classic definition in his brief and concise article "Sul concetto di tipologia architettonica" (1962).[2] Of course, a number of different misunderstandings with their respective consequences can be traced back to Argan's essay. These misunderstandings concern the fundamental appraisal of the place and importance of typology in regard to design practice and methods, and the even more clouded issue of the systematic value of the type and its importance to the historical dimension of architecture.

Argan's essay first appeared, in its original short form, in the *Festschrift* for Hans Sedlmayr. Since his Borromini studies in the 1930s, Sedlmayr—even if working from completely different premises—had been close to the problems of architectural typology, and was considered in the 1930s the chief proponent of the iconology of architecture. It is questionable whether, or to what degree, Argan wanted or was able to take into account the discussions of structuralism in Germany since the end of the 1920s. There are no explicit references. Conjectures in the light of the dedication to Sedlmayr remain unresolved. However, Argan does undoubtedly relate his efforts at interpretation to the specific state of the then current art historical discussion of methods. With an eye toward Italian art history, Argan describes his analysis as a contribution to the criticism of idealism. He tries, on the other hand, to draw a parallel with what was then the most up-to-date and the most discussed viewpoint in the discipline: the *typology* of *architecture,* he says, corresponds for the most part with the *iconology of the pictorial and sculptural arts*. This explicit parallel places Argan's essay in that series of works (Krautheimer, Wittkower, Bandmann) concerned with a specific iconology of architecture. The publication of the essay in the *Festschrift* for Sedlmayr can be adequately explained only in this light.

* * *

Quatremère de Quincy's article is distinguished, as usual, by analytically precise wording and the systematic organization of the arguments (concept definition, etymological derivation, explanation of the history of the concept, discussion of word usage, and, only then, remarks specific to architecture). It is no accident that Quatremère de Quincy conceived of and planned his *Encyclopédie méthodique: Architecture* as a necessary, field-specific extension of the great encyclopedia of Diderot and D'Alembert. In keeping with this more general context, the distinction between type and model bears characteristics from epistemology and from general systematic thought—which had been just as well known and as much discussed in architectural circles, *mutatis mutandis,* since the early days of Vitruvianism between Alberti and Barbaro. This is not the place to reach that far back in history; Nevertheless, it can be said with confidence that the definition of the concept of the "type" in Quatremère de Quincy is just as unthinkable without the precedent of the classical philosophical question of *form and matter* as the discussion of typology altogether would be without the preceding efforts to integrate Euclidean geometry into architecture. Simply remembering the conceptual correspondence between type and figure (*typos/figura*) should surely suggest much additional thought.

By the same token, one also comes upon shortcomings in Quatrèmere de Quincy's distinction between type and model. To his perhaps overly abstract and for the present too philosophically conceived definition of the type, one can at least contrast a compromised formula—yielded in the context of defining architectural drawing as an extension of Vitruvian exegesis—in which the pure geometric form requires "sensuous" mediation in visible lines (*lignes sensuelles*). . . . There is very probably, then, a possibility of graphically representing "typologies" and of applying and using them indirectly in design. Here Quatremère de Quincy reveals his Platonic side! He was no doubt thoroughly aware of the schematics customarily used at the time—half-abstract, symbolic formulas (almost in a *plan de masse*). Apparently, he did not want to depart from his main distinction to go into these "transitional forms" in his article, which was aimed at a systematic attack. To put it differently, that Quatremère de Quincy foregoes an analysis of the existing practical equivalents of typology of his day is accounted for by the decidedly theoretical orientation of the *Encyclopédie méthodique.*

In this light, Argan's attempt to limit the distinction between type and model all too exclusively to architectonic realities (which occurs predominantly against the previously mentioned background of assigning function and content) seems a two-fold obfuscation. Quatremère de Quincy always kept the two viewpoints clearly separated. And for just this reason, in a second part near the end of his article (not sufficiently considered by Argan), he took up the discussion of contingency and conventionality, through which the embedding of the type in historical reality and in a specific time inevitably occurs. If this second part—which comes astonishingly close to a hermeneutical point of view—of Quatrèmere de Quincy's definition had been sufficiently heeded, the discussion of typology could not have been posed *against* artistic individuality and *against* historicity, but would have had to have been conceived of as a regulative principle enmeshed in history and context.

Now it is also true, however, that in Italian discussions of typology, led chiefly by architects, such positions have been worked out, in part independently. And as a result, it is precisely in these discussions (specifically within the so called rationalist tradition) that *history as a problem* has been rediscovered, and in a much more clearly refined way than postmodernism is able to manage, relying as it does on a superficial conception of mimesis, as invoked by Argan, or on mere imitation.

⁜ ⁜ ⁜

In this climate of distinctions and analyses, Quatremère de Quincy finally, with full awareness of the rich tradition in art history, takes up his argument. This becomes even more apparent as his other articles (on architecture, character, convention) and further writings, such as *Considerations morales sur la destination d'ouvrages de l'art* (1815), are included in the analysis. The more comprehensively Quatremère de Quincy argues, the clearer his tendency to attack the one-sidedness of a purely "historical" and positivistic approach to history. In this manner he criticizes the usual treatment of mimesis. Starting from the fact that nothing exists without predecessors ("Il faut un antecédent a tout. . . ."), he turns against literal interpretations of imitation, aimed at the model and its repetition, and against imitation based on its positivistic form: "Ils méconnoissent tous les degrés d'imitation morale, par analogic, par rapports intellectuels, par application de princips, par appropriation de manieres, de combinaisons, de raisons, de systemes, etc." What are required, then, are fundamental, systematic, analogic, rational, and combinatory kinds of processes in the context of the encounter with history. And here it becomes clear that Quatremère de Quincy argues from the position of one who is aware of the possibility of misapplication and trivialization in handling this fundamental problem in architecture, and who realizes he has been confronted with such misuse. The *problem of appropriate usage* thus overshadows, at least partly, the systematic intention with which Quatremère de Quincy discusses the concept of typology.

One is much closer now to that "extreme" example of contemporary typological effort that, once more in a misleading way, has been touted as the "pièce de résistance" of all attempts at formalization. Durand's table "Ensemble d'édifices resultant des divisions du quarré, du parallèlogramme, et de leurs combinaisons avec le cercle," published in his *Précis des leçons*, is commonly seen as an example of that narrow conception of typology that turns to the solid basis of the universal language of geometry to apply it in as unadulterated a manner as possible to concrete architectonic objects themselves. That Durand related ("pure") geometric configurations directly to the *design process* emerges clearly both from his publishing the table in the relevant tract of the *Précis* and also from the immediate juxtaposition of geometric figure and architectural type in the second edition of the table (1813).

Yet a closer examination shows that Durand by no means represents *only* a counterposition to Quatremère de Quincy's "historical" discussion of the concept of typology. Not even Durand speaks *only* of a "geometrical reduction of architecture." On the contrary, he is concerned with clarifying the relationship in architecture between a concrete (historically) existing typology and the *general form* based on the universal laws of geometry. What resembles, in the table of 1802, a purely "Euclidean" development of a form, entirely in the mainstream of the attempts at classification that had been extremely popular since the eighteenth century, turns out under closer scrutiny to be a very carefully developed attempt to legitimize more complex architectonic configurations. Despite the elementary nature of the geometric figures shown, even in these simple forms, one can make out the architectonic thought behind them. Durand reveals this himself in the revised, 1813 version of the table, where simple ("pure") geometric figures and their architectonic correlates, in the form of fully developed types, are presented together in the same illustration.

*   *   *

The decisive point about this observation is that quite probably even within his demonstrative figure arguing on "purely typological" grounds, and indirectly within the bounds of his design methodology, Durand maintains the connection with precise, historically contingent objects, which was regarded as given at the time and thus placed at his disposal, clearly in sight. On the other hand, the design method was intended in fact to lead to concrete results, which in their turn constituted the history of architecture.

An analogous, contrasting consideration must also be added to Durand's efforts in the history of architecture. Just as the *Précis des leçons* was intended to satisfy the *systematic* requirements of the designing architect, the *Recueil et parallèle des tous les édifices anciens et modernes* of 1800 was to make the *history* of architecture available to him. In keeping with his own systematic intentions—though this time with a different orientation than in the *Précis*—Durand intended to work *formally* on the historical material as well. Furthermore, this had to be done so that both comparability of forms and applicability of concrete design work were always guaranteed in the process of reducing them to the essentials (that is, in representing typological diversity) as well as in the process of standardizing both measures and means of graphic representation.

In both undertakings—the systematic as well as the historical—Durand shows himself ready to compromise. Neither is his systematic-geometrical approach exclusively abstract, nor does his history remain unsystematic. History is not played off against systematics. Rather, the basic presuppositions of dealing with systematics and with history are both considered in order to meaningfully introduce typology, the "theory of figures," as an intermediate court of appeal. The realization of this project, in accordance with the distinction between type and model tossed into the balance as a weighty argument by Quatremère de Quincy, remained at that time unfulfilled. And therefore—in the light of these theoretical efforts, in other words, *before* putting them into practice—at the other end of the discussion of typology a good deal of autonomy was necessarily granted. In any case, introducing typology to design practice would not (as, for example, Zevi seems to do) replace the creativity of the design process that would necessarily follow, but rather would merely set out more demanding conditions and premises. The self-evident interaction with these conditions has been lost to the architect in the new mythos of the unbound desire for invention. (Even the doctrine of mimesis had decisively limited this!) This myth leaves the architect wholly at a loss, so that architecture is then surrendered ever more completely to accidents and to forces foreign to architecture itself.

In its appeal to general geometrical forms, Durand's diagram also shows that an identification of architectonic figures with functions and interpretations was premature at the least, prior to the confrontation—to be sought from within contemporary design itself—with fully developed or developing traditions. The theory of character can set a similar contextual condition. Quatremère de Quincy expressly mentions that the type must receive its conventional application *(emploi / usage naturel)* according to necessity *(besoin)* and natural constitution *(nature)*. So architecture does not come about by blind translation of geometries. The circle of the argumentation is rounded out when one considers that elsewhere, namely, in his *Considerations morales sur la destination d'ouvrages de l'art,* along with other conventions of varying degrees of necessity, Quatremère de Quincy draws on those basic Vitruvian concepts *(firmitas / utilitas / venustras)* that have for so long acted as regulative principles in architecture. Once more, in such cases it is not a matter of his pinning architecture down to its societal actualizations or its indispensable historicity. Instead, he is concerned with defining the remaining freedom, within and despite this conditioning, that guarantees the artist the ability to function effectively and the possibility of affecting society, and in this way passes on to him a precisely defined role.

In light of this broadened consideration of the work of Quatremère de Quincy, it further becomes apparent that the discussion of typology is by no means a matter of simplification or standardization or of a reductive model of architectural invention. On the contrary, we must perceive in his work an intelligently developed construct in which the link is ensured between the systematic and the historical or conventional (and therefore always societally oriented) limitations of architecture in their reciprocal dependence.

Editors' note: Illustrations and references to illustrations have been omitted.

› Notes

1 English translation in *Oppositions* 8 (1977): 148–50.
2 First published in Munich, 1962. Now in the *Enciclopedia Universale dell'Arte* (Venice). English translation. "On the Typology of Architecture," by Joseph Rykwert in *Architectural Design* (December 1963): 564–65. Editor's note: see also N45 in this Reader.

53 Micha Bandini

Typological theories in architectural design (1993)

Micha Bandini, 'Typological theories in architectural design', from: Ben Farmer and Hentie Louw (eds), *Companion to Contemporary Architectural Thought*, London: Routledge, 1993, extracts pp. 387–393.

The word typology means the study of types. Typology is concerned with those aspects of human production which can be grouped because of some inherent characteristics which make them similar. The theory of typology is thus that of conceptualizing those categories.

The issue of types and typology becomes of fundamental importance in artistic production whenever the artist is confronted with, on the one hand, the weight of historical precedent and, on the other, artistic invention. If an artist is interested in contributing to the culture of human artefacts he or she will have to confront the problem of type, whether choosing the avant-gardist position of rejecting history, or accepting the continuation of tradition.

It becomes obvious, then, why typology is of central interest to architecture, since architecture cannot exist in a vacuum but will always be found in a context which is often pregnant with historical references. These are precedents which designers might want either to follow or to distance themselves from, but which, nevertheless, because of their nature, condition the act of creative invention itself.

It is of cultural significance that typology becomes relevant in architecture every time the following two issues are simultaneously present: when similar, but different, architectural objects are needed to house similar functions (for example, banks, schools); when the validity of a dominant stylistic convention is being challenged. Thus typology assumed primary significance at the end of the eighteenth century, when the classical tradition of architectural composition was confronted by the emerging needs of an industrializing society; it was again in the forefront of the architectural debate during the 1920s and the 1930s, when the so-called Modern Movement was expected to provide an alternative aesthetic for an ever-increasing number of building requirements. And typology once again became important in the late 1960s and the early 1970s, when a number of architects began to question both the validity of the Modernist aesthetic and its solutions.

*   *   *

To this, two different answers have been traditionally given. The first assigns to type an ideal role, that of a mental construct which is not embodied in any specific form but which is adapted and elaborated by the designer, so that invention can coexist with tradition and the authority of precedents. The second sees type as a tool for the composition of schematic objects which might become real architecture if the needs of social and economic production require their particular conformation.

The first answer is usually attributed to Quatremère de Quincy who, following the Neo-Platonic tradition of neo-classicism, defined 'type' as an a priori which can be further transformed by the designer to fit his imagination and the requirements of the brief (Quatremère de Quincy 1788–1825). The second answer comes from J.N.L. Durand who, following contemporary theories of taxonomy in the natural sciences, believed that the nature of a type is that of a classifiable form, composed from primary architectural elements which, combined with the laws of descriptive geometry, can produce a model to be copied (Durand 1802).

But while the conventions of a tradition characterize these two positions as opposites, a closer reading of Quatremère and Durand shows an absence of that rigid schematization which had been the main feature of their posthumous interpretation.[1] Thus when Quatremère makes the distinction between type and model he is not only reaffirming the predominance of the ideal over the contingent, he is also indicating the need to provide, through an inspiring mental construct, a workable indicator for practising architects. Likewise, J.N.L. Durand, who declares the importance of a 'model' rooted in history in both the *Précis des Leçons* (1802), where he indicates a geometrical compositional procedure, and in the *Recueil et parallèle des tous lés édifices anciens et modernes* (1800) where he traces their historical lineage. Thus Durand's conceptual justification of the 'model' is reached through analysing the tradition of the formation of certain types and through successively elaborating on them with the belief, common to the culture of his time, that if the classical language had been able to sustain architecture over the previous centuries then it would be within that tradition of composition that the requirements of the nineteenth century were likely to be met.

It is from this mixed heritage that the theory of typology came to represent within the polemic of the Modern Movement both the perfectibility of the industrially produced mass object and the ideal timeless perfection of certain forms. Muthesius in his advocacy for a better industry, Le Corbusier in his conception of a minimum unit in the composition of a larger 'Unite', and Ernst May, Alexander Klein and the second CIAM congress (1929) in their search for a minimum housing standard, all shared that tradition which chose to keep open the ambiguity between type and model because of the workability of the latter and the formal authority of the former.

Most contemporary evidence now shows that these architects, while taking part, theoretically, in the avant-gardist polemic against history, in their practical work often elected to invent on the basis of a tradition which allowed the linking of contemporary creativity with an awareness of the formal richness of the past. But the way in which this manner of working was received, codified and transmitted by critics and historians to others, in order to make it more palatable and useful, is rather different. The flexibility, one could almost say the ambiguity, which was built into early Modernist theorizations was not incorporated in those narrower recordings of architecture which saw type only as a non-specific concept, and model only as a very convenient way for appropriating precedents.

Thus type, in the reductive exception it acquired through its post-Second World War vulgarization, came to be almost synonymous with two trends of thought: either with functionalism, which was negatively equated with the *Existenzminimum* research, or with the classification, and possible further production, of previous architectural examples.

* * *

Typological debates became very important in Italy, perhaps because immediately after the Second World War history became central to architectural debate. The reason for this was not just that the country needed to obliterate the representational ambiguities of its immediate Fascist past by linking itself to the rationality of Modernism and to its Enlightenment roots, but also because younger designers, searching again to ground architecture within specific cultural and geographic settings, questioned the ['internationality'] of the Modern Movement and its legitimacy as a 'model' valid for all times and in all contexts.

For a while the debate between model and type seemed to lean on the Neo-Platonic interpretation of type, especially because this was the thesis of an authoritative article by G.C. Argan which has appeared in different versions since 1965 and which achieved its ultimate status when it became the entry on 'type' in the *Enciclopedia Universal dell' Arte*.[2]

Argan's argument, in equating the role that typology serves in architecture with that of iconology in art, not only followed the art-criticism hypothesis current at the time, but also made hypothetical suggestions to those Italian architects who were searching for a rationale from which to operate.

His three-tiered argument, used frequently by those who support the idealist interpretation on type, starts by stating:

> Type is characterized as a set of rules deduced through a procedure of reduction of a series of formal variants from a base-form or from a communal scheme. If type is the product of this regressive procedure, the found base-form cannot be understood as a mere structural framework, but either as the internal framework of form in its autonomous artistic value or as the principle which includes in itself not only all the formal configurations from which it has been deduced but also the possibility of further variations and even the complete modification of the structure of the given type.
>
> (Argan 1958:3)

Argan then proceeds to demonstrate that type is an integral part of any artistic creation first by stating that 'typological series are not formed in history because of the practical function of buildings but because of their configuration', and second by making the hierarchy of architectural scale the conceptual means by which such formal configurations may be subdivided into categories. In order to do this he chose three all-encompassing categories: 'the first which includes entire configurations of buildings, the second [which comprehends] large building elements, and the third [which is concerned with] decorative elements' (Argan 1958:4).

The attractiveness of Argan's article is due not only to its intrinsic appeal but also to the way the argument builds up towards a process which closely resembles, in its internal logic, the one which gives rise to rationally based design. It could be reasonably hypothesized, then, that what came to be understood by those European architects who were inclined towards this design approach, and they were the majority, as a basis for a typological debate was:

1   that type is an idea and not a precise form, which means that it can be elaborated upon;
2   that this modifiable concept is similar, in the internal logic of its historical deployment, to the internal logic which the architect employs when creating the forms of his or her projects;
3   that through the analogical combination of the two (the type-ideal-form and the architect-ideal-form) the designer could approach the pressing problem of history; and finally
4   that the procedure through which all of this could be achieved would be to follow a design process which would be careful to identify the appropriateness of different hierarchical scales of composition both in appraising and in designing buildings.

These ideas seemed especially relevant, during the 1960s and the 1970s, for the Venice School of Architecture where a number of influential teachers came to regard the investigation of the typological structure of a city as a prerequisite for a morphological intervention into it. Within this tradition of enquiry, begun by Giuseppe Samonà,[3] and furthered by Saverio Muratori, with a detailed survey of the Venetian urban context (Muratori 1960), Aldo Rossi chose typology as the main topic of discussion for the academic year of 1963–4 (Rossi 1963–4). In this way a long series of contributions began through which his approach to typology developed and changed.

While it is clear that Rossi, in this early phase, saw building typology as the repository of the permanent morphological features of the city, the role he attributes to type in respect to the boundaries of architecture is more ambiguous. Does type possess socio-anthropological connotations, which the designer can access through its analysis and elaboration, or is such a method doomed to failure and can architecture only be pursued within an autonomous position? Rossi's contemporaneous 'architecture of silence' seems to further the second hypothesis, especially because it is pursued in conjunction with his concept of the city formed of parts formally concluded where, in the urban structure, building typologies provide the networking tissue and monuments the exceptions. Rossi writes (almost paraphrasing Argan):

> Type is thus a constant and manifests itself with a character of necessity; but even though it is predetermined, it reacts dialectically with technique, function and style as well as with both the collective character and the individual moment of the architectural artifact.
>
> (Rossi 1976:41)

If Rossi's initial concept seems to draw on the ideal aspect of type, particularly emphasizing the ethical correctness of typology as the appropriate 'political' compositional device,[4] he would, later on, relax into a more all-embracing attitude which would focus on those aspects of the relationship between urban morphology and building typology (as, for example, with 'memory') which the designer could use in order to transform the urban context through his or her own creative sensibility.

But in those years of confusion, when general political issues became mixed up with the intellectual difficulties which architects were encountering in understanding their role in society, liberating themselves from the Modern Movement straitjacket while simultaneously seeking to give 'form' to their projects, these kind of compositional approaches provided security. Thus a 'political' working document, drawn up during the academic year 1967–8 by a group of students tutored by Massimo Scolari, characterized type as a principle of architecture based on formal analysis; twenty years later Scolari would write in appraising this phenomenon:

> Even the definition of 'type as a principle of architecture' was only apparently a theoretical statement. In Rossi's architecture this was, immediately and from the very start, a not reducible model; and it was so close to the idea that it remained ambiguously poised between simplicity and oversimplifcation. To the latter belong all the replicas and the variations produced by the imitators.
>
> (Scolari 1985:45)

While Rossi pursued, through the ideal type, his own idea of architecture, in the same years Carlo Aymonino saw typology more as part of that current of thought which drew on the rationality of both the Enlightenment and the Modern Movement. To him, building types are architectural hypotheses, 'useful to all just because necessary'. Thus 'type becomes the reference point of the emerging urban structure'; however, 'the boundary between "type" and "model" would often be weak and the prototype will later become the type to be confirmed in the subsequent built examples' (Aymonino 1976:76–7).

*   *   *

Particularly interesting in this respect is the *excursus* of the French followers of the typological school. Notwithstanding their allegiance to J.N.L. Durand, Wittkower and Aymonino, who had become the legitimizing authority for their writings,[5] to them the distinction drawn between analysis and project, so important for the political and cultural correctness of previous elaborations, became of secondary importance. Instead they seek to derive the project from the analysis of its urban components (Panerai 1979:14).

Such attitude is very evident in the work of P. Panerai, as, for example, when he writes:

> But it is not only up to the project to enlarge the knowledge of the city, which would not be negligible, we must interrogate ourselves on the usage of typology, and ask ourselves if such work could, at a certain point, be of any utility in the process of designing. First of all typology is useless if one does not have any intention of making use of it. Why waste time observing part of a city, understanding the constitutive mechanisms of its tissue, if the hypothesis from which the design process springs is that of a *tabula rasa* operation or a bulldozer operation. If one continues to believe that there

is a time for analysis and another for the project which will simply put logical forms to the 'objective' data given by the analysis, then one understands that analysis and project are but two moments, two faces of the same theoretical reflection, of the same responsible attitude towards the city. Urban analysis, and this is the thesis here defended, goes hand in hand with the criticism of those interventions which tend to demolish the city, to violate it, to annihilate it. Without such criticism urban analysis would be nothing but an alibi.

(Panerai 1979: 14)

Bernard Huet's belief in an architecture which sees itself mainly as contributing to the structure of the city is at the centre of most research pursued at the Institut d'Etudes de Recherches Architecturales in Paris. There, a series of studies was spawned on the typo-morphological relationship underlying the structure of French cities. 'L'architecture urbaine' (as this approach is labelled) is seen as a political tool to contrast speculative developments, and a teaching method is proposed as a way to anchor design to a cultural and ideological dimension. It is interesting to note that Huet's response to the problem of mass teaching is conditioned by his belief in the supremacy of typology over other theoretical tools. This extends itself to the point that typology becomes the source of all architectural education, as when he writes:

All the practical problems given to the students to solve should be considered in terms of urban quantity and repetition of type rather than in terms of the development of subjectivity based on the new and original. Compulsory typology must be a necessary beginning and not an end in itself for architecture consists in going beyond it.

(Huet 1978)

The methodology of the French approach to typological questions seems to me particularly well exemplified by Castex and Panerai' s study of the city of Versailles, where four analytical levels of investigation became the basis for reading the city. This prescriptive framework, which in its hierarchy strongly resembles Argan's interpretative categories, constitutes both the strength and weakness of these researches.[6] Castex, Depaule and Panerai seem to acknowledge the inherent ambiguity of their approach, for example when they write with respect to one of their later research projects:

Among different possible ways of reading the city, we do consider the city as an architectural artefact which can be divided in distinct elements in order to emphasise differences. Such differences, which refer to different levels of meanings, have to be interpreted in the light of evidence external to architecture. In particular we are referring to the relationship between spatial organization and social practices, this being for us of primary importance. In order to do so we will be using the notion of model both from an architectural point of view . . . and from a cultural one. . . . From this stems the apparent ambiguity of our work: it is a morphological study, but referred to examples belonging to a specific historical context, it is an architectural study, but at the urban scale, it is spatial too, but concerned with social aspects.

(Panerai et al. 1980:8–10)

The reputation of the typo-morphological approach is contemporaneous and linked with the emergence of the 'Tendenza' after the thirteenth Biennale of Milan, because those who recognized the necessity of a 'rational' and 'theoretical' framework for design approached the relationship between architecture and the city as a priority, and resorted to typology as being representative of a system of analytical investigation in which the project could be anchored. I think it is interesting to note here that the more widespread this attitude the looser the boundaries of its system of reference became, so that, by the end of the 1970s – either under the banner of 'rational' or of 'typology' – one could find a series of very different designs. These ranged from the purely morphological ones to those who saw 'the relationship between building typology and urban morphology' as still belonging to the alternative political climate of urban renewal of the late 1960s. Particularly representative of the formal approach to typology is Rob Krier's *Stadtraum in Theorie und Praxis* (1975), where the notion of urban space seems embodied by that of spatial type, the vessel of all functional, symbolic, social and historical contents. Krier's geometric characterization of spatial types through history clearly aligns itself within the tradition established by J.N.L. Durand.[7]

*   *   *

Editors' note: illustrations and references to illustrations have been omitted.

› Notes

1   See Oechslin 1986 for a most illuminating analysis of both conceptions.
2   It is interesting to note that the English version of the *Enciclopedia* omits this specific entry.
3   Samonà's lifelong interest in the typological question is best represented in the long introduction to the collection of his essays (see Samonà 1978:11–52).
4   For example, Rossi writes:

> The structural value of typology – and thus its prominence in architecture – is a compositional factor; it concerns first of all a choice, a tendency. . . . In order to make a typological choice it is necessary to make some references, these references are part of the choice or tendency. . . . in architecture, typological indifference means disorder. I do not refer to expressionistic disorder but to the disorder of not-architecture of non-choice.

(Rossi 1979)

and also: 'The problem is to design new parts of the city choosing typologies able to challenge the status quo. This could be a perspective for the socialist city' (Rossi 1979).
5   In this respect it is illuminating to read Panerai 1979.
6   Castex and Panerai's analysis, notwithstanding its historical dimension, is largely based on four categories: the overall form of the city in relation to the territory and with the stages of its growth; the big, monumental, atypical insertions within the urban tissue; the relationship of housing to work-place; and, finally, the single residential configuration.

7   The variety of design positions represented within the so called 'rationalist' camp is simplified well in *Rational Architecture Rationelle* (Archive d'Architecture Moderne (AMM) 1978), a book presenting a series of projects which take on board the relationship between architecture and the traditional city. It includes a paper by A.Vidler (1976) which underpins the approach theoretically. He introduces the thesis, an interesting one notwithstanding the circularity of its argument, that a third typology (the one just presented by the rationalist approach) is equipollent to the previous two – the one that 'returned architecture to its natural origins' and the one that 'assimilated architecture to the world of machine production' (Vidler 1976:28). Of the AAM activities and intellectual overtones, I think the article by Santelli (1981) is representative; in this article a correct urban rehabilitation is seen as being possible only if architects follow traditional typologies in their reconstructions.

› Bibliography

Argan, G.C. 'Typology', *Enciclopedia Universale dell'Arte* 1, Vol. XIV, Venice: Fondazione Cini.

Aymonino, C. (1976) *Il Significato della cittá*, Laterza.

Durand, J.N.L. (1802-5) *Précis des leçons d'architecture donnees à l'Ecole Polytechnique*, Paris.

Huet, B. (1978) 'The teaching of architecture in France 1968–1978: from one reform to the next', *Lotus International* 21.

Muratori, S. (1960) *Studi per una operante storia urbana di Venezia*, Rome: Institute Poligrafico dell Stato.

Oechslin, W. (1986) 'Premises for the resumption of the discussion of typology', *Assemblage* 1 (October): 37-56.

Panerai, P. (1979) 'Typologies', *Les Cahiers de la Recherche Architecturale* 4 (December):3–21.

Panerai, P., Castex, J. and Depaule, J.C. (1980) *Formes urbaines: de l'îlot a la barre*, Paris; Italian edn 1981, *Isolato urbano e città contemporaneo*, Milan: Clup.

Quatremère de Quincy, A.C. (1788-1825) 'Type', in *Dictionnaire d'architecture: encyclopédie méthodique*, Vol. III, part 2, Paris.

Rossi, A. (1963–4) 'Considerazioni sulla morphologia urbana e la tipologia edilizia', in *Aspetti e problemi delta tipologia edilizia*, Venice: Venice University.

—— (1976) *L'architettura della città*, Bari: Laterza; trans. 1982 *The Architecture of the City*, Cambridge, Mass.: MIT Press.

—— (1979) *L'architettura della città*, Bari: Laterza; trans. 1982 *The Architecture of the City*, Cambridge, Mass.: MIT Press.

Samoná, G. (1978) *L'unita architettura urbanistica: Scritti e progetti 1929-1973*, ed. P.Lovero, Milan: Franco Angeli.

Santelli, S. (1981) 'Réhabilitation et règles typologique', *Archive d'Architecture Moderne* 21.

Scolari, M. (1985) 'The typological commitment', *Casabella* 509/510 (January/February).

54 Guido Francescato

Type and the possibility of an architectural scholarship (1994)

Guido Francescato, 'Type and the possibility of an architectural scholarship', from: Karen A. Franck, Lynda H. Schneekloth (eds), *Ordering Space: Types in Architecture and Design*, New York: Van Nostrand & Reinhold, 1995, extracts pp. 255–258.

*　*　*

Relational typologies, the subject of this chapter, are less straightforward. *Relational* connotes the idea that type epitomizes the relationship between architectural form and utility. This connection is distinctive of architecture and lies at the core of its enterprise, but it has been difficult to identify and to describe how type embodies it. Indeed, a great deal of puzzlement about what is meant by type stems from the interpretations given to relational typologies by architects and critics alike, which prompts some authors to label type as a "confusing" notion (e.g., Pérez-Gómez 1991). In general though, two main classes can again be identified. The first represents the highly personal views of type espoused by such designers as Aldo Rossi and the Kriers. Leon Krier, for example, seems to think of type as a formal property of the elements of a composition, the finished building being the result of a process of assembling a typology of selected components. This is explicitly shown, for example, in his plans for a school in St. Quentin en Yvelines.

Rossi (1982) merges a similar notion of type with what has been called an "autobiographical" approach, which depends on "personal experiences, memories, even fleeting impressions" (Doordan 1989, 59) and "on the juxtaposition of memory and reason" (Moneo 1978, 36). The result is a vigorous, evocative, but highly idiosyncratic architecture, perhaps the inevitable consequence of a view of type that depends so strongly on a personal interpretation of history. Indeed, Moneo suggests that Rossi's work is based on types born in the architect's imagination, reflecting "a past that may not have existed" (1978, 37). This is a crucial insight, because, as I will discuss later, the canonical view of type holds that its foundations are to be sought in history – and there can be no history of a past that did not exist.

Krier's and Rossi's notions of type (and similar ones) are highly prescriptive; that is, they express the view that contemporary architects must recover forms from the past, especially urban forms, that have been lost through the antihistorical posture of the Modern Movement and the profit-making orientations of capitalist societies. In this sense, their view is certainly nostalgic. But even though in many ways it is responsible for muddying the waters of a general discourse on typologies, it is nevertheless important – no matter how problematic the interpretations and the actual projects that emerged from it. The reason is that these designers view architectural objects as the result of a process that begins by considering entities (types) already possessed of formal *and* functional aspects. This stands in sharp contrast to the cause-and-effect relationship of programmatic requirements and architectural form that had been postulated by functionalism, and affords a linkage to more descriptive ideas of type.

The second class of interpretations of relational type reaches back to the formulations proposed originally by Quatremère de Quincy in his well-known, seminal, but frequently misinterpreted article for the *Encyclopédie méthodique* ([1825] 1977). Quatremère's article was firmly founded on the Neoplatonic ideas of Laugier's (1753) "primitive hut" as the root-principle or origin of architecture (Vidler 1977, Lavin 1992).[1] This article was intended as a manifesto extolling the virtues of the neoclassical tradition and opposing the perceived excesses of baroque and rococo and the pre-Romantic symbolism of such architects as Boullée and Ledoux. Moreover, the notion of art as mimesis, as imitation of nature, hovers in the background of Quatremère's argument, though it must be recognized that he was not bound to the notion of imitation in a positivistic sense; on the contrary, he criticized literal interpretations based on a pedestrian reproduction of preexisting form.

A contemporary reading must strip Quatremère's essay of its Neoplatonic overtones and prescriptive qualities, which were relevant to the polemics of the time but are not germane to the debates of the present. Regrettably, this has not often been the case, which has led to critiques of the notion of type as a prescription for banal and reductive convention (Bandini 1984; Pérez-Gomez 1991) or as a rigidly ideological principle that requires adherence to the concept of origin or primitive cause (Bell 1991).

Quatremère's discussion of type is articulated around the following themes: (1) a careful distinction between *type* and *model;* (2) the recognition of the inescapable relationship between objects and their *historical precedents;* and (3) an emphasis on the connection between *form* and *use.*

The first theme is crucial not only for understanding Quatremère's paradigm, but also for addressing a number of recent critiques objecting to the perceived restrictiveness of type. Quatremère writes that "all is precise and given in the model; all is more or less vague in the *type*" ([1825] 1977, 148). In his view, the *model* is clearly a form to be repeated, copied, and imitated, and therefore more appropriate to the crafts or, in our time, to the technologies of industrial production, than to architecture. The word *type,* on the other hand, suggests "the idea of *an element which ought itself to serve as a rule for the model* . . . an object after which each [artist] can conceive works of art that *may have no resemblance* [to the model]" ([1825] 1977; emphasis added).

Second, the relation between objects and their historical precedents represents, beyond the Neoplatonic ideas of "origin and primitive cause," the recognition that form is not the product of the artist's imagination unfettered by knowledge of prior forms. On the contrary, form results from operations performed on prior forms, or better, on ideas of prior forms – that is, on relationships embodied in prior forms. Hence, history becomes the necessary underpinning of the generation of form.

Finally, the third theme in Quatremère's discussion links the historical evolution of a type to the use for which an object is intended, suggesting that there are forms that tend to support a specific function, while others, whatever their aesthetic merits, are simply inimical or inappropriate to the intended purpose. Not surprisingly, this is the theme that already in the nineteenth century, through Durand's (1805) theories, began the process that eventually led to the programmatic determinism of the Modern Movement.

In Quatremère's thinking one already finds the germ of the important idea that type is both limiting and liberating: limiting, because designers cannot avoid the constraints imposed by social use and the physical environment, which are the initial *raison d'être* of their work; liberating, because they are not compelled to slavishly repeat historical models. The significance of this thought becomes apparent when dealing with the dilemma designers constantly face: whether to produce forms to which the public is already accustomed and which it presumably "wants" (Michelson 1968) or to invent new forms.

For Quatremère, then, type represents at the same time the architectural intention or purpose ("the original reason of the thing"), the generator of form ("an element which serve(s) as the rule for a model"), and the container of tested functionality ("has its type in use and nature") ([1825] 1977, 148–50). Although type belongs to the domain of visual form, it is not a mere icon or image but a composite of form and function. And precisely because it contains the relationship between form and use (or better, one possible such relationship), it is also a carrier of architectural knowledge ("a sort of nucleus about which are collected . . . the development and variations of forms to which the object is susceptible") (148).

This is undoubtedly a highly abstract, complex, and somewhat ambiguous formulation. But it is also evocative and persuasive precisely because, in its intricacy and vagueness, it reflects the absence of certainties, the complex interplay of nonexplicit and frequently conflicting goals, and the difficulty of predicting outcomes that so essentially characterize design. It suggests that knowledge in architecture is likewise uncertain but is also attainable (through the study of precedent) and communicable (by means of historical analysis). The ambiguity of Quatremère's formulation need not be construed in a negative sense. For example, Kahn (1991) has proposed an interpretation based on contemporary concepts of metaphorical structure, which points out the critical value inherent in the tensive relationship between such perceived opposites as convention and innovation or likeness and difference. She suggests that this relationship is indeed essential to the production of form.

Argan (1963, 1965) is credited with reproposing Quatremère's definition of type. However, Moneo (1978) submits that Argan's interpretation was, in an important aspect, diametrically opposite to Quatremère's, while the latter, true to his Neoplatonic orientation, thought of type as an *a priori* entity, Argan viewed it largely as the result of a search for commonalities among real works of architecture, therefore as an *a posteriori* examination aimed at uncovering the "inner formal structure" of a series of such works. Argan, as a historian, was primarily interested in the descriptive and taxonomic qualities of type and only incidentally in those that may affect the generation of form.

Argan made a distinction between "the moment of the typology," which he regarded as a link between the architect and historical precedent, a sort of passive form-receiving by the designer, and "the moment of formal definition," which he viewed as the active, form-giving stage in the production of architectural works. He seemed to imply that form was the result of operations outside the domain of typology, operations still ruled by the logic of function and economics as "determinants" of form. Moneo indicates that, in this, "he revealed his respect for Modern Movement orthodoxy" (1978, 36), that is, for the doctrine that viewed form as the result of operations performed on the functional requirements of the architectural program, not of operations performed on an entity – the type – which already contained a formal response to those requirements.

It is important to understand that Argan's emphasis implies a notion of type that focuses mainly on the formal aspects of architecture. In his writings, for example in an examination of the relations between the social, economic, and intellectual climate of the Weimar Republic and the work of Gropius and the Bauhaus, he eloquently links the formal aspects of that work to the cultural context in which it was produced, as the best historians have always done (Argan 1951). But this is not the same as explicating the connection between form and use, which would have been the corollary of a view of type consistent with Quatremère's definition. In the case of the Bauhaus and its architectural production, and particularly in the instance of the *Siedlungen* in Dessau-Törten and Berlin-Siemensstadt, exploring the connection between form and use would have led him to analyze the public meaning and social acceptance of that work and, ultimately, what Robinson (1991) calls its "political and moral consequences."

Still, though Argan seems to have misread one of Quatremère's principal points, it was he who reopened the discussion of type and redefined it as the "generator of form" *(progetto di forma)*. In so doing, in fact, he began to turn the focus of architectural discourse away from a purely functional perspective and opened the door to the rethinking of the design process that was to follow.

* * *

Editors' note: illustrations and references to illustrations have been omitted.

› Note

1   Quatremère himself was an intellectually conservative, if not downright reactionary, man. Jacques and Vidler (1977) report that students at the Ecole des Beaux-Arts twice rioted and had to be evicted by the police during his eulogies for architects Bonnard and Delabarre, respectively. It is then ironic that Quatremère's view of type was resurrected by Argan (1963, 1965), surely a most refined and progressive historian, and taken up and further developed by a number of architects who have been in the forefront of the critique of both the Modern Movement and contemporary consumer society, especially in Italy.

› Bibliography

Argan, G.C. 1951. *Walter Gropius e la Bauhaus*. Turin: Giulio Einaudi Editore.
Argan, G.C. 1963. On the typology of architecture. *Architectural Design* 33 (12): 564–5.
Bandini, M. 1984. Typology as a form of convention. *AA Files* 6: 73.

Bell, D. 1991. Nomads. In *Type and the (Im)possibilities of Convention*. Midgård Monographs 2: 19–31.

Doordan, D.P. 1989. Changing agendas: architecture and politics in contemporary Italy, *Assemblage* 8: 69.

Durand, J.N.L. 1805. *Précis des leçons données à l'Ecole politéchnique*. Paris: Chez l'Auteur.

Kahn, A. 1991. Toward a nonoppressive interpretation of the concept of type. In *Type and the (Im)possibilities of Convention*. Midgård Monographs 2: 107–13.

Jaques, A. and Vidler A. 1977. Chronology: the Ecole des Beaux-Arts, 1671-1900. *Oppositions* 8: 151-7.

Laugier, M.A. 1753. *Observations sur l'architecture*. Paris: Desaint.

Lavin, S. 1992. *Quatremère de Quincy and the Invention of a Modern Language of Architecture*. Cambridge, Mass.: MIT Press.

Michelson, W. 1968. Most people don't want what architects want. *Transactions* (July-August): 37-43.

Moneo, R. 1978. On typology. *Oppositions* 13: 23–45.

Pérez-Gómez, A. 1991. Architecture is not a convention. In *Type and the (Im)possibilities of Convention*. Midgård Monographs 2: 11–18.

Quatremère de Quincy, A.C. [1825] 1977. English trans.: Vidler, A. 1977. Type. *Oppositions* 8: 147–50. Published originally in Architecture. *Encyclopédie Méthodique*, vol. 3. Paris: Panckoucke.

Robinson, J. 1991. Premises, premises: architecture as a cultural medium. In *Type and the (Im)possibilities of Convention*. Midgård Monographs 2: 11–18.

Rossi, A. 1982. *The Architecture of the City*. Cambridge, Mass.: MIT Press.

Vidler, A. 1977. The production of types. *Oppositions* 8: 93.

Architecture and the City

55 Aldo Rossi

The architecture of the city (1966)

Aldo Rossi, *L'architettura della città*, Padua, Marsilio, 1966. Extracts here from: Aldo Rossi, *The Architecture of the City*, 'Chapter 1: The structure of urban artifacts', Cambridge-Massachusetts: MIT, extracts pp. 35, 40–41 and 56–61, translation by Diane Ghirardo and Joan Ockman.

*   *   *

› Typological questions

The city as above all else a human thing is constituted of its architecture and of all those works that constitute the true means of transforming nature. Bronze Age men adapted the landscape to social needs by constructing artificial islands of brick, by digging wells, drainage canals, and watercourses. The first houses sheltered their inhabitants from the external environment and furnished a climate that man could begin to control; the development of an urban nucleus expanded this type of control to the creation and extension of a microclimate. Neolithic villages already offered the first transformations of the world according to man's needs. The "artificial homeland" is as old as man.

In precisely this sense of transformation the first forms and types of habitation, as well as temples and more complex buildings, were constituted. The *type* developed according to both needs and aspirations to beauty; a particular type was associated with a form and a way of life, although its specific shape varied widely from society to society. The concept of type thus became the basis of architecture, a fact attested to both by practice and by the treatises.

It therefore seems clear that typological questions are important. They have always entered into the history of architecture, and arise naturally whenever urban problems are confronted. Theoreticians such as Francesco Milizia never defined type as such, but statements like the following seem to be anticipatory: "The comfort of any building consists of three principal items: its site, its form, and the organization of its parts." I would define the concept of type as something that is permanent and complex, a logical principle that is prior to form and that constitutes it.

One of the major theoreticians of architecture, Quatremère de Quincy, understood the importance of these problems and gave a masterly definition of type and model:

"The word 'type' represents not so much the image of a thing to be copied or perfectly imitated as the idea of an element that must itself serve as a rule for the model. . . . The model, understood in terms of the practical execution of art, is an object that must be repeated such as it is; type, on the contrary, is an object, according to which one can conceive works that do not resemble one another at all. Everything is precise and given in the model; everything is more or less vague in the type. Thus we see that the imitation of types involves nothing that feelings or spirit cannot recognize. . . .

We also see that all inventions, notwithstanding subsequent changes, always retain their elementary principle in a way that is clear and manifest to the senses and to reason. It is similar to a kind of nucleus around which the developments and variations of forms to which the object was susceptible gather and mesh. Therefore a thousand things of every kind have come down to us, and one of the principal tasks of science and philosophy is to seek their origins and primary causes so as to grasp their purposes. Here is what must be called 'type' in architecture, as in every other branch of human inventions and institutions. . . . We have engaged in this discussion in order to render the value of the word *type*—taken metaphorically in a great number of works—clearly comprehensible, and to show the error of those who either disregard it because it is not a model, or misrepresent it by imposing on it the rigor of a model that would imply the conditions of an identical copy."

In the first part of this passage, the author rejects the possibility of type as something to be imitated or copied because in this case there would be, as he asserts in the second part, no "creation of the model"—that is, there would be no making of architecture. The second part states that in architecture (whether model or form) there is an element that plays its own role, not something to which the architectonic object conforms but something that is nevertheless present in the model. This is the *rule,* the structuring principle of architecture.

In fact, it can be said that this principle is a constant. Such an argument presupposes that the architectural artifact is conceived as a structure and that this structure is revealed and can be recognized in the artifact itself. As a constant, this principle, which we can call the typical element, or simply the type, is to be found in all architectural artifacts. It is also then a cultural element and as such can be investigated in different architectural artifacts; typology becomes in this way the analytical moment of architecture, and it becomes readily identifiable at the level of urban artifacts.

*   *   *

› The complexity of urban artifacts

*   *   *

I also wish to emphasize my reservations about a certain language and reading of the city and urban artifacts which present a serious obstacle to urban research. In many ways, this language is linked with naive functionalism on the one hand and a form of architectural romanticism on the other. I refer to the two terms *organic* and *rational,* which have been borrowed by the architectural language and which, although they possess an indubitable historical validity for making distinctions between one style or type of architecture and another, certainly do not help us to clarify concepts or somehow to comprehend urban artifacts.

The term *organic* is derived from biology; I have elsewhere noted that the basis of Friedrich Ratzel's functionalism was a hypothesis that likened the city to an organism, the form of which was constituted by function itself. This physiological hypothesis is as brilliant as it is inapplicable to the structure of urban artifacts and to architectural design (although the application to the problem of design is a subject in itself and requires a separate treatment). Among the most prominent terms of this organic language are *organism, organic growth, urban fabric*. Similarly, in some of the more serious ecological studies, parallels between the city and the human organism and the processes of the biological world have been suggested, although quickly abandoned. The terminology, in fact, is so pervasive among those in the field that at first sight it seems intimately tied to the material under consideration, and only with some difficulty is it possible to avoid the use of a term like *architectural organism* and substitute for it a more appropriate word like *building*. The same can be said for *fabric*. It even seems that some authors define modern architecture *tout court* as organic, and by virtue of its powerful appeal this terminology has passed rapidly from serious studies to the profession and to journalism.

The terminology of the so-called rationalist variety is no less imprecise. To speak of rational urbanism is simply a tautology, since the rationalization of spatial choices is by definition a condition of urbanism. "Rationalist" definitions have the undoubted merit, however, of always referring to urbanism as a discipline (precisely because of its character of rationality) and thus offer a terminology of clearly superior usefulness. To say that the medieval city is organic reveals an absolute ignorance of the political, religious, and economic structures of the medieval city, not to mention its spatial structure. To say, on the other hand, that the plan of Miletus is rational is true even if it is so general as to be generic and fails to offer us any real idea of Miletus's layout (beyond the ambiguity of confounding rationality with what is a simple geometric scheme).

Both of these aspects are aptly characterized in Milizia's comment cited earlier about functional organization and beehives. Thus, even though this terminology undoubtedly possesses a certain poetic expressiveness, and as such might be of interest to us, it has nothing to do with a theory of urban artifacts. It is really a vehicle of confusion, and it would be useful to drop it altogether.

Urban artifacts, as we have said, are complex; this means that they have components and that each component has a different value. Thus, in speaking of the typological essence in architecture we said that it "has its own role to play in the model"; in other words, the typological essence is a component element. However, before attempting a typological reading of the city based on a theory of urban artifacts and their structure, it is necessary to proceed slowly to some precise definitions.

Exactly how are urban artifacts complex? A partial answer has already been given with respect to the theories of Chabot and Poète. One can agree that their statements relative to the soul of the city and the concept of permanence go beyond naive functionalism and approach an understanding of the quality of urban artifacts. On the other hand, little attention has really been given to this problem of quality, a problem which surfaces mainly in historical research, although there is already some progress in the recognition that the nature of urban artifacts is in many ways like that of a work of art and, most important, that a key element for understanding urban artifacts is their collective character.

On the basis of these considerations it is possible to delineate a type of reading for urban structures. But we must begin by posing two general sets of questions: First, from what points of view is it possible to read the city; how many ways are there for understanding its structure? Is it possible to say, and what does it mean to say, that a reading is interdisciplinary; do some disciplines take precedence over others? Obviously, these questions are closely linked. Second, what are the possibilities for an autonomous urban science?

Of the two questions, the second is clearly decisive. In fact, if there is an urban science, the first group of questions ends up having little meaning; that which today is often defined as interdisciplinary is nothing other than a problem of specialization and occurs in any field of knowledge. But the response to this second question depends on a recognition that the city is constructed in its totality, that all of its components participate in its constitution as an artifact. In other words, on the most general level, it must be understood that the city represents the progress of human reason, is a human creation par excellence; and this statement has meaning only when the fundamental point is emphasized that the city and every urban artifact are by nature collective. I am often asked why only historians give us a complete picture of the city. I believe the answer is that historians are concerned with the urban artifact in its totality.

› Monuments and the theory of permanences

Clearly, to think of urban science as a historical science is a mistake, for in this case we would be obliged to speak only of urban history. What I mean to suggest, however, is that from the point of view of urban structure, urban history seems more useful than any other form of research on the city. Later I will address the contribution of history to urban science in a more detailed way, but since this problem is particularly important it would be useful to make a few specific observations right away.

These concern the theory of *permanences* as posited by both Poète and Lavedan. This theory is in some respects related to my initial hypothesis of the city as a man-made object. One must remember that the difference between past and future, from the point of view of the theory of knowledge, in large measure reflects the fact that the past is partly being experienced now, and this may be the meaning to give permanences: they are a past that we are still experiencing.

Poète's theory is not very explicit on this point, but I will try to summarize it briefly. Although he presents a number of hypotheses among which are economic considerations that relate to the evolution of the city, it is in substance a historical theory centered on the phenomenon of "persistences." These persistences are revealed through monuments, the physical signs of the past, as well as through the persistence of a city's basic layout and plans. This last point is Poète's most important discovery. Cities tend to remain on their axes of development, maintaining the position of their original layout and growing according to the direction and meaning of their older artifacts, which often appear remote from present-day ones. Sometimes these artifacts persist virtually unchanged, endowed with a continuous vitality; other times they exhaust themselves, and then only the permanence of their form, their physical sign, their *locus* remains. The most meaningful permanences are those provided by the street and the plan. The plan persists at different levels; it becomes differentiated in its attributes, often deformed, but in substance it is not displaced. This is the most valid part of Poète's theory; even if it cannot be said to be completely a historical theory, it is essentially born from the study of history.

At first sight it may seem that permanences absorb all of the continuity of urban artifacts, but in reality this is not so, because not all things in the city survive, or if they do, their modalities are so diverse as often to resist comparison. In this sense, according to the theory of permanences, in order to explain an urban artifact, one is forced to look beyond it to the present-day actions that modify it. In substance, the historical method is one that isolates. It tends not only to differentiate permanences but to focus entirely on them, since they alone can show what a city once was by indicating the way its past differs from its present. Thus permanences may appear with respect to the city as isolated and aberrant artifacts which characterize a system only as the form of a past that we are still experiencing.

In this respect, permanences present two aspects: on the one hand, they can be considered as propelling elements; on the other, as pathological elements. Artifacts either enable us to understand the city in its totality, or they appear as a series of isolated elements that we can link only tenuously to an urban system. To illustrate the distinction between permanent elements that are vital and those that are pathological, we can again take the Palazzo della Ragione in Padua as an example. I remarked on its permanent character before, but now by permanence I mean not only that one can still experience the form of the past in this monument but that the physical form of the past has assumed different functions and has continued to function, conditioning the urban area in which it stands and continuing to constitute an important urban focus. In part this building is still in use; even if everyone is convinced that it is a work of art, it still functions quite readily at ground level as a retail market. This proves its vitality.

An example of a pathological permanence can be seen in the Alhambra in Granada. It no longer houses either Moorish or Castilian kings, and if we accepted functionalist classifications, we would have to say that this building once represented the major function of Granada. It is evident that at Granada we experience the form of the past in a way that is quite different from at Padua. In the first instance, the form of the past has assumed a different function but it is still intimately tied to the city; it has been modified and we can imagine future modifications. In the second, it stands virtually isolated in the city; nothing can be added. It constitutes, in fact, an experience so *essential* that it cannot be modified (in this sense, the palace of Charles V in Granada must be counted an exception, since precisely because it lacked this quality it could so easily be destroyed). But in both cases the urban artifacts are a part of the city that cannot be suppressed because they constitute it.

In choosing these two examples, I have defined a persistent urban artifact as something very similar to a monument. I could in fact have spoken of the Doge's Palace in Venice or the Theater at Nîmes or the Mezquita of Córdoba, and the argument would not change. In fact, I am inclined to believe that persistence in an urban artifact often causes it to become identified as a monument, and that a monument persists in the city both symbolically and physically. A monument's persistence or permanence is a result of its capacity to constitute the city, its history and art, its being and memory.

We have just distinguished between a historical or propelling permanence as a form of a past that we still experience and a pathological permanence as something that is isolated and aberrant.

In large measure the pathological form is identifiable because of a particular *context,* since context itself can be seen either as the persistence of a function over time or as something isolated from the urban structure, that is, as something which stands outside of technological and social evolution. Context is commonly understood as referring primarily to residential sections of the city, and in this sense, its preservation is counter to the real dynamic of the city; so-called contextual preservation is related to the city in time like the embalmed corpse of a saint to the image of his historical personality. In contextual preservation there is a sort of urban naturalism at work which admittedly can give rise to suggestive images—for example, a visit to a dead city is always a memorable experience—but in such cases we are well outside the realm of a past that we still experience. Naturally, then, I am referring mainly to living cities which have an uninterrupted span of development. The problems of dead cities only tangentially concern urban science; they are matters for the historian and the archaeologist. It is at best an abstraction to seek to reduce urban artifacts to archaeological ones.

So far we have spoken only of monuments, inasmuch as they are fixed elements of the urban structure, as having a true aesthetic intentionality, but this can be a simplification. The hypothesis of the city as a man-made object and a work of art attributes as much legitimacy of expression to a house or any other minor work as to a monument. But perhaps this carries us too far afield; I mainly want to establish at this point that the dynamic process of the city tends more to evolution than preservation, and that in evolution monuments are not only preserved but continuously presented as propelling elements of development. This is a fact that can be verified.

Moreover, I have already attempted to demonstrate how function alone is insufficient to explain the continuity of urban artifacts; if the origin of the typology of urban artifacts is simply function, this hardly accounts for the phenomenon of survival. A function must always be defined in time and in society: that which closely depends on it is always bound up with its development. An urban artifact determined by one function only cannot be seen as anything other than an explication of that function. In reality, we frequently continue to appreciate elements whose function has been lost over time; the value of these artifacts often resides solely in their form, which is integral to the general form of the city; it is, so to speak, an invariant of it. Often, too, these artifacts are closely bound up with the constitutive elements, with the origins of the city, and are included among its monuments. Thus we see the importance of the parameter of time in the study of urban artifacts; to think of a persistent urban artifact as something tied to a single period of history constitutes one of the greatest fallacies of urban science.

The form of the city is always the form of a particular time of the city; but there are many times in the formation of the city, and a city may change its face even in the course of one man's life, its original references ceasing to exist. As Baudelaire wrote, "The old Paris is no more; the form of a city changes more quickly, alas, than the heart of a mortal." We look upon the houses of our childhood as unbelievably old, and often the city erases our memories as it changes.

The various considerations we have put forward in this chapter now permit us to attempt a specific reading of the city. The city will be seen as an architecture of different parts or components, these being principally the *dwelling* and *primary elements.* It is this reading that I will develop in the following pages, beginning with the concept of the *study area.* Since dwellings cover the major portion of the urban surface and rarely have a character of permanence, their evolution should be studied together with the area upon which they are found; thus I will speak of the *dwelling area*.

I will also consider the decisive role played by primary elements in the formation and constitution of the city. This role tends to be revealed through their character of permanence in the case of the monuments, which, as we will see, have a very particular relationship to primary elements. Farther on we will investigate what effective role primary elements have in the structure of urban artifacts, and for what reasons urban artifacts can be said to be works of art or, at least, how the overall structure of the city is similar to a work of art. Our previous analysis should enable us to recognize this overall composition of the city and the reasons for its architecture.

There is nothing new in all of this. Yet in attempting to formulate a theory of urban artifacts that is consistent with reality, I have benefited from highly diverse sources. From these I consider some of the themes I have discussed—function, permanence, classification, and typology—to be particularly significant.

* * *

Editors' note: footnotes have been omitted.

56 Leon Krier

The reconstruction of the city (1978)

Leon Krier, 'The reconstruction of the city', from: *Rational Architecture Rationelle*, Bruxelles: AAM Editions—Archives d'Architecture Moderne, 1978, extracts pp. 38–39 and 41–42.

› The architectural project

The present book does not pretend to be a complete documentation of the exhibition "Rational Architecture" which we have organised in 1975 in London.

We rather want to outline, to sketch very generally a debate, which—with a growing precision and through drawings and written documents—concentrates on the renewal of Architecture in general and of the European city in particular.

"The new is no more new". This graffiti which could be read on the building site of the Centre Pompidou in Paris could well document the end of an era.

The sad results of an obsessive drive towards mere technical innovations leaves us today to contemplate the cut stones of a rue de Rivoli, or the masonry walls of a rural building with more interest and pleasure than the noisy structures of a cultural machine which tries to hide its social emptiness by an ephemeral and prestigious formalism.

The period of post-war construction appears today to have also been a period of intellectual stagnation.

After this darkest and most devastating period of European Architecture, the building crisis and the contemplation of the damages which have been caused to the city and necessarily to the country-side, seem now to revive the minds of the most progressive architects with a new breath which is both critical and optimistic.

In this crisis of construction, the architectural project has regained all its millenial dignity as a thinking instrument. It becomes now clear that the architectural reflection can at this precise moment only be undertaken through the practical exercise in the form of a critique or in the form of critical project.

The Charter of Athens

One can say that in the post war years, the European cities have been more destroyed both physically and socially than in any other period of their history, including the two world wars. Our generation is both witness and victim of a cultural tragedy to which there is no precedent in history. The radical commercialisation of urban land becomes now even a menace to the architectural profession. The architects as servile executors of grand speculation and the large building monopolies have lost their traditional credibility as creators of a better tomorrow. Building, once a promise, constitutes now a threat for the collectivity.

When the cultural models of the modern movement as formulated in the "Charter of Athens" found their way into legislation, they became instrumental in the process whereby urban space and the city as a whole became commercialized, became included into the cycles of profit maximisation.

It is true that in the pamphlets, manifestos and other expressions of modern architectural culture, no notion has been so much stressed as "space", "total space" (Mies van der Rohe) "espace indicible" (L.C.). The escape into vague and confused formulations has historically coincided with the loss of precise urban space as, the street, the square, the colonnade, the arcade, the court, etc. . . . The obsessive emptiness of modern urban spaces (Plaza of the Three Powers-Brasilia), their isolation from any urban fabric is probably the best illustration of the profound character of parlementary democracy and in general of the destruction of the public realm in a totally administrated world.

The overstressing of the historical centres through peripheral growth and the following breaking up of their structures by the mechanical means of transport (as a result of zoning) have enforced the decomposition of the city as a complex spatial continuum.

"The city as a system of spaces is being replaced by a system of bodies" (J.F. Geist, "Passagen"), whose order is solely regulated by administrative prescriptions. The Inspector General of the German army has commented on this state of affairs with a biting irony. "Today, discipline is no more measured on the formal level, but purely on the functional level" *(Der Spiegel*, 9 July 1969). Adorno has compared the autonomy of bureaucratic procedure with that one of bourgeois art, in that its motivation is no more dictated by Reason, i.e. utility, commodity etc . . ., but that it perpetrates itself according to its own dynamic.

The endless reports and regulations on isolated technical problems—real orgies of quantitative thinking—have been accompanied by a generalised decay of our environment. The overloading of the architect with mountains of technical data and apparently value free cultural models, finally his confrontation with the chaotic products of the building industry, confuse the architect as much as his potential client.

The brutal class character of this cultural promiscuity, is once more demonstrated by the latest experiments of the English building industry in the new city of Milton-Keynes. The fact to call "city" this confusion of town and country will remain a mystery as long as anyone of his inhabitants will remember what the country on one hand and the city on the other used to promise. It cannot be by a mere chance that the name of the greatest capitalist economist should resound so conspicuously in its name.

Here the loss of the last bit of cultural autonomy has turned the architects into the ruthless executors of the building industry.

The merchandise character of these housings is no more disguised, but disgustingly displayed by the architects. The schools have well prepared the last generation of architects [for] their ideological roles. It seems now that a radical change could only be instrumented in these schools.

Against this overwhelming reality, the XVth Triennale in Milan organised by Aldo Rossi represented the first major alternative position from the ranks of the profession. The projects exhibited and the theoretical implications gathered in the book "Architecture Razionale" confirmed in the words of Massimo Scolari a new architectural tendency.

This tendency included architects from Europe, the U.S.A. and Japan but also the renewal of the historic centre of Bologna etc. . . the catalogue which I present here also includes projects already shown at the Triennale. In this case however, the exhibits were not chosen because they are particularly representative of their author's work, but because, when seen together, they represent a new architectural movement, a critical attempt at the *Reconstruction of the European city*. For this very reason I have not included in this catalogue works by the New York Five, Venturi, etc. . . who—although present at the Triennale and however brilliant their artistic œuvre—would rather confuse the typological and morphological discipline which are the central themes of Rational Architecture.

In Italy, it seemed for a moment that the conservative critique under the leadership of Bruno Zevi had achieved to lower the discussion to a mere level of style, ignoring demagogically the complex arguments put forward by this new movement.

› Architecture

We want to state very clearly that Rational Architecture is not concerned with the revival of the Rationalism of the 1920ies. It is, as Scolari explains, primarily to do with the revival of Architecture "tout court". If its theoretical basis is to be found in the philosophical Rationalism of the enlightment its primary concern should now lay with the re-creation of the public realm.

In a late capitalist economy however, every contribution to a complex theory of the city and its architecture must remain fragmentary, in the same way as the efforts to save the historical centres from physical and social destruction will remain fragmentary as long as the economic and social basis for a renewed urban culture are missing. A rationalist theory of the city and of its architecture represents for that reason a modest step in a society, which is more and more incapable of resolving its own contradictions in a creative way. If then this theory should not become reduced to a style, to a mere introspection of its formal principles, it has to be part of an integral vision of society, it has to be part of a political struggle.

The problem of Rational Architecture can therefore not be one of choreography. It cannot find its motivations in a "state of mind", in the fictions of artistic or technical progress but in the reflection on the city and its history, on its social use and content. The revolutionary element of this new Architecture does not lie in its form but in the model of its social use, in its coherency, in the reconstruction of the public realm.

To clarify this radically new position, it is important to take a critical attitude in relation to Modern Architecture in particular and in relation to the bourgeois production of Architecture in general.

* * *

Technical progress and industrialisation of building

In the 1920s the growing industrialisation of building was largely seen by architects as being the basis for a new architecture, for a new quality. However with all the disposition we have inherited from the 19th Century to believe in technical progress as the key to social progress, we can say now that modern building technology is still at the level of the experiment and an ephemeral progress leaves us today with a building technology which in many ways is more primitive than at any moment in Western civilization.

Industrialisation has neither created quicker building techniques nor a better building technology. Far from having improved the physical conditions of the worker, it has reduced manual labour to a stultifying and enslaving experience. It has degraded a millenial and dignified craft to a socially alienating exercise.

Industrialisation has neither reduced the cost of production. Far from being socially economical in the long term, it has been the most radical means to include building into vast cycles of industrial production and consumption, its profound motivation having been the maximisation of profits. As the manual and artisanal culture of building became destroyed, the intellectual and theoretical corpus of Architecture had to collapse in a society, whose very base of existence, the artisanal production, became eliminated.

The failure to refound Architecture and Building in any other discipline than in its own history and in itself has been sufficiently demonstrated in the last 5 decades, it makes us now understand that the recuperation of a dignified mode of production, the reconstruction of an artisanal building culture will be the basis of any new architectural culture, of a new collective language.

The conception and form of a rationalist architecture will lie in the organisation of the building production. The vulgarity of late capitalist architecture is as much caused by the random profusion of building types as by the endless invention of building materials and construction systems; not an outcome of rationalisation but of maximisation of profits. I suppose that the restriction to a few building materials and the elaboration of an urban building typology will create a new architectural discipline of simple nobility and monumentality.

History of architecture—history of types

Against the anti-historicism of the modern movement we repropose the study of the history of the city. The narrow rationalism of modern architecture is expanded to understand the city in all its typological components. The history of architectural and urban culture is seen as the history of types. Types of settlements, types of spaces (public and private), types of buildings, types of construction. The bourgeois concept of architectural history—basically concerned with the monument—is extended to include the typological complexity of the urban fabric, of the anonymous buildings forming the flesh of the city, the skin of its public space. The buildings which are not so much the result of high art but of building tradition. The roots of a new rationalist culture are to be found here, as much as in [J.N.L.] Durand's Typology of institutional Monuments.

› A dialectic of types

The physical and spatial unity of the traditional city is understood as a result of the maximal interaction of these types.

The dialectics of buildings and urban spaces, of solid and void, of private and public realm can no more be exclusively seen as the result of political, social and economical constraints, but as the result of rational intention of culture.

› The city within the city

Urban life and the quartier

If we repropose as a political choice the dynamism of urban culture as against the conservatism of suburbia, this has to be seen as an integral part of a democratic and socialist vision of society. The traffic problems which have been created by centralisation on regional and national scale can initially only be resolved on a political level through the new definition of the city within a rational organisation of the territory and finally through the reorganisation of the city into units of complex and integrated functions: quartiers, districts, homogeneous areas (Bologna), functional communities (E. Saarinen). Here work, leisure and culture are integrated into compact urban districts. The size of these districts is both a physical and a social one. It can only be checked on the historical model.

The "Art of Building Cities"

The "Art of Building Cities" has to find its way into legislation. The complex architectural scheme, precise types of urban space (*streets, avenues, squares, arcades, colonnades*) will have to replace the two-dimensional zoning spaces. A functionally complex and visually simple spatial continuum has to replace the contemporary system of disintegrated functions and buildings: inside a precise relationship of building-typology and morphology of urban spaces, we re-establish a dialectic of public buildings (monuments) and urban fabric. This relationship has been explored by architectural archaeologists and is now becoming instrumental in the urban renewal of Bologna, in buildings and projects shown in this book.

The method we are slowly elaborating is both precise enough to create built and spatial continuity and general enough to allow great functional flexibility and change. It is a method where time and memory become part of a dialectical composition.

Public realm and politics

In these new projects the form of the public realm is the prime concern. The public realm as a finite, unitarian, rational space. *Place* becomes the lieu where the individual identifies himself as a being with full cultural and political responsibility.

*   *   *

57 Rob Krier

Typological and morphological elements of the concept of urban space (1979)

Rob Krier, 'Typological and morphological elements of the concept of urban space', from: Rob Krier, *Urban Space*, New York: Rizzoli, 1979, extracts pp. 15–17.

› Introduction

The basic premise underlying this chapter is my conviction that in our modern cities we have lost sight of the traditional understanding of urban space. The cause of this loss is familiar to all city dwellers who are aware of their environment and sensitive enough to compare the town planning achievements of the present and the past and who have the strength of character to pronounce sentence on the way things have gone. This assertion alone is of no great service to town planning research. What has to be clearly defined is what should be understood by the term urban space and what meaning it holds within the urban structure, so that we can go on to examine whether the concept of urban space retains some validity in contemporary town planning and on what grounds. 'Space' in this context is a hotly disputed concept. It is not my intention here to generate a new definition but rather to bring its original meaning back into currency.

› Definition of the concept 'urban space'

If we wish to clarify the concept of urban space without imposing aesthetic criteria, we are compelled to designate all types of space between buildings in towns and other localities as urban space.

This space is geometrically bounded by a variety of elevations. It is only the clear legibility of its geometrical characteristics and aesthetic qualities which allows us consciously to perceive external space as urban space.

The polarity of internal-external space is constantly in evidence in this chapter, since both obey very similar laws not only in function but also in form. Internal space, shielded from weather and environment is an effective symbol of privacy; external space is seen as open, unobstructed space for movement in the open air, with public, semi-public and private zones.

The basic concepts underlying the aesthetic characteristics of urban space will be expounded below and systematically classified by type. In the process, an attempt will be made to draw a clear distinction between precise aesthetic and confused emotional factors. Every aesthetic analysis runs the risk of foundering on subjective questions of taste. As I have been able to observe from numerous discussions on this topic, visual and sensory habits, which vary from one individual to the next, are augmented by a vast number of socio-political and cultural attitudes, which are taken to represent aesthetic truths. Accepted styles in art history—for example, baroque town plans, revolutionary architecture etc—are both useful and necessary.

However my observations indicate that they are almost always identified with the social structure prevailing at the time in question. Certainly it can scarcely be proved that, because of the wishes of the ruling classes and their artists, the stylistic canons of the period in European art history between 1600 and 1730 appeared almost to be determined by fate. Of course for the historian every period of history forms a unit with its own internal logic, which cannot be fragmented and interchanged with elements at other periods at will.

* * *

Our age has a remarkably distorted sense of history, which can only be characterised as irrational. Le Corbusier's apparent battle against the 'Académie' was not so much a revolt against an exhausted, ageing school as the assumption of a pioneering stand in which he adopted its ideals and imbued them with a new and vigorous content.

This so-called 'pioneering act' was a pretended break with history, but in reality was an artistic falsehood. The facts were these: he abandoned the tradition current until then that art supported by the ruling classes enjoyed the stamp of legitimacy and, being at an advanced stage of development, materially shaped the periods which followed. It was a revolt at one remove, so to speak, for the 'Académie' lived on, and indeed came itself to share the same confused historical sense as the followers of the revolution.

* * *

The example of the baroque town layout has already been mentioned, and the question raised of the identity of form, content and meaning. We must be more exact in asking:

1 Was the resulting form the free expression of the creative artist?
2 Alternatively, were the artistic wishes of the employing class imposed on the artist, and was he forced to adopt their notions of form?
3 Do contemporaneous periods exist, which on the basis of different cultural traditions in different countries or continents where similar social conditions prevail, produce the same artistic solutions?
4 Alternatively, are there non-contemporaneous periods which led to fundamentally different artistic solutions, each being a stage in the development of the same cultural tradition in the same country under the same conditioning social factors?

In this series of permutations, the following factors are relevant: aesthetics, artist, patron, social environment, leeway given to artistic expression, formal restrictions imposed by the patron, formal restrictions imposed by the social environment, fashion, management level of development, technology and its potential applications, general cultural conditions, scientific knowledge, enlightenment, nature, landscape, climate etc. We can conclude with a fair degree of certainty that none of these interrelated factors can be considered in isolation.

With this brief outline of the problem, we should just add a word of caution about an over-simplistic undiscriminating outlook. It is certainly worth trying to establish why certain kinds of urban space were created in the 17th century which we now identify with that period. And it would be even more interesting to examine the real reasons why 20th century town planning has been impoverished and reduced to the lowest common denominator.

The following classification does not make any value judgements. It enumerates the basic forms which constitute urban space, with a limited number of possible variations and combinations. The aesthetic quality of each element of urban space is characterised by the structural interrelation of detail. I shall attempt to discern this quality wherever we are dealing with physical features of a spatial nature. The two basic elements are the street and the square. In the category of 'interior space' we would be talking about the corridor and the room. The geometrical characteristics of both spatial forms are the same. They are differentiated only by the dimensions of the walls which bound them and by the patterns of function and circulation which characterise them.

58 Carel Weeber

Formal objectivity in urban design and
architecture as an aspect of rational planning (1979)

Carel Weeber, 'Formele objectiviteit in stedebouw en architectuur als onderdeel van rationele planning', *Plan* (Amsterdam), 11, 1979, extracts pp. 27–29, 31–32 and 34–35, translation by Kevin Cook.

* * *

This article[1] will discuss the formal quality of architecture, and will do so from the point of view of urban design; for the destruction of this discipline is largely to blame for what I consider is the sorry state of architecture today. Architecture thrives thanks to urban design, not the other way round. As long as the appearance of cities remains dependent on architects, it will be at risk.

› The unpredictable architect

Functional quality standards are laid down by governments in the form of regulations for builders (and users); but architects have little time for them. They tend to see rules and regulations as curbs on their creative freedom, a mentality that is bound up with the romantic image of the architect-as-artist. This self-identification leads to frustration which makes today's architects unpredictable designers – an unproductive factor in the development of architecture as a social product.

Not only do they dread functional regulation, but they see no opportunity to be involved in reproducing its logic (the 'experimental housing' fiasco). The image of the architect-as-artist includes the notion that design is a wholly individualistic activity. As a result, a system of rules governing form is not tolerated. Over the years this has left architecture – just like art – in a vulnerable and arbitrary position.

* * *

Architecture has been pushed into a corner, and now seems able to justify its existence only through other disciplines. It has been sociologised, ecologised, biologised, semiologised, politicised, psychologised, anthropologised, economised and historicised . . . This way of building leaves no room for architectural and urban space, or control of appearance. And yet its whole focus is supposed to be on people, living at their own scale, in their own place, with their own car on their own plot. If architects are willing to behave like rational, realistic artists, they will eventually be able to shed the masks of other disciplines and once again supply regulated products that they have helped supervise and that can be fitted into society as architecture.

*　*　*

Owing to various recent developments, urban design no longer exists as a discipline in its own right; and this is one of the main reasons for the current malaise. The quality of urban design and architecture in the late 1950s was sufficient reason for the journal *Forum* to claim that the two should no longer be separate. As *Forum* saw it, urban design should cease to exist as an independent discipline and instead be integrated into architecture. . . . [Today,] design issues are mainly discussed verbally, in terms of perception. Yet this does nothing to solve the formal, conceptual problem. Cities cannot be designed by describing how they are perceived – just as a cookery book would be useless if it simply contained descriptions of how the dishes tasted, rather than recipes. Urban design – and architecture – are all about recipes.

› Operative disciplines

What I am referring to here is the instrumentality of methodologies that are devised within disciplines – in this case, the methodologies that must be implemented to ensure quality control in the production process of spatial planning, especially as regards the visual quality of the environment to be created.

Today's urban designers have a predilection for methodologies that describe the intended visual qualities verbally, in terms of goals. Material implementation is left to the next stage of planning: architecture. This is not an operative methodology, for the perceptual qualities described in terms of goals do not survive the change of medium – from writing to drawing – that is inherent in the planning process. Verbal meanings turn out to be different from meanings expressed in spatial forms, or at least cannot be directly translated into them. Based on a subjective principle, this methodology has cut the heart out of urban design, namely its formal objectivity. Only if this is restored can a satisfactory operational relationship with architecture be re-established.

This largely verbal methodology must be abandoned, if only because it is no easy matter to achieve a consensus on perceptions of quality during the planning process; and, in my view, operational planning processes depend on consensus. This means developing formal visual techniques whereby visual qualities can have an objective impact in planning terms. In this connection, something may be deemed objective if there is a consensus about it. The question, of course, is whether this is possible at such formal levels. I believe it is. Rightly or wrongly, numbers can easily produce consensus, and not just among technicians. Anyone involved in planning knows this, and is well aware how it can influence the 'softer' participants in the process – usually the designers, who have to give way, especially if their arguments are solely based on 'perceptual value'.

So, for this reason alone, we need to develop rational formal planning techniques. Objectivity is an essential part of planning, if only because this is procedurally so complex; for all kinds of different people are involved in the process, successively and simultaneously, in time and space. As a component of spatial planning, urban design is inevitably a matter of institutions and lengthy procedures. Plans must be sustainable over time if they are to qualify as plans. They can therefore be considered eminently objective if they are so internally (formally) self-evident that the character of the plan can be adopted by what is built and reproduced within it.

The history of urban design contains examples of urban patterns that display this objective character. In these patterns, artefacts such as buildings and infrastructures — all of them vehicles for shifting meanings, values and functions — are ranked alongside urban open spaces such as streets, squares, avenues, boulevards and so on.

› Urban plans, not traffic plans

I believe it is the job of urban designers to design urban morphology using formal concepts that are known or assumed to be capable of absorbing urban meanings, values and functions. The prevailing view has been that urban plans are above all derived from (urban) functions, often with the emphasis on traffic regulation. Yet we are gradually coming to realise that this does not really work, and may actually be an illusion. Surely, although we may not consciously acknowledge it, our designs are based on formal representations of these functions that have evolved over time. This is because most urban functions are too ambiguous to serve as starting points for design. Many different kinds of function can be accommodated within one and the same form.

This ambiguity means that designers must resort to another instrument: the formal concept. Consciously acknowledging this fact — which Functionalism unfortunately obscured — opens up prospects and opportunities for redeveloping formal architectural and urban design techniques. The emphasis here must be on the production of objective characteristics, which initially, and above all at the planning stage, can focus on the visual resources inherent in two (planar) dimensions.

Although urban design is ultimately a three-dimensional reality, the focus of consensus in planning terms is on two-dimensional presentation. In other words, representation of the urban plan on a map can already (thanks to its own internal two-dimensional self-evidence) provide a legitimate basis for consensus, without raising the issue of three-dimensional perceptual quality — but only on certain conditions, which we will return to in a moment.

So the question is, can this be done — and, if so, how?

Since I cannot provide an answer to this here, let me simply refer to a historical urban pattern that in my view fulfils the criterion of formal objectivity: the grid city.

› A grid city – like Barcelona

The formal concept based on regular, two-dimensional geometric repetition of rectangles or squares to form grids is a planning type that has been applied in Asia, Europe and colonised countries. The best-known example in Europe is Cerdà's 1859 plan for Barcelona, where in the repetition and continuity of urban spaces building is determined by alignment and a predominant building height. In this city, building is a self-explanatory process. A typical feature of the plan for Barcelona is that, once a formal pattern has been laid out on the map, the character of the plan is adopted and reproduced in the built reality. The appearance of the city is thus determined by the character of the plan, and what is to be built in future can be read from what has already been built. This process sidesteps the issue of individual taste, for the resulting appearance is self-evident and hence is not perceived as a straitjacket; on the contrary, it is confirmed over and over again. Nor is it geomorphically constrained.

Cerdà's plan survived intact for a century – an unchallenged piece of urban design. This goes to show that urban design can anticipate later architecture. The problem of situation no longer arises at the architectural level, and is not passed on to the next stage of the planning process. I believe this is a *sine qua non* for planning methodologies, in which the 'master plan → zoning plan → development plan → building' sequence must be viewed as a problem-solving process.

There is another lesson to be learned from Barcelona. All over the world, for all kinds of reasons, there is a growing demand for high-rise buildings, which can now also be seen in Barcelona at various intersections with major traffic arteries. This has undermined the objective character of the plan, for building height is now a subjective factor. The inevitable result is a succession of tugs-of-war within planning agencies. And here in the Netherlands, in the absence of formal objectivity in today's urban design, the same thing is unfortunately happening left, right and centre. But in Manhattan – another grid city – skyscrapers have been built so extensively that the new building height has become an objective part of the plan.

I will now sum up the main features that make the grid plan objective:

- straight lines and right angles
- geometrically bland – not tasteless! – repetition and continuity
- a dimensional grid known to be suitable for producing specific types of buildings and public open spaces
- an open-plan character in terms of more specific formal elaboration and grouping of functions; the plan is always both finished and unfinished, and the grid has no intrinsic final size, no initial or ultimate form
- plot division is normally based on right angles and alignment
- perhaps the most important feature: the grid is not so much a design for a city as a design of a pattern for a city – just as a system of drainage ditches in a polder is not a design for urban plots, but may still be suitable for this purpose. This means that an urban plan need not be seen as the design for a city, but as a design for an objective urban formal system, with planning consensus initially achieved in terms of a two-dimensional map. This may also apply to districts of cities and landscapes; in other words, it is not a scale-dependent methodology.

* * *

› Back to an autonomous formal urban design plan

The visual quality of cities is primarily determined by the visual qualities of public space, in which the appearance of buildings plays a part, but not a key part. The urban design plan will have to be reintroduced as an independently planned formal entity, without speculation on the visual qualities of the buildings. It will have to fulfil a number of criteria, some of which are tentatively set out below:

- The plan is primarily a formal, objective, two-dimensional composition, aimed at the ordering of public urban space whose forms are associated with visual types that are embedded in the culture of urban design and architecture.
- The designed urban morphology anticipates future building typologies.
- The plan is indifferent to future functional patterns. Among other things, dimensions will mainly have to be based on the visual form that is to be created, rather than functions (such as those of traffic). However, like other functions, these will have to be appropriately fitted in when the time comes.
- The 'master plan → zoning plan → development plan → building' sequence is a problem-solving process. This means that problems arising at the various stages must not be passed on to subsequent stages for no good reason. For instance, the problem of situation must not be left to the building stage, but must be solved within the urban design plan. At present, the shortcomings of urban design as a discipline are such that almost all problems are passed on to the next stage, namely the architect. It is almost as if urban designers were setting puzzles for architects to solve.
- Regulation of appearance must not be part of the planning procedure. This paternalistic instrument, which frustrates the development of architecture, has never been shown to improve the character of cities; on the contrary, it has a blunting and, because of its policing function, conservative impact. Furthermore, since it is not a public process, it cannot be part of the architectural debate. Despite frequent claims to the contrary, it does not enhance architectural quality. It is therefore vital to make sure that regulation of visual character does not become an aspect of urban design – unfortunately this now seems to be happening in a number of places.

› Note

1 This is a new version (specially revised for *Plan* by the author) of a lecture he gave during 'Lessons in Architecture: designers discuss today's buildings', a course organised in Delft by the *Stichting Post-Doctoraal Onderwijs in het Bouwen* (Foundation for Postgraduate Education in Building) in June 1979.

Logical Construction
and Autonomy

59 Giorgio Grassi

The logical construction of architecture (1967)

Giorgio Grassi, *La costruzione logica dell'architettura,* Padua: Marsilio, 1967, extracts pp. 27–30, translation by Stefania Boccaletti with the editors.

> Chapter one

*   *   *

4

To talk about rationalism in architecture – and therefore of reason, and the forms and techniques inherent in the concept – means to refer mainly to epistemology: in other words, in the case of architecture it means to refer back to the scientific foundation of architecture itself. This is equivalent to proposing that only one science of architecture can exist in the present moment, and it needs to constantly merge analytical study of the past with that of the present. However, this science cannot be defined solely by its objective: as a matter of fact, it is simultaneously defined by the specific nature of its method.

At this point it is necessary to discuss what I consider to represent the fundamental methodological principles of research into rationalism in architecture.

Because of the specific connotations of the rationalist thought we see that the intent of this research is primarily directed toward the **syntactic** aspect of architecture, namely toward its logic of 'construction'.

On the other hand, there is recourse to the concepts of rationalist thought that are theoretical paradigms of deductive thinking: in this sense, the problem of construction in architecture is perceived in these theories as a process of the **logical construction** of architecture.

As a consequence of the general significance inherent in analysis of the problem of cognition, and the specific meaning connected with this investigative procedure which enables it to represent recurring and generic elements; and because of the interface between 'analysis' and 'project design', given their mutual purpose within the concept of an architectural rationalism; architecture is primarily conceived in terms of its characteristic 'construction', or in contrast as a process following a logical order of succession, or more precisely a logical syntactic character.

It is demonstrable that this concept is linked to the category of **formal theory**, where the term 'formal' does not refer to the meaning of architectural forms, but to their constitutive **types** and **orders** (as they present themselves). Consequently one can posit that research in the theoretical field of rationalist thought in architecture is inclined towards the construction of a manifest theory of architectural form: this aspect will become clear from an examination of exemplary discourse.

It is (therefore) clear that this represents a delimiting choice with regard to the many factors that contribute to the full complexity of human endeavour; it determines the efficacy of certain constant elements which, when all is said and done, characterize this agenda. It is therefore a conscious choice, which comes to be identified with a particular conception of the 'meaning' of architecture, which is the basis for a specific idea of architecture and design relative to the temporal 'experience' of architecture in the present.

I will talk later about this particular aspect of the meaning of architecture and its origins in rationalist thought when I discuss normative systems . . . but we must clarify this decision more specifically in relation to a 'formal' conception of architectural theory. Here, an explicit view is taken about the **meaning** of forms: that in particular is to address the issue of the role taken by fundamental architectural elements, definitively focused on the issue of the process by which the architecture is defined, both in terms of analysis and in terms of the (design) project itself.

It is precisely as a consequence of this choice informed by the 'meaning' of forms that the 'problem of architecture' acquires a 'definitive' character which is particular to both the theoretical construction and the 'logical evidence' of rationalist architecture (seemingly referencing a form of intellectual solidarity).

Consequently, if analysis tends to determine a series of objective propositions, their formal responsiveness and communicative sense (as well as a design process understood as the production of form generated by a succession of choices), are to be understood as a structural syntactic calibration more particularly focused on **formal** issues related to the construction of theory.

To establish, here, a relation between the architectural processes of Rationalism and those of logical thought, in order to sketch out parallels between the two, seems less useful than a concrete examination of theoretical work. This, on the other hand, will bring to light formal elements as they are to be read correctly within the specificity of the architectural design process. At this point we can, in some measure, observe that in architecture logical reasoning coincides with a theory of rationalism.

However, in talking about the characteristics of work that investigates the theoretical construction of the architecture, we have to take account of the fact that it generates two forms of conceptualization: those that result from analysis and observation as **descriptive** concepts, and those concerned with process, that is to say **logical** concepts. However, it has never been possible to entirely determine theoretical works in these terms, because these concepts have always been tangled up and overlaid in theoretical constructs. We cannot really just talk about, for example, the process, without also discussing the results emerging from it, which are in turn derived from observation.

We can nevertheless say, if only in general terms, that any work aiming to analyse architecture represents an attempt to constitute its logical foundations, whereas all attempts to construct rule-based norms represent an effort to predetermine logical foundations for design.

In this context, and with these aims in mind, certain characteristics inherent in design work stand out. In particular one should emphasize the strictly cognitive objective of works that seek to **describe** a form of architecture, and in addition the **importance** attached to the 'construction' of these works as that is informed by their taxonomic **classification**.

Indeed, classification itself represents the clearest convergence between method and objectives, and between logical thought and architecture. This is to emphasize the syntactical aspect of an architecture that investigates combinatory form without concerning itself with constituent identity; with which of the possible combinations will actually be implemented, or with evaluation of their efficacy in practice.

In addressing individual syntactic elements, classification also concerns itself with the potential structure of a **serial order.** This provides a more definitive framework than a purely 'analytical' [conception of form], and in doing so constitutes the fundamental point of departure of this study.

In the following chapters we will discuss descriptions, classifications, and systems of rules: the first two will be understood as attempts to construct a logical foundation for 'architecture', whereas the last is instead an attempt to set out a logical foundation for 'design'.

*   *   *

60 Ezio Bonfanti

Elements and construction: a note on the architecture of Aldo Rossi (1970)

Ezio Bonfanti, 'Elementi e Costruzione: note sull'architettura di Aldo Rossi', *Contraspazio*, vol. II, 10, October 1970, pp. 19–28 (also published in: Marco Biraghi and Michelangelo Sabatino (eds), *Nuovo e Moderno in architettura*, Milan: Bruno Mondadori, 2001, among other sources). Extracts translated by Stefania Boccaletti with the editors.

› Critique and self-description

*   *   *

A further limitation concerns the relation between theory and design, despite Rossi's specific insistence on their mutual inseparability (he in fact went as far as to contend that: 'the most important artists concentrated more on theory than on actual making'). I find myself in complete agreement with him on this point, but intend to limit my analysis solely to his buildings and projects. First and foremost one should recognise that choosing architecture [itself] as the focus for this investigation is the most direct way to discuss the relationship between theory and practice; as architecture should lack nothing compared with theory. This is the logical consequence of theory intended to both be a foundation for design and an inquiry into architecture's own rationale; to avoid the 'constant reinvention of the wheel, which is a typical mistake of minor architects who refer to experiences external to real ones; in order to reject extra or inter-disciplinary deviation and [to deny] the ideology of abdication (often fuelled by questionable Marxist assumptions). Design theory should [instead] be a complete project enabling 'anyone who has at any given point in time thought about and designed buildings, to be able to explain their architectural decisions'. This should (in principle) allow them to 'clearly formulate (the sources) from which their architecture, our architecture, was conceived'.

*   *   *

› A reading scheme for analytical architecture

Aldo Rossi's architecture immediately projects the characteristics of a unique sharpness, recognisable identity, and programmatic quality. A more accurate analysis will reveal that the programmatic character of his work is in fact less rigid than it would at first appear – for instance, we should (really) not talk of a 'schematic' character to his work, which appears predominant at a first glance.

The problem is to interpret the tension between logical rigour and fantasy, which allows him to consider both without one ever *compensating* for the other. This issue runs in parallel to those directly investigated in Rossi's (architectural) theory. Even in his theoretical work, the concepts of 'logic' and 'autobiography' (that is those concepts which are inseparable from one's own personality, personal life, and feelings or emotions) seek to *compensate* each other, but instead (my contention is) they should be *added* to one another. What emerges as autobiographical in his architecture and its accompanying theory is subjected to rational analysis.

Reason does certainly not alter the initial intent or 'autobiographical' character of the work – we witness the same difficult relation to rationality experienced by the Surrealists. The unconscious, the fantastical and even the pathological, were translated into art as an explicit answer to the Marxist imperative [that argued] 'an excess of reason' in an expanded conception of reality, could not be achieved by eluding or disguising these issues. By refusing the logic of 'compensation': the averaging out of opposing terms or their amalgamation in a proposition where they are 'happily merged' – that is, dissolved and unrecognisable; it is still possible to retain the terms of the conversation. Rossi's architecture may be analysed in this sense, but that does not mean it is *facile* [or without consequence]. His architecture openly displays – as suggested earlier – its (particular) character as a *composition of elements*.

*   *   *

› 'Pieces' and 'parts'

*   *   *

To consider the 'blind wall' as a 'piece' may appear to subvert its identity as a recognisable and generic component of architecture. However, it takes on a distinct meaning in Rossi's architecture as intrinsic to the construction of an (enclosing) envelope, one that defines the consequent architecture and excludes other possibilities. In his architecture there is similarly no alternative (except in certain early projects) to the portico or *galleria*. This choice is related to the conceptual identity of the 'opening' (or aperture). Doors and windows – when they are not dealt with porticos or arcades – are invariably 'carved out', (that is) they are always subservient to a materially substantive architecture and their shape and proportion refers to an archetypal notion of 'doors' and 'windows'. As a result in Rossi's work, strip windows or even the use of 'curtain walling' are (notably) absent. In this manner key characteristics of Modern architecture are set aside; although influenced by Gropius – his *Villa ai Ronchi* [in Versilia] was inspired by Gropius' houses in Dessau – Rossi never made use of that lexicon.

*   *   *

It is important to recapitulate and remind ourselves that in Rossi's work *elements* are not just individual 'pieces' but actually also (a set of) 'parts' according to the distinction previously outlined. This distinction is in the first instance possible because of the formal simplicity of such finite architectural 'parts': if we consider a prism with a triangular base we already have a perfect relation between piece and part. The other members of the set of forms employed are not much different from the basic elements to which I have already referred. They are all derived from the following: an essentially cubic rectilinear volume, though subjected to a wide range of fragmentations, excavations, and erosions; the drum – cylindrical or elliptical and capped where necessary by a cone (Parma and Sannazzaro), or a dome (Scandicci); a linear typology, often very thin; the city gate (developed in the portico fronting the Triennale exhibition, or those beside the large cylindrical towers of the Scandicci city hall project), and perhaps several other formal types.

*   *   *

› The additive method

The process of design proceeds by *serialising* or *superimposing* elements depending on whether one studies the composition in plan or elevation. This is very significant in my view: in fact I believe that Rossi has pursued this additive process to such a radical degree in order to attain original results not readily comparable with received precedents. The use of parataxis – to attenuate, or even eliminate, connections and mediations – is a characteristic procedure we can find in literature, art, and even modern architecture (emerging in the 1700s when, as Kaufmann noticed with a degree of arbitrariness, certain characteristics such as the 'gradation' typical of 'Renaissance and Baroque systems of order', disappear). Incidentally, emphasising Rossi's debt to Modern Architecture also helps to play down certain generic but insistent claims that his work is inspired by Classicism; his particular use of basic architectural elements does not support a comparison with Classicism. Parataxis is, however, extended to a further extreme and in a particular manner. It is not just a refusal to, even partially, interpenetrate different parts (a condition which in the project for Scandicci is only made more unsettling by the use of stone cladding to connect the Union's office to the two wings articulating the composition), but more importantly it is his use of finite parts of the architecture as compositional elements of the building. The determination to pursue this agenda initially produced compositions (consisting) of purely detached elements.

*   *   *

[This predilection for] simple and regular forms can be separated from any autobiographical association; they are didactically irresolvable since *they may look like they were 'found' rather than chosen* which constitutes a form of circular logic we also find in Boullée. When asked why he liked regular forms, Boullée replied: 'because they are simple and regular' – a tautology so evidently clear as to implicitly convey a precise argument.

Clearly (Rossi's) simple forms and quotations have a similar role. It is not just that simplified forms can be considered to have exceeded [literal] quotations (this theme of the recurrence and persistence of elemental forms needs to be further developed), but they are also elements, forms, and artefacts coming from unmediated sources. They cannot simply be invented or configured – one by one – within the process of design.

* * *

› Choice and history

The fundamental difference resides in the issue of *choice*. Choice is already implied in the process of analysis of urban conditions and its relation to design. These are processes that also have a didactic value; that can affect the communication of ideas and collaborations; as such they can configure [the] Tendenza and give it an instrument to control its development. Pushed to its logical limit, choice is also charged with autobiographical elements, memories, associations, even weaknesses and limits, which are unavoidably part of one's personal history.

* * *

The role [in design] of an informed choice, as Rossi explains, implies an engagement with the history of architecture (and art) that is in radical contrast to that of other [historians].

'The works accumulating in the history of architecture constitute [and define] architecture' – Rossi has recently affirmed – 'however even amongst this collection, choice is a necessary requirement and even amongst these works *tendenza* remains meaningful: I believe this to be an authentic historicism having nothing in common with a false historicism that reduces history to mere historiography and denies the thought and action required for effective and active implementation'. This [argument] reinforces a concept that Rossi had already written about on many occasions. In 'Architettura per i musei' (Architecture for Museums) for example, which can be read as a piece entirely dedicated to this topic, he declared that: 'Roman monuments, Renaissance palaces, castles, Gothic cathedrals all constitute architecture – they are part of its overall construct – and as such they will always come back, not so much in history and as memory, but rather [in the form of] elements of design'.

This is in evident contrast to the position emphasised by Manfredo Tafuri following [publication of] his *Theories and History of Architecture*. In that book he distinguished between an 'operational critique' (acting in combination with *tendenza* to unify 'thought and action'); an approach 'substituting analytical rigor with pre-conceived value judgments, ready for immediate action'; and a (new) variant, a 'typological critique', with which Aldo Rossi was identified as a leading exponent.

There is a substantial difference (of opinion) that cannot be bridged between Tafuri's 'instrumental historiography' and Rossi's defence of his own work as 'authentic historicism'. 'As a design tool history is sterile, it can only offer predictable solutions' writes Tafuri. It is a marginal caveat then to point out that Rossi was the first to denounce the formalistic qualities within a certain *Tendenza*, as too literal and distanced a proposition (attributes stemming in his view from a critique of Kahn). This attitude was very clearly stated in his article of 1956 (published) in *Societa*, where he discriminated between a progressive, and a sterile reactionary, Neo-classical tradition. Tafuri however is adamant: '. . . today we are forced to read the history of architecture not as an extensive collection of codified values, but rather as a repository of utopias, failures, and betrayals' which prompts a 'faith in violent ruptures, jumps in the darkness and challenges taken without any certainty of success'.

Against history understood as a series of fractures, a distant past with which we cannot be reconciled, stands Rossi's idea of the past displayed and encrypted in the city, that is in the continuity of architecture's disciplinary *corpus*: 'it makes no sense to say that the problems of ancient architecture are different from ours' . . . 'we can say that in the history of architecture and the city there are no ruptures'.

*　　*　　*

61 Aldo Rossi

Introduction (1974)

Aldo Rossi, 'Introduzione', from: Hans Schmidt, *Contributi all'architettura 1924–64*, Milano: Franco Angeli Editore, 1974, extracts, translation by the editors.

*   *   *

Hans Schmidt always stressed that in his personal opinion Adolf Loos was his sole and categorical point of reference. Both [architects] are distinguished, despite clear differences in personality, by their conception of architectural 'reason' exemplified in the radical nature of their fully resolved designs. The logic of their architectural language is stronger than any style with which they could be identified. In the final year of his life Schmidt emphasised once again that his fundamental agreement with Loos' ideas; particularly the notion that 'the form cannot change without a change of technology'; which had led him to move away from the exaggerated formalism expressed in his earlier buildings. This was to repeat a view already expressed in 1941 that: '. . . without Loos, perhaps our architecture would have remained no more than an interesting game of talent'.[1] The radical nature of his examination of particular themes surfaces in several remarks made throughout his life as an architect – for example his defence of rational architecture against the accusation of monotony. In doing so he not only refuted the rather ambivalent psychological undercurrent to this controversy, but in his argument, closely linked to his conception of the role of the architect, he went one step further – basically he is set against stupidity [as he sees it], whether generated by bourgeois eclecticism or democratic piety. Schmidt reminds everyone that (for him) 'the question of monotony is not an aesthetic problem, but one of society.'[2]

*   *   *

Rational architecture, according to Schmidt, has nothing to do with aesthetics or morals, or how we choose to live; it is the only logical response to real and existing problems. Given this perspective Hans Schmidt's polemical involvement with Hugo Häring's architecture is revealing. At a seminar with students from the ETH in Zurich he derives from his examination of Häring, particularly convincing and illuminating arguments regarding his own work. The question is, in principle, a clear one where Häring's organic and naturalistic architecture proves to be the antithesis of Schmidt's realism, representing [as it does] an entirely different architectural system. Despite Häring's conception of construction and composition being entirely technical issues, on the Garkau estate [farm] for example he observed the animals, their movements and positions, and studied work sequences on the estate, bringing everything together into a valid and definitive final form. In the [contrasting] so-called 'flexible variant' of organic architecture, the function of a building is defined independently from its function over time. Hans Schmidt counters [this conception]: 'I could, on the contrary, argue that the 'flexible' building is not flexible in itself, but that the life within it is flexible. Therefore the building in itself has to be the ultimate functional-building. Human society and the built environment (occupied by man), are two different things.'[3]

The ultimate conception of a functional building is reflected architecturally in Hans Schmidt's typological rigour; accordingly he calls to account Klein's small-minded fixation with the key functional sequences [of activities] in housing, [an approach] which in principle represents Häring's point of view. Writing in 1923, Adolf Behne in one of his most important treatises about functional architecture, had already emphasised the intrinsic importance of this question (in architecture):

> Häring and Scharoun sometimes choose different widths for their corridors, allowing them, like living arteries, to narrow, to shrink, in places where there is less traffic. This is all right provided that traffic always follows this same path until the death of the building, that the same conditions prevail as on the first day, in the same way as is the case for blood corpuscles in an organism. But it is wrong, and the functional becomes anti-functional as soon as the traffic finds different conditions – such as through a change of owner or when purpose alters traffic requirements – whereby it could be the heaviest in precisely those places where the plan requires it to be lightest.
>
> Thus in view of the fact that an individual item, even if it functions excellently in and for itself, and even if it is completely adapted to an infinitely manifold nature, is not adequate for society's living requirements, it indeed closes itself to them because it is exaggerated for the sake of uniqueness in space, time, and personality and is not open to duration, change, and multiplicity. In such a case it is questionable whether the mechanical structures of rectangularity are not socially more correct in functional terms![4]

This [view of the] uniqueness of architecture, this emphasis on an individual identity, questions the rationality of architecture or counters it with a logic that is unacceptable to Hans Schmidt. The thought that a well-proportioned, right-angled space, designed equally for everyone, could be replaced by a tailored space, that generic form in architecture could be replaced by a 'purpose made' design, fitting like a glove but only for one particular hand, would mean to privilege an individualistic character for architecture [in general]. But this would negate its process of development and separate architecture from [wider] social problems: architecture is always required to serve a general purpose and its objectives must always be directed towards society. If we consider the purpose of architecture [as a discipline] we can overcome the functionalism inherent in, for example, Klein's functional activity sequences or Häring's [conception of] flexible form. A truly progressive architecture aims not to hinder the life which enables it in the first place.

This view of freedom is closely linked to the defence of rational architecture against the accusation of (so-called) 'monotony'. Hans Schmidt has had, like many others, to listen to the familiar rhetoric against 'monotony': people have different needs, families come in different sizes and therefore they need a variety of different flats. Contributing to a discussion in Berlin Hans Schmidt commented on this issue: 'If you have got the money for all these complications, then build a bigger / larger house – you can do that – and then leave it to people how they structure their lives and how they want to express their own complicated preferences.'[5]

The representation of one's own conflicts attests to the personal freedoms of each individual and does not fall into the ambit of the state's responsibility; neither is it the architect's job to provide a didactic framework for this (circumstance). Attempts to pursue this have, time and again, led to a delightful funfair architecture, no more no less.

Rationalism here becomes a question of personal freedom because it is the architect's responsibility to create an environment that enables particular problems to be solved while interfering as little as possible with the private sphere. Schmidt, for example, accuses De Stijl of having conceived the house in pictorial terms, constructing walls as if paintings and compelling the occupants to indulge in a [total] work of art. As a reaction to De Stijl's pictorial wall-planes, and to the rather questionable and misplaced desire of formalist aesthetes who see in architecture a vehicle to project an ideal way of life, Hans Schmidt, with a vehemence very likely rooted in his longstanding concern with this question, a concern still of programmatic consequence today, insisted on the neutrality of the 'wall':

> Whether we hang picture postcards or oil paintings on these walls; whether we hang nothing, like the Japanese, or we paint them with frescos as in the Middle Ages; this is in the first instance completely irrelevant – it is a question of individual taste and individual means.[6]

*   *   *

After becoming conscious of the close association between the immaterial and material aspects of form, Hans Schmidt partly renounced and overcame [his identification with] the early Modern Movement, because, as he once outlined in a discussion with students in Lausanne, his accord with Loos' thinking led him to refrain from the formalism which had characterised his early projects.

In reality Schmidt, in this self consciously critical search for the meaning of 'architecture', moves away from [the notion of] a clearly defined style in order, from then on, to allow his projects to be led by the logic of architecture [as a discipline]. In this sense the Liestal competition illustrates the whole spectrum of Schmidt's architectural development.

Few [architects' drawings] from the 1930s exhibit a similar starting point, one reduced to the essential, if diagrammatic, representation of a building as the implementation of an essentially typological structure: for example one only needs to remember the closed volumes, provided with only the most immediately necessary openings, where columns and gable ends determine the structure. In this project Schmidt appears to reconcile apparently opposing aspects of his work and interests; a project which though simple and accessible, with minimal means concludes the whole complex of themes [related to the concept] of rational architecture.

Throughout his subsequent career, beginning with his studies of the architecture of the Enlightenment at the ETH in Zürich and inspired by the radical phase of the Modern Movement [in moving] towards a Socialist Realism, Hans Schmidt believed that the development of ideas can be brought forward with each concrete proposal, with each design project, given their mutual orientation towards [social] reality.

Realism is therefore, for Hans Schmidt, a deepening of his own rationalism – his project for Liestal carries a legacy of his early projects published in ABC. It is consequently important to recognise the close relationship between Schmidt's ideological convictions and his architecture. There are only a few artists in whose work theory and design demonstrate a similar coherence and reciprocity to that found in Schmidt's work, where both were combined in a unified intellectual framework . . . and this provides the foundation of Schmidt's radicalism. Only mediocre and superficial artists are unable to describe and reflect on their own work: typically the clarity of the design is synonymous with the clarity of thought. This initial lucidity is rarely to be found in the field of architectural criticism; and in this respect it may be that Adolf Behne had a strong influence on Schmidt. Speaking informally at the ETH in Zurich, shortly before his death, Schmidt explained Behne's thinking very succinctly. I would therefore like to cite one of Behne's passages, in which he explains rational architecture very precisely as an 'architecture of meaning'. In this short passage the whole controversy with regard to Klein and Häring, and their conception of an organic and functionalist architecture, [a debate] which is reflected in Schmidt's work and in that of all those who recognise in rational architecture the architecture of our time, is addressed:

> The rationalist is no more indifferent to purpose than the functionalist. Although he does not have the perspective of the Baroque genius opposing purpose, he avoids the tyrannical rule of purpose. As the functionalist looks for the greatest possible adaption to the most specialized purpose, so the rationalist looks for the most appropriate solution for many cases. The former wants what is absolutely fitting and unique for the particular case; the latter wants what is most fitting for general need, the norm. The former is all for adaption, relation, formlessness growing from selflessness, and mimicry; the latter is also for personal will, self-consideration, play, and form.[7]

Moving on from the [deployment of] form aimed at function and adaptability one arrives at another, more general form, described by Behne, for which at a social level, the [requisite] aesthetic and formal principles are still valid – whereas satisfying individual needs would, accordingly lead to anarchy.

*   *   *

In 1964 Hans Schmidt, developing his controversial opinion about the lack of unity between architecture and urban design, writes:

> We speak of monotony not only with regards to individual buildings, but more particularly with urban design in mind. But this question was addressed in the 'mass' construction of cities during the last century. It is consequently not necessarily a trait of industrialised building. As a remedy against monotony in urban planning today we generally see a desire to create the greatest possible variation in the architecture, in the scale, and in the arrangement of buildings. As a result in many cases we find residential areas lacking urbanity and running the danger, in seeking the greatest possible diversity, of a new form of monotony, namely disorder and anarchy. In the end, the question of monotony is not an aesthetic problem, but one of society. The most famous cities of the past, demonstrate the artistic potential of uniformity. The Rue de Rivoli in Paris; Bedford Square in London and the frontage of St Mark's Square in Venice, were erected in an absolutely 'uniform' architecture. The Paris we know and love regulated the architecture of its Boulevards in the form of a singular and uniform pattern of building. Why don't we speak of monotony there? In all these cases their uniformity has a particular artistic motivation. The Buildings, Streets and Squares form the city as a social organisation. What we would otherwise perceive as being monotonous is transformed to manifest an inherently artistic quality.[8]

I believe that the persuasiveness of this passage lies in the particular clarity of its diagnosis: 'In the end, the question of monotony is not an aesthetic problem, but one of society.'

Just as with 'humanist architecture' and other related concepts, often the defence of the 'humanity' of architecture is nothing more than the aesthetic projection of an incapability to build in accord with reality.

*   *   *

In his search for a technical language of form, for the rationality inherent in artefacts, Schmidt deliberately resorts to repeating Loos' guiding principle:

> We work as well as we can without pausing for a moment to think about the form. The best form is always there already and no one should be afraid of using it, even if the basic idea for it comes from someone else. Enough of geniuses and their originality. Let us keep on repeating ourselves. Let one building be like another.[9]

That 'one house is like the other'. Adolf Loos has, following this logic, described the architect's task in designing housing. Even though the problems here are of a general nature, they always also concern modern man in the contemporary city. Schmidt's argument, directed at civil servants concerned about monotony, is similar in kind: 'If you have more money, then spend it, not on ugly ornament or nonsensical buildings, but on bigger houses, so that people can enrich their lives, according to their own desires.'

Editors' note: See also, Bruno Flierl (ed.), *Hans Schmidt – Beiträge zur Architektur*, Zürich: gta Verlag, 1993.

› Notes

1   Adolf Loos, Typescript, 11 February 1941. Trans. Torsten Schmiedeknecht.
2   'Modular Coordination in Architecture', extracts from a presentation given at TU Delft, published in *Werk* 1972, n. 10, p. 560. See also N 37 in this Reader.
3   'Gab es den Funktionalismus wirklich? Ein Gespräch mit Hans Schmidt', in: *Canapé News*, ETH Zürich, 1970/1971, p. 12
4   Adolf Behne, *Der moderne Zweckbau*, Frankfurt/M./Berlin 1964, p50. Editor's Note: trans. Michael Robinson from Adolf Behne, *The Modern Functional Building* (Santa Monica CA: Getty, 1996) p. 129.
5   Aldo Rossi, 'Hans Schmidt und das Problem der Monotonie', in *Werk-archithese*, 197, n. 17/18, p. 11.
6   Hans Schmidt, *Beiträge zur Architektur: 1924–1965*, Berlin 1965, p. 56.
7   Adolf Behne, *Der moderne Zweckbau*, Frankfurt/M./Berlin 1964, p59. Editor's Note: Adolf Behne, *The Modern Functional Building*, op. cit. p. 138.
8   'Modular Coordination in Architecture', op. cit. p. 560. See also N 37 in this Reader.
9   Adolf Loos, *Trotzdem: 1900–1930*, Innsbruck, 1931, pp. 141, 144. Editor's note: Rossi's pagination is incorrect. The quotation is taken from pp. 145/146. We have preferred to use Michael Mitchell's translation of 'Heimatkunst (1912)' from Adolf Loos, *On Architecture*, eds. Adolf and Daniel Opel (Riverside CA: Ariadne Press, 2002) p. 117. Rossi's translation of the last phrase is 'One house is like the other', which he repeats.

62 Luigi Snozzi

Design motivations (1975)

Luigi Snozzi, 'Entwurfsmotivationen', Martin Steinmann, Thomas Boga (eds), *Tendenzen. Neuere Architektur im Tessin*, ETH Zürich: Institut für Geschichte und Theorie der Architektur (gta), 1975, extracts p. 164.

*   *   *

My training makes it impossible for me to conceive of an "idea of architecture" in any other way than by construction: in fact, all of my attempts to approach the significance of architecture were based upon observations and experiences made during the design process, in particular in the attempt to solve constructive problems.

In constructive practice, for example, there are recurring themes: the roof, the openings, how the building is supported by the terrain, etc. All of these elements of a building, which define its relationship to "nature", are in fact extremely complex. This is true on the technical level alone, as can be seen by thumbing through any construction manual. These difficulties indicate basic problems affecting the very nature of architecture. A deeper investigation of these questions raises the problem of the relationship of man to nature in different terms each time.

The architect must supply an answer to this problem of the relationship [between man and nature]: such an answer is a prerequisite to any [physical] intervention.

At this point I should like to quote briefly from a talk I gave to the Architecture Department in which I attempted to illustrate concisely my design course and a few concepts which I find essential to design.

. . . whenever I design – be it a stable, a path, a house or a neighborhood – I cannot help referring to a city. My personal relationship to the city is a function of many factors, mainly my political-ideological views.

They are the basis for my thoughts and acts, therefore also my designing and teaching. Their main content is the rejection of a consumerist, utilitarian and efficiency-obsessed view of contemporary society.

The implications of this viewpoint include some basic positions with respect to design:

a) An attempt to find a new spatial organization seeking to regain and reintroduce values that are totally alienated today: the value of land as an inalienable common good, geographical and cosmic values, the changing of the seasons, the value of those elements needed for man's survival, (such as water, air and light), the value of history and tradition, of human labor, etc.

b) My view of schools of architecture, which must maintain their full autonomy from professionalism: this professionalism is in the service of the false needs endemic to the consumer society.

In the final analysis, architecture is a problem of form. For this reason, it is my view that the designer must approach the problems of architecture starting from form. Thus, other approaches (sociological, economic, etc.), which in recent years have provided architects with an avenue of escape from their true responsibilities, must be excluded. It is my contention that the failure of the architect in contemporary interdisciplinary work is due mainly to his lack of depth in his own discipline.

The concept of the territory as our field of intervention can be understood as part of a long transformation process in which man converts nature to culture. This is true both of so-called "natural" and "constructed" landscape, of which the most highly evolved form is the city.

A preoccupation with this concept of the territory led me to reject such protectionist views as adaptation and camouflage, extremely widespread in our official culture, as exemplified by both committees to protect the environment and monuments as well as in present-day architecture and planning practice.

For example, the real problem is not the insertion of a building into the environment, but rather the creation of a new environment. Likewise, a new structure should not be incorporated into the historically preserved city, but rather, the city should be integrated into a new spatial context, a new city.

Finally, let me mention a few points of reference which play an important role in the design process:

a) Reference to history;

b) Reference to "New Architecture" as the last unifying element in architectural history, whose main interest was housing construction; a subject whose critical appraisal is still of the utmost urgency: categorical rejection of vulgar functionalism as expressed by the equation form = function;

c) The analytical study of the city in all its topographical, historical and formal components;

d) The study of typology and morphology.

*   *   *

63 Giorgio Grassi

Architecture as craft (1979)

Giorgio Grassi, 'L'architettura come mestiere', *L'architettura come mestiere et altri scritti*, Milan: Franco Angeli, 1980, from: Richard Burdett and Wilfried Wang (eds), *9H,* 8, 1989, extracts pp. 42–44 and 47–49, translation by Winston Burdett and Richard Burdett.

*   *   *

What, then, is the critique Tessenow indirectly makes of contemporary architecture—the last manifestation of romantic eclecticism and those new experiences apparently intended to reveal absolute rationality? It is the same criticism that we can make today.

These two worlds; the romantic and the rational, that are so contradictory nevertheless have points in common. In their different ways their formal research excludes that concrete bond with daily life that is uniquely expressed by the evocative quality of architectural forms. Their reading never succeeds in satisfying us. For the most part they offer us confused sensations rather than persuasive modes of thought; after alluring us with their premises they often disappoint us. The few exceptions (as in the case of the Modern Movement, for example), the few who have been able to free themselves of these premises, have all started anew from the beginning, reopening a dialogue with history which cuts across the elementary conditions of their work. As stone-masons or carpenters, some have discovered in the origins of their experience the very structure of architecture, its most certain and fixed point of reference[1]: once again, architecture as craft.

The elements of this craft are quite clear. Indeed, the only reasonable definition worth repeating is that architecture constitutes all architectures, all those that have been conceived and all those that have been realised, together with their principles and theories: architecture is all of these. Of course a definition of this kind carries certain limitations. Not everything man has built or will build for himself is architecture—neither the Hegelian "house built as a fundamental type", nor the primitive hut; nor the modern fantasies of science fiction. Moreover architecture is an experience which (within the limits defined by its beginning and possible end) must be evaluated on its own terms.

According to this definition, the individual and collective aspects of each artist's work are found within architectural practice. "In the end industrial work [the craftsman's work] is always inadequate. When it is very good, it consists of fifty per cent stupidity and fifty per cent intelligence. The best industrial work considers both equally valid and knows perfectly well how absolute things elude us, and says to itself: that which is intelligent is as stupid as that which is stupid is intelligent. We have to be certain, and at the same time doubtful about our certainty, in order to produce the best industrial work". With these words on the different roles involved in work, Tessenow defines a clear-cut boundary between the limits of custom (in which each part and principle is a concrete and commensurable fact and thus participates in the collective realm) and the limits of the individual (where each individual tension is translated into the finished work, but little can be said about this barring the fact that it reveals our interest in that work). Architecture, perhaps, exists at the meeting point of these two lines; but the fact that in most instances they remain distinct in no way detracts from the veracity of the craftsman's work, which we recognise as the foundation of architecture.

The protagonist of one of Conrad's stories, the only survivor aboard his ship after it has escaped a fearful hurricane, says of himself: ". . . I was like a mad carpenter making a chest: even if he is convinced that he is the King of Jerusalem, he will always make the chest according to the rules of his craft".

And so, in designing a house we may even imagine that we are making who knows what; that we are penetrating, let us say, the seven walls of the temple of Jerusalem, or the mysterious house of Golem, or the castle of Argol, hewn from the living rock, or the Pantheon itself the model of all architecture. But we will always end up making a house. And the principal rule will be that the house as such should not be violated or contradicted.

As we design a house we may also think of the splendour of princely dwellings, and seek to reproduce their order and dignity. We may also think of the simple and uniform essential quality of medieval habitations and imagine ourselves, as architects, the principal artificers in the common labour of *Existenzminimum*; the problem of *housing for all* may also be awarded a place of honour among the compelling motivations which generate architecture; equally, we may dream of beehives and houses with gardens. But there is a limit beyond which our fantasticating or our serious thoughts lose all value; and this limit is the house as it is read through time, the house in its generality, defined and specific. The principal rule will be, precisely, that of not contradicting.

All the elements of our work and study are contained within this *principle of non-contradiction;* the relationship with history, the relation to the city and its permanences, with its typologies, destinations, and so on. This constitutes a reconstruction of the discipline of architecture; and its relationship with *style,* the definitive moment of an architectural work, and of any attempt at generalisation or archetypal reduction. Each architectural work will be a stone that is added to the construction of the discipline. Style not in the sense of historical category, but rather as something common to all the solutions to specific problems developed over the course of time: the house, public space, the street, the public square, etc.

But to return to the workshop, we can see that it possesses another element that is essential for architecture, an element which can only manifest itself positively in a concrete undertaking; that is the idea of a *collective work.*

Among the familiar definitions of architecture there is one that is particularly important, attributed to Mies van der Rohe: "architecture is the visible expression of a point of view that others wish to share". I know of no definition that is as rich in concrete promises, and surely this quality springs from its being so accessible, for its being, in fact, nothing less than an open invitation. It thus presupposes the idea of collective work.

Now collective work, in the sense of the workshop or an architectural laboratory, is possible only insofar as there exists, so to speak, a state of fixed tension; that is, a rationalisation of the process of design so that every proposal finds a commensurate response. Such a process certainly can claim no linear simplicity. For example, it assumes that in any given work the logical processes and abstract concepts (such as formal order or truth) are perceived as concrete objects, as experiences, in the same manner as building techniques and methods of construction. We should add, though, that the truth of such assumptions does not need to be established by persuasion and convention, but can be observed in history, in the experience of the past, and in the obstinate determination of our predecessors to give things an ever more distinct meaning.

*   *   *

To assert, for example, that in architecture there are physical principles that no longer have anything to do with building construction and technology—perhaps they have determined those principles and certainly, up to a given moment, constituted their clearest explanation—is in effect to recognise omission as one of the processes of formal definition that are proper to architecture. Such principles have become with time autonomous laws of architecture. Tessenow's argument which I have just quoted refers particularly to the *omission of the constructive moments*—and in this connection we might recall the fable of the old master builder and the timber door.

In referring to this, Tessenow takes for granted that it implies a more advanced phase, a more evolved stage in which architecture has become an autonomous *art,* a particular activity that in time defines itself and its laws. From this point of view omission occupies a role far more important than that of mere negation in the work of design; omission indeed creates new links and establishes new hierarchical relationships among design elements, reflecting, first of all, the autonomy of architectural figuration.

We may illustrate this process with reference to Tessnow's Klotzsche school project. Think of the portico that surrounds the central court and compare it with the exposed structure of the lateral wings. Clearly the starting point for this design is the portico in its full height—a reference, filled with a rural dignity, to Weinbrenner's Kaiserstrasse. In this case the portico is the unifying element that brings together the different buildings around the courtyard. However, as a structural element it can be read as a formal gesture that ties together the different parts of the complex through the rhythm of the facades. This structure becomes modified in the project; it is reduced to a pure and simple representation of its constitutive elements—the vertical emphasis of the dense columns and the horizontal emphasis of the architrave—to the point that it totally loses its value as a load-bearing structure, in effect annihilating itself as such and becoming instead the suggestion of a completely autonomous figuration. This is carried to the point of creating an image composed of a multitude of vertical posts fixed in an ordered way in the ground—like the scenic apparatus of a fair ground made ready for the tournament—which characterises the design and becomes the most general evocative component of the project itself. Beginning with a formal idea that is both so rich and also so specific, this architecture is eventually evaluated in terms of a particular image of nature, or better, from a particular historical position of man's dominance over nature. Undoubtedly this is the most significant aspect of the project. Tessenow does not deny the structure; he assumes it to be such from the start; he then turns it around and carries it back to the formal idea in which the structural element is no longer of relevance. We may say, indeed, of this structure that all that remains of it is a *heraldic emblem*.

There is a close relation between the notion of omission and what we commonly mean by *formal simplification*. The one designates what is to be eliminated, and the other what is to be highlighted and brought to the fore. The process that both entail is obviously the same. Formal simplification, too, aims at revealing elements of generality in architecture and at reaffirming what we have called the principle of non-contradiction. Simplification as such is not an alternative way of making architecture. It is, rather, a necessary condition. It cannot be taken as a phase in the process of formal definition. It is the process itself. It cuts across the entire experience of architecture as a particular type of progress, which can only be accounted for [. . .] with reference to the specific cognitive character of architecture.

*   *   *

Editors' note: This essay, 'L'architettura come mestiere', was first published as an introduction to the first translation into Italian of Tessenow's *Hausbau und dergleichen*, in *Osservazione elementari sul costruire,* Milan: Franco Angeli, 1974.

› Note

1   I am referring to the apprenticeships of both Mies van der Rohe and Tessenow, which were so decisive for their later development.

64 Oswald Mathias Ungers

Architecture's right to an autonomous language (1979)

Oswald Mathias Ungers, 'Architecture's right to an autonomous language', from: Paolo Portoghesi (ed.), *The Presence of the Past—Venice Biennale 1980*, London: Academy Editions, 1980, pp. 319–323.

Architecture nowadays is mostly conceived as an ecological, sociological and technological function. Economical problems like effective usefulness, profitability and economizing, are brought to the forefront by the operators and are declared to be the theme and content of architecture. Attention is given to taking an objective view of the plan's progress and creating standard architectural elements.

However it is useless continuing to discuss architectural problems if it is only a question of satisfying the existing requirements in the most rational way. If that were the case it would be better to abandon the field of architecture to producers who are more capable than anyone else of rationalizing the operational process.

It is equally difficult to derive a formal structural project from mere social conditions, since one cannot trust sufficiently either in the behaviour and habits of a single person's life or in the general public's feelings. In most cases people's good sense has turned out to be a failure as an artistic metre. Social factors naturally influence architecture, but careful analysis of people's habits and customs does not necessarily lead to the choice of an architectural form as well. Any architect who consults a sociologist must realize that the latter will simply exert the right of making a critical analysis and judgement of someone else's creative product, which does not belong to him.

The pretensions of Economy and Sociology are joined by those of Technology. There can be no doubt that the invention of new materials and the arrival of new building methods have enriched the world of construction. This fact, however, must not lead us to overestimate the thinking about construction, which is the case with those who spread the mistaken vision of the engineer as the artist-builder of the future.

When Lissitzky, one of the leaders of Constructivism, claimed there to be a link between the engineer and the architect, asserting that the introduction of new materials and construction methods was enough to make "the opus rise as an independent result," this was certainly a statement comprehensible in the enthusiasm first aroused by the opening of new constructive possibilities. All the same, another architecture cannot be born from the consequences of a material or a logical constructive idea; at best a technical work is born.

I do not deny that economic conditions, sociological requests and constructive requirements have an important part in the carrying out of a building. They are real factors, to which the activity of building is attached. But the overestimation of these factors and the consequent idea that that is all architecture is for must be rejected. The work's destination does not contain in itself elements of formal choice. The wishes arising from it can only cause modifications in the arrangement, but the practical destination can in no way condition architecture in such a way as to compromise the laws belonging to it. Over and above the laws of construction, the consideration of human necessities and the effective usefulness is the imperative requirement of formal shape, and this is where the architect's spiritual responsibility resides. The total failure of modern architecture in transmitting the cultural models of our times into formal symbols is proof of the lack of spiritual values and contents.

Since architecture is engaged in a continual process of dialectical tension between creative willpower and intellectual calculation, conception and functional acceptance, imagination and reality, every theory tends to distinguish between practical knowledge and experience and intellectual know-how.

Two theories have thus emerged in the debate about the essence of architecture, each unacceptable to the other. The first inserts architecture into a general theory about art as a special field of artistic activity. The second, on the other hand, considers architecture to be autonomous: it has much in common with a general theory about art but in principle is clearly distinguished from it.

The first theory has essentially been in existence since the 16th century and is based on Vasari's work on the "Vite de' piu excelenti pittori, scultori ed architettori italiani." Vasari believed that the arts of painting, sculpture and architecture merge in the ability to draw, and they thus had the same origin. The concept of "Beaux Arts," or Fine Arts, came into being as a result.

With the passage of time came the development of principles from the idea of Fine Arts that can be seen in the impartial character of the arts:

- No theory of Beauty should refer to aims of any kind: art should be impartial.
- The Beauty thus conceived should act on all the sensorial perceptions and should stimulate both visual and acoustic reactions.
- The idea of what is beautiful came to be formed as part of a general concept of life centred on the solicitation and investigation of sensorial experiences. Architecture was inserted in this concept of Beauty.

The alternative theory, according to which architecture is an independent art and must thus be considered only in relation to the art of building, is based in general on Kant's "Critique of Judgement." Here, for the first time in the philosophy of art, he distinguishes between the free arts, the "pulchritudo vaga," and the subordinate arts, the "pulchritudo adhaerens." In this way he separates pure art from applied art.

This means that architecture is counted among the subordinate arts, seeing that its existence has an intention and an aim.

This separation has conditioned architectural thinking right up to the present day, this also explains why those who glorify the concept of architecture as "pulchritudo adhaerens" display such a passionate hatred for fine appearances, formal effect and ideal function. One can also understand why the distinction between "pure art" and "art with a purpose" has caused general controversy among architectural theorists, spreading the tendency to consider pure art as an object without any function and disqualifying all activities linked to a purpose, like architecture: they are judged to be imperfect and alien to art. Those whose opinion it is that architecture is art are slandered as formalists, individualists and utopians.

The concept of "applied art" became strongest in Germany, under the formula of "art with a purpose" and "functionalism." It has turned into the predominant idea in architecture and has stayed the same to the present day.

Anyway, the basic principles of this concept belong to the average intellectual baggage of every layman who is interested in the subject. They can be summed up in the following points:

- A building is only beautiful if it fulfills its functions in the best possible way.
- A building that fulfills its functions is beautiful as well, and
- An art object derives its form from its function. Thus all art objects, including buildings, are the result of an industrial or artisan production process. They are included in artistic handicrafts and not in art, and the same goes for architecture.

The last axiom was made popular by Semper in his book "Style in the technical and tectonic arts." His influential theoretical treatises on material conformity and on the imprint of function on building methods form the basic toolkit of modern architecture. They were most accurately reflected in the teaching of the Bauhaus. The professional preparation here was based on the didactic principle that if an object can be designed, then anything can, or, as Gropius put it: "The starting-point for any kind of design—be it a chair, a building, a city or even a regional development—should be, as a matter of principle, identical." In this way architecture became no more than a part of the production process. Faced with this declaration of failure for architecture proclaimed by so-called "Modernism," it is worthwhile reproposing reflection on the original values of architecture. Firmitas, utilitas, venustas, that is, stability of construction, appropriate arrangement of space and external beauty, are on the other hand the three equally important principles with which Vitruvius defined architecture. Any theory that wants to give serious reasons for the overall meaning of architecture is still concerned with these principles. Although different aspects dominated at different times—first the constructive mentality prevailed, then the way of articulating the space, then the formal points of view—it is nevertheless certain that these three elements: construction, space and form, are the true basic elements of architecture. Their right to autonomy exists independently from the social, political and economic conditions that present themselves now and then.

I would like to pause briefly to consider these three principles and their autonomous meaning in the field of architecture.

› Form

Form describes the visual quality of architecture. It is decided by formal laws that are expressed in the building's visible appearance; it takes its vocabulary from the specific law of formal relations and does not depend on external influences. The formal language of architecture is not—as is commonly assumed—a function of empirical conditions in whatever way they present themselves, but it expresses the aesthetic value of architecture as a specific fact. It has its own ratio, and it is only in this way that the concept of rational architecture—which has been much debated in recent times—should be understood. Formal language's means are the laws by which bodies and space are formed. This is the language of architecture, which arouses a marvellous feeling. Architecture's expressive capacity transforms what is useful into something spectacular, that is, into art. With the aid of formal language, functions and constructions are transformed artistically just as sounds are transformed into music, words into literature and colours into paintings. The communication of ideas and experiences by way of the language of form is one of architecture's basic premises.

› Space

The concept that a building is suitable for use only if it is employed for its original purpose seems obvious. This theory, however, which seems so evident, has for some time not only been doubted but also, especially in the criticisms of the so-called rationalists, has been the object of the most heated controversy. The real reason for this lies in the fact that even obstinate technocrats and functionalists must gradually realize that spatial conditions cannot be decided with exactitude, and that there is a great variety of types of buildings for which no perfect form can be found. Apart from this, buildings are often used for different purposes than the ones originally foreseen.

Thus doubt keeps on growing: should form be adapted to function or should it be the opposite, function to form?

There are abundant examples in the history of architecture of social and religious institutions which have developed in spaces previously in existence. The British Parliament, for example, where the government and the opposition sit opposite each other, derives from the fact that the first parliamentarians held their sittings in a Medieval Choir. The French and German parliamentary systems, on the contrary, are based on the confrontation between the lone orator and his listeners, which corresponds to the form of Greek theatre. Originally the first type of space came from liturgical requirements and the second from those of Greek drama. Neither of the two uses had the slightest relationship with a functional arrangement for the workings of a parliament. Many examples could be cited so as to demonstrate how different functions from the ones originally foreseen have been transferred into existing spaces and have adapted their forms. Therefore the validity of certain spatial forms does not only depend on the functions, and the building's typology clearly prevails over its functions. The functions adapt themselves to the type of building, which can be conceived as a completely self-sufficient and autonomous project. This means that the creative element in architecture certainly cannot be its function, but rather the idea of the building, the real project, for it is the architectural archetype that defines the building. When it is a question of architectural language the function is secondary; it is simply a means of reaching an end, and not the end in itself. Let's take this formula to its limit: architecture is not dependent on the end, not because it is not utilizable, but in the sense that its particular dimension expresses itself independently from external constrictions.

› Construction

Architecture's third component is construction, "firmitas." What seem like good reasons sustain the supremacy of construction over space and form. The first is that architecture is basically the ability of composing different constructive elements, like walls, supports, ceilings, roofs, etc., into a whole. To this, however, can be added the knowledge that use and function change in the course of time and that for this reason the construction should obey logical and mathematical laws exclusively.

The real debate on the aspect of architecture had already begun in the 19th century and spread to the problem of architecture conceived as the exclusive product of logical constructions and building technique which conformed with the type of material. The debate concerned the idea of engineering and building ethics that were expressed in concepts like honesty, clarity, cleanliness and genuineness. Adherence to reality was obviously much less important at the beginning of the 18th century, when appearance (which meant appearance of beauty) counted more than reality, and when hypocrisy was highly approved of. Under the influence of the theories and treatises of Kant and Semper a construction was considered true to reality only when its structure and visible appearance corresponded accurately with the building project and with a use of the elements that was in line with the material. This doctrine was gradually dropped after many years of dogmatic domination, and people began to realize that the form of a building contains in itself much more than the correct use of materials or the mathematics of static structures. It was discovered that architecture could be the bearer of spiritual values and that it was capable of expressing emotions just like any other art.

After a long period of doctrinal dependence on the dogmas of modern architecture, what counts nowadays is that architecture should be accepted again as an art. In this way, architecture links up again with its tradition and with its true social mission after a series of deviations, misunderstandings, mistaken interpretations and libels. Like all the other arts, architecture is capable of freeing man's surroundings and existence from grey daily banality and from the vulgarity of reality, it can transcend the constraints of material necessity.

In this way architecture not only contributes to a notable extent in modelling man's surroundings, but also takes on once more its due humanist responsibility.

65 Livio Vacchini

The necessity for uselessness. Remarks on a conversation (1987)

Livio Vacchini, 'La necessità dell'inutile. Appunti per una conversazione', from: *Livio Vacchini – architetture 1970/1987*, Exhibition Catalogue, Vicenza: Cripta ex convento dei Teatini, 1987, extract pp. 4–7, translation by the editors.

*   *   *

To be an architect means to give form to a necessity. How does form arise?

It does not fall from the skies, driven by a vague inspiration, but it does evolve from the application of principles and rules. Abstract principles have a dogmatic character but also a personal applicability, and stem from reflection about the construction of theories for different aspects of life and the real world. Rules, however, are grounded in reason and determine the cultural climate in which we live.

The form to which we assign constructed artefacts is dependent on a coherent realisation of the principles chosen and on our interpretation of given rules. Without rules there is no freedom of expression, and the perfection of a work of architecture is measured by the degree of rationality with which it corresponds to this prescription.

Our practice is therefore located within a pre-determined logical system which has always remained the same and which we call the 'classical'. Our designs refer to works made previously, and our work is generally concerned with 'transformation' of that which already exists.

I am often called a classical architect, and I am indeed flattered by this, but the definition makes little sense, because all of us architects are classicists, there is no other option.

If I am being asked for the rules of the game, my answer is that I don't know of anyone who summed them up better than St. Thomas [Aquinas]:

- Integrity – the form of a building must be sufficient within itself, it must be an end in itself.
- Totality – the different parts of a building must not be fragmented. There are no [singular] details.
- Symmetry – the different parts must be in balance with each other, they must correspond and be proportionally in harmony with each other.

- Charisma – the building has to be unique, unrepeatable and original and it must carry a personal signature.

The rules I have cited live in my practice like the branches of a tree, supported by the trunk. The trunk is symbolic of an obsession to look at anything in the world with regards to how it is connected to the ground, how it has a centre, and how it opens up to the sky.

The 'rule' decries that every object consists of three parts, and for more than twenty years my work has been grounded in the interpretation of this proposition in all of its inexhaustible richness.

› The rule as instrument

The rule not only permits pragmatic planning and its formal materialisation, but also communication, the transport of ideas and the building of a tradition.

Language is the element which connects architects of a school or an epoch: it is the distinctive way in which each of us gives order to their ideas. This is generally called style, and an epoch's style is nothing other than the combination of the particular styles, with the styles of those dominating who had the biggest influence on their time.

Over recent years the culture of building has often risked losing its sense of continuity and desire for totality: all too often, intellectual anarchy and individual exhibitionism predominate. It seems to me that today the desire for a common language is growing again. The purity of language expands the possibilities of communication, insofar as that culture is the expression of a common order.

Eclectic internationalism is now opposed by a universal [global] culture, which is diffuse and spreads everywhere. The response to individual experimentation lies in a fixed repertoire and the safety of norms.

› The use of technology

Every building is characterised primarily through its method of construction: its form varies depending on the technology applied in its realisation.

This means that the choice of construction method is crucial. It is fortunate that, together with scientific progress, building methods and technologies change over time. Correspondingly, the appearance of buildings changes so that the development of construction methods instigates evolution in architecture.

I do not know of any great architect who did not develop the technical solution of their time to its utter perfection. Our attention to the constructive aspect of building must know no limits and we must not tire of our engagement with it. I am not saying, however, that architectural work should be reduced to a question of technology, because after all, great works of engineering are by no means architecture. At the inception of our work there is always a concept and the desire for its expression. Expression evolves from the idea, but form evolves from the structure. Astonishingly, ideas change in relation to technology, and vice versa.

If I look at my work over the past twenty-five years, it strikes me that the development of my thinking always corresponded with a particular way of 'making'.

The authenticity of an idea is always and only verified by constructive facts, and consequently the work of the great masters is characterized as the expression of technology pushed to the boundaries of perfection.

66 Hans Kollhoff

The myth of construction and the architectonic (1991)

Hans Kollhoff, 'Der Mythos der Konstruktion und das Architektonische', from: Hans Kollhoff (ed.), *Über Tektonik in der Baukunst*, Braunschweig/Wiesbaden: Friedr. Vieweg & Sohn, 1993, extracts pp. 9, 10–13 and 19, translation by the editors.

Examining today's building activities or experiencing the 'pleasure' of having to sit on a competition jury, one realises the alarming absence of what I would call a 'feeling for the architectonic': that is how a house sits on a slope, next to a river, lake or the sea, or is situated in a street. Similarly [one can question] whether or not the house is self-contained or seeks a relationship with its context; whether it gives the impression of solidity promoting a feeling of serendipity, or whether it permanently confronts us with details that question the unity of the house, because each is vying for its own independent identity, consequently raising a concern that the whole thing will collapse like a house of cards.

The pioneers of modernism did certainly have this feeling for the architectonic, if only subconsciously, and when we compare Peter Behrens' AEG turbine hall with the Bauhaus Building by Walter Gropius, we can see how finally the urge for abstraction prevailed, over material sensitivity. It is therefore useful to concern ourselves with the architectural categories available at the beginning of the twentieth century. Among these we can count tectonics.

* * *

The more journals and magazines create a media-frenzy about architecture, the more our idea of architecture seems to evaporate. The more the term 'architecture' is monopolised by other disciplines, the more devoid of content it becomes for the architects themselves.

The [new] world of CAD already seems to be more complex and exciting than our meagre traditional architecture; moreover it seems more scientific and precise. Consequently the problem of legitimisation faced by the architect designer assigns to construction the role of manifesting architecture's last fundamental 'truth'; consequently its transfiguration diverts attention from our deeply rooted insecurity regarding belief in technological progress. Given the primacy of construction as a supposedly objective category, architecture comes to epitomise the rapidly changing development of technology in our time. A global orientation towards the future is seen to evolve into the world of machine aesthetics, space shuttles and microchips, leaving behind the ballast of history. Architects' eyes glint: move out of the mud, the earthen, the slippery and imprecise, into the clinically hygienic world of high technology.

But is it possible to relate architecture in this manner to the world of applied technology, or does architecture not rather, to paraphrase an essay by Julius Posener, belong to the 'world of objects'? Does architecture identify with a reality which can, in the last instance, only be understood by the specialist, or is it part of everyday life, part of the familiar and the ordinary?

Posener writes that an apparatus instils fear, objects inspire confidence. Objects are distinguished by their proximity to our body: the blanket we wrap around ourselves, the suit, the dress, the chair, the bed, but also the room, the house. Mankind desires surroundings he can comprehend, with which he can empathise, particularly when technological developments take place beyond the boundaries of our sensory perception.

Similarly, we dislike reductive exposure to the merely techno-functional. In the same way that our inner bodily organs and skeleton are enclosed by flesh and skin in order to evolve as body and to become a person, we do not expect to encounter a house as an accumulation of constructive elements or as a collection of pipes and tubes, whatever pragmatic sense they may have in themselves. In viewing a house, the integrity of its structure and the utility of its services are not my primary concern. The Modernist dictum of 'honest' construction, in this case, has been exaggerated and perverted. Even 'constructionist architecture', as Stefan Polónyi once called it, is exposed to the elements, to cold, fire and most importantly to corrosion; therefore it [also] has to be enveloped, wrapped, faced, in one word: clothed. A dressed architecture, which has been a [habitual] subject of architectural theory since Gottfried Semper, is a fact. We have to get used to it, even if it has, given the profession's demise into a decorative art and craft, become suspect. But neither escape into high-tech fantasies, nor into the past, are going to assuage the dilemma of the fact that a house, including its extremities, has [now] to be wrapped in a 120mm thick layer of Styrofoam, before a covering finish is applied.

It seems the monolithic building only exists as an exception at our latitude. It is, in any case, pure fiction that the architecture of antiquity, or that of the Middle Ages, was monolithic. Marble was always used as a facing. Interiors were always rendered. With the development of available technology for the refinement of surfaces in [the application of] expensive timbers, metals and stones, the trend to layered facades in our century has become generally accepted. Aided by skeleton construction the wall has been freed from its load bearing function, now serving only as protection from the elements and as insulation.

The wall constructed from one or two materials fulfilled every function – structure, insulation, waterproofing. The layered wall, in contrast, consists of a number of elements each fulfilling their different and separate functions. Thus a multitude of specialists come on site, whose interventions have to follow a precise building sequence. Between the trades there are [now] extreme differences in degrees of precision, and this requires tolerances and increases the necessity for joints. The invention of the silicon application syringe is perhaps the most effective [craft tool] of the second half of our century. Inaccuracy is not least, programmed by law via building regulations and normative criteria.

On a daily basis we are confronted with new products, which all comply with these 'norms' and which are technically, looked at in isolation, more or less accomplished. However, try selecting from this confusing array on offer, in order to make a judgement and put together a house. Take a window: in our university institute we have a collection of samples from which we can easily comprehend the state of the available technology. This is impressive. But I would not use any of these windows in a building. They are generally ungainly and all contain features that may be problematic, whether in terms of overall appearance or for reasons concerning the combination of materials, proportions, profiles and colour. You could say, I'll design my own window and get it fabricated by a good craftsman. When dealing with a small house this is surely the best method. But in larger projects, because of cost and [specification] guarantees, you are forced to choose from readily available products on the market. You will have problems convincing your client to choose a more expensive, if more elegant, window, if they can have a technically highly developed mass product, with relevant certificates and appropriate guarantees.

The laws of the market obviously compel the architect to choose products increasingly at odds with a conception of architecture that doesn't envisage itself as the art of wrapping or packaging. The building industry has reached a degree of technical specialisation that can only be refined in the detail. Consequently, if we follow the advertising brochures, innovations are not taking place [so much] in the arena of technical performance, but, in the broadest sense, in the 'realm of the decorative': corrugated metal sheets are currently available in twenty correspondingly layered pastel tones; bricks are being 'flamed' to imbue 'life' into an industrial product which used to be inherent in the manufactured product; timber glazing bars are being glued onto thermo-insulated window panes.

It would be wrong to blame the building industry for this, because there is obviously a demand for these absurdities. With the denial of the ornament man is left without any 'emotional access' to his artefacts, and, so to speak, these self-referential, abstract bodies, are beyond our tangible experience. There remain two last resorts: either the building itself becomes an ornament and sits as if a giant earring in the landscape or the city, or we find a way to infuse 'life' back into industrial products. Why are there not more demands on the market from architects, particularly from those with a tendency to withdraw sulking into their corner of 'craft building'? Is it not the case that the futility of the market only reflects the helplessness of architects?

* * *

The shift from an interest in 'surface' to one in the material (body) suggests that architecture becomes identified with our own physical experience. Heinrich Wölfflin conceives the organisation of the human body as the form through which we understand physical presence. Here the basic elements of architecture are determined by our own experiences: 'We can even empathise with the properties of a mute piece of stone. Because what we share with this stone are the relations between weight, balance, durability and so on. All these relationships are worth expressing'. This, for Wölfflin, is the basic theme of architecture.

* * *

Where, today, do we find such a tectonic sensibility? And are there, indeed, examplars which not only retained this within modernism, but that thematised it directly? Without a doubt, we must first mention Auguste Perret, who, in his proposal that 'technology, seen poetically, leads to architecture', succinctly summed up the theme of our symposium. Perret, like no other [architect], resisted the temptation of the abstract cube on the one hand, and that of a fascination with the naked concrete or steel grid, on the other. His work combined modernity and nineteenth-century tradition in an exceptional manner. Are we still capable of the same today? Or are all our efforts, to artistically master the technological possibilities of our time, to demonstrate them in an authentic architecture which does not only satisfy the intellect but also our feeling for materiality, bound to fail? Can we any longer comprehend our technically optimised constructions as 'structure' in the [classical] sense of Perret or Mies van der Rohe, and as a prerequisite for tectonic expression? Or is there now only a tectonic of the 'mass' form left, following which, according to Adorno, tradition no longer provides an unquestionable canon for the artist, and every work of art is now burdened with an unavoidable self-consciousness?

Reproduction and Tradition

67 O. M. Ungers

What is architecture? (1964)

O. M. Ungers, 'Was ist Architektur?, *archplus*, vol. 39, 179, 2006, extracts pp. 13–18, translation by the editors.

*   *   *

Which topic should a newly appointed Professor of Architecture discuss in his inaugural lecture? Which key question is a suitable point of departure for the teaching I would like to develop here in this school? When I began to consider these questions I realised how difficult it is to put the subject with which we concern ourselves here, and which we think we know so well, into words. I therefore cannot avoid at the outset the fundamental question: what does architecture mean?

At first it may seem to you as if it was futile to pose such a general and well-rehearsed question. But, try yourselves to give an answer. What is architecture? What actually is that thing we name day in and day out? We speak of architecture with certainty, we make architecture, we regard it and we struggle [to understand] it. But what does this term mean? Are we dealing with a craft, with a science or [perhaps] even an art? Or, is not the difficulty of finding an exact definition caused by the fact that architecture is neither the one nor the other, but all three together. If you ask a mathematician what mathematics is he will be able to give you a straight answer. He will say that mathematics is the science of numbers. This is a solid definition, terminologically clear and unambiguous. It is, however, impossible to make an equally binding statement as to what architecture is.

*   *   *

› The architect as arch-technician

Archi in Greek signifies 'the first and the highest'.

*   *   *

This would imply that one could translate the term 'archi-tect' as arch-technician. Accordingly it follows that the architect has an inherent ability to permanently bring together [otherwise] individual parts into a complete whole, to which is assigned a significance that goes beyond the merely useful.

› Technos – craft, science, art

As discussed previously, the second part of the word architecture is derived from the Greek *technos*, which still underpins our contemporary understanding of technology, which has evidenced a change in meaning over time. Today we understand technology only as process (the means applied with which a result is achieved). The term consequently describes an activity, the technical qualities of its execution – in other words, the process of production. This represents a significant reduction of the original Greek meaning. Literally, *technos* translates more accurately as 'with artifice' or as 'artistically appropriate' and concerns in its original sense the converse of the natural. It is that which man invents, and achieves through the employment of reason, and that which is not nature. It is thus an act of *techne* when man appropriates natural materials, when he collects stones and cuts wood to size in order to build a shelter against the elements, as much as when he builds a hearth or arranges reed mats to sleep on. All these activities, which concern 'craft', are united under this term.

Beyond that *techne* also designates those activities with which man deploys the forces occurring in nature, in order to generate energy by using wind and hydropower (for example). In order to exploit these forces to full effect man needs more than just instinct. A certain aim, or intentional functionality, can only be achieved if knowledge precedes it and may be transferred into a consequently useful result. These are [properly] the concerns of science.

Thirdly, man's desire to act is furthered by his intent in having an idea, something he desires to give expression to. This idea is neither directly useful, nor can it be achieved in the sense of a pursuit of function. The desire to project ideas motivates man to acquire a 'Gestalt'. This not only enables man to conceive something as real, but also to 'read' it retrospectively. In giving a meaning to things, man also animates the object in his own image. This desire for meaning moves man to 'design' his environment. This is also *techne*.

In this sense *techne* is an achievement grounded in its own practice. One cannot for example simply state that one is 'designing' something to achieve a higher speed. The resulting streamlined form is a stipulation one can fulfil, but not something one can 'design'. One can optimise this stipulation but there is no optimum or conclusive design. Design is never definitive, or all-inclusive, since it is dependent on an idea which can change at any time. Only [fine] art is the representation of an idea.

* * *

Technos consequently designates the art of craft, restricted to the use of natural materials to serve man's needs. Secondly, *technos* constitutes the art of science, concerned with the systematic channelling of natural forces for particular uses. And thirdly, to be systematic, we can designate *technos* as the practice of the arts expressed in artistic creation that stems from generic ideas.

› Purposefulness, material conviction, and design

It follows that we can now designate the term 'architecture' to that process which combines craft, technology and art in a mutual intent. One could say that in architecture three fundamental demands are required: usefulness, truth to materials and design execution (*Gestaltung*). To reverse this contention, architecture is only that which satisfactorily fulfils all three conditions. I would now like to test the conviction of this statement.

If, for instance, material and use interact, without doubt a product emerges. But if only material and design come together, we realise [instead] a work of art. And if, finally, only use and design are combined, then nothing will be created because these abstract terms can only take on a concrete form in the presence of material and construction. Architecture is thus neither merely the fulfilment of purpose nor pure art.

*   *   *

› Architecture as a binding art

Most writing on aesthetics designates architecture as a circumscribed or bound art, as opposed to the 'free' arts of music, poetry, painting and sculpture. Furthermore it is often contended that architecture is the mother of all arts. But how in particular is architecture 'materially constituted'? And what makes architecture the mother of all arts?

*   *   *

The more interesting question concerning what makes architecture a compound art is not easily answered. Having an obligation to purpose and material cannot be meant exclusively, because materiality is also fundamental to other arts. But what if this idea [about architecture] was merely a cliché based on a misinterpretation, stubbornly persisting within the literature on the fine arts. I would like to remove this misunderstanding according to which architecture is a 'bound' art and prefer to speak of architecture as a 'binding' art. If the perfect participle [bound], primarily expresses a compulsion, is replaced by the present participle 'binding', the meaning is changed decisively. Architecture as a binding art is therefore the active art of connectivity.

With this re-interpretation it is possible for architecture to move beyond its dependence as a pseudo-art or pseudo-technology, to take on a meaning and intent, which in the first instance only applies to architecture itself. Thus architecture is able to fulfil the encompassing meaning of *archi* and *technos* in the sense of an 'arch-art' and 'arch-technology', hierarchically placed above the arts and technology.

› Rules and their prerequisites

How can architecture justify this role? And how can it succeed in binding together such different requirements and problems?

To answer this question we may envisage architecture as an orchestra. Every musician can be a virtuoso on their own instrument, he can do what ever he pleases, but whenever several musicians play together they can no longer play whatever they like according to their own whims, which would produce a disastrous cacophony. Even if the individual played correctly and sensibly, as a whole and in playing together it would make no sense. Playing together is only possible when prior rules are agreed, according to which everyone knows what, or what not, to do. Only then can a collective sense be achieved.

It is not so different in architecture, where distinct elements associated with different conditions, come together to make a constituent whole. Nothing can be held together without rules. Thus, one of the essential attributes of architecture is to construct a framework of rules.

› Everything is composition

We have established that architecture, given the application of rules, designates an ability to bring conventionally independent requirements like use, material and design, into relation with each other; and furthermore that it binds together different imperatives. These may be firstly: the desire for a proportional arrangement in which repetition is the simplest form of rhythm – which, however, becomes more complex through spatial layering; and secondly for a sense of an integration into a single unit in order to achieve an overall composition.

This can be based on different principles, namely:

1. Symmetry, in which coordination occurs evenly.
2. Proportion, in which the individual parts or stages are set in particular relation to each other.
3. Axial arrangement in which one or more parts are directionally orientated.
4. Contrast, which makes visible the differences between individual elements.

In order to establish rules, composition seems to be an essential requirement. And vice versa, if architecture is the art of establishing rules, then we can say that with this attribute is linked the need for composition. Generally composition involves the bringing together of parts into a whole and we talk of a composition when several different parts are brought into a wider order or framework and therefore achieve a coherent singular expression. If, for example, several buildings are combined to form a street or a square, this is inherently a composition.

Consequently anything can be subject to composition – no matter whether it is a purpose, a construction, a façade, or a space to be composed. Because anything and everything can be related in compositional terms, the ability to compose is the prerequisite for any intellectual activity. Insofar as reality is determined by an intellectual aspect to experience, then this reality is part of a composition. Nothing makes sense without being composed. Without composition, we could not even communicate, because language is enabled by composition. Composition is thus primarily associated with creativity and stands at the onset of any act of design. If architecture and composition are equivalent terms, then architecture can be seen as the mother of the arts, both of the binding arts and the 'bound' arts. It is therefore understandable that we can speak of the tectonic structure of music, of poetry, but also of nature itself. We can therefore establish that without composition there is no architecture. To finally answer the question posed at the beginning, 'what is architecture'? Well architecture is composition – an answer which, in this truncated form reads like a predetermined programme in danger of sounding like an advertising slogan and apt to degenerate into a formulaic term – too similar perhaps to 'form follows function', the slogan of functionalism.

*　*　*

Editors' note: Inaugural Lecture, TU Berlin, Summer Semester 1964.

68 Aldo Rossi

Architecture for museums (1968)

A. Rossi, 'Architettura per i musei', Guido Canella et al., *Theoria della progettazione architettonica*, Bari: Dedalo, 1968, from: Aldo Rossi, 'Architecture for Museums' (Architettura per i musei), *Aldo Rossi – Selected Writings and Projects*, Dublin: Gandon, 1983, extracts pp. 14, 17–20, 21–24 and 25, translation by Luigi Beltrandi.[1]

The creation of a design theory is the first objective of an architectural school before all other types of research. A design theory is the most important and creative moment of every architecture, thus in an architectural school, a theory of design course should be its driving force.

One could remark on the rarity of existence of design theories, or in other words, rational explanations of how to make architecture. One stumbles across some writings on this matter, perhaps by the most naïve or the greatest of men. Above all one notices how these people who take a few principles of a theoretical line become so uncertain of those theories as to never wish to verify them, in what is the most important moment of any theory. In other words, the relation between a theoretical vision of architecture and the making of architecture. In the end one can only say this: that for some a theory is only a rationalization of a previous action—therefore it tends to be a norm rather than a theory.

At the risk of appearing naïve, I propose to trace a truthful and appropriate theory of design, in other words forming a theory of design as an integral part of a theory of architecture.

*   *   *

I will now briefly state what I mean by 'architecture'. I mean 'architecture' in a positive sense, as a creation inseparable from life and society, a great deal of which is a collective happening. The first men in building themselves dwellings, created a more favourable space for their existence. In building themselves an artificial climate, they followed an aesthetic intention. They began architecture by creating the rudiments of a city. Architecture is therefore integral with the forming of a civilization, and is a lasting necessity and universal happening. The basics of architecture lie in the creation of a space for comfortable life, together with aesthetic intention. Enlightenment writers take up this view when they refer to the primitive hut as the positive foundation of architecture. Therefore architecture is created with the forming of the city and in time dwellings and monuments are created. Dwellings and monuments, private and public events, are the reference terminology for the study of the city which have imposed themselves from the beginning and constitute the principles of classification of an Aristotelian analysis of the city. Architecture and the city detach themselves from any other science because they propose themselves as an adaptation of nature, having been once natural elements. This type of definition runs the length of the history of architectural thought and can be summed up in the definition of Viollet le Duc as a *creation humaine* and in the more recent one of Levi-Strauss that describes the city as *chose humaine par excellence.* On reflection, nothing stuns one more than those great man-made objects that run across the countryside, as architecture that sets itself up as a transformation from nature to man-made work. The whole of the city and its surroundings then play a part in this construction. They are part of architecture. Carlo Cattaneo once talked in this way of the city as an artificial homeland for man and stated that one cannot understand the reality of the countryside or the surroundings of cities without realizing that they are an enormous deposit of spent energy. This deposit of spent energy represents, in time, the real formation of a city. When Francesco Milizia attempted to make a definition of the city (I quote Milizia because of his characteristic enlightenment approach towards architecture) he took up the question of the definition of architecture in relation to other art forms by taking his definition back to the eighteenth century naturalism, and wrote: *Architecture lacks that model formed by nature, but it has another formed by man, by following natural industry in the building of the first dwellings.* By considering architecture in this manner he is forced to discard the image of naturalistic imitation and returns to a historical vision.

I have described the principles of an architectural theory which I have already developed in other writings. One has now to ask oneself what are the implications of an informative process of this analysis, and what are, in general, the forms of contributions that architectural theory makes to design. In other words, what is the relevance, what worth has the knowledge of certain principles for design? I think one can answer, in the first instance, that they are tournaments of the same process, and effectively when one is designing one has knowledge; therefore one comes close to a theory of design the more that one defines a theory of architecture. In this way all ancient and modern architects have taken up, at a time, analysis and design in their writings.

But, if architectural principles are permanent and necessary, how can they then become the history of different and real architectures? I think one can only say this: that principles in architecture, insofar as their foundations are concerned, have no history, they are fixed and unchangeable; but solutions are constantly changing, and so do the answers that architects give to these real solutions. I had better make a distinction between the difference in character of the questions and answers.

One has to distinguish between the city and the architecture of the city as a collectively made object, and architecture for its own sake, architecture as a technique, as an art form that is ordered and passed on in a traditional way. In the first instance it is a collective process, slow and traceable over a length of time, in which the whole of the city, society and humanity with all its different forms play a part. In this way the urban evolution, the changing face of the city, is a slow and indirect process which needs to be studied by following its laws and peculiarities. Think about the different layers that constitute a city in its coherence and to those reactions that create new elements.

In this way the study of a city can be compared to the study of a language: in particular it is clear that the study of a city sheds light on analogies with the study of a language, especially in the complexity of the process of modification and permanence. I am referring to de Saussure on the development of linguistics. A theory of the city, an urban science, treated in these terms, can only be separated with difficulty from an architectural theory; especially if one accepts the first hypothesis: that architecture is born out of, and is one with, the traces of a city. But by this formation, and by its continuous involvement with the urban context, even architecture elaborates certain principles, and transmits itself by certain laws, that make it autonomous. It elaborates a doctrinal body.

Let us look for a moment at a monument, the Pantheon. Let us leave behind the urban complexity that precedes this architecture, for in a way one can refer to the project of the Pantheon, or directly to the principles, to the logistical terminology, that precedes its design. I believe that the lesson one can learn from this terminology is as much a part of the present as the lesson learnt from a modern architectural work. For one can compare two works and see how the whole of the architectural argument, in all its complexities, reduced to its basic terms, can be incorporated into a single argument.

Architecture then presents itself as a mediation of events and happenings; the unalterable principles are few, but the answers that the architect and society give to the problems encountered in the course of time are many. The unalterability is due to the rational and seducing character of architectonic terms. *If unity has to exist in architecture, it cannot happen by applying a number of different forms to it, but only in the search for that form that is the expression of – and is prescribed by reason.* These are the words of Viollet le Duc, but they could be from any other rational architect, for in architectural history this situation is so apparent as almost to be defined as a characteristic.

Alessandre Laborde, in his work consecrated to the French monument, like Quatremère de Quincy, praised artists of the late eighteenth century and early nineteenth century for having gone to Rome to study and experience the unalterable principles of those more advanced studies, thus following the footsteps of antiquity. The architects of the new school presented themselves as scholars perceptive to the real events of their science, architecture.

Architecture then followed a steady path because its teachers were concerned with the forming of a logic of architecture based on essential principles. *There are both artists and servants; artists are used to observation and criticism.* One takes this approach to architecture as a science of logically formed principles, of a compromise of architectural events; and therefore, basing it principally on monuments, one tries to verify by means of certain chosen architects both ancient and modern. Architecture, Le Corbusier wrote, means the formulation of clear problems, everything depends on this, and this is the decisive moment. This idea can be found in the thoughts of both ancient and modern masters, and is almost obsessive in the writings of Adolf Loos who declared that architecture can only be described and not drawn. This type of logical formulation permits a characteristic description of great architecture. The Pantheon can be described, the buildings of the Secession cannot. Now, I ask myself, how is it possible to formalize all this, how can one arrive at a theory of design from a series of terms that form the basis of an architectural theory? Architecture has to be brought back to itself. I refer to all those statements and arguments that wish to establish whether architecture is an art or a science: of these many create false problems for they have no solution. On the other hand, one must not explain architecture on borrowed knowledge external to it.

Now, without wishing to pass quickly from a theory of architecture to a theory of design, I shall state what I consider to be the fundamental points of a design theory.

They are firstly the study of monuments, secondly the argument on form and the physical world, and lastly the study of the city; or better a new bilateral conception of urban architecture.

On the first point, the study of monuments, the Modern Movement, but not its masters, has created a kind of terrorism against it, as if it is almost impossible to talk about it. Tafuri, because of this, has stated that masters such as Le Corbusier, Loos and others have always talked about monuments and the importance of their study, whilst the scholars, in particular such authors as Giovannoni, have been responsible for proposing an environment as the alternative to the monument. I have to admit that in the first decades of the twentieth century there was a justified reaction against that stupid historicism, that so-called imitation of the antique, and the eclectic use of historical styles; but today one can clearly resubmit oneself to the study of monuments without compromising one's position.

*   *   *

The discussion on the second point I mentioned, on the problem of form, is a difficult one, full of ambiguities. I will simply say that by form I mean a precise sign that is found in reality and is the measure of a process of transformation. In this way architectural form is something closed and perfect, still part of a logical terminology. Because of this I believe that the Roman aqueducts, for example, are form and sign, which precisely modify a type of reality and define the image that we have of that reality. Naturally, in referring to a Roman aqueduct, rather than another work, I am making a certain choice and this choice is part of my poetry. It is natural that one could substitute for a Roman bridge another man-made work, but an example such as this seems to me an interesting one for it refers to an insertion in a natural world, and points out the particular meaning of an historical event. I am personally fascinated by the development of late Enlightenment thought. Even in its more modern forms, as the polemic of the finished and completely finished, form proposes itself as a sign of mobility of events as classical and neoclassical thoughts, or more recently developments of formal logic in neo-Aristotelian thought. But on this third point, form has a new field which rightly belongs to the theory of design, which the designer cannot forget. I am referring to the city, to the study of the construction of the city. I have called all this 'architecture of the city', and I am again referring to the physical form of the city, to its construction and to the city as a man-made object. These are not only problems of urban context. We have attempted an analytical study of the city, of its formation, of its most important phenomena, and the nature of urban events.

I believe that before setting out how the foundation of a theory of the city can also be the basis for a new architecture one should closely look at how the problem of the city, the urban context, etc., has come up in Italian architecture as an overriding problem. This is necessary to see the real importance, and also to see the distortion or the double aspect which it has taken, on the one hand with the problem of the construction of the new city, of the understanding of the ancient one, of the basis of architecture and, on the other, with the problems of environment, of conservation, etc.

At University at the end of the war, we found ourselves faced with a particular aspect of the crisis of the Modern Movement; this aspect regarded the problems of designs and the teaching of design. The Modern Movement had based its theories of design on certain fixed points: they were method and function. On these points much had been written; one knew its importance, especially of function, and the vastness of the problems that they encompassed. The crisis of functionalism soon became the crisis of that same poetry of rationalism and of organic architecture.

On the other hand urban studies were being undertaken before attempting to look at the scientific aspects of the problem; it was almost a state of mind, one did not know to which work and what writer to refer. Certain experiences, like those of Le Corbusier, were almost ignored. At this point a very important book came out (I am referring to the Italian context, but if this context wasn't still today a little isolated, it could also apply to the rest of *Europe*)—*L'Urbanistica e l'arvenire della citta*.

I now refer to all those works that for the first time proposed something different: going against a static situation and showing a different basis for our studies. This basis was the city, seen for the first time in its entirety, as a continuous line of evolution. It gave a decisive shove to the petty moralism that unfortunately still presides in urban studies. The city became an event of such importance that we must come to terms with it, even and especially from the architectural point of view.

If one looks at the issues of *Casabella Continuità* of the time, one sees the development of this polemic, and the re-examination, made by a group of young Italian architects and Ernesto N. Rogers which never turned away from the more problematic aspects of architecture. A larger examination runs parallel with this renewed interest in the city, conducted from inside architecture, but of the same architecture which makes up our cities. To me it seems necessary to study and indicate the principal aspects of neoclassicism as the formative moment of an Italian city in a European sense: Milan.

Certain projects of the Napoleonic plan of Milan, and the plan itself, were recognizable by certain pre-eminent architectural characteristics. These projects were a unity at a time when a political choice of a progressive nature encountered a rational architecture, transmittable from one society to another, and from one country to another. Thus a new value to an architectural culture was being stated, but maybe also a new architecture was being constituted.

From all this stems the idea of a city where the monuments represent fixed points of human creation; tangible signs of the action of reason, and collective memory. When the dwelling becomes the real problem for man's way of life then day by day he improves and organizes the space in which he lives according to his basic necessity. Thus, the structure lays itself out in different ways by following the laws of dynamics of a city, but always with these fixed elements, the dwelling and those primary elements, the monuments. These differentiations inside the city do not correspond simply to specific functions even if they include some of them. A city is made up of urban events of different natures, which are conceived differently.

I believe that this conception is already a way of making architecture as much as a way of understanding it. I believe that differences of design in themselves can be taken out of this distinction and not only by designing fragments of a city, but concerned with architecture in itself.

The highest measure of an architect will still be the monument, just because the monument is the final sign of a more complex reality; it is the sign upon which one reads something that cannot otherwise be said, for it belongs to the biography of the artist and the history of society.

The functionalist conception is overturned; function is an instrument in architectural experience. I still believe in the ability of building a system in the teaching of design from the development of this theory of the city.

But I cannot end this study without mentioning the problem which I believe to be fundamental for us architects and for a theory of design—I am referring to the subjective element.

Just as one sees the relations between a theory of architecture and a theory of design we have to see the relations that exist between a theory of design and the subjective contribution, if one wants an autobiography of an artist.

In other words, if one was to put into practice what was stated at the beginning, quoting Raymond Roussel, *How I have made some of my architecture* in fact it is indispensable that in making this or that determinate architecture one does not wish to express to someone else something of his—at least if one is not completely second rate. But how does one reconcile this contribution with those rational principles, upon which I have insisted, with a classical-rational matrix? Certainly in a more complex way than can be brought together by those theories where subjectivity is the only way of producing and where a system is ambiguously produced.

On the other hand, he who looks for poetic elements of rationalist architecture cannot detach himself from what Lessing said: *Increase in clarity has always been, for me, an increased beauty,* and still one could take the famous statement of Cezanne as a manifesto, *I paint only for museums.* In this statement Cezanne clearly declared the need for a painting style, following a logical and rigorous development, and placing itself inside the logic of painting verified in museums.

But the development and the verification offered by museums does not alter the subjective element of a work; that belongs to human quality. One can be detached from what Lessing, described as a 'Modern Aristotelian', wrote

> *Any genius is a born critic . . . and establishing that criticism and regulations can repress the genius is to agree that examples and practice can do the same. This not only means to isolate the genius in himself, but to shut him up at his first attempts; he who reasons in the right way is also capable of invention . . . he who wants to invent has to be capable of reason, and it is only the ones that are unable to do both that believe the two can be separated.*

*   *   *

To conclude: rigorous argument about architectural design has to be based upon a logical foundation; and it is this, in its most general form, which is the rationalist position towards architecture and its building. I believe in the possibility of an education which is covered by a

ALDO ROSSI

system where the world of form is as logically clear as any other architectural notion, by considering this as meaning as transmittable in architecture as in any other form of thought.

Architecture was born out of need, now it is autonomous; in its highest form it creates museum places which are drawn upon by technicians to be transformed and adapted to the multiple functions and needs to which they have to be applied.

Thus one has to educate oneself about the analysis of the basic constructive character of a project and this is how a design theory must propose itself.

› Note

1   This essay – 'Architettura per i musei' – is based on the seminar of the theory of architectural design given at the Istituto Universitario dell' Architettura di Venezia, in the 1965–66 academic year.

69 Leon Krier

The age of reconstruction (1980)

The reconstruction of the European city (1980)

Leon Krier, 'The age of reconstruction', from: *Leon Krier Drawings 1967–1980*, AAM, 1980, extracts pp. xv and xxv–xxxi.

* * *

> ## The age of reconstruction

A CITY CAN ONLY BE RECONSTRUCTED IN THE FORM OF
STREETS AND SQUARES AND URBAN QUARTERS.
THE QUARTERS MUST INTEGRATE ALL FUNCTIONS OF URBAN LIFE,
IN AREAS WHICH MUST NOT EXCEED 35 HA AND 15.000 PEOPLE.
THE STREETS + SQUARES MUST PRESENT A FAMILIAR CHARACTER.
THEIR DIMENSIONS + PROPORTIONS MUST BE THOSE OF THE BEST + MOST
BEAUTIFUL PRE-INDUSTRIAL CITIES.
SIMPLICITY MUST BE THE GOAL OF AN URBAN PLAN,
HOWEVER COMPLEX THE URBAN GEOGRAPHY AND TOPOGRAPHY.
THE CITY MUST BE ARTICULATED INTO
PUBLIC + DOMESTIC SPACES.
MONUMENTS + URBAN FABRIC.
CLASSICAL ARCHITECTURE + VERNACULAR BUILDINGS.
SQUARES + STREETS
AND IN THAT HIERARCHY.

* * *

> ## The reconstruction of the European city

* * *

Zoning and politics

The politics of industrial infrastructure has been based on the spatial (territorial) separation of functions.

All industrial states independently of their ideology have promoted and imposed the functional ZONING of the cities and countryside with equal brutality and pseudo-scientific arguments against whichever resistance of urban or rural populations.

Functional Zoning is not an innocent instrument; it has been the most effective means in destroying the infinitely complex social & physical fabric of pre-industrial urban communities, of urban democracy and culture.

Functional Zoning of city and countryside has been an authoritarian project corresponding nowhere to a democratic demand.

Zoning is the ABSTRACTION of city & countryside. We know now, that an anti-urban philosophy condemns ipso facto the countryside.

One cannot destroy the cities without also destroying the countryside.

Zoning is the ABSTRACTION of communities; it reduces the proudest communities to mere statistical entities, expressed in numbers & densities.

Zoning, dictated by big industry and their financial and administrative empires, can be fought only by democratic pressure that demands the reconstruction of urban communities where RESIDENCE, WORK and LEISURE are all within walking distance.

*   *   *

The quarters

A large or a small city can only be reorganised as a large or a small number of urban quarters, a federation of autonomous quarters.

Each quarter must have its own centre, periphery and limit. Each quarter must be "A CITY WITHIN THE CITY".

The QUARTER must integrate all daily functions of urban life (dwelling, working, leisure) within a territory dimensioned on the comfort of a walking man, not exceeding 35 ha in surface and 15000 inhabitants.

Tiredness sets a natural limit to what a human being is prepared to walk daily and this limit has taught man all through history the size of rural or urban communities.

There seems on the contrary to be no natural limit to the size of a functional ZONE; the BOREDOM which befalls man while driving a car has made him forget any sense of physical limit.

*   *   *

Building and architecture

Building is the material culture of construction. As a craft, it is concerned with the construction or domestic structures, of workshops, of warehouses, of engineering works, it is generally concerned with the erection of the urban fabric, of building blocks which form the streets of the city, its retaining walls, bridges etc. Building culture is basically concerned with the repetition of a few building-types and the adaptation to local conditions of use, of materials and climate.

Architecture is the intellectual culture of building. As an art, it is concerned with the imitation and translation of the elements of building into symbolic language, expressing in a fixed system of symbols and analogies the very origin of Architecture in the laws of nature and in human intelligence and labour.

The very condition of Architecture to exist is to attain to material and above all to intellectual permanence.

It can be no business of Architecture to express ever-changing functions.

Certain building-types merely become associated with certain functions and celebrations and it is up to sculptural or pictorial iconography to help and sustain these associations.

Architecture is only concerned with the erection of public buildings and monuments, with the construction of public squares.

For classical architecture the notions of progress and innovation do no longer exist, because it has solved all technical and artistic problems in solidity, in beauty, in permanence and commodity.

City architecture building

It is only a dialectic of Architecture and Building, of Classical and Vernacular cultures, of public and domestic that can endow human settlements with the dignity of a collective culture.

Only a great functional complexity can lead to a readable, clear permanently satisfying and beautiful articulation of the urban spaces and quarters, of the city as a whole.

Simplicity and evidence must be the goal of the very complexity of the urban plan and silhouette.

A city articulated into

public and domestic spaces
monuments and urban fabric
Architecture and building
squares and streets

and in that HIERARCHY.

Vernacular and classicism

Classical and Vernacular cultures oppose the production and consumption of futile objects.

Classical and Vernacular do not erect class distinctions but distinction between collective and individual, between monuments and urban fabric, public palace and domestic dwelling.

Classical and Vernacular cultures are based on the repetition of a few fundamental CONSTRUCTIVE and FUNCTIONAL TYPES which are the universal expression of human activities, of collective and individual work and pleasure.

Architecture and Building as Classical and Vernacular cultures are based on imitative systems of production, on artisanal tradition, where intellectual and manual faculties are exercised in harmony and not in contradiction.

In an artisanal culture, material or intellectual innovations become accepted only for their technical or artistic improvement and not as a result of a freewheeling imagination. This process of slow and constant clarification and elaboration involving all the skills and intelligence of the individual artisan or artist are the source of true pleasure of authentic culture.

Classical Architecture as the symbolic elaboration of vernacular building does not know INNOVATION as a virtue. It does not know Styles but one Style which is fixed and immutable in its typological and morphological essence, but infinitely varied in their realisation, as are all objects of nature.

Architecture and Building are not objects of consumption. They can only be reconstructed in a perspective of material permanence.

Without such permanence, without architecture transcending the lifespan of its builders, no public space, no collective expression as craft or art are ever possible (Hannah ARENDT).

* * *

Neo-rationalism in Retrospect

70 Manfredo Tafuri

History of Italian architecture, 1944–1985 (1982)

Manfredo Tafuri, *Storia dell'architettura italiana*, Torino: Giulio Einaudi editore s.p.a., 1982, from: Manfredo Tafuri, *History of Italian Architecture*, Cambridge Massachusetts: MIT, 1989, extracts pp. 135–139 and 141–146, translation by Jessica Levine.

› The "case" of Aldo Rossi

Gabetti and Isola, Canella, and Gae Aulenti thus used different means to induce a state of fatigue in the materials of language, thereby evoking extreme unpleasantness and intellectual *sensiblerie*. Among the paths left open by the themes discussed in Rogers' arena, there remained the search for the principal elements of the architectural process, a search that led to a liberation from fixed contexts and a movement toward a horizon where private and collected pasts merged. Aldo Rossi was the protagonist of this search: an architect who, beginning in the mid 1960s, presented himself as the most watched and discussed "case" both in Italy and on the international scene, the only "school leader" capable of constantly fueling around his own works and self a controversy and an interest that ended by affecting the very concept of architecture. We have already seen that Rossi was one of Rogers' students, active in the group of writers working for *Casabella continuità*, the designer of one of the most polemical projects presented to the competition for the office district of Turin, and of the "bridge" executed for the 1964 Triennale of Milan. But the complexity and exceptional coherence of his work soon placed him outside of contingent polemics: Rossi did not intend to dirty his hands in controversy; his *poiesis* refused to compromise with reality, since the only way to return to the "ancient house of language" was by maintaining an attitude of surly indifference.

It is undeniable, however, that Rossi's poetics contained a secret reaction to the *desengaño* that Italian architects experienced in the sixties. This too indicated that he was interested in themes and forms that had been swept away by a moralistic gust of wind just after the war. At the twelfth Triennale of Milan, Rossi exhibited a project for the restructuring of the zone around Via Farini: it was an optimistic project, meant to refashion an identity for the suburbs. But the year was 1960, and this optimism soon proved unfounded. In the same year, Rossi's villa in Ronchi, Versilia, hailed the "discovery" of Adolf Loos, whom Rossi celebrated in 1959 in an article in *Casabella*. As he began his search for primary forms, Rossi reflected upon Loos's work as well as that of Max Bill; these forms were exiled from the urban sphere, but spoke of their exile in order to propose a theory of the city as the *locus* of collective memory. There followed in 1964 the competition project for the Teatro Paganini in Parma, in 1965 the monument for the Partisans in Segrate, in 1966 the competition project for a residential complex in San Rocco in Monza, done in collaboration with Giorgio Grassi, and a book, *Architecture of the City*. On the one hand, there was an attempt to redefine urban science through an encounter with the French school's geography; on the other hand, there was the evaporation of the image in search of the pressure point where one can draw from memory a real epiphany of signs. The triangle, the cube, the cone: these obsessive, stripped figures kept reappearing in Rossi's projects. They were not finalized for the sake of an abstract elementarist search, but attempted to circumscribe the source of form in progressively smaller circles. *Desengaño* had become eloquent. It was necessary to turn one's back on the "noise of the world" in order to contemplate places whose alienation had become sacral—the golden suburbs, reminiscent of Sironi's, that appear in Rossi's designs, such as places where life seemed suspended—the project for a new cemetery in Modena of 1971, and also the metaphysical courtyard at the De Amicis school in Broni of 1970. Rossi's projects began to flounder, sinking increasingly into a new realm of images whose source was De Chirico, frozen in spaces abandoned by time, and Böcklin's "unhappy vision." The Gallaratese block, the elementary school in Fagnano Olona of 1972, the projects for the town hall of Muggiò of 1972 and for Villa Bay in Borgo Ticino of 1972, were contrasted with designs, collages, and rallying cries of the seventies. The assembled forms referred to the astonishing fixity of Giorgio Morandi's objects: a hidden eye explored the form-giving act, spying on the hand and mind of the artist, and encountering, in the deepest memories, only words already spoken, but now aligned in sinister fashions or piled in disorderly heaps.

Nor did it matter that the search for a primordial essence was constantly being frustrated. On the contrary, this led to a ceaseless renovation of the game of transformation, played by materials reduced to their zero degree. This was demonstrated in the successive versions of the project for the Modena cemetery, in Rossi's returning to already tested forms in order to make them converse with each other, in the different versions of his "analogous city," and in the insistent way that the spectral presence of *San Carlo Borromeo* menaced architectural assemblies, with or without "domestic objects." The imagined project concerned a new collective need in a universe that was robbing individual action of its element of fantasy. But whoever immerses himself in imaginary realms today—as Blanchot has warned us—is forced to annul space and time, to send them deep into the nothingness of "literary space." This annulment is indecent and provocative. It has nothing to do with the classical *Entsagung*; it is based on the amoral principle of abstention. Not coincidentally, Rossi's work provoked choruses of indignation, as well as unreflecting love. Yet Rossi had the courage to contemplate this "nothing," to project its impalpable signs onto a magic urn, the mirror of a dream that was being narrated in public. Rossi's *mémoire* was heir to the overwhelming autobiographical trend of the fifties, but it preferred archaic silence to the opulence of Gadda's rhetorical flourishes. For this reason, its introspection was expressed in a humorous and thoughtful work, the Teatrino Scientifico, or little theater of 1978. The Teatrino, which features in its triangular pediment a clock permanently set at five o'clock (in the evening?), is a small temple in the shape of a "little house," the only one appropriate to hold Rossi's architectural works, which are arranged there as permanent and movable sets. The space of representation coincides with the representation of space: Rossi wished to convince himself of this with his metaphysical theater.

But this coincidence had already been announced in the "agitated silence" of the inner courtyard of the school in Fagnano Olona and in the "museum in the shape of a baptistry" that appeared in the competition project for the office district of Florence of 1977. Representation was everything: it was useless to worry about secondary meanings in inaccessible realms. The city—in spite of Rossi's statements to the contrary—revealed itself as a simple pretext. But it was also true that representation presupposed models, archetypes, and figures as points of reference. Rossi's typological research is confined, not coincidentally, to self-description: the type, motionless, does not make history, its repeating and being repeated recall Tessenow's will for *naïveté*. In this way, Rossi's universe may still be experienced as a labyrinthian landscape in which misleading tracks, left by the memory of the artist, confuse the visitor. Architecture is placed fearfully in the balance: its reality, never denied, is perversely bound to the unreal. Lissitzky's Proun changed the course of direction, but continued to fluctuate in an ineffable universe.

Rossi's words assumed the dignity of alchemical signs especially in the projects, designs, and engravings he did in the seventies. In *The Elba Cabins* (1973), in *The Copernican City*, and in *Memories of Florence*, an obstinate magus refuses to look into the Galilean telescope, and instead manipulates an esoteric alphabet. Rossi's rigorism was the condition of his imaginary realm: it sought to demonstrate that alienation can be narrated, that whoever knows how to become a child can escape aphasia. One must be a sublimely irresponsible individual—and this is precisely the point. It explains Rossi's resorting to infantile schemes or to a geometric elementarism reminiscent of Durand's tables: typical, in this regard, were the project for the Palazzo della Regione of Trieste of 1974, homage to an *Aufklärung* without time, and the Teatro del Mondo, which was moored as a poetic and fleeting apparition next to the customs pier in Venice in 1979.

Yet "Dieses ist lange her / Now this is long gone" was the title of an engraving that Rossi did in 1975, in which, as in his watercolor "Architecture Assassinated"—dedicated, perhaps polemically, to this writer—he presented his dreams in a state of collapse. It was, however, a frozen collapse: the fragments dangling or projected into empty space remained immobile. The loss was not painful: the traveler was prepared for it. The "bridge," a supersignifying metaphysical figure that, in projects ranging from the 1964 Triennale to the monument in Segrate and the Gallaratese block, presented itself as connecting inconceivable extremes—memory and history, sign and meaning, the individual and external reality—broke and flew off into space, carrying with it the fragments of a painful will for knowledge.

› Rigorism and abstinence: toward the 1980s

It is only possible to decipher Aldo Rossi's alchemical alphabet as a normal dictionary if one sees his work as tautological. "A rose is a rose is a rose is rose . . ." Giorgio Grassi's "logical construction of architecture" stayed within the boundaries of pure reiteration. While Rossi represented his heartbroken exploration of "origins" with a confession of repeated failure, Grassi resigned himself to a search for "essences" and noumena extracted from a fixed grasp of primary forms. For him, logic coincided with the classical—not the classical as exemplified by Goethe's insatiable resignation, but that of Winckelmann's atemporal perfection, identified with the spectral reiterations of Weinbrenner's Langestrasse in Karlsruhe and Hilberseimer's laconic images. Grassi's research was initially tangential to Rossi's, and the two collaborated on a few works: the hotel at the mountain pass of Monte Croce Comelico of 1963, the ISES quarter in Naples of 1968, and the San Rocco quarter in Monza of 1966. But Grassi's work later differentiated itself from Rossi's by a will for knowledge turned in on itself. His projects for a laboratory to manufacture equipment for biological research in Paullo of 1968, for the restoration of the viscount's castle in Abbiategrasso of 1970, for a residential unit also in Abbiategrasso of 1972, for riverside residences in Pavia of 1970–73, and for the secondary school in Tollo all question typologies such as the courtyard and portico, and compositional strategies such as symmetry and rhythmic constancy. They aspire to the blank page; the controversy surrounding what Grassi called "disconnected parody" was resolved in a display of rigorist certainties. It is, moreover, undoubtedly true that the linguistic purification accomplished by Grassi had remarkable consequences. In the plan to salvage the historical center of Teora in Avellino and in the recent project for the reconstruction of the Prinz Albrecht Palais in Berlin, both done with Agostino Renna, the attempt to commemorate Karl Ludwig Schinkel's classical dream was not intended to be pleasurable, and the dessication of forms reached a dignity rich in implications. And with the recent project for the restoration of the Roman theater in Sagunto, Giorgio Grassi's poetics took another qualitative leap forward, demonstrating the fertility of the laconic vocabulary it had chosen.

It is significant that ideas like Grassi's can be evaluated in contrast with the evil contemporary city. Silence can, of course, be resounding when surrounded by noise; it remains to be seen whether that silence can really express something besides the simple will to know, and whether the testimony it offers can have more than the mere value of a symptom.

It should not be surprising that the methods of Rossi and Grassi succeeded in creating a "school." Those who turned to them were in general anxious to find the great mother again, to rest by returning to the womb of Architecture, and to divorce themselves from the miseries of contingency. The didactic success of these two men was a litmus test revealing the anguish and "void of values" pressing in upon the younger generation; that success does not, however, justify the attempt to construct a *tendenza* by putting Rossi's wandering signs on a par with Leon Krier's research, Aymonino's eclecticism, Dardi's eloquence, Ludwig Leo's machinism, or Adolfo Natalini's "continuous monuments," as was done at the fifteenth Triennale of Milan in 1973, under the formula "Rational Architecture."[1] For Rossi, who was responsible for the international sector of architecture at that Triennale, it was a matter of a large collage, which arranged fragments according to a technically organized surrealism. For the facile exegetes, it was a new church in which to burn incense; for the opposing factions, it was an "exhibit on the Starace model" and a return to terms dangerously reminiscent of totalitarian rhetoric.

In reality, Rossi, Grassi, and their immediate circle were not the only ones trying to construct architecture with its own elements and *of those elements only*. If the work of the GRAU members, after the project for the Florence archives, was disappointing, the work done by Franco Purini and Laura Thermes, by the Roman group Labirinto and especially by Paolo Martellotti, and by a few of Quaroni's students revealed itself to be similar, at least in its attempt to define a universe that mirrors itself in the limitations of form. They achieved, in the best cases, an autonomy of language dialectically spoken to the other by the self, and in the worse cases, a segregation presumptuously satisfied with its own immobility.

An insatiable demand for rigor, offset by sudden moments of lyrical abandon, found its way into the stacks of designs produced by these new purists. And, whether they, like Purini, focused on a configuration of events testing the consistency and elusiveness of compositional materials, or whether—as with the Labirinto in reconstructing the Calcografia Nazionale in Rome in 1973–75—they experimented with values inherent in the calculated distortion of visual structures, their program included a self-imposed behavior and approached moralizing. "To take a generation out of the running," Purini and Thermes wrote, "one has only to encourage youth to cultivate the myth of total moral 'integrity': thus they will not know how to accept and practice compromise, certainly not of the petty kind, but of the sort which defines politics as the art of the possible, as the dialectic of the real." Ritual was equated with the obstinate search for the laws determining form. Moreover, an "integrity" without purpose and also without social outlets must eventually be colored with mysticism. The rigor of "words" sets limits to the "frivolous": not coincidentally, it becomes more and more confined to design. The professional abstinence to which, for objective and subjective reasons, that generation seemed condemned, invited reason to travel to the limits of the permissible: in "designed architecture"—the goal and prison of whoever wanted to claim, "I, too, am Piranesi"—narcissistic practices abounded, as well as calls for a totality of values otherwise unobtainable. The Kafkaesque atmospheres created by these occasionally refined graphic universes have something coherent about them (perhaps too coherent): in empty space, they made words resound and set forth superfluous laws.

That all this, moreover, could create a climate suitable for the reproduction and autonomous life of these rituals was demonstrated by projects like the detailed plan for the new university in Cagliari of 1977–78, formulated by the group coordinated by M. Luisa Anversa and Marcello Rebecchini, and by the result of competitions like those for the office district of Florence of 1977 and for the construction of a piazza on the site of the old military bakery of Ancona of 1978. The competition in Florence no longer gave rise to musings on the destiny of the "terziario" services sector or to bodies concerned with encompassing and condensing nuclei to restructure the national countryside. Marco Porta, working with Purini, Emilio Battisti, Cesare Macchi Cassia, and collaborators, tried to make his project harmonize with Gregotti's university system, adjacent to the new office district, as well as with the marks that history had left on the region. A sum of themes emerged: the rotation of axes, the variation of the walled boundary, and the strongholds emerging from an ideal centuriatio. Vocabulary inferred from the work of Rossi, Gregotti, and Purini formed a lexicon, as was demonstrated by the projects of the Vernuccio group, the Rosa-Cornoldi-Sajeva-Manlio Savi group, the Polesello group, and in some ways by the Angelini-Dierna-Mortola-Orlandi group.

One of the big Italian competitions after the war, for the office district of Florence—characterized by an announcement that seemed expressly to recommend abstraction to the competitors—did not give rise to a debate between diverging ideas, nor to any significant methodological or formal reflection. The most prestigious competitors stayed within their own "manner": this was true of Giuseppe and Alberto Samonà, Aymonino and Rossi, Fiorentino and Anversa, and even of James Stirling, who was associated here with the Castore group.

In fact, even designed architecture was too limited to contain the universes of the totality of form that constituted the goal of a humanism resulting from the forced acceptance of the marginality of language.

One can take coherence even further in dealing with one's own assumptions; one can turn architectural forms into an imaginary landscape free from the weight of matter. One can, in fact, express with the traditional instruments of engraving, watercolor, and oil paint, the secret aspiration to relive—necessarily as a dream—mythical seasons governed by divine language. And so it happened that Massimo Scolari and Arduino Cantàfora staged their own sublimations with great skill, while a team of younger designers of uneven graphic skill sent a stream of dreamy sketches to private Italian galleries, which accepted them in the hope of forming a new market. In Rome, Bologna, and Milan (as well as New York), exhibits of the designs and engravings of Rossi, Purini, Scolari, Martellotti, and Dario Passi came one after the other, while the "Artistic Encounters" led directly, in 1977–78, to a competition—"Interrupted Rome"—which invited the new international of the imaginary to measure its own fantastic disseminations against places preserved on Nolli's plan. The "need for architecture" thus survived, encouraging skillful collages (such as Nicola Pagliara's architectural works), impatient experimentalism, hymns to "classical" attitudes, songs addressed to the ephemeral, and the "posthumous" violation of inhibitions.

Forced to engage in "parallel actions," the protagonists of this architectural moment thus remained balanced on the ridge separating the *locus solus* of self-reflection from the noisy agora. But they could not partition, consume, and attack the materials of form and history without consequence. The old discipline of "architecture" saw its ruins on a game table surrounded by young players about to make "new techniques" concrete. These players did not, however, despair as they faced the ruins of certainties that had sustained modes of intervention capable only of self-reproduction. The problem was one of controlling differences that were fragmenting the discipline, without imagining them to be precipices in which to sink one's anguish. Faced with a "power" expressing itself in several dialects, no "synthesis" could hold firm; this was also true of the synthesis that began with the theme of form, then aimed at the problem of reform, the golden *domus* of the *Bauen* could therefore be saved without "refounding" and without confounding pleasure with play. It was necessary to proceed "without a home."

At the beginning of the eighties, all that has so far constituted our history appeared to be a "negative prologue" to the new tasks that were taking shape. The "delirious constructions," the story of which we have tried to narrate, were refracted into several languages: urban management, techniques for the reuse of existing structures, construction economics, design on various scales, and formal games. The emphasis initially placed on the "project" had turned into a "criticism of the project," leading to a crisis of models and to the ineffectiveness of passwords: this was the less than negligible result of the intellectual work accomplished by Italian architectural culture during the preceding decades.

› Note

1 Editors' note: all footnotes and references to illustrations have been omitted, with the exception of this extract of the original footnote 3 from Chapter 10 in Tafuri's text: 'The exhibit[ion] did, however, make the mistake of artificially uniting under the unfortunate term of *tendenza*, architectures of opposing *tendenze*: in this respect, the exhibit was in perfect agreement with Portoghesi's exhibit[ion] for the Biennale of Venezia of 1980. Let us mention, therefore, for the benefit of those who are still fond of the term *tendenza*, that Massimo Scolari, who was responsible for it, when recently questioned, said that in 1973 he was making an ironic Dadaist "gesture."'

71 Fritz Neumeyer

A return to humanism in architecture (2002)

Fritz Neumeyer, 'A return to humanism in architecture', from: Hans Kollhoff, *Architektur*, Prestel, 2002, extracts pp. 19, 22–23 and 26, translation by Chris Charlesworth.

*   *   *

If we look at the role of architecture as a medium for making cognition manifest and as a storehouse for knowledge and experience, it is striking that architecture has primarily been called upon to exemplify logical relationships connected with the nature of *physical objects*, about which it is also possible to make precise statements through language. Seen from this perspective, architecture can be understood as the exemplification of the idea of structure just as our concept of system is an exemplification of the "architectonic" itself. The interpretation of architecture as the objectification of the "grand" system of divine reason or universal harmony was based primarily on the visible logic of loads and load-bearing elements as expressing a physical relationship of component parts which make up a solid and self-contained whole.

The meaningfulness of architectural form, in which loads and load-bearing elements are in the same relationship as cause and effect, has also become a model for thought. According to Descartes everything is rational and well founded if we proceed step by step as if we were building a house. Kant sees "architectonics" as the very "art of the system" *per se*. Science is the structural system underpinning reason. That is why science—one could add: just like architecture—is "also merely" the art of building. Kant's famous key proposition: "The whole is thus a well-structured organism (*articulatio*), and not an aggregate (*coacervatio*)" defines a concept of structure that corresponds to the idea of a well-ordered and well-proportioned organic building. Architectonics is thus an abstract symbol of structure, and denotes systematic forms of knowledge and cognition that have been expressed in conceptual terms. Its elementary logic is part of the aesthetics of all built objects. The architectonic of reason thus also takes its legitimation from the symbolic power of its built order, or, to put it another way, from the "aesthetic" power of the system.

*   *   *

Architecture gives rise to the law of vision that states space is visually fixed. For Alberti it follows that the abstract system of rules governing lines, planes, and three-dimensional bodies is also the characteristic tool used to create an effect with architectural form. Like the *theatrum mundi*, the perspective box is the space in which all sensory events take place before our eyes and which is at the same time the anatomical terrain of architecture. This model seems to eliminate the world as the space in which things happen and to adapt it to the observer, who, as the "one perceiving," takes on the role of putting things in their place within the whole.

Like no other art, space-creating, space-defining architecture expresses a reality that is both logical and aesthetic, a reality we relate to not only as an observer but also as a participant. In the same space, which the architectural work of art creates as an aesthetic experience, we are also physically present in a space-time identity. We can enter the space depicted by a painting only in our imagination; in reality we remain outside this space. In architectural space, we are present in the reality of our existence, not just in our imagination. It is precisely this aspect of direct unmediated experience that made modern painters such as Mondrian or [van] Doesburg envious of architecture, with whose help alone the unachievable "great dream" can become reality, namely to finally "place the person not *in front of,* but *in* the painting."

"Architecture for thinkers" refers to the art of placing a person into his own image through spatial enclosure. This happens when we succeed in creating a separate spatial sphere around ourselves and, based on the ideal forms inherent in human intuition, in giving that space corresponding form through a "symbolizing" phenomenon in reality. This would then produce powerful architecture which, as Goethe so beautifully put it, would force us back "in the gentlest possible way into ourselves," because—we could add, following Nietzsche the great unmasker of humankind's ulterior motives—it flatters our artistic "instincts." Alberti probably had something similar in mind when he said of the relationship between convention and innovation: "For battling against the habitual in many respects does bring gratitude, but conforming with it is also of benefit and very advantageous."

Nietzsche called the "desire for simplicity, intelligibility, regularity, and clarity" a powerful "instinct," which "is at work in all sensory activities and reduces, regulates, assimilates etc., the wealth of true (unconscious) perceptions and only *presents them to our consciousness* in this pre-prepared form. This 'logical', this 'artistic' activity takes place incessantly."

Using fixed forms to reflect a vital human instinct that is concerned both with our physical awareness of stability and with how we experience space is part of architecture's representational power. And the desire to deliberately unsettle these impressions, or even turn them upside down, is directly connected to this power. Deeply embedded in human nature is a trust in the elemental stability of mass, a feeling for weight, pressure, and resistance as part of our experience of our own bodies. For that reason, architecture can trigger a very lively invocation of our memories of physical security and strength.

It is exactly the same with space, which enters our awareness and our memories as an experience of free movement of our bodies. The "pedestrian-friendly city," which is under discussion once more after our experiences with the "car-friendly city," is a comment on the potency of this capacity for memory. No matter how much we love our cars, we are not willing to sacrifice the urban spaces that allow us unhampered physical movement. The "living quality of space," which August Endell spoke of in 1907 in his "Schönheit der Stadt," is created by people, because "open space is divided up by moving bodies, [and] distance and size take on a new meaning." The way we experience space through our own bodies enables us immediately to adapt to space and in our imagination to fill it with our movements. Thus, for example, a long space, such as the nave of a church, suggests forward movement; a symmetrical space constantly brings our thoughts back to the center and vice versa letting them drift in all directions. Also the distinction between a broad urban square and a sunken square, which depends on the siting of the buildings dominating the square and capturing the eye, ultimately follows this pattern. Because squares that are not accessible to this act of the imagination give us nothing to go by in terms of size and shape, we experience them as being without scale and therefore desolate.

*　*　*

Regaining architectural form on the outside and inside of buildings, the formal principles governing the design of buildings as enclosed space, sculpted volume and interplay of surfaces that go beyond empty abstraction, but also beyond a new machine aesthetics based on modern media technology or sensation-hungry aestheticism is a task which today will seem disconcerting only to architects who have become alienated from architecture.

Architecture is lost to those architects who are in love with images, who regard the wall as a no man's land and offer it as an advertising space for rental to any media that can generate "images" and messages, because they are no longer capable of mastering the architectural categories of surface that are needed to generate an "image of architecture" with these means on the wall. Architecture is lost to those architects who are in love with objects and who place their buildings in space as sculptural objects, which then spread out into the space in a spectacular way, but cannot themselves create space because those objects are no longer able to generate a space-solid figure. Architecture is lost to those architects who are intoxicated with space and cannot see architectural space as an encounter between inside and outside, the self-contained and the expansive, and who will not accept the idea of an urban square as being a genuine architectural symbol and creative experiential dimension, because they have lost the feeling for the peculiarities of the border that defines space and the structural categories of a pictorially fixed architectural form of space.

*　*　*

72 Mary Louise Lobsinger

The new urban scale in Italy – on Aldo Rossi's
L'architettura della città (2006)

Mary Louise Lobsinger, 'The new urban scale in Italy – On Aldo Rossi's *L'architettura della città*',
Journal of Architectural Education, vol. 59, 3, 2006, extracts pp. 28–30 and 35.

› Introduction

In Italy, the mid-1960s saw the publication of several book-length studies and numerous articles
by architects offering critical interpretations of the contemporary city. Most of these texts took
the radical social and physical transformations of the Italian postwar city as the point of departure
for assessing the legacy of modernist urbanism and for speculating upon the city's future form.
Within this intellectually lively and contentious field of inquiry, Aldo Rossi's *L'architettura della città*
(The Architecture of the City) of 1966 stands apart for the clarity of the author's intentions.
L'architettura della città was written in the mode of a treatise in which the author strives to put in
place the principles for a science of urbanism. The thesis of his book was informed by and
responded to a polemical debate over the scale and form of the city within Italian architectural
discourse of the early 1960s. In other words, the architect's thinking about the city evolved within
a specific historical context identified in the first instance as postwar Italy. It responded in part to
the perceived dissipation of urbanism as a discipline within an interdisciplinary field of study. The
following essay examines the events that compelled Rossi to undertake the task of defining the
terms for analyzing the city and situates his thesis within the contours of the urban debate during
this period.

Despite the fact that Rossi states his purpose quite clearly in the first chapter, the reception
of the book, particularly in the Anglo-American world, tended to translate his theory for an
autonomous urban science as evidence supporting preoccupations with architectural autonomy.
For example, when in 1976 the American architect Peter Eisenman introduced Rossi to a select-
reading audience, he claimed that the publication of *L'architettura della città* played an influential
role in the evolution of the concept of autonomous architecture.[1] The context for this claim was
provided by the English language translation of the Spanish architect Rafael Moneo's essay on Rossi
in *Oppositions* magazine. It was an interpretation already once removed from the original source.
Autonomous architecture was again the subject of a monographic issue of the *Harvard Design Review*

of 1984 in which Claudio D'Amato published an article on *L'architettura della città*. Celebrating the fifteen-year anniversary of the Italian publication, D'Amato situated the book historically within the architectural milieu of the early 1960s. His effort to retrieve Rossi's book from the proponents of architectural autonomy was overshadowed by the numerous articles on autonomy and the publication of architectural drawings from the *Autonomous Architecture* exhibition held at the Fogg Art Museum in 1981. On the other hand, Mary McLeod's review of the English translation of the book acknowledged the Italian sociopolitical context and importantly presented the book as a set of parameters for research that "in no way dictate his specific formal choices.[2] While the fortune of Rossi in the architectural culture of the 1970s and 1980s has yet to be fully examined, suffice to say that in its initial North American reception, the book reflected the concerns and theoretical propensities of a milieu foreign to its inception and purpose.

The reception of *L'architettura della città* can, in part, be attributed to a set of straightforward circumstances beyond the interests extended in the secondary literature on Rossi. It is a simple fact that the book made its English language debut in 1982, reversing the order of sequence in which it appears in the development of Rossi's architectural thought and design. Rossi's early career comprised jointly authored competition projects and texts as well as a professional profile based largely on teaching, researching, and writing about architecture and urbanism. While pursuing research on the city, he built very little. In contrast, by the time *L'architettura della città* appeared in English, Rossi the architect had acquired an international reputation and was well established as the front man for *la Tendenza* (the tendency). It should also be noted that the English translation was preempted by the publication of *A Scientific Autobiography,* a book of substantially different intentions, written from a distinctly personal point of view, and reflecting a completely different period in his life and career.[3] Adding to the confusion is the fact that Rossi's earlier publications were for the most part unavailable to non-Italian reading audiences. Given this, the city book reads as a singular statement representing an overarching theoretical proposition distinct from and even set against his later more personal writings. Overlooked in the favorable reception of his drawings and the promotion of architectural autonomy is the book as a thoroughly researched and learned response to very specific events. Rossi was well aware of the disconnection between the book's conception and its later reception outside of Italy. In a lecture given to an American audience in the mid-1970s, he acknowledged that the book had been written in response to a polemic within Italian architecture and he admitted that time had since "liquidated" that debate.[4] This paper steps aside from the reception of *L'architettura della città* in foreign contexts to track the debate that motivated Rossi to write a book defining the principles for a science of urbanism.

It is worth repeating the well-known fact that *L'architettura della città* was published by the Padua-based Marsilio Press in 1966. Its English translation appeared some sixteen years later, well after the historical context and the debate motivating the architect had passed. Rossi's notes and published writings from the mid-sixties confirm his goal to write a treatise for a theory of urbanism, a treatise that, following those of the enlightenment, assigned classifications that described specific urban phenomena and posited precise terms for analyzing changes in urban structure. Rossi's focus on urban form, particularly its history and the complex totality of forces, exemplified the construct of the urban artifact, as well as his critique of naive functionalism evolved within the contours of the reformulation of architectural modernism in Italy during the 1950s. Perhaps most significantly, *L'architettura della città* is evidence of the transition within elite, meaning largely academic, architectural debate in Italy during this period. In general, this transition can be characterized as a turn from investigating the continuity and tradition of architectural modernism and the critique of modernism as a style toward the problems of the city and town planning. The book illustrates Rossi's belief in the continuity and progressive evolution of modernism and elaborates a concept of function that includes broadly construed criteria such as societal, psychological, and historical. Rossi attempts to establish a method of analysis inclusive of such criteria. Rossi's thesis also responded to specific points of debate integral to the polemic over the expanding scale of the Italian city and the emerging discipline of urbanism.[5]

Within Italian postwar architecture, the shift to urban issues and the problems of the contemporary city has a distinct profile that tracks the repositioning of the architect's role. During the 1950s and early 1960s, Italian architectural discourse turned from questions about the expressive potential of architecture and concerns with the object to the querying of the architect's contribution to the field of urbanism. While the formation of urban design as a discipline is a history yet to be written, it can be stated that the Italian debate about urbanism paralleled the growing pains of the new discipline during these years. It was further motivated by the perceived failure of postwar reconstruction to stem the unruly development of Italian cities and to provide adequate housing for the influx of workers from rural areas, particularly from the poverty stricken south to cities of the industrial triangle of Milan, Turin, and Genoa. Although the expansion of the city had been a concern prior to the war and during the reconstruction, by the late 1950s exponential population increase and problems attending the geographic reorganization of the city exacerbated the social transformations wrought by Italy's economic miracle (ca. 1957–1963).[6] For example, during the height of the boom years, the population of Rome increased by more than a million inhabitants putting pressure on city infrastructures, particularly on the historic center. The swollen peripheries of cities such as Milan, Turin, and Rome comprised an uncontrolled mix of developer- and state-sponsored housing quarters and commercial and industrial buildings.[7] Subject to rampant land speculation and building practices largely unregulated by law, the accelerated rate of change profoundly affected the configuration of Italian urban centers. It changed ways of life and places of living, catapulting largely traditional social forms into an urbanized society of mass consumption. The forces of change accompanying the boom sponsored the emergence of a mobile mass society, transforming Italian cities into centers and peripheries of uneven development. In the early 1960s, architects viewed the challenge of this unwieldy sociogeographical configuration as a call to reassess professional responsibilities and the discipline of architecture.

Aligned with the shift to the city in critical architectural discourse was a subtle transfer in influence from Ernesto N. Rogers to educators and architects such as Giuseppe Samonà, Dean of the *Istituto Universitario di Architettura di Venezia* (IUAV), and Ludovico Quaroni, an architect-urbanist who taught at several universities during this period.[8] As editor of *Casabella continuità* throughout the 1950s until 1964, Rogers profoundly influenced Italian architectural culture. He also mentored a whole generation of young architects at *Casabella's* Centro studi (study center) and through his teaching at the Polytechnic of Milan. At *Casabella,* the promotion of Aldo Rossi and

MARY LOUISE LOBSINGER

Francesco Tentori to editors in 1961 signaled the changing of the guard. Quaroni and Samonà were, on the other hand, contemporaries of Rogers who had worked at the urban scale and were active members of the *Istituto Nazionale di Urbanistica* (National Institute of Urbanism). Samonà authored the influential book on modern urban development titled *L'urbanistica e l'avvenire della città negli stati europei* (Urbanism and the Future of the City in the European Countries) published in 1959. During the 1950s, Quaroni had co-coordinated several of the most important postwar housing projects such as the Tiburtino Housing District (1949–1954) in Rome and the new town of La Martella (1951–1954) near Matera in southern Italy. Although the received configuration of postwar Italian architecture typically pits the North, specifically Milan, against the so-called Roman School, this geographic description does not stand up to close scrutiny in this case.[9] The affiliations between Romans, Milanese, Venetians, and others involved in the polemic over the new scale of urbanism were not drawn by local associations. For example, one of Rossi's key collaborators and staunch supporters was Carlo Aymonino, an architect associated with the Roman School in postwar years who taught in Venice as well as in Rome during the early 1960s. It was Samonà and Giancarlo De Carlo who were invited from Venice and Milan to participate in the seminars discussing the idea of *la città territorio* held at University of Rome in 1963. Between 1959 and 1965, the debate over urbanism escalated into a polemic that crossed two generations of architects. The publication of Rossi's *L'architettura della città* in 1966 demarcated the conclusion of a wide-ranging debate in Italian architecture about the form, the history, and the future of the contemporary city.

› Italy circa 1962: the dynamics of urban scale

Of the many articles Rossi published in the early 1960s, "Nuovi problemi" (New Problems) of 1962 most succinctly captures the conditions of urban change confronting Italian architects. In this article, Rossi characterizes the previous ten years of urban growth as having radically transformed Italian cities to such a degree that the physical distinctions between the city proper and its surrounding countryside no longer existed.[10] Confirming a widely held view, Rossi stated that the word "city" insufficiently described the emerging amorphous nature of urban form. From this, he concluded that the economic, social, and spatial factors governing urban form should be interpreted as a "metropolitan area" that functions largely as a job market. The identification of the emerging urban dynamic as dependent on employment referred to a key force propelling city growth, the mass immigration from rural Italy to the city. Over the next four years, Rossi sought to identify the specific nature of the forces acting upon the city, and this goal stood in contrast to architects preoccupied with describing the effects of population growth and the unraveling of the city's periphery. For Rossi, the emerging city form and its social and physical configurations presented architects with precise new tasks.[11]

It was a well-repeated observation during this period that the consequences of urban expansion challenged architects to define their role within the field of urbanism. For example, at the seventh meeting of the *Istituto Nazionale di Urbanistica* in 1959, participants argued for a conceptual shift in the relation between architecture, urbanism, and town planning.[12] The title of the conference *Il volto della città* (The Face of the City) identified two aspects of the contemporary city that concerned architects. The first suggests that the visual impact of architecture had altered due to changed perceptual modes brought about by new means of mass communication and increased mobility. The spatiality and temporality of the new urban dimension rendered irrelevant a frontally viewed architecture. Second, the structure of the postwar city had developed according to fundamentally different necessities; roadways, commuters, and consumers' desires, for example, now dictated urban development and architectural form. Architects were advised to think in terms of "architectonic planning" and to consider architecture at the scale of planning. As one participant suggested, architects should conceive of an *architettura della città* or an architecture at a scale that would confront the expanded visual and physical dimensions of the Italian city.[13]

*   *   *

Italian reviews of *L'architettura della città* acknowledged Rossi's intent to formulate an "objective science" of urbanism as a response specific to critical academic discourse of the early 1960s. The reviews welcomed Rossi's erudition and recognized the integral relation between his use of history, city form, and politics. Giorgio Grassi characterized the book as a product of debates internal to the teaching environments at the School of Architecture at the Polytechnic of Milan and IUAV and judged it slightly provincial in focus.[14] As one might expect, he applauded Rossi's attack on organic and functionalist theories as well as on the more recent behaviorist readings of the city. Vittorio Gregotti welcomed Rossi's use of urban geography and the political analysis that, as he put it, established the *autonomia scientifica della scienza urbana* (the scientific autonomy of urban science).[15] However, he warned readers against Rossi's rigid point of view, too focused on a limited idea of architecture. Carlo Aymonino championed Rossi's political agenda and commended his attempt to disentangle various ideologies – functionalist, naturalist, and preservationist paradigms, for example – from the social groups, laws, and politics that actually determine urban form.[16] Less enthusiastic was a review published in *Città-società* that judged Rossi's prose turgid and, misconstruing the aim of the book, complained that it failed to deal with the problem of urban scale or to deliver guidelines for design.[17]

In 1966, Rossi's book replied to the Italian polemic over the new urban scale. The book was not, as some interpreters would have it, a broad-brush rejection of modernism or the Modern Movement, nor was it a pitch for an autonomous architecture. It countered naive functionalism with the complex functions – sociopolitical, economic, and aesthetic – of the urban artifact and made an important contribution to the critical reappraisal of the urban propositions of the Modern Movement. Rossi articulated an analysis of the structure of the city that stemmed from "the recognition that the city is constructed in its totality."[18] He objected to modes of interpretation brought about by increased specialization–sociological, functional, and economic – that by ignoring the primacy of form, relegated the city as a physical entity to a secondary role. The book contested the emptying out of the specificity of urban form and its deep connection to history for abstract analyses pursued in so-called interdisciplinary studies. Rossi privileged architecture as a key aspect of the city as an urban artifact and as the primary physical evidence of the complex forces acting on the city. Architecture as a concrete fact or as an artifact, in the full cultural sense of the word, not only produced knowledge about the city but, by means of detailed analysis, it also evidenced the forces acting within and upon the city. Other disciplines could only describe or theorize the city, while architecture was the physical evidence of myriad forces acting upon the city. For Rossi, no other discipline could lay claim to such tangible authority. It rendered urbanism the status of an independent discipline comprising the architecture of the city.

Within postwar Italian critical discourse, the year 1966 undoubtedly demarcates a watershed. The one side is characterized by tumultuous debates about the city and the future of modernism, polemics galvanized by experiments within schools of architecture and played out in journals, seminars, and competitions. Rossi's book was one among many signaling the summation of the debate over the contemporary city and its new urban scale. Publications by architects such as Vittorio Gregotti, Carlo Aymonino, Alberto Samonà, Manfredo Tafuri, and Giancarlo De Carlo confirmed the intensity of research activity and, perhaps more significantly, the theoretical propensities Italian architects brought to their querying of architecture and the city.[19] After 1966, the issue of the city dissipated as architects turned their attention elsewhere, becoming caught up in political upheaval and the transformation in Marxist thought that would influence, on one hand, an intransigent ideological critique of architecture and, on the other, feed the pop radicalism of the neo-avant-garde. Meanwhile, Rossi's book became a major influence in architecture schools such as the Polytechnic of Milan or Eidgenössische Technische Hochschule (ETH) in Zurich as well as abroad where it was translated into several languages. More famously, the book supported a strand of Italian architectural inquiry fundamental to the emergence of *la Tendenza* on the international scene in the 1970s. The publication of the book, despite its formation within a highly specific context and its much later reception within Anglo-American circles, marks a significant moment in and contribution to the history of critical architectural discourse. As a theory of urbanism, it put into motion the querying of architecture and urbanism as inextricable as well as a conception of disciplinary autonomy fundamental to architecture theory from the 1970s onward.

› Epilogue

At forty years following the publication of Rossi's *L'architettura della città,* one is compelled to ask if his research and thesis hold any value for current urban and architectural discourse. Is his pursuit of the principles for an urban science an outdated task? Are Rossi's regard for the significance of form as evidence of historical processes constructing the reality of the city and his skeptical view of gigantism in scale as primarily concerned with abstraction, conceits that have no place within current processes of globalization, or the academic discourse celebrating emergent urbanisms? These latter are frequently evidenced by examples of decentralization, the documenting of large-scale urbanized areas underpinned by the pretense of the positive outcome of self-organizing systems, and informed by the cross-pollination of the various design disciplines, particularly landscape and urbanism. I believe that there are some parallels to be drawn between the pre-occupations that galvanized *la nuova dimensione* and current modes of describing emergent urban conditions and its search for alternatives to motivate design invention. Notions such as the plan as process, the privileging of systems, and infrastructure, thought to liberate form and enable open and nonpredictive evolution of urban potentials, are comparable to the current description of the attributes of urbanization sponsored by complex adaptive systems.

* * *

Editors' note: Illustrations and references to illustrations have been omitted.

› Notes

1 Peter Eisenman, *Oppositions* 5 (Summer 1976): 1. All translations are by the author unless otherwise indicated.

2 Mary McLeod, "The Architecture of the City," reviewed in Design Book Review 3 (Winter 1984): 50.

3 See Aldo Rossi, *A Scientific Autobiography* (Cambridge, MA: MIT/ Oppositions Books, 1981).

4 Aldo Rossi Papers, Getty Research Institute Special Collections and Visual Collections Accession 880319, Box 9, File 132.

5 See Aldo Rossi, *L'architettura della città* (Padua, Italy: Marsilio, 1966), p. 37.

6 See Paul Ginsborg, *A History of Contemporary Italy: Society and Politics 1943–1988* (New York: Penguin Books, 1990), pp. 210–254.

7 There is a close connection between transformation of the postwar Italian city and the subject matter of Italian films during this period. See the use of the city, buildings, the periphery, and borgate in Pier Pasolini's *Accattone* (1959), Michelangelo Antonioni's *La notte* (1961), or Vittorio De Sica's *Rocco e i suoi fratelli* (1963), for example.

8 Samonà began teaching at IUAV in the mid-1930s, where he was chair from 1945 to 1971. Quaroni taught urbanism at several universities from the mid-1930s onward. From 1955 to 1964, he taught at University of Florence, and from 1964 to 1981 he held a position at University of Rome.

9 For example, Bruno Zevi is not recorded as having participated in any of the major events associated with the urban debate during this period. Although he had been a key contributor to Italian architecture particularly during the immediate postwar years, he had little to do with the encounter between architecture and urbanism in the late 1950s and early 1960s. However, Tafuri later credited Zevi with coining the term *urbatecture* in the mid-1960s.

10 Aldo Rossi, "Nuovi problemi," *Casabella Continuità* 264 (June 1962): 3.

11 Ibid.

12 "Il volto della città." VII Convegno nazionale dell'Istituto nazionale urbanistica, *Urbanistica* 32 (December 1960): 5–8.

13 Ibid., p. 6.

14 Giorgio Grassi, Review of *L'architettura della città*. Architettura libri no. 2/3 (July 1966): 98–99.

15 Vittorio Gregotti, "Aldo Rossi: L'architettura della città." il verri 23 (1967): 172–173.

16 Carlo Aymonino, "Per la formazione di una scienza urbana. L'architettura della città. Chi sceglie in ultima istanza l'immagine di una città? Qual è il ruolo della politica?" *Rinascita* 27 (July 2, 1966): 21–22.

17 Piero Bulgheroni, "L'architettura della città." *Città-società* (December 1966): 108–11.

18 Rossi, *L'architettura della città*, p. 50–51.

19 For example, Vittorio Gregotti published *Il territorio della architettura* (The Territory of Architecture), Carlo Aymonino *Origini e sviluppo della città moderna* (Origins and Development of the Modern City), and Alberto Samonà *La nuova dimensione urbana in Francia. I "grandi ensembles" e la modificazione della forma della città* (The New Urban Dimension in France. The Grand Ensembles and the Modification of Form of the City). Through the early 1960s, Giancarlo De Carlo published among other writings the proceedings from several of his seminars on urbanism such as *La pianificazione territoriale urbanistica nell'area Milanese* (Planning Territorial Urbanism in the Milan Area) of 1966.

73 Pier Vittorio Aureli

Rossi: the concept of the locus as a political category of the city (2008)

Pier Vittorio Aureli, 'Rossi: the concept of the locus as a political category of the city', from: Pier Vittorio Aureli, *The Project of Autonomy – Politics and Architecture within and against Capitalism*, New York: Princeton Architectural Press, 2008, extracts pp. 53–55, 56–58, 62–64, 66 and 68–69.

› Rossi: the concept of the locus as a political category of the city

The construction of an alternative to the capitalist city and the proposal of an autonomous architectural culture thus meant, above all, the constitution of a theory of the city. In the 1950s Italian architecture had been mainly a matter of increasing *professionalismo* (literally, professionalism). It was an attempt to link a still artisanal dimension of design and building techniques with the urgent demands of modernization created by the rapid advance of postwar capitalist development. In the 1960s, however, with the reemergence of political struggles and new social conflicts, the necessity appeared in all disciplines, including within the internal discourse of architecture and urbanism, to find a way toward cultural and conceptual renewal. Instead of simply advancing in tandem with the further modernization of architecture and the city, the need for renewal became visible as a demand for a theoretical refoundation of architecture in relation to the city.

In the 1950s and early 1960s the main protagonists of the intellectual debate in architecture had been Bruno Zevi, an architectural historian, critic, and founder of the Movement for Organic Architecture (APAO); Giulio Carlo Argan, an art historian and author of several important contributions to the theory and historiography of modern architecture; and Ernesto Nathan Rogers, an architect and leader of the BBPR office and director of the prestigious magazine *Casabella continuità* from 1953 to 1964. Their contributions may be summed up as a critical recuperation and cultural reinvention of the theoretical objectives of the Modern Movement, especially as the latter were represented by three different directions: Frank Lloyd Wright's organic architecture (supported by Zevi), Walter Gropius's pedagogical program at the Bauhaus (supported by Argan), and the ethical legacy of CIAM (supported by Rogers).[1] This recuperation was to some degree intended by all three theorists as a political project, aimed at a new cultural and historical legitimation of the liberal trajectory of the Modern Movement as the only path to a democratic architecture and city.

But it was against the ideological pretensions of this nexus of liberalism, democracy, and modernism that the refoundation of architectural theory would take form in the 1960s in the thinking of the next generation, above all architects like Aldo Rossi and Andrea Branzi, both born in the 1930s and reaching intellectual maturity at this moment. For these new protagonists, the cultural proposals advanced by intellectuals like Zevi, Argan, and Rogers were still bound to a reformist view of the relationship between politics and architectural thought. They aimed at a recovery of the modern city in terms of the negative political, cultural, and formal instrumentalities and ideologies that had been brought into being by capitalist development: respectively, spatial humanism as a way of making the new forms of habitation more acceptable, new technologies as a way of distributing social equality, and coexistence between the old and the new as a way of manifesting an ethical pluralism. What these committed intellectuals did not, and could not, put into question was their own unwavering trust in the continuing progress of democracy; they were unable to question the structural foundations of this assumption. The basis of the postwar democratic city – both the real one and the one imagined by these "liberal" architectural thinkers – was not simply political economy of capitalism, however, but also its ideological representations. The latter especially took the form of a rediscovered "humanism," which became the mantra of socially *engagé* intellectuals.

With the rhetorical abuse and exhaustion of professionalism and humanism in the early 1960s, and in the face of the advancing process of integration of social relations within the context of contemporary capitalist development, there were, in the view of the new generation of intellectuals, two theoretical paths that appeared as potentially valid alternatives in architecture: on the one hand, a political affirmation of the autonomy of architectural *poiesis* in the form of the reinvention of categories such as typology and place (Rossi); and on the other, a critique of the ideology of the capitalist city as this ideology manifested itself in the postwar recuperation of the Modern Movement and a new wave of technological avant-gardism in the 1960s (Tafuri and Branzi). In spite of their sometimes radical differences, these two positions may be said to have converged in the necessity of a theory that consisted not in the autonomy of the discipline, but in the autonomy of a political subject committed to the formulation of a cultural alternative to the bourgeois domination of the capitalist city. Theory was always against ideology, as Tronti affirmed in these years. If ideology coincided with the blind belief in progress, with faith in the evolution of society for the better, theory, as Tronti quoted from Paul Klee, was *sichtbar machen* – making visible, that is, the construction of a clear analytical and political point of view based on the solid ground of concrete conceptual categories.[2] But in making visible what was invisible, theory was also meant to go beyond the critique of ideology, to resolve itself in the project.

*   *   *

Having been deeply influenced by the writings of Antonio Gramsci, especially Gramsci's reflections on the role of intellectuals – whom the political philosopher had defined as autonomous yet organically linked to party institutions and thus responsible for the creation of its hegemonic forms of culture – Rossi joined the Italian Communist Party in 1956, at the time of the Twentieth Party Congress in the Soviet Union and the invasion of Hungary, a moment when many leftist intellectuals were instead leaving the party. His intellectual formation between 1954 and 1964 as a politically engaged architecture student and regular contributor to Rogers's magazine *Casabella continuità* included the writing of a series of articles in which he came to see architecture no longer as a product of masters but as an integral part of the evolution of urban phenomena.[3] Carlo Aymonino, an architect who directed the design department of the IUAV in the 1970s and was close to Rossi, has said that what characterized their generation was primarily the replacement of architectural history interpreted within an arthistorical perspective by urban history understood in relation to political development.[4] If this is so, then we may say that Rossi represented a paradigmatic case, and his pioneering essays on Milanese neoclassicism and the architecture of the Enlightenment, his monographic writings on architects like Loos and Behrens, and his case studies of cities like Berlin, Hamburg, and Vienna aimed to establish a new, autonomous field of research in which architectural form was conceived as the primary means of constituting the politics of the modern city.

Rossi's hypothesis of autonomous architecture involved more than the rejection of the naiveté of functionalism, nor was it just a call for disciplinary specificity. It was rather a search for a rational language: a theory of form liberated from the sequence of formal styles in the service of the dominant bourgeois institutions. His rediscovery of the architecture of rationalism was an attempt to recuperate and reappropriate the legacy of the bourgeois city as the form of the socialist city. In his first important essay, entitled "Il concetto di tradizione nel neoclassicismo milanese" (The concept of tradition in the architecture of Milanese neoclassicism),[5] he analyzed the relationship between the politics of the Napoleonic government of Milan and its specific architectural language. This language had its formal expression in the Jacobin rationalism of Luigi Antolini's design for the Foro Bonaparte. What Rossi saw in this architecture, and in other monumental buildings and urban interventions of Napoleonic Milan, was the will of the bourgeoisie to assert and represent itself as the dominant new class vis-à-vis the old aristocracy. The architecture of the neoclassical city was thus for Rossi primarily a political choice by the Milanese bourgeoisie concerning the new institutions of power, who understood them as means to define and realize its idea of public space. The bourgeois class thus gave expression to its existence and status through its appropriation and reinvention of the classical tradition. In Rossi's view, it was time for the socialist city to likewise construct its own tradition by appropriating and reinventing the legacy of *its* predecessor, namely the city of the bourgeoisie.

It was in the context of his effort to define the civic realism of a socialist architecture that Rossi revisited the history of European bourgeois rationalism from the eighteenth to the twentieth century – from Boullée to Loos. This project reached its theoretical culmination in 1973 with Rossi's organization and curatorship of the Fifteenth Triennale in Milan, which Rossi devoted to a survey on "rationalist" architecture in the twentieth century, both before and after World War II.[6] In contrast to the general design exuberance of the 1960s, Rossi reappropriated the tradition of rationalism not in the fashion of the Modern Movement, as a normative and functional language, but rather as an affirmation of a potentially autonomous architecture opposed to the hybrid and technologically heteronomous forms being churned out by neocapitalist urbanism at this time. In commenting on his choice of references and examples for the Triennale, Rossi wrote: "[W]e have here incorporated some texts by and references to Ludwig Hilberseimer, Adolf Behne, and Hans

Schmidt because they have a particular meaning within the legacy of the Modern Movement. These texts are valid because they have confronted the contradictions of bourgeois architecture from a socialist perspective."[7]

For Rossi it was important to continue the modern tradition of Hilberseimer, Behne, and Schmidt not as a generic and open-ended movement, but as a political and cultural project, a *tendenza*[8] – a recognizable architectural development aiming to establish an alternative to the capitalist city. Within this framework, what was needed, according to Rossi, was not a change of architectural style or urban form, but the elaboration of a new theoretical point of view on the city and architecture. Its aim should be the primacy of political choices over technocratic ones. In this sense, Rossi's elaboration of an autonomous architecture coincided with his proposal of a theory of the city capable of challenging what he saw in the early 1960s as capitalism's new form of urban project: its totalistic planning of the city, with its concomitant celebration of technology. For Rossi, the premise of a contemporary theory of the city should be the city as a site of political choices – as a concrete geography of places irreducible to the totality and continuity of urbanization.

* * *

. . . Rossi insisted on the concreteness of the urban artifact, of the architecture of the city, as the most relevant and precise instrument of urban analysis and design. Instead of looking to the city as an undefined, neutral ground shaped only by the categories imposed by the accelerating forces of urbanization, Rossi proposed to see the city as a place formed by politics. From this standpoint, only an analysis of architecture could reveal the city's immanent separateness, that is, its constitution of parts not reducible to the common denominator of technological development.

The two conceptual categories of such an analysis were typology, understood as knowledge concerning the constitution and evolution of urban forms; and the individuality of the urban artifact, understood as the concreteness of architecture in its actual material manifestation. If typology for Rossi was the "science" through which it was possible to assess the nature and evolution of the city according to an analysis irreducible to any monolithic idea of urban development, the individuality of the urban artifact was the moment of decision in which typological principles were applied to the real city. The field in which typology met the individuality of the urban artifact was neither urban planning, with its abstract, diagrammatic representations, nor "townscape", with its iconic representations of urban scenes, but rather urban geography, with its concept of the *locus*. By *locus* Rossi meant the geographic singularity of architecture's constitution, understood not just as empirical evidence but as a universal structural condition.

Greppi has recently recalled that a major appeal of Rossi's position for the radical Left was his strong interest, unusual among architects at the time, in urban geography as a critical framework opposed to townscape.[9] During these years Rossi was intensely studying the major authors of the French urban geography school, including Marcel Poëte, Maurice Halbwachs, Jean Tricart, Georges Chabot, and Max Sorre. These scholars were interested in reading urban space both as a field of fragmenting forces and as a whole whose evolution still had a discernible structure. With his reference to the studies of Sorre, Rossi construed the idea of *locus* as a manifestation of singular points within the overall framework of the city. As he writes in a crucial passage of *L'architettura della città*, "[A] geographer like Sorre could suggest the possibility of a theory of spatial division and, based on this, postulate the existence of 'singular points.' The *locus*, so conceived, emphasizes the conditions and qualities within undifferentiated space which are necessary for understanding an urban artefact."[10] In this sense, it is possible to say that for Rossi the *locus* constituted the very limit of any intervention or interpretation of the city.

In his opposition to planning and his defense of the idea of the *locus*, Rossi thus implicitly opposed the techno-capitalist conception of urbanization latent in planning practice. The city was a plurality of parts that did not add up to any totality, especially one imposed by the capitalist forces of integration. In this sense, it was possible to interpret the category of place as a *political* category, which, by virtue of the separateness that it evoked, *de facto* opposed the broad-scale subjugation of the territory to the totalizing forces of capitalist development. The embrace of the *locus* and of other concepts similarly characterized by their singular nature – for example, monumentality and collective memory, so pervasive throughout *L'architettura della città* – thus should be understood not as an effort to recuperate a traditional view of the city, but instead to establish a new political reading. By proposing a lucid theory that rendered the city immune to the anxiety of capitalist change and innovation, Rossi seemed to be suggesting that there was a possibility of looking at the city as an arena of decisive and singular events whose defined forms could pose a challenge to the urban phenomena and flux surrounding them.

At the same time, it was possible to use this theory to analyze these singular events in terms of their deeper structural consequences, in terms of their profound role in the collective experience of the city. To look at the city as a manifestation of collective urban memory was to go beyond what was empirically visible and perceive the dialectical conflict between constituent and constituted forces. In this sense, demolitions, reconstructions, and disruptions became events through which the actual history of the city could be traced. According to Rossi, these phenomena were what really constituted urban development. In this context, the aim of an autonomous theory of the city was to assess the real dynamic of discontinuous events, beyond their iconic visibility, beyond the superficial image of the city.

*   *   *

For Rossi and his colleagues, therefore, the city's technological advancement coincided with its political decadence. In this sense, there was more than an incidental analogy between Rossi's idea of autonomy and the Autonomist positions of Panzieri and Tronti. All were attempts to demystify capitalist development by opposing to the continuity of economic development the separateness of both society and the city. These formulations challenged the primacy of economic determinants over political action. To the tendentious abstractions of economic programming and capitalist planning, Rossi, like Panzieri and Tronti, counterposed a reality based on the tension between antagonists. For the Operaists, this conflict played out in the political and institutional forms that the working class evolved out of its own experience; for Rossi and his colleagues, it played out in the form of the individuality of the urban artifact, the singularity of the locus, and the idea of the city of separate parts.

* * *

Architecture for Rossi could not fail to be an expression of the power of the dominant class, but in making decisions for the city, the dominant class could not do other than position itself with respect to the forces antagonistic to it. Rossi's project proposed to be a new civic monument, one that by virtue of its strong critical presence immediately referred to its adversary. Yet while the dominant class sought to evade political responsibility for its role within the development of the capitalist city, Rossi sought to reveal this role, making explicit that all buildings in the city were inevitably representations of power: "There are no buildings of opposition," Rossi wrote, "because the architecture *that is going to be realized* is always an expression of the dominant class."[11] Consequently, it was necessary for the project to exhibit through its own formal devices an argument with respect to power. Only on the basis of such a clear formal proposal was political choice possible, that is, for the community "to decide collectively in favor of one kind of city and to reject another one."[12]

This was the framework within which originated the austere and simple formal language that was to characterize the rationalist project of Rossi in the years ahead. Instead of using novel styles and images that could be consumed along with the new technologies. Rossi opted for a rigid grammar of forms. These forms did not aspire to be anything else but themselves. They thus shifted attention to the *locus* as a symbolic and geographic singularity, a state of exception within the city, posing a challenge to the open-ended space of the capitalist city-territory. Analogous to Tronti's autonomy of the political, which was an inquiry directed not at the autonomy of one part of society with respect to another but at the autonomy of power itself, Rossi's autonomy of architecture was above all about the establishment of urban concepts that posited the supremacy of politics over the city's accelerating economic development.

› Notes

1. The most important written contributions to the Italian theoretical debate on architecture and the city before the 1960s are the following: Bruno Zevi, *Saper vedere l'architettura: Saggio sull'interpretation spaziale dell'architettura* (Turin: Einaudi, 1948): Giulio Carlo Argan, *Walter Gropius e la Bauhaus* (Turin: Einaudi, 1951); and Ernesto Nathan Rogers, *Esperienza dell'architettura* (Turin: Einaudi, 1958).

2. Tronti, *Operai e capitale*, p. 303: "*Sichtbar machen* means to make visible: to say clearly so as to be understood, even at the risk of not interpreting very well things that are intrinsically obscure."

3. On the political formation of Aldo Rossi and his relationship with Communist culture, see Pier Vittorio Aureli, "The Difficult Whole: Typology and Singularity of the Urban Event in Aldo Rossi's Early Work, 1954–1963," in *Log* 9 (2007), pp. 20–41.

4. Carlo Aymonino, *Il significato della città* (Padua: Marsilio, 2000), p. 4.

5. Aldo Rossi, "Il concetto di tradizione nel neoclassicismo milanese," Società 3 (1956). Reprinted in Rossi, *Scritti scelti sull'architettura e la città* (Milan: Città Studi Edizioni. 1975), pp. 1–24.

6. See Ezio Bonfanti et al., *Architettura razionale* (Milan: Franco Angeli, 1973).

7. Aldo Rossi, Introduction, in Bonfanti et al., *Architettura razionale*, p. 16.

8. *Tendenza* is a Gramscian term. It refers to the potential of a cultural movement to express the hegemonic line of the dominant class.

9. Greppi made the following observation in an interview with the author in October 2007: "At the time of the publication of his [early] writings and his major book *L'architettura della città*, Rossi was not yet known for

his projects, but more for an idiosyncratic reading of the city based on urban geography. The latter was irreducible to the blind technocratic approaches that were fashionable at that time – those of the city-territory and townscape, on the one hand, and the megastructure on the other."

10 Aldo Rossi, *The Architecture of the City*, trans. Diane Ghirardo and Joan Ockman (Cambridge, MA: MIT Press, 1982), p. 103.
11 Rossi, *The Architecture of the City*, p, 116 (my italics).
12 Ibid.

74 Angelika Schnell

The socialist perspective of the XV Triennale di Milano.
Hans Schmidt's influence on Aldo Rossi (2010)

Angelika Schnell, 'The socialist perspective of the XV Triennale di Milano. Hans Schmidt's influence on Aldo Rossi', *Candide. Journal for Architectural Knowledge*, 2, Bielefeld: Transcript Verlag, extracts pp. 35–51, 55–59 and 67–70, translation by Fiona Fincannon.

› Architettura Razionale

1973 was an important year in Aldo Rossi's career. Seven years after the publication of his much-noted book *L'architettura della città*, he made his definitive entrance onto the international stage, as principal curator of the XV Triennale di Milano.[1] *Architettura Razionale*, the title of that exhibition, sounded quite provocative at the time because it reawakened ambivalent memories of Gruppo 7, the avant-garde group cofounded by Giuseppe Terragni. In admiration of Le Corbusier, the group had given itself the name Movimento Architettura Razionale (MAR) in 1928, only to change it just two years later to Movimento Italiano per l'Architettura Razionale (MIAR); under that name it publicly endorsed Italian Fascism.

But this reference was part of the agenda, for it was considered that the rationalist legacy of modern architecture had to be vaunted as such, in programmatic opposition to functionalism, which to a certain degree was considered modernism's bad legacy. On the very first pages, the accompanying exhibition catalog quoted (in Italian translation) Adolf Behne's definition from *Der moderne Zweckbau* of 1926, in which he undertakes to make the conceptual distinction between rationalism and functionalism, one that will be crucial for the postwar Rationalists:[2] "Nothing is more self-evident than that a rationalist should stress form. Form is nothing more than the consequence of establishing a relationship between human beings. For the isolated and unique figure of nature there is no problem of form. Individuals, even individuals in nature, are free. The problem of form arises when an overview is demanded. Form is the prerequisite under which an overview becomes possible. Form is an eminently social matter. Anyone who recognizes the right of society recognizes the right of form."[3]

The Italian curators apparently concluded that Rationalist Architecture, therefore, is (still modern) architecture that understands every architectural problem first and foremost as a problem of form and not as a problem of technical and social functions from which form was, in the end, to follow.[4] As an oppositional concept, Rationalism is liberated from the bonds tying it to modern science, technology, and economics, and can once more bring to architecture that which modernism had supposedly given up on: spirit or soul, art, history, autonomy.[5] In conformity with this agenda, the architect Arduino Cantafora delivered the corresponding image, *La città analoga*, in which the models for a Rationalist Architecture are assembled in a sort of ideal urban landscape; it includes one of Rossi's projects, the 1965 monument to the partisans in Segrate.[6]

In spite of Behne's definition of form as "an eminently social matter,"the Triennale paved the way to a formalism that was accompanied by a "new classicism,"[7] which established an autonomous architectural language that was apparently free from political and historical ties. This new classicism sought to bring about a return of the rational and timeless elements of architecture and the city, on the basis of a "third typology,"as Anthony Vidler put it only a little later: "Columns, houses, and urban spaces, while linked in an unbreakable chain of continuity, refer only to their own nature as architectural elements, and their geometries are neither naturalistic nor technical but essentially architectural. It is clear that the nature referred to in these recent designs is no more or less than the nature of the city itself, emptied of specific social content from any particular time and allowed to speak simply of its own formal condition."[8]

Vidler's definition of Rossi's and other Rationalists' concept of type was apparently confirmed by them. It is well known that Rossi's neoplatonic definition of type in *L'architettura della città* is based on that of Antoine Chrysostôme Quatremère de Quincy: "The word type presents less the image of a thing to copy or imitate completely, than the idea of an element which must itself serve as a rule for the model."[9] By adopting this definition, Rossi was associating himself with the Rationalists, who emphasized the links to the philosophy and architecture of the Age of Enlightenment. This is substantiated by Rossi's other statements and, above all, by his translation into Italian of Etienne-Louis Boullée's *Architecture. Essai sur l'art.* (At that time, in the mid-1960s, Boullée was seemingly almost an alter ego for Rossi.) Elsewhere, he writes: "Ultimately, we can say that type is the very idea of architecture, that which is closest to its essence".[10]

Yet Rossi's understanding of type and Rationalist Architecture also has other aspects and interpretations that he himself brought into play. Often he brings to bear on the concept of Rationalism an additional concept that has a relativizing, complementary, refining, or deepening effect depending on the theoretical background and purpose.[11] Particularly in his early years, in the 1950s and 1960s, he was already seeking a theoretical definition of Rationalism that was to be simultaneously "realistic" and "concrete." Rossi's first essay in architectural theory, on the classicist architecture of Milan,[12] already makes it clear that he—at the time a staunch member of the Partito Comunista Italiano (PCI)—interprets the rationalism of this architecture as time-specific and not timeless. Class struggle, social and societal problems, and questions of use are equally important to architecture and urban design, and yet, according to Rossi, architecture is not derived from them. The "architecture of the city" also has permanent elements ("elementi permanenti"[13]). In order to develop a precise theory for it, Rossi studied Structuralism, among other things, and the French sociologist Maurice Halbwachs's theory of collective memory.

This network of different influences on Rossi's thought, Surrealism amongst them, has had the effect of making his architectural theory hard to grasp, diffuse; critics have described it as "mysterious"[14] and as an "alchemistic alphabet."[15] The search for the lowest common denominator of Rossi's architectural theory, therefore, is understandable, even if this reduction renders it impossible to take account of the ambiguities of his thought. Two factors—first, the participation in the Triennale by a large number of contemporary international architects, including Oswald Mathias Ungers, James Stirling, the New York Five (Peter Eisenman, Charles Gwathmey, John Hejduk, Richard Meier, and Michael Graves), Leon and Rob Krier, Adolfo Natalini, Bruno Reichlin, Fabio Reinhart, and, of course, Aldo Rossi and Giorgio Grassi; and second, Leon Krier's reorganization of the exhibition under the same name, with almost the same participants[16] in London's Art Net Gallery just two years later—have confirmed the perception that Rationalist Architecture was a powerful postwar movement, principally in western Europe and North America, a movement that helped form regain its rightful place—simple, clear, geometrical form above all, independent of any "social content," as Vidler expressed it.[17]

› The socialist perspective

However, the intention of the curators of the Triennale was quite different. The catalog of the Milan exhibition contains objects and references that cannot be accounted for by simply asserting that Rationalist Architecture can be explained through formalism and the use of basic geometric forms. It is first and foremost Rossi's introduction to the catalog that is instructive.[18] It acknowledges the secret star of the exhibition: Hans Schmidt and the architecture of the German Democratic Republic [East Germany or GDR].

In the introduction, Rossi clearly points to Schmidt and to a socialist definition of architectural type, a definition that is not aesthetic, but social. Rossi presents type—or rational form—neither as archetype nor as lasting architectural form, but as the product of collective work. And as such, it is beyond any aesthetic criticism, for example, of its monotonous appearance. There and in other essays written in the first half of the 1970s, Rossi forthrightly adopts one of Hans Schmidt's arguments that repeatedly emphasizes that monotony and monumentality in architecture do not call for aesthetic debates, but social debates. In the introduction to the Triennale catalog, it is to the "socialist perspective" that Rossi declares his allegiance, and not to timeless, abstract laws of form, which he elsewhere dismisses as schematism.[19]

However, the socialist perspective does not provide a more coherent or realistic definition of type at all. Hans Schmidt, upon whose theory Rossi's is based, had himself long sought such a definition. In his search, he had performed several feats of reasoning due more to the need to adapt to the political situation of the time than to a strictly scientific or logical reflection on the subject of type. The contradictions to which Schmidt falls victim are therefore Rossi's contradictions too. However, there is no trace of them at the beginning of the 1970s, or more specifically, during the Triennale exhibition.

*   *   *

One thing is certain, though, and that is clear from his introduction: Rossi's goal is not a Rationalist Architecture that is to be understood as a timeless aesthetic. A short time later he explains that the catalog begins "with a panorama of the modern movements in architecture in order to question their relations to today's architecture." (He is referring to the picture by Cantafora already mentioned.) This is definitely not meant to introduce a blind "encomium of modernism," but instead to make it clear that modernism "has given architecture an opportunity to engage with the modern world in a concrete way." And for this reason he and his comrades-in-arms "selected a few texts by authors like Hilberseimer, Behne, and Schmidt who are particularly significant with regard to modernism in its complexity; for it is primarily through them that we can today recognize the value of comparing all the architectural contradictions in the bourgeois world with the perspectives of the socialist world."[20]

Such sentences hardly point to a "new classicism" or to the immutability of basic geometric forms, which Ungers, for example, has praised.[21] Make no mistake, Rationalist Architecture is presented—at least in this text by Rossi—as socialist architecture, meaning that architecture has a mission in society and should "engage with the modern world in a concrete way." And the "work of the Halle-Neustadt collective represents precisely the model for such a Rationalist Architecture," which, as he writes, he finds "very impressive" "as a type of collective work that is independent of the results achieved."[22]

With this statement, Rossi distances himself from those conceptions of Rationalist Architecture that situate it in relation to buildings or to a formal language. Instead, he is speaking here about the production process as non-individualized design. A collective is responsible for the prefabricated high-rises in Halle-Neustadt, a group that can obviously create something together, something that is "independent of the results achieved,"[23] something that on the one hand, as a collective, has a critical and rational distance to the products that it has created, and on the other, reflects the societal forces of the GDR, and therefore points far beyond itself.

Rossi is here referring to two things. First, he is referring to his own statements about architectural type, understood as the product of a collective, which, while derived from urban structures, as Vidler explained, never loses its social and societal reference, even when consciously leaving it behind.[24] Second, Rossi is referring to Hans Schmidt's definition of type, presented in the texts that Rossi had had translated, into Italian. This definition is based exclusively on the collective of a socialist society. And therefore a very particular architecture was associated with it: monumental, uniform, and in a comprehensible style. However, Schmidt's method of arriving at this definition was tortuous, and in the end it was not compatible with the GDR's prefabricated high-rises. As Manfredo Tafuri wrote in his obituary, Schmidt was unable to resolve an important contradiction, namely the one between the "reclamation of form" and its "avant-garde dissolution."[25] This contradiction makes it clear that in the twentieth century no way was found to return to time-honored types on the basis of industrial production.

*   *   *

› Conclusion

Looking at the prefabricated high-rises of the former GDR today, one has to rate as very naive Schmidt's trust that the artistic forces in socialism would lead to an urban architecture comparable with the facades on Piazza San Marco in Venice or Rue de Rivoli in Paris. But Schmidt was in error not just from an aesthetic viewpoint. He refused to acknowledge the contradiction that Tafuri had pointed out: his concept of type, which addressed the whole building, the whole facade, the entire complex of an urban structure (which usually derived from the past) was incompatible with industrialized construction and therefore with the purely technical and economically determined "dissolution of form."

Rossi did not accept this contradiction either, for in an article for *werk-archithese,* he summarized Schmidt's theses and concluded: "For Hans Schmidt, construction cannot be distinguished from construction techniques, which he described as the character of architecture." According to Rossi, this "character"—as we know, Schmidt speaks of style—cannot be arbitrarily superimposed from the outside but instead results from the knowledge of the "inner rationality of things."[26]

The facades' uniform design is therefore legitimated by Rossi too through an "inner rationality of things." This can only be socialist society itself, which resolves the conflict between the individual and society by simply ignoring the individual:

> The really progressive standpoint of architecture lies in not hindering the life that it itself enables. This notion of freedom is tightly linked to the defense of what is called the monotony of rational architecture. Like many others, Hans Schmidt had to listen to the same old story about monotony over and over again; people have different needs, there are different-sized families, and so apartments of different sizes are required. Hans Schmidt responded to this question during a debate in Berlin: ". . . if you have the money for all these complications, then build a bigger house—you can do that—and then leave people free to arrange their lives as they please and to represent their own complications." This representation of personal conflict is therefore part of the individual's freedom; it is neither the responsibility of the state nor of the architect to create a pedagogic space. Such attempts always ended in theme park architecture, funny up to a point, but nothing more than that. Here, rationalism becomes a real problem of freedom. The architect should provide a comfortable ambience, solve certain problems, and interfere as little as possible in the private sphere.[27]

Monotony and uniformity are therefore the external characteristics of a Rational Architecture that is the expression exclusively of the body politic, denying individual needs by designating them the problem of the individual; Schmidt refers to them rather derogatorily as "complications." In so doing, Rational Architecture creates for the individual the freedom to live as he or she pleases behind de-individualized facades. The facades, however, are the expression of political and economic conditions. Their design and construction process must therefore be de-individualized too, and this Rossi emphasizes in his introduction to the Triennale catalog, even though he never achieved it himself, as he neither planned nor built in a socialist state.

In a highly industrialized capitalist state, planning and building tend to use the façades to express the individuality of the owner. This holds true even when the opposite is intended through self-imposed disciplined design. The attempt to tame the "tiger" of capitalism through conscious formal reduction—through "monotony"—is duplicitous if all the design, planning, and construction processes are based on capitalist production. The contradiction between the reclamation and dissolution of form that Schmidt was unable to overcome, is even more difficult to resolve in a capitalist society than in a socialist state. This is because a concept of type that refers to the totality of the building and thus usually to historical examples, comes up against fabrication technologies and financial models that can realize this concept merely as caricatures; our inner cities are full of them today.

In consequence, Rossi's notion of type does not work as a design theory; in fact, in spite of his assertions to the contrary, Rossi developed only the beginnings of a theory of design. However, his definition of type can be understood as a theory of a new historiography of architecture. Instead of regarding type as an abstract idea to be materially implemented in different ways, Rossi defines ways the other way round: as a concrete work that has become an idea, that is, the idea of collective creation. Particularly in his later texts, and above all in his *Scientific Autobiography*—Rossi's last theoretical publication of any significance—it becomes ever more clear that for him, type is not a product of the *Arché,* not an *Urform,* but a product of maturity. Therefore, although he is committed to an evolutionary model, it is not an evolutionary model that describes and analyzes the history of architecture in an objectifying manner, but instead one that describes the process of how the perception of architecture is formed. According to this model, it is not when and where something began that is important, but instead only what has become of it since then—an accepted building type, for example. In his theory of collective memory, Halbwachs called this process "formed memory."[28]

Rossi addressed Halbwachs's position in *L'architettura della città.* However, he did not simply adopt Halbwachs's theory. It was in a process of collective remembering that Rossi anticipated his own architecture, which at least in retrospect would allow for the de-individualization of architecture. About his cemetery of San Cataldo in Modena, he writes: "Early in 1979 I saw the first wing of the cemetery at Modena being filled with the dead, and these corpses with their yellowish-white photographs, their names, the plastic flowers offered out of family and public sympathy, gave the place its unique significance. But then after many polemics it went back to being the great house of the dead where the architecture was a scarcely perceptible background for the specialist. In order to be significant, architecture must be forgotten, or must present only an image for reverence which subsequently becomes confounded with memories."[29]

By this time, Rossi had long since ceased to articulate the perspective of a socialist architecture or city. Yet even though this reference is missing, it remains clear that Rossi was constantly seeking a theory of type that understood type as a product of society and not as mere formalism. Rossi's *Architettura Razionale* is more multifaceted than established historiography admits.

Editors' note: illustrations have been omitted.

> Notes

1 The curators of the XV Triennale di Milano were, in addition to Aldo Rossi: Ezio Bonfanti, Gianni Bragheri, Rosaldo Bonicalzi, Giorgio Grassi, Franco Raggi, Massimo Scolari, and Daniele Vitale.

2 This was the conceptual distinction upon which Heinrich Klotz too would rely: "Surely the trend in contemporary architecture referred to as 'Rationalism,' as initiated by Aldo Rossi and Oswald Mathias Ungers, has proved itself the most successful answer [. . .] to Functionalism." Klotz 1987: 211 [Engl. trans. Fiona Fincannon].

3 Behne 1996 [1926]: 137.

4 Revealingly, during these years, Rossi often declared Hugo Häring's architecture to be the main representative of a functionalist architecture, an architecture that seeks to replace the "the universal unit of measurement of architecture" with an "individual yardstick" by creating designs that can be "drawn over the hand like a glove, but only over this one particular hand." Rossi 1978b: 11 [Engl. trans. Fiona Fincannon].

5 Numerous authors confirm this perspective, which culminates in the assumption that Rossi had availed himself of archetypical forms. For example, Vittorio Magnago Lampugnani writes: "When the Italian Aldo Rossi called for a rational, neutral, ascetic 'architecture of the city' in his manifesto L'*architettura della città* and developed his own artistic idiom through the obsessive repetition of the same archetypal elements . . ." Lampugnani 1986 [1978]: 183f [Engl. trans. Fiona Fincannon].

Ingo Bohning analyzed the window openings in Rossi's Gallaratese complex in Milan: "The window itself is simple, a wood-framed casement window painted white, with a crossbar. [. . .] It is a matter of that type of window that we have called [. . .] archetypal because of its conscious simplicity, and because of the archetype that it contains." Bohning 1981: 107 [Engl. trans. Fiona Fincannon].

Bernard Huet writes: "By its typological conspicuousness and its effects of logical presence, the architecture should evoke the silent and archaic permanence of the archetypes that fuel the collective memory of a society." Huet 1984: 21.

Alexander Tzonis and Liane Lefaivre find that "Rossi's meaning of analogy was close to the way in which associations between objects were perceived by depth psychology." Tzonis and Lefaivre 1992: 58.

And lastly, Peter Eisenman suggested the immediate connection between Rossi's work and Carl Gustav Jung's theory of archetypes in his introduction to Frampton 1979, principally Part II: 6f.

6 See pages 38/39. [Editors' note: this note refers to omitted illustrations.]

7 Lampugnani 1986 [1978]: 184–189 [Engl. trans. Fiona Fincannon].

8 Vidler 1998 [1976]: 14.

9 Quatremère de Quincy 1999 [1832]: 254.

10 Rossi 1982 [1966]: 41.

11 The author's PhD dissertation carefully uncovers all the different elements in the network of influences on Rossi's theoretical work, Schnell 2009.

12 Rossi 1956. This very illuminating essay was translated into German in its entirety for the author's dissertation.

13 The concept of the "permanent" is a key concept in L'*architettura della città*. It also appears in: Rossi 1978 [1970]: 35, among others.

14 Tzonis and Lefaivre 1992: 58.

15 Tafuri 1989 [1986]: 141.

16 Actually, Leon Krier, the curator of the exhibition, excluded the American contributions; the exhibition was, after all, subtitled "The Reconstruction of the European City." Krier also suppressed any obvious references to the avant-garde of the early twentieth century.

17 It is surprising enough that later, the Rationalist movement would even be identified by some as part of postmodernism, indeed, that the concept of Rationalism could be established as a positive concept at all after the Second World War (without taking account of any philosophical critiques like those of Max Horkheimer and Theodor W. Adorno, for example, in *Dialektik der Aufklärung*). However, this development must be seen primarily in the context of the dichotomy between Rationalism and Functionalism.

18 The introduction to the Triennale catalog was translated into German for the first time for the author's PhD dissertation.

19 Evident in: Rossi 1959, for example.

20 Rossi 1973: 16 [Engl. trans. Fiona Fincannon].

21 "The square and cube elements are immutable components of human existence." Ungers 1990: 110 [Engl. trans. Fiona Fincannon].

22 Rossi 1973: 17 [Engl. trans. Fiona Fincannon].

23 At first, this statement sounds astonishingly similar to that of a younger contemporary of Rossi's. In Delirious New York in 1978, Rem Koolhaas also celebrates a collective effort by architects, taking Rockefeller Center as his example. Thanks to their constant reciprocal critique and reciprocal monitoring, they achieve an "honesty and integrity of design" that an individual, ensnared in conceitedness and "philistinism" would never have been able to achieve. Nonetheless, there is a difference. Koolhaas bases his own design theory on Surrealist techniques, namely écriture automatique, with the help of which "creatures beyond all suspicion" are to be created through the collective unconscious. Cf.: Koolhaas 1999 [1978] 195f; Breton-Collinet 1986: 206; Schnell 2005:78–82.

Rossi, who claims to have a great deal of admiration for Surrealist artists—particularly for Andre Breton, Max Ernst, Georges Bataille, and Raymond Roussel—never goes as far as Koolhaas does, to proclaim that he wants to conquer the unconscious. None of the attempts to interpret Rossi's work in this way can be reconciled with Rossi's own explanations, according to which he has remained a life-long Rationalist, and wanted to maintain control over design. This includes the now famous interpretation by Peter Eisenman, who relates Rossi's concept of the città analoga to Carl Gustav Jung's theory of archetypes, which was rejected by Rossi himself a few years later in his Scientific Autobiography. Nothing indicates this attitude more clearly than his contribution to the XV Triennale di Milano.

24 On various occasions, Rossi referred to Andrea Palladio and his typological reinterpretation of the central plan that derives from religious architecture and which Palladio implemented to build private residences. In spite of this new use—which Tafuri called heretical—the reference to the past remained, according to Rossi. "It is clear, for example, that the central plan is a fixed and constant type in religious architecture; but even so, each time a central plan is chosen, dialectical themes are put into play with the architecture of the church, with its functions, with its constructional technique, and with the collective that participates in the life of that church." Rossi 1973 [1966]: 41.

25 Tafuri 1972: 552f. [Engl. trans. Fiona Fincannon].

26 Rossi 1978b: 12 [Engl. trans. Fiona Fincannon].

27 Rossi 1978b: 12 [Engl. trans. Fiona Fincannon].

28 Halbwachs developed this thought with the aid of his analysis of the sites in the Holy Land: "For us, it is not important whether or not these traditions linked to the holy sites are true to life, whether they accord with earlier occurrences. We accept them as such, as formed memories, investigate them from the time when they first appear and throughout the centures that followed. If collective memory means—as we believe it does—essentially a reconstruction of the past, if it correspondingly adapts its picture of events that took place in the past to the religious convictions and spiritual needs of the present, then the knowledge of what actually took place becomes at best of secondary importance, and otherwise entirely superfluous. The reality of the past, an unchangeable template to which one has to conform, no longer exists." Halbwachs 2003 [1941]: 20f. [Engl. trans. Fiona Fincannon].

29 Rossi 1981: 45.

› References

Behne, Adolf. 1964 [1926]. Der moderne Zweckbau. 1996. The modern functional building. Michael Robinson, trans. Santa Monica, CA: Getty Research Institute for the History of Art and the Humanities.

—— 1964 [1926]. Der moderne Zweckbau. [. . .] Berlin/Frankfurt am Main: Ullstein. ENGLISH: 1996. The modern functional building. Michael Robinson, trans. Santa Monica, CA: Getty Research Institute for the History of Art and the Humanities.

Bohning, Ingo. 1981. "Autonome Architektur" und "partizipatorisches Bauen". Zwei Architekturkonzepte. Basel?Boston/Stuttgart: Birkhäuser.

Breton-Collinet, Simone. 1986. "Die Erfindung der 'Erlesenen Leiche'". In: Karlheinz Barck, Hg. Surrealismus in Paris 1919-1939. Ein Lesebuch. Leipzig: Reclam.

Frampton, Kenneth, ed. 1979. Aldo Rossi in America: 1976 to 1979. [Exhibition catalog.] New York: Institute for Architecture and Urban Studies.

Halbwachs, Maurice. 1941. *La Topographie légendaire des évangiles en Terre Sainte*. Paris PuF. [. . .]

Huet, Bernard. 1984. "Aldo Rossi, or the exaltation of reason". In: Aldo Rossi. *Tre città (Three Cities): Perugia, Milano, Mantova*. [Quaderni di Lotus 4 (Lotus Documents 4).] Milano: Electa.

Klotz, Heinrich. 1987. *Moderne und Postmoderne. Architektur der Gegenwart*. Braunschweig/Wiesbaden: Vieweg.

Koolhaas, Rem. 1994 [1978]. *Delirious New York*. Rotterdam: 010 Publishers.

Lampugnani, Vittorio Magnago. 1978. "Auf dem Weg zu einer faschistischen Architektur? Formale Tabuisierung und Machtdarstellung im Bauen". *Die Zeit*, Nr.49: 52. Reprint in: Lampugnani 1986.

—— 1982. "Weiße Vernunft oder graues Gefühl? Zur Architektur-Diskussion in den USA / Der unsinnige Begriff, 'Post-Moderne'". *Frankfurter Allgemeine Zeitung*, 20. November 1982, Nr. 269: 25. Reprint in: Lampugnani 1986.

—— 1986. *Architektur als Kultur. Die Ideen und die Formen. Aufsätze 1970–1985*. Köln: DuMont.

Rossi, Aldo. 1956. "Il concetto di tradizione nell'architettura neoclassica milanese". *Società*, XII , Nr. 3, 474–493.

—— 1956. "Il concetto di tradizione nell'architettura neoclassica milanese". *Società*, XII , Nr. 3, 474–493. DEUTSCH: In Schnell 2009.

—— 1959. "L'ordine Greco". Casabella Coninuitá, Nr.228, Giugno 1959, 14-16. ENGLISH: 1990. "The Greek Order." In: Andreas Papadakis / Harriet Watson. *New Classicism*. London: Academy Editions. DEUTSCH: In Schnell 2009.

—— 1966. *L'architettura della città*. Padua: Marsilio. [. . .] ENGLISH: 1982. *The Architecture of the City*. Diane Ghirardo and Joan Ockman, trans. [Opposition Books.] Cambridge, MA: MIT Press.

—— 1970. "I caratteri urbani della città venete". In: A.A.V.V. *La città di Padova*. Roma: Offina Edizioni; also in: Rosaldo Bonicalzi, ed. 1975. *Scritti scelti sull'architettura e la città. 1956-1972*. Milano: Clup. [. . .]

—— 1973. "Introduzione a *Architettura Razionale*". In: Bonfanti et al. 1973 [partial translation only]: 1983. "Rational Architecture". In: *Aldo Rossi. Selected Writings and Projects*. John O'Regan, ed. [Exhibition catalog. Blue Studio Architecture Gallery, Dublin (16.–31.5.1983)] London: Architectural Design, 54–57. DEUTSCH: In Schnell 2009.

—— 1978a. "Das Konzept des Typus". In: *ARCH+ 37*, April 1978: 39–40.

—— 1978b. "Hans Schmidt und das Problem der Monotonie". In: *werk- archithese*, Nr. 17/18, Mai/Juni 1978: 11–12.

—— 1981. *A scientific autobiography*. Lawrence Venuti, trans. The Institute for Architecture and Urban Studies and The Massachusetts Institute of Technology. Cambridge, MA: MIT Press. [. . .]

—— 1990. "The Greek Order". In: Andreas Papadakis / Harriet Watson. *New Classicism*. London: Academy Editions.

—— 1982. *The Architecture of the City*. Diane Ghirardo and Joan Ockman, trans. [Opposition Books.] Cambridge, MA: MIT Press.

—— 1973. "Introduzione a *Architettura Razionale*". In: Bonfanti et al. 1973 [partial translation only]: 1983. "Rational Architecture". In: *Aldo Rossi. Selected Writings and Projects*. John O'Regan, ed. [Exhibition catalog. Blue Studio Architecture Gallery, Dublin (16.–31.5.1983)] London: Architectural Design, 54–57.

—— 1978a. "Das Konzept des Typus". In: *ARCH+ 37*, April 1978: 39–40.

—— 1978b. "Hans Schmidt und das Problem der Monotonie". In: *werk-archithese*, Nr. 17/18, Mai/Juni 1978: 11–12.

—— 1981. *A scientific autobiography*. Lawrence Venuti, trans. The Institute for Architecture and Urban Studies and The Massachusetts Institute of Technology. Cambridge, MA: MIT Press.

Schnell, Angelika. 2009. *Die Konstruktion des Wirklichen – Eine systematische Untersuchung der geschichtstheoretischen Position in der Architekturtheorie Aldo Rossis*. Dissertation. Staatliche Akademie der Bildenden Künste Stuttgart.

Tafuri, Manfredo. 1972. "Hans Schmidt – ein 'radikaler Architectkt'". Werk, Oktober 1972.

—— 1986. *Storia dell'architettura italiana, 1944-1985*. Torino: G. Einaudi. ENGLISH: 1989. *History of Italian Architecture. 1944-1985*. Jessica Levine, trans. Cambridge, MA: MIT Press.

Tzonis, Alexander / Liane Lefaivre. 1992. *Architecture in Europe since 1968*. New York: Rizzoli.

Ungers, Oswald Mathias. 1990. "Verpackung für die Phantasie. Würfelgedanken". *Daidalos*, Nr. 35, März 1990.

Vidler, Anthony. 1976. "The Third Typology." *Oppositions*, Nr. 7, Winter 1976. Reprint in: Michael Hays, ed. 1998. *Oppositions Reader. Selected Readings from A Journal for Ideas and Criticism in Architecture 1973–1984*. New York: Princeton Architectural Press.

POSTSCRIPT

Hans van der Heijden

The heroism of rationalism?

> I

I grew up in a country that regards itself as innocent. The generation of my grandparents had resisted the German occupation of the Netherlands. For my parents' generation World War II and the bombing of Rotterdam are traumatic memories. However, the atrocities of Dutch imperialism in Indonesia and South Africa are remote, geographically and historically, and erased from collective memory. Historical understanding in the Netherlands is shallow. Four hundred years ago, the Dutch river Delta was largely un-urbanized marshland where agricultural production was impossible. Even today, what few prehistoric, Roman and medieval archeological relics remain are safely buried in the mud. As a young architect, I was taught to work *at* constructing a contemporary landscape, rather than working *in* or *with* a territory. Everything looked possible. There was still a major shortage of housing that was ascribed to the damage of World War II. This was still the context from which the Superdutch architects emerged in the 1990s. With high spirit and unfailing good cheer they supplied the country with their 'sugarmodernism' and, supported by generous state subsidies, exported their problem-free design ethos to exotic places. Superdutch architecture was a product of a nation of traders.

My German friends inherited a different history. Their feelings of guilt may well be as unjust as Dutch innocence and perceived victimization, but there was no way they can afford to neglect the history of their country. The critical reconstruction of Berlin that developed in the 1990s had none of the positivist rhetoric of the contemporary Superdutch. The Berlin Wall had just fallen. Answers had to be found to the complex new political reality following *Die Wende*. These inevitably attracted a degree of melancholy, given the ambivalence attached to reunification. The objectives of the German bourgeoisie and the Kreuzberg squatters coincided in a practice of cautious urban renewal in which German 'history' was neither preserved (there was little left anyway) nor declared sacrosanct. Berlin's critical reconstruction had to demonstrate the vitality and political self-awareness of German culture – this time without a Marshall Plan.

In the critical reconstruction of Berlin, architecture was confirmed as a discipline that negotiates the relationship between collective decisions and private action; while even today, Rotterdam celebrates its state of perpetual instability and regards the city as available land, ready to build on. In Rotterdam the cultural meaning of architecture has been elusive.

Today, German and Dutch architects share a European market. Our generation is facing another reality. Big themes have gone. All the museums necessary have been built. No more theatres are needed. Our cities are completed. Like many European colleagues of different nationalities we assume that our field of work must be the anonymous volume of urban expansion that our predecessors were unable to restrain: the post-war *Plattenbau* (pre-fabricated concrete estates in East Germany); the *Banlieu* (on the French urban periphery); the urban sprawl of the Veneto and Southern Switzerland, and the Flemish 'Nebula City'. These urban realms are not well understood. Although they appear undesirable and weak in architectural form, they won't go away. They are part of our reality and, contingent with our hopes and fears, have become part of our city, so to speak. Interventions are called for in a considered order of priority.

> II

Looking back at a century of rationalism in architecture, rationalism has never been offered as, or aspired to, the status quo. It constitutes an ongoing engagement with ideas concerned about two particular topics: the question of urban form and the production of urban buildings. This Rationalism is about architecture and cities – asking *which* architecture and *what* city? Its ambitions are not inconsiderable. Rationalism attempts nothing less than to construct continuity between ideological objectives regarding our habitat and clear operative methods of design practice, and as such negotiates between collective intent and private enterprise. Rationalist 'tools' focus on the history of architecture, its analysis and its evidence of design methodologies. Rationalist architectural discourse seeks to demystify and depersonalize architecture, and in that particular sense engages the profession in political debate. Rationalism is practiced as a legacy of the European Enlightenment and Berlin has been a productive arena, both historically and following *Die Wende*.

> III

Whether in conceptualizing the city or in the production of its buildings, rationalist paradigms have shifted over the last 50 years. Urbanism has moved from the priority given to urban expansion towards a renewed interest in the historic city, whilst attitudes towards construction have moved from the axis of industrialization and standardization towards architectural craftsmanship and contextualism. This paradigm shift has been evident, although not exclusively, in various texts identified as rationalist – Le Corbusier's *Ville Radieuse* displaced by Aldo Rossi's *The Architecture of the City*. The rhetoric of the *machine a habiter* was set aside when Rossi's *Teatro del Mondo* was towed into the Venice lagoon in 1979.

This is more than a caricature. It cannot be underestimated how a rationalist conception of reason has developed, through its rhetoric and imagery, into a position not to be disregarded. Rossi's *teatro* was imprinted on the retina: the world would have looked different without it. Through iconic symbols of this kind rationalism earned a degree of heroism. Its causes were worth fighting for. The arrival of the *Teatro del Mondo* in Venice asserted the claim that architecture from that moment on would be about the reinterpretation of historic urban, and architectural, models.

Meanwhile, the antique city is well protected. Our history and our urban monuments are cherished. *La Ville Radieuse* is no longer an option. Contemporary architecture is expected to carry a strong personal signature. Uniqueness has replaced the anonymity of craftsmanship and industrial standardization alike. Early twentieth-century rationalist architecture has passed into history. Perhaps confusingly, that episode, once regarded as antagonistic to the historic city, has meanwhile provided its own canon and set of listed monuments. Our urban heritage incorporates conflicting ambitions, appearing as fragmented and without order. Relics from different periods have gained similar status. Urban and suburban residential areas have become part of the same urban constellation. Handcrafted buildings adjoin mass-produced structures, contrasting uniqueness with utter blandness. The line between high and low culture has become blurred.

Rossi's appreciation of urban space as a collection of primary artifacts against a backdrop of the unstable volume of normative building has become unworkable for architects working with the existing urban realm. Surrounded by a multidirectional aggregation of historic urban material, they still ask: *what* city and *which* architecture?

› IV

The renewal of the post-war urban realm, derided by Rossi's contemporaries and allegedly unpopular with its inhabitants, serves as a case in point. This is a task architects can hardly afford to avoid, if only for its sheer extent. Fifty per cent or more of the housing stock of any Western European country is likely to have been produced after 1945. How well do we know and understand this urbanism, its architecture and the construction systems that served to produce it? What are the methodological criteria for interventions in these areas? What is a plausible long-term investment scenario? Or put more directly: should the resistance to blind ground floor facades be taken as phantom pain (given the loss of the urbanity of streets and squares) or as a desire to reintroduce such urban figures? And, should the rejection of an architectural vocabulary, the consequence of standardized construction systems, be an alibi for the creation of a new well-crafted architecture at odds with the appearance of this context?

› V

One can still aspire to a rationalist contribution to architectural design and professional discourse in our reassessment of the European post-war urban realm where a balance between collective and private initiatives is required. The alleged social and architectural weakness of this 'city' seems largely unsubstantiated. Again, the same questions remain topical: *what* city and *which* architecture is to be sought? Meanwhile, architecture has to retain its credibility in this polemical debate. An architectural discipline promoting its own enthusiasm will not readily be recognized for its capacity to handle the scale, requisite negotiations and compromises involved. Architecture will have to give up its naiveté and come to terms with the incipient alienation of the post-war estates, with cities as they are and not what they should be, and with designs that 'maintain' cities and buildings as much as define or redefine them.

This may be profitable work and serve a good cause, but it is also intrinsically un-heroic, at least in comparison to the buildings of previous generations of architects. Emblems that transform such an unspectacular architecture into an unarguable position as decisively as Rossi's *teatro* are, however, not yet imaginable.

David Dunster

Rationalism

As with most architectural terms, Rationalism carries ideas which are not party to either philosophy or religion, specifically its use in nineteenth-century France that privileges pure geometrical forms and later attempts to conceptualize a system of buildings as architecture, and then in the twentieth century various further attempts to systematize building according to industrial principle in pursuit of scientific knowledge. To this sense, post-world war thinking added, refuting the modernist refusal of architectural history as precedent, forms of Rationalism based upon two ideas concerning type and cities. Former attempts to free architecture from simple emotion and extend its discursive territory into 'science' could be questioned, just as the idea that science stood for one specific process might be suspect. In particular cases the term 'Rationalism' was a principle, though one understood personally in the works of Rossi and Ungers.

It would appear that in the history of concepts, their exact meaning changes often radically, across time. If 'science' can no longer be used to include all that scientists do, it should not come as a surprise that Rationalism also has a chequered history depending upon who uses it, when, and in what context. For some, now, a Rationalist work apes the forms of Neo-classicism, to others the history of architecture includes modernism and thus cannot simply pursue plagiarism. This latter meaning seems to be that which promises the more inventive work. Which raises the question, what can be invented within that position?

Because architecture lacks a cognate verb, to 'architect' something is clumsy in all European languages, I shall use the term design, itself full of unavoidable ambiguities. What the newer Rationalists have included is a recognition that what designers feel cannot be erased from a process of design even if personal perceptions are then subject to the thoughts forming the basis of their architecture. Aldo Rossi's work is unthinkable without his experience of life in his home city, Milan, nor can Ungers' work be separated from his love of architecture of late Rome as he found it in the remains of Cologne, Trier or Aachen. With this observation one common characteristic of all Rationalisms, that a result can be repeated through time and place, appears untenable. A possible defense returns to that geometric basis favored by the Enlightenment, so that Rossi's work outside Milan is not a simple commentary on Milan, though it repeats the use of the large column, pitched roofs, and square windows. Thus, Rationalism as now understood does not refuse a personal signature. With Ungers, the use of grids, of Russian Dolls, and urban analysis similarly signify.

These two architects stand as the basis of contemporary Rationalist work though their best work is easily copied. However, the better work being built now expands into many voices. As so often in the history of the Arts, what Rationalists stand for counters direct personal expressionism despite my observation above. It is because what one architect sees is necessarily different from another, that Rationalism as it now stands is far from homogeneous or repetitious. There does appear to be a rejection of structure as the main determinant of form, though masters like Alvaro Siza can play with structure in ways that Ungers and Rossi would not. There is also no particular reverence for materials as the main determinant of form, and further, the plan is no longer privileged. This last separates the Rationalists at work today from architects trained under the Smithsons observation: 'Mies is great but Corb communicates'. Rationalists recognize the primacy of form in architecture, and continue to seek it. Some Gods are dead, atheism lives now as a belief.

Hans Kollhoff

Tectonics

Defying the 'virtues' of abstraction, and in parallel with the urge for *Großform* (mass form) and free-standing 'sculptural' artefacts, a tendency to ornament surfaces has become prevalent. The banality of an office block is being down-played with recourse to coloured and layered panes of glass, and the meaningless box of a museum is decorated with colourful rods, in order to loudly attract attention: look, something is happening here!

Gottfried Semper's theory of 'cladding' is habitually cited, but often misconceived since for Semper the cladding, which gave the raw artefact architectural dignity in distinguishing it from mere 'building', was tectonic. It structured and articulated the architectural whole in accordance with anthropomorphic qualities, distinguishing between top and bottom, back and front, and supporting or suspending etc., in order to ultimately confront us with a surrogate body with which to identify.

The nature of construction, and the manner in which a multitude of different parts are joined to form a coherent whole, is of particular significance, here. Cladding, for Semper, was precisely not simply about 'wrapping' or 'enclosing', but rather proposed a delicate play between constructive (indeed functional) facts and visual appearance, unified in material experience.

If a large unstructured form for most people carries the connotations of a threat, in contrast tectonic articulation creates an emotional identification with the architectural artefact. Maybe this is possible with manifold decoration or wrapping – exemplified by Frank Gehry in Bilbao – but does this form remain 'architectural'? I would argue that this is not the case. For me this (display) belongs to the realm of fashion – which seems to want to coerce architecture.

In my understanding, architecture is not subject to the trends of fashion, even if architecture seems to resist contemporary market forces. The invention of a glass gherkin as a high-rise building will remain precisely that, and it will only serve to generate differentiated glass gherkins, without any possibility of asserting a generally valid basis for the development of an architectural convention.

As long as we indulge in play on the (urban) periphery: beyond the city gates (as it were), where since the nineteenth century all developments in conflict with the 'evolved' urban fabric have been deposited – army barracks and hospitals or railway stations and world expos; there are no boundaries for the unconventional. But when we move towards the historic city and towards the city centre (here in Europe), then architectural convention quite rightly demands its role as (an aspect of) collective memory; a record located beyond individual invention establishing a (representative) standard, which the individual 'idea' cannot fulfil – consequently to be banned from the '*Centro Stòrico*'.

Beyond postmodern appropriation of images, a structural logic has established itself, firstly with the tectonic layering of stone facades and the abstract grid of open joints; then in brick facades with deep reveals in the brick bond, and finally with conventional double-skinned rendered walls with flat tectonic relief. In pointed stone construction we can still distinguish the individual slab in relief, and in high-rise buildings the brick bond hides the prefabricated element necessary for such structures. The rendered 'house' manifests the ideal of the seemingly monolithic building (without joints), but here tectonic articulation is only in part justified or determined by [the actual] construction; rather it structures the artefact according to anthropomorphic criteria.

All this is technically possible today, despite all the [predictable] economic, technological and aesthetic reservations. Having reached this point, we experience a longing for more architectural unity, which requires considered attention to the detailing of profiles; of the moulded base; the stringcourse and the eaves cornice. Suddenly we find ourselves in the company of historic architects from the nineteenth and early twentieth century, from whom we are now only separated by their 'relaxed' application of ornament (which we now often pursue in cooperation with visual artists). Sometimes we are successful in this, when we achieve a coherent whole without having negatively interfered with each other's expertise.

The *Weltsaal* (Universal Hall) in the German Foreign Office in Berlin exemplifies this – not only were the 'pictures' by Gerhard Merz integrated into the tectonic articulation of the interior walls, but more to the point they emerged from functional and spatial requirements (of acoustics and for extension). Furthermore the original hall construction and lighting scheme were rectified without obliterating the interventions from the 1950s and 1960s (by the Central Committee of the *Sozialistische Einheitspartei Deutschlands*).

Translated by the editors.

Leon Krier

Rational-Architecture-Rationelle 1975–1978

My principle motivation for organizing the *Rational Architecture* exhibition, held in March of 1975 at Peter Cook's Art Net Gallery and in June 1975 at the ETSAB in Barcelona, was to act as a corrective to Aldo Rossi's 1973 Triennale exhibition titled 'Architettura Razionale'. The name was too good to be wasted. Rossi had invited a range of architects from around the world, very few of whom fitted an elusive category which Rossi and his assistants spent very little effort explaining. His writings too were literary essays around the theme of Architecture and the City with very few clues as to what these manifested technologically, typologically, structurally, socially or even materially. I thought Rossi was an interesting painter-designer, but his architectural lexicon was too limited to pose a serious challenge to the reigning polymorphous and omnipotent modernisms.

Without comment the Triennale aligned the Communist housing blocks of the GDR with Michael Graves' purist experiments for the Rockefellers. I was invited to the exhibition even though I had still only a sketchy notion of what I wanted to do architecturally and urbanistically. Like myself most participants, if interrogated individually, would have had a clear answer on what they didn't want to do, but none displayed any ambition to design more than individual buildings, be they tiny cottages, mile long slabs or mile high towers. None showed interest in a strategy of how to overcome the shortcomings of Modernism. There were interesting critical theories afloat, ranging from Theodor Adorno to Jane Jacobs, but I strongly felt that criticism was worthless if it wasn't backed up by an alternative general theory of how things should be done: how to confront and reform a worldwide and all-embracing phenomenon which corroded all notions of the city, architecture, technology and society as we knew it. I came to realize that although I had had the privilege of growing up in superlative traditional cities and landscapes, and continued to live in such environs, the design skills and philosophy I had been taught were condemning that environment to utter disappearance.

If the despair of seeing my hometown eroded by criminally immature ideas and equally bland buildings had awoken me, the situation of having to teach a studio at the AA in 1974 forced me to collect myself. I started to build a theory of which I alone seemed to feel the implacable urgency.

The various 'schools' of urban thinking formulated by Bruyère, Alphand, Sitte, Stuebben, Saarinen, Wagner, Henrici, Fischer, Giovannoni, Hegemann, Gruber, Piacentini, Muratori, had rendered conceptions of typology and morphology operative. The doctrine and practice were literally devastated by the Second World War and compromised by subsequent undeserved political discredit. Their academic followers reduced this methodology to merely analytical instruments that served to read 'historical structure' but which were unable to inform contemporary design and construction. Pier Luigi Cervellati was the most lucid inheritor of the discipline with his formidable and forgotten book *Tipologia e Morfologia della Città Storica* (1972). Unfortunately, he restricted the use of the traditional design *corpus* to restoring and repairing historic towns and buildings, unable to see its fundamental relevance for the conception of new towns and buildings.

I decided to teach traditional urban and architectural design methods not as ideology, political science or art-history, but as applied technology. Technology based and defined by the use of natural building materials, dictated by local climate, topography and human skills. A technology shaped by human scale and resources, one able to build lasting settlements and a socio-cultural order that transcends political and economic trends. The blind expansion and pervasive dominion of fossil-fuel dependent mechanization and the ensuing hegemony of 'hyper' or mega-structural scale had to be resisted. This was an intuition born of despair.

The 1978 *Rational-Architecture-Rationelle* bilingual catalogue reproduced the pedagogic structure of the exhibition. Projects were not displayed under the name of the architect but in the typological category that the particular project demonstrated and illustrated: the urban Street, Square, Block, Quarter, Park, Public Building and Urban Fabric, Public Works, Monuments and Networks. Aymonino's Gallaratese, Gregotti's Quartieri Zen and Stirling's Runcorn were included primarily for opportunistic reasons, simply because there were no better examples available from that generation of architects.

The overall objective of my Rational Architecture exhibition was to prove that, even though many of the designers were opposed to the idea, they were consciously, or unconsciously, participating in the Reconstruction of the European City, the lasting rational and humane city, in leaving behind the catastrophic experiments of Modernism.

Contributors

Nicholas Bullock is Emeritus Reader in Architectural and Planning History at Cambridge, a Fellow of King's College and teaches in the Graduate School of the Architectural Association. He has written on housing and planning in nineteenth- and early twentieth-century Germany and France and on aspects of Modernism both between the wars and after 1945. He published *Building the Post-War World, Modern Architecture and Reconstruction in Britain* in 2002 and is currently writing a book on architecture, urbanism and the modernisation of post-war France.

David Dunster, sometime Roscoe Professor of Architecture at the University of Liverpool, has taught at Kingston Polytechnic, University College London and South Bank University. He chaired the RIBA Research Trust Awards, was the founding editor of *The Journal of Architecture* and contributes regularly to *The Architectural Review*. He has lectured and published widely in the USA, Europe and Australia. He organised the Student Design Charette at the first World Architecture Festival in Barcelona October 2008, and was a judge in subsequent WAF events. He was a member of the first CABE Design Review Panel for four years and a founding member of the Liverpool Urban Design Conservation, Architecture and Planning advisory panel to the Planning Department of Liverpool City Council.

Henk Engel is an architect and Associate Professor at the Faculty of Architecture in Delft. He is a co-founder of the office De Nijl Architecten, which has been involved in various forms of urban transformation since the beginning of the 1980s. At the Faculty of Architecture, Engel teaches architecture theory, design and research. For the past ten years, he has led the research program 'Mapping the Randstad Holland'. He is editor of the publication series 'OverHolland', which publishes the results of the Randstad research and other related studies. Aside from his built work, he has published various design studies as well as scholarly work on De Stijl, CIAM, Team 10 and the Tendenza. 'Theo van Doesburg & the destruction of architectural theory', in the Tate Modern catalog *Van Doesburg & the International Avant-garde*, was published in 2009.

Hans van der Heijden graduated as an architect and urbanist at TU Delft in 1988. He founded biq in 1994 and is biq's practice design director. In 2008 he published *Architecture in the Fractured City*. From 2009 to 2010 he was the curator of the debate series ArchitectureCases of the Rotterdam architecture centre AIR. He is an editor of the Dutch Architecture Yearbook. His designs include the restoration of the Bluecoat arts centre in Liverpool, the urban renewal of Eindhoven Lakerlopen and the rehabilitation project for Rotterdam Ommoord. biq projects have been displayed at the travelling international exhibition 'Architecture of Consequence' and the Venice Bienale 2012.

Thilo Hilpert is a publisher and sociologist as well as an architect and urban planner. His architectural work and writing is focused on a critical perception of the Modern Movement and its tradition. He has written books and many articles on design methodologies, urban design and the history and theory of modern architecture. His selection of urban design projects was published in *Town in Mind: Urban Vision*. In his recent 'The Utopias of a Blue Planet' in *ARCH+* Post-Oil City he discusses architectural and urban theories since 1960 in relation to the current global environmental crisis. Thilo Hilpert is Guest Professor in Szechuan, China.

Hans Kollhoff was born in 1946, in Lobenstein (Thuringia), Germany. He studied architecture at Karlsruhe University from 1968 and graduated in 1975. From 1975–1978 he received a DAAD grant to study at Cornell University, New York. In 1978 he founded his own practice in Berlin, and from 1978–1983 he was an assistant at the Faculty of Architecture and Design, TU Berlin. In 1984 his practice went into partnership with Helga Timmermann. Between 1983 and 1989 he held visiting and temporary professorships at HdK Berlin (83–85), Dortmund University (86–87) and ETH Zurich (87–89). Between 1990 and 2012 he was Professor for Architecture and Construction at ETH Zurich. He currently has practices in Berlin, Rotkreuz (CH), Rotterdam and Florence. In 2004 he was appointed president of the *Internationale Bauakademie Berlin*. A volume of his collected essays on architecture, *Das architektonische Argument: Texte zur Baukunst*, edited by Fritz Neumeyer, was published by GTA Verlag in 2010.

Leon Krier is an architect, urbanist and design consultant. He studied architecture at the University of Stuttgart and subsequently became assistant to Jame Stirling in London, 1968–70 and 1973–74. In 1971–72 he was also project partner with J. P. Kleihues in Berlin. Leon Krier has taught at AA School in London, Princeton University, the RCA in London. He has been Jefferson Professor of Architecture, University of Virginia and visiting Professor at Yale intermittently since 1990. His built projects include: New town of Poundbury Masterplan and architectural coordination for Duchy of Cornwall and HRH The Prince of Wales, 1988 onwards; Justice Palace, Luxembourg, 1990–97; Citta Nuova, Alessandria, Italy, 1995–99; Cayala, Guatemala City, 2003 onwards; The New Tor Bella Monaca Quarter, Rome, Italy 2010 onwards. Publications include: *Rational Architecture Rationelle*, 1978; *Albert Speer: Architecture 1932–42*, 1985 and 2013; *The Completion of Washington DC*, 1986; *Atlantis*, 1987; *The Architecture of Community*, 2009; *Drawings for Architecture*, 2009.

Andrew Peckham teaches architecture at the University of Westminster; current research interests focus on the publication of architecture and the culture of rationalism. His 'Cataloguing Architecture' is forthcoming in *Literatures, Libraries, and Archives* and he is currently working on a new book *Architecture and its Imprint*.

Charles Rattray read architecture at the University of Edinburgh and worked in practice for a number of years including a period with Sir Leslie Martin. He is a Senior Lecturer at the University of Dundee, an Editor of *Architectural Research Quarterly* (Cambridge University Press) and a regular contributor to other architectural journals. With Andrew Peckham and Torsten Schmiedeknecht, he edited *Rationalist Traces* (Wiley, 2007). His essay on the Dutch architectural practice Geurst en Schulze introduces a monograph on their work to be published by Quart, Lucerne, in 2013.

Torsten Schmiedeknecht is a senior lecturer at the School of Architecture, University of Liverpool. He is an architect and has worked in practice in Germany, Greece, France and the UK. Aside from his research into Rationalism, recent and forthcoming publications include papers on architectural competitions and their impact on mainstream architecture, as well as edited volumes on the relationship between fame and architecture.

Document credits

The authors and publishers gratefully acknowledge the following for permission to reproduce material in the book. Every effort has been made to contact and acknowledge copyright owners. The publishers would be grateful to hear from any copyright holder who is not acknowledged here and will undertake to rectify any errors or omissions in future printings or editions of the book.

Note: Full publication and extract details given in main documents.

'The rationalist legacy: complement and contradiction'. Copyright authors.

'Rationalism: a philosophical concept in architecture' (1987). Copyright author. First published in *Modernity and the Classical Tradition: Architectural Essays 1980–1987,* MIT, 1989.

'Rationalist tendencies in nineteenth-century architecture'. Copyright author.

'The Architects of modernism and their texts: an introduction to the history of modern architecture 1922–1934'. Copyright author.

'Architecture, rationalism and reconstruction: the example of France 1945–55'. Copyright author.

'The neo-rationalist perspective'. Copyright author.

(1) 'The foundations and development of architecture' (1908). Copyright J. Paul Getty Trust (1996). Excerpts from the English-language translation of ''The Foundations and Development of Architecture'' were originally published in Hendrick Petrus Berlage, *Thoughts on Style, 1886-1909*, trans. Iain Boyd Whyte and Wim de Wit (Los Angeles: Getty Research Institute, 1996).

(2) 'Architecture' (1910). Courtesy Wilfried Wang and Arts Council England.

(3) 'Toward an architecture' (1923). Copyright J. Paul Getty Trust (2007). Excerpts from the English-language translation of 'Argument,' 'Airplanes,' 'Automobiles,' 'Mass Production Housing,' 'Eyes Which Do Not See…,' and 'Mass Production Housing,' were originally published in *Le Corbusier, Toward an Architecture*, trans. John Goodman (Los Angeles: Getty Research Institute, 2007).

(4) 'Regarding economy' (1924). Reprinted from *Raumplan Versus Plan Libre: Adolf Loos and Le Corbusier, 1919–1930*, 'Regarding Economy', pp. 137–138, 138, 140 and 141. Copyright (1988), with permission from IOS Press. Translation courtesy Francis Jones.

(5) 'Yes and no: confessions of an architect' (1925). From *The Original Drawings of JJP Oud 1890–1963*, catalogue published by the Architectural Association, 1978. Copyright permission Architectural Association Publications.

(6) 'Type-needs type-furniture' (1925). Copyright ADAGP/Fondation Le Corbusier.

(7) 'Architecture' (1926). Gruppo 7, *Oppositions* Fall 1976, pp. 89–92, © by permission of The MIT Press.

(27) 'What would concrete, what would steel be without mirror glass' (1933). Neumeyer, Fritz, translated by Mark Jarzombek, *The Artless Word: Mies van der Rohe on the Building Art*, 200-word excerpt from page 314, © 1991 Massachusetts Institute of Technology, by permission of The MIT Press. Courtesy Mies van der Rohe Estate.

(28) 'Structure and architecture' (1935). Pagano, Giuseppe, 'Struttura e Architettura', *Dopo Sant'Elia* (Milano, 1935). Courtesy Editoriale domus S.p.A., all rights reserved.

(29) 'The new architecture and the Bauhaus' (1935). Gropius, Walter, *The New Architecture and The Bauhaus*, pp. 30–38, 111–112, © 1965 Massachusetts Institute of Technology, by permission of The MIT Press. World (excluding US) rights: Faber & Faber Ltd.

(30) 'Mass produced buildings' (1924). Copyright ADAGP/Fondation Le Corbusier. Courtesy The Open University.

(32) 'Collective design' (1924). Courtesy Verlag Lars Muller.

(33) 'Principles of Bauhaus production [Dessau]' (1926). Conrads, Ulrich, *Programs and Manifestoes on 20th-Century Architecture*, 250-word excerpt from page 96, © 1971 Massachusetts Institute of Technology, by permission of The MIT Press.

(34) 'The new world' (1926). Courtesy Stiftung Bauhaus Dessau.

(35) 'Building' (1928). Conrads, Ulrich, *Programs and Manifestoes on 20th-Century Architecture*, 1080 words, pp. 117–120, © 1971 Massachusetts Institute of Technology, by permission of The MIT Press.

(36) 'Theory and design in the first machine age' (1960). Copyright Reyner Banham 1960. Reproduced by kind permission of Mrs Mary Banham and Shelley Power Literary Agency Ltd.

(37) 'Modular co-ordination in architecture' (1964). Courtesy Madleen Lamm.

(38) 'The fine red thread of Italian rationalism' (1978). Copyright Mondadori Italy and courtesy author.

(39) 'Building modern Italy' (1988). Copyright and courtesy author.

(40) 'Polemical rationalism' (1991). Etlin, Richard A., *Modernism in Italian Architecture, 1890–1940* (Cambridge, MA and London: The MIT Press, 1991). Copyright and courtesy author.

(41) 'Rationalism, Mediterraneità, and the vernacular' (2010). Copyright and courtesy author and Routledge.

(42) 'Architecture for barbarians – Ludwig Hilberseimer and the rise of the generic city' (2011). Copyright and courtesy Architectural Association Publications and author.

(43) '"Everything in the state, nothing against the state": corporative urbanism and Rationalist architecture in fascist Italy' (2012). Copyright and courtesy author and Routledge.

(44) 'Architecture and ideology' (1957). Copyright Rizzoli International Publications Inc.

(45) 'On the typology of architecture' (1962). Courtesy Architectural Design/Wiley. Copyright translation Joseph Rykwert.

(46) 'The question of style' (1969). Copyright and courtesy author.

(47) 'The new architecture and the avantgarde' (1973). From Hays, K. Michael (ed.), *Architecture Theory since 1968*, 1600 words from pp. 131–134 and 137–139, © 1998 Massachusetts Institute of Technology, by permission of The MIT Press.

(48) 'The third typology' (1978). Copyright (1977) and courtesy author. Courtesy AAM Publications.

(73) 'Rossi: the concept of the locus as a political category of the city' (2008). Copyright and courtesy author.

(74) 'The socialist perspective of the XV Triennale di Milano'. Copyright original text author. Copyright English translation *Candide*. 'Hans Schmidt's influence on Aldo Rossi' (2010). A longer version of this essay was first published in *Candide. Journal for Architectural Knowledge*, No. 2 (7/2010), Transcript, Bielefeld. The full text can be downloaded at www.candide-journal.net.

'The heroism of rationalism?' Copyright author.

'Rationalism'. Copyright author.

'Tectonics'. Copyright author.

'Rational-Architecture-Rationelle 1975–1978'. Copyright author.

Index

building(s) 109–10; industrialisation of 181, 272; typification of 79–80
Bullock, Nicholas 180–5

CAD 312
Canella, Guido 217, 218, 336
Caniggia, Gianfranco and Maffei, Gian Luigi: *Interpreting Basic Building* 230–3
Cantàfora, Arduino 191–2, 341, 361, 363
Cartesian rationalism 16, 22
cartography 237
Casabella continuità 22, 188, 194, 217, 235, 336, 348, 353
catalogue architecture 153
Cervellati, Pier Luigi 377–8
choice: and history 290
Choisy, Auguste 28
CIAM (Congrès Internationaux d'Architecture Moderne) 34, 35, 37, 188, 191; Athens Charter (1933) 92–5, 270–1; congresses 42, 43; and corporativist urbanism 174–8; founding of 40; Italian involvement in 176–7; La Sarraz declaration (1928) 35, 122–5, 160
cities 84–6, 87–8, 91, 117–18, 132, 190–1, 253, 262–81, 324–5, 326–8; analogous 191–3; architecture of 271–2, 326; and Athens Charter 92–5; and CIAM 191; complexity of urban artefacts 263–5; concept of the locus as a political category of 353–8; corporativist 174–8; formal objectivity of urban design 277–81; grid 279–80; Hilberseimer and rise of generic 170–2; historic heritage of 93; history of types 272–3; monuments and the theory of permanences 265–8; and Neo-Rationalists 237; operative disciplines 278–9; physiognomy of 85; quarters 226, 273, 331, 348; reconstruction of 268–73, 330–3; Rossi and architecture of 262–8, 346–52, 356; as site of new typology 221, 225–6; study of as study of a language 325; urban plans 279; urban space concept 274–6
city hall: and prison 226
cladding 375
classical rationalism 15–18, 200
classicism 22, 332–3; new 200, 224, 361, 363
classification 286

closed form 110
Cocteau 65
collective design 138–9
collective needs: and architecture 75–6
collective work 301–2
Collectivism 44
colour 63, 90
Colquhoun, Alan: 'Rationalism' 15–24
commercial buildings 118
Como 176, 177
composition 321–2
Conrad, Ulrich 36
construction 100–3, 121, 284–91, 298, 307–8, 310, 375; and form 117–19; logical 284–6; myth of and the architectonic 312–15
Constructivism 304
corporativist urbanism: and CIAM 174–8
craft: architecture as 300–3
Cubism 66, 110, 135
Cuvier, Georges 25

D'Amato, Claudio 347
Dardi, Nino 217, 236
de Baudot, Anatole 162
de Saussure, Ferdinand 194–5, 325
De Stijl 37, 208, 209, 235, 294
decorative art 64
design theory 192, 287, 323, 326–9, 365
Doordan, Dennis, *Building Modern Italy* 158–61
Doric architecture 77
Dunster, David 373–4
Durand, Jean-Nicolas-Louis 24–5
Durand, J.N.L. 24–5, 26, 222, 245–6, 246–7, 249, 254, 258; *Précis* 24, 25, 249
dwelling area 268
dwelling houses 84–5, 132

eclecticism 18, 19, 36, 49
economic system: and La Sarraz declaration 122–3
economy 57–60
Eiermann, Egon 39, 41
Eisenman, Peter 190, 346
Elsässer, Martin 150
empirical rationalism 15–16, 22
Endell, August 345
engineers 103, 105, 138, 304
Enlightenment 17, 23, 24, 235–6
environment, notion of 237

industrialised building: heavy versus lightweight models 183–4
industrialization 136, 272
International Style 41, 42–3, 148, 151, 210
internationalism 40
Italian Neo-Rationalists 234–40
Italian Rationalism 71, 73, 156–7, 158–61, 162–4, 166–8, 234
Italians: involvement in CIAM 176–7
Italy 44, 66, 158–61, 250; history of architecture 336–41; importance of typological debates 250–2; new urban scale in 346–52; rural architecture in 77–8

Jeanneret, Pierre 120–1
Jencks, Charles 188
Johnson, Philip 41, 42

Kahn 258
Kant, Immanuel 343; 'Critique of Judgement' 305
Kaufhaus Schocken (Stuttgart) 39
Kaufman, E. 235
Klotzsche school project 302
Kollhoff, Hans 375; 'The Myth of Construction and the Architectonic' 312–15
Korn, Arthur 42, 148
Kosel, Gerhard 42
Krier, Leon 221, 256, 362, 377–8; 'The Age of Reconstruction' 330–3; 'The Reconstruction of the City' 268–73
Krier, Rob 189, 254; 'Typological and Morphological Elements of the Concept of Urban Space' 274–6

Laborde, Alessandre 325
Lansburgh, G. Albert 163
Laugier, M.A. 25, 26, 222, 257
Le Corbusier 22, 33, 40–1, 43–5, 105–7, 109, 151–2, 159, 201, 223, 224, 275, 325; *The City of Tomorrow and Its Planning* 87–8; and classicism 22; and Cocteau 65; *The Decorative Arts of Today* 64; 'Five Points Towards a New Architecture' 32, 120–1; and floor plan 106; journey to Rome 44–5; and *L'esprit nouveau* 32, 34, 35, 105, 159; 'Mass produced buildings' 134–5; and modern metropolis 109; Mundaneum project 40; *Plan Voisin* 32, 44; *The Radiant City* 34; rationalism of 109; 'Three

Reminders to Architects' 43; and use of standards 106; *Vers une architecture* 32, 34–5, 43, 54–6, 172, 184; Villa Savoye 42; *Ville Contemporaine* 192; *Ville Radieuse* 42, 44, 189, 191, 371
Le Havre, reconstruction of 185
Ledoux 24, 211, 257
Leonidov 41
Lessing 328
Libera, Adalberto 160–1, 166
light: relationship of building materials to 90
Lissitzky, El 33, 36, 38, 304–5
Littoria 176
Lobsinger, Mary Louise: 'The New Urban Scale in Italy' 346–52
locus, as a political category of the city 353–8
Lodoli, Carlo 17, 177
Lods, Marcel 6, 182, 183, 184
logical atomism 20
logical construction 284–6
Loos, Adolf 292, 296, 325, 336; *Architecture* 51–3; 'Regarding Economy' 57–60

machine 28, 105, 124, 135, 140, 221, 223, 224
Manhattan 280
Marullo, Francesco 171
Marx, Karl 171
mass production 88, 134–5, 153, 154, 223–4
mass production housing 54–5, 56
May, Ernst 42
mechanization 131, 135
Mediterranean 166–8
Mendelsohn, Erich 39, 111, 118
Messel, Alfred 118
metropolis, modern 109
Meyer, Hannes 39, 40, 42, 43, 148; 'Building' 143–5; 'The New World' 141–2
Mies van der Rohe 22, 27, 33, 34, 37, 38–9, 42, 110, 118, 201, 209, 210, 301; 'Building' 115–16; 'The Dwelling of our Time' 42; 'Industrial Building' 136–7; 'Office Building' 113–14; 'Remarks on my block of flats' 122; *Weissenhofsiedlung* 38–9, 43; 'What would concrete, what would steel be without mirror glass' 126
Milan Triennale: (1936) 159; (1964) 189, 336, 338; (1973) 189, 234, 271, 339, 355, 360–5, 377